ASSESSING THE WORLD TRADE ORGANIZATION: FIT FOR PURPOSE?

The WTO recently celebrated twenty years of existence. The general wisdom is that its dispute settlement institutions work well and its negotiation machinery is going through a phase of prolonged crisis. *Assessing the World Trade Organization: Fit for Purpose?* overcomes this myopic view and takes stock of the WTO's achievements while going beyond existing disciplinary narratives. With chapters written by scholars who have closely observed the development of the WTO in recent years, this book presents the state-of-the-art in thinking about the WTO's performance. It also considers important issues such as the origins of the multilateral system, the accession process and the WTO's interaction with other international organisations. The contributions shed new light on untold stories, critically review and present existing scholarship and sketch new research avenues for a future generation of trade scholars. This book will appeal to a wide audience that aims to better understand the drivers and obstacles of the WTO's performance.

MANFRED ELSIG is Associate Professor of International Relations and Deputy Managing Director of the World Trade Institute, University of Bern.

BERNARD HOEKMAN is Professor and Director, Global Economics at the Robert Schuman Centre for Advanced Studies, European University Institute, Florence.

JOOST PAUWELYN is Professor of International Law and Co-Director of the Centre for Trade and Economic Integration at the Graduate Institute of International and Development Studies, Geneva, and Murase Visiting Professor at Georgetown University Law Center.

ASSESSING THE WORLD TRADE ORGANIZATION

Fit for Purpose?

WORLD TRADE FORUM

Edited by

MANFRED ELSIG

World Trade Institute, University of Bern

BERNARD HOEKMAN

European University Institute, Florence

JOOST PAUWELYN

Graduate Institute of International and Development Studies, Geneva

CAMBRIDGE
UNIVERSITY PRESS

CAMBRIDGE
UNIVERSITY PRESS

University Printing House, Cambridge CB2 8BS, United Kingdom

One Liberty Plaza, 20th Floor, New York, NY 10006, USA

477 Williamstown Road, Port Melbourne, VIC 3207, Australia

4843/24, 2nd Floor, Ansari Road, Daryaganj, Delhi – 110002, India

79 Anson Road, #06–04/06, Singapore 079906

Cambridge University Press is part of the University of Cambridge.

It furthers the University's mission by disseminating knowledge in the pursuit of education, learning, and research at the highest international levels of excellence.

www.cambridge.org
Information on this title: www.cambridge.org/9781107193222
DOI: 10.1017/9781108147644

First published 2017

A catalogue record for this publication is available from the British Library.

Library of Congress Cataloging-in-Publication Data
Names: World Trade Forum (2015 : Bern, Switzerland) | Elsig, Manfred, editor. | Hoekman, Bernard M., 1959– editor. | Pauwelyn, Joost, editor.
Title: Assessing the World Trade Organization : fit for purpose? : World Trade Forum / edited by Manfred Elsig, World Trade Institute, Bernard Hoekman, European University Institute, Florence, Joost Pauwelyn, Graduate Institute of International Studies, Geneva.
Description: Cambridge ; New York : Cambridge University Press, 2017. | Includes index.
Identifiers: LCCN 2016053993 | ISBN 9781107193222 (hbk)
Subjects: LCSH: World Trade Organization – Congresses. | International trade – Congresses. | Commercial policy – Congresses.
Classification: LCC HF1385 .W635 2015 | DDC 382/.92–dc23
LC record available at https://lccn.loc.gov/2016053993

ISBN 978-1-107-19322-2 Hardback

CONTENTS

FIGURES

TABLES

CONTRIBUTORS

TODD ALLEE is Assistant Professor of Government and Politics at the University of Maryland. His research focuses on international organisations, international trade, the World Trade Organization (WTO), foreign direct investment, dispute settlement and territorial conflict resolution. He is the author of *The Democratic Peace and Territorial Conflict in the Twentieth Century* (with Paul K. Huth, Cambridge University Press) as well as more than 20 articles and book chapters that employ political economy approaches and quantitative methods to explain the origins, escalation, and settlement of trade, investment and territorial disputes. His current research explores the design of trade and investment agreements using a variety of statistical- and text-analysis methods. His work has been published in journals such as the *American Political Science Review, International Organization, World Politics, World Economy, International Studies Quarterly* and *Journal of Conflict Resolution.*

DIRK DE BIÈVRE is Associate Professor of international politics at the University of Antwerp. He obtained his PhD in social and political sciences at the European University Institute in Florence in 2002 and did post-doctoral research at the Max Planck Institute for Research on Collective Goods and the Mannheim Centre for European Social Research of the University of Mannheim. In 2014–2015, he was a visiting fellow at the Department of Government of the London School of Economics and Political Science. His research interests include EU trade policy, interest groups and the World Trade Organization. He has published, among others, in *Journal of European Public Policy, British Journal of Politics and International Relations* and *World Trade Review*. Together with Arlo Poletti, he recently co-authored the ECPR monograph *Judicial Politics and International Cooperation: From Dispute Settlement to Deal-Making in the World Trade Organization.*

CHAD P. BOWN is a Senior Fellow at the Peterson Institute for International Economics in Washington, DC and a Research Fellow at CEPR in London. Bown was formerly a tenured professor of economics at Brandeis University, where he was on the faculty for twelve years. He served as senior economist in the White House on the Council of Economic Advisers and most recently as a lead economist at the World Bank. He also spent a year in residence as a visiting scholar at the WTO Secretariat in Geneva. Bown is a member of the Council on Foreign Relations and since 2011 he has co-directed, with Petros C. Mavroidis, an annual programme of scholars providing legal-economic assessments of WTO case law and jurisprudence published with Cambridge University Press. He currently serves on the editorial boards of a number of professional journals in economics, law and trade policy.

CÉDRIC DUPONT is Professor of International Relations at the Graduate Institute of International Studies, Geneva. He is a Senior Research Fellow of the Berkeley Asia Pacific Economic Cooperation Study Center (BASC) at the University of California at Berkeley and an Associate Editor for Europe of the Journal Business and Politics.
He has written extensively on regional integration developments in Western Europe, on domestic–international linkages in international negotiations and on game-theoretic modelling in political science. His current research focuses on the political economy of trade and finance, on the governance of world and regional integration processes and on regional integration in Asia and the Pacific.

MANFRED ELSIG is Associate Professor of International Relations and Deputy Managing Director of the World Trade Institute, University of Bern. He is the Director of the National Centre for Competence in Research Trade Regulation. He holds a PhD from the University of Zurich in political science. His research focuses on international political economy, international organisations, international courts, preferential trade agreements and European trade policy. He has taught at the University of Zurich, the University of Geneva, the Graduate Institute of International and Development Studies, the London School of Economics and Political Science and the Thunderbird School of Global Management. His work has been published in journals such as *International Studies Quarterly*, *European Union Politics*, *European Journal of International Relations*, *Review of International Organizations*, *Review of International Political Economy* and *World Trade Review*. He is the co-editor of *Governing the WTO: Past, Present and Beyond Doha* (Cambridge

University Press, 2011) and *Trade Cooperation: The Purpose, Design and Effects of Preferential Trade Agreements* (Cambridge University Press, 2015).

JOSEPH MICHAEL FINGER has worked at the United Nations Conference on Trade and Development, the US Treasury Department and the World Bank. Since retiring from the World Bank he has served as Resident Scholar at the American Enterprise Institute, as consultant to developing country governments, to the United Nations Food and Agricultural Organization, the UN Millennium Project Task Force on Trade, the UK Department for International Development and the Asian Development Bank. Dr Finger has taught at universities around the world, and specialises in the law and the economics of the GATT/WTO system in relation to development, on trade management instruments and their national governance, on the commercial value of intellectual property in poorer communities and on the coordination of development support and the rules-making function of the WTO. Dr Finger is author or editor of nine books, and author or co-author of 150 articles and reviews.

JUDITH L. GOLDSTEIN is the Janet M. Peck Professor of International Communication and the current chair of the Department of Political Science at Stanford University. Her research focuses on international political economy, with a focus on trade politics. She has written and/or edited six books including *Ideas, Interests and American Trade Policy* and more recently *The Evolution of the Trade Regime: Politics, Law and Economics of the GATT and the WTO*. Her articles have appeared in numerous journals. Her current research focuses on the political requisites for trade liberalisation focusing both on tariff bargaining and public preferences. In addition, she is engaged in the analysis of a large survey panel, which focuses on how economic hard times influence public opinion. Goldstein has a BA from the University of California, Berkeley, a Master's degree from Columbia University and a PhD from UCLA.

ROBERT GULOTTY is an Assistant Professor in the Department of Political Science and the College of the University of Chicago. His research focuses on the politics of international trade and investment, including the political economy of regulatory cooperation in trade agreements, the politics of exchange rates, and the origins of the global trade regime.

BERNARD HOEKMAN is Professor and Director, Global Economics at the Robert Schuman Centre for Advanced Studies, European University Institute in Florence, Italy. Prior positions include Director of the International Trade Department and Research Manager in the Development Research Group of the World Bank and economist in the GATT Secretariat. A graduate of the Erasmus University Rotterdam, he obtained his PhD in Economics from the University of Michigan. He is a CEPR Research Fellow where he co-directs the Trade Policy Research Network and a senior associate of the Economic Research Forum for the Arab countries, Iran and Turkey. His research focuses on trade and development, international trade agreements, trade in services and international regulatory cooperation. His most recent publication is *The Global Trade Slowdown: A New Normal?* (London: CEPR Press and VOXEU, 2015).

TOBIAS HOFMANN is Assistant Professor of Political Science at the University of Utah. He is a graduate of the University of Konstanz and holds a PhD in Political Science from the Free University of Berlin. Tobias Hofmann's work examines the political economy of international institutions, with a focus on multilateral and preferential trade agreements as well as European integration. He is particularly interested in the design, use and effectiveness of institutions related to compliance and the settlement of trade disputes. His publications include 'Caving in or Sitting it Out. Longitudinal Patterns of Non-compliance in the European Union' (*Journal of European Public Policy*, 2012, with Tanja A. Börzel and Diana Panke) and 'Obstinate and Inefficient: Why Member States Do not Comply with European Law' (*Comparative Political Studies*, 2010, with Tanja A. Börzel, Diana Panke and Carina Sprungk).

DOUGLAS A. IRWIN is the John Sloan Dickey Third Century Professor in the Social Sciences in the Department of Economics at Dartmouth College. He is author of *Free Trade Under Fire* (Princeton University Press, fourth edition 2015), *Trade Policy Disaster: Lessons from the 1930s* (MIT Press, 2012), *Peddling Protectionism: Smoot-Hawley and the Great Depression* (Princeton University Press, 2011), *The Genesis of the GATT* (Cambridge University Press, 2008, co-authored with Petros Mavroidis and Alan Sykes), *Against the Tide: An Intellectual History of Free Trade* (Princeton University Press, 1996) and many articles on trade policy in books and professional journals. He is a Research Associate of the

National Bureau of Economic Research and has also served on the staff of the President's Council of Economic Advisers.

SOO YEON KIM is Associate Professor of Political Science at the National University of Singapore. She holds a PhD in Political Science from Yale University and a BA in Political Science and International Relations from Yonsei University. She is the author of *Power and the Governance of Global Trade: From the GATT to the WTO* (Cornell University Press, 2010). Her current research focuses on production networks, multinational firms and the politics of free trade agreements in Asia; the politics of compliance in WTO disputes; and rising powers in the global economy. Soo Yeon Kim's recent publications include *Regional Trade Governance* (with Edward D. Mansfield and Helen V. Milner, 2016) in Tanja Börzel and Thomas Risse, eds. *The Oxford Handbook of Comparative Regionalism* (Oxford University Press, 2016), and with Mark S. Manger, *Hubs of Governance: Path Dependence and Higher-Order Effects of Preferential Trade Agreement Formation* (Cambridge University Press, 2016).

JOOST PAUWELYN is Professor of International Law at the Graduate Institute of International and Development Studies in Geneva, Co-Director of the Institute's Centre for Trade and Economic Integration, and a Visiting Professor at Georgetown Law Center. He specialises in World Trade Organization (WTO) law and Foreign Investment Law, and advises governments and non-state actors in WTO dispute settlement and investor–state arbitration. Previously, he was Senior Advisor with King & Spalding LLP, a tenured professor at Duke Law School, a Visiting Professor at both Stanford and Harvard Law Schools, as well as legal officer at the WTO from 1996 to 2002. He was appointed to the roster of WTO panelists and as arbitrator under Free Trade Agreements and the Energy Charter Treaty. He is also a member of the ICSID Panel of Conciliators. He is Co-Editor-in-Chief of the Journal of International Economic Law.

KRZYSZTOF J. PELC is William Dawson Scholar and Associate Professor in the Department of Political Science at McGill University. He works on the political economy of international trade. His book *Making and Bending International Rules* is forthcoming at Cambridge University Press.

ARLO POLETTI is Assistant Professor of International Public Policy at the University LUISS Guido Carli in Rome. His research focuses on the political economy of trade policy making, WTO judicial politics, the politics of international regulatory cooperation and interest groups' lobbying. He obtained a PhD from the University of Bologna, and was a post-doctoral researcher at the Department of Political Science of the University of Antwerp. He has published on these topics in *Journal of Common Market Studies, Journal of European Public Policy, Regulation & Governance, West European Politics, Comparative European Politics* and other outlets. He is also the author of a monographic study *The European Union and Multilateral Trade Governance: The Politics of the Doha Round* (Routledge) and co-author of a forthcoming ECPR Press book, *Judicial Politics and International Cooperation: From Dispute Settlement to Deal-Making in the World Trade Organization.*

JULIA QIN is Professor of Law at Wayne State University in Michigan and Tsinghua University School of Law in China. She has also taught as Visiting Professor at the University of Michigan Law School, Washington University in St. Louis, and Seoul National University in South Korea. She received her LLB from Peking University, and her LLM and SJD degrees from Harvard Law School. Her work focuses on the law and policy of the World Trade Organization and special issues concerning China and the WTO. Her recent publications include *Accommodating Divergent Policy Objectives under WTO Law: Reflections on EC–Seal Products* (AJIL Unbound, 2015), *The Conundrum of WTO Accession Protocols: In Search of Legality and Legitimacy* (Virginia JIL, 2015) and *Reforming WTO Discipline on Export Duties: Sovereignty over Natural Resources, Economic Development and Environmental Protection* (J. World Trade, 2012).

FRIEDER ROESSLER completed his legal training in Germany, and afterwards worked for the World Bank, the General Agreement on Tariffs and Trade (GATT) and the World Trade Organization (WTO). In 1989, he was appointed Director of Legal Affairs of the GATT. Mr Roessler's main task at the GATT and the WTO was to advise dispute settlement panels and prepare drafts of their reports. He was also closely involved in the legal aspects of the Uruguay Round negotiations and participated in the legal drafting process at the end of the Round. After leaving the WTO in 1995, Mr Roessler joined the faculty of law of Georgetown University in Washington, DC. From 2001 until 2012 Frieder Roessler served as the first Executive Director of the Advisory Centre on WTO Law (ACWL). Mr Roessler has published extensively in the field of international trade law.

LUCA RUBINI is Reader (associate professor) in International Economic Law and deputy director of the Institute of European Law at Birmingham Law School. He served as référendaire (law clerk) with Advocate General Jacobs at the European Court of Justice in 2002–2003. He has held visiting positions at the European University Institute, the Institute of International Economic Law (Georgetown), the World Trade Institute (University of Bern) and Bocconi University. He is a fellow of the Centre of European Law, King's College London. He has law degrees from the Catholic University, Milan (JD) and King's College London (MA, PhD).

GIORGIO SACERDOTI is emeritus professor at Bocconi University in Milan where he was professor of international law from 1994 and Jean Monnet Chair in European law from 2004. In his writings and teaching he focuses on international trade and investment law, arbitration and adjudication. From 2001 to 2009 he was a Member of the WTO Appellate Body which he chaired in 2006–2007. He was previously Vice President of the OECD Working Group on bribery and presided over the drafting committee of the OECD Anti-bribery Convention of 1997. A member of the Milan Bar, he is an active commercial and investment arbitrator, a member and chair of several tribunals under the ICSID Convention, on whose arbitrators' list he has been for many years, and of other arbitral institutions rules.

L. ALAN WINTERS is Professor of Economics at the University of Sussex, a Research Fellow and former Programme Director at the Centre for Economic Policy Research in London, and a Fellow at the Institute for the Study of Labor in Bonn. He was formerly Chief Economist at the British Government's Department for International Development, as well as Director of the Development Research Group, Economist, and Division Chief and Research Manager in the World Bank. He is Chief Executive Officer of the Migrating Out of Poverty Research Programme Consortium, Chairman of the Board of the Global Development Network and a member of the Council of the UK's Economic and Social Research Council. He is currently the editor of *The World Trade Review*. He has advised, inter alia, the OECD, the Commonwealth Secretariat, the European Commission, the European Parliament, UNCTAD, the WTO and the Inter-American Development Bank.

AYDIN YILDIRIM is a PhD candidate in Political Science at the University of Antwerp. He is a member of the research group Antwerp

Centre for Institutions and Multilevel Politics (ACIM). He received his Master's by Research (MSc) degree in Politics and International Relations from the University of Edinburgh in 2013 and previously obtained his Bachelor of Arts degree in Political Science from the University of Houston. He is currently a guest fellow at the Max Planck Institute Luxembourg for International and European Law. His main research interests are the World Trade Organization, international political economy and international trade. He is in the final phase of his PhD dissertation that examines the impact of the globalisation of production chains – i.e. the so-called global value chains – on WTO Members' propensity to comply with their WTO commitments.

PREFACE

The World Trade Organization (WTO) has celebrated twenty years of existence. To mark this occasion we invited leading scholars from political science, law and economics to Bern to participate in the World Trade Forum in September 2015. The focus of attention was on what the WTO has achieved as an organisation or, simply put, whether 'it is fit for purpose'. We learned in this process how disciplinary 'goal posts' differ and how performance is assessed in varying ways. We hope this volume will inspire a new generation of scholars to focus critically on the WTO's achievements.

We benefited greatly from the exchange among the participants and wish to thank all of them for their inputs, which resulted in this volume. We hope that readers will find some of their intuitions about how the WTO can be assessed, confirmed or challenged. This volume is not the definitive resource when it comes to assessing the overall performance of the WTO, but is rather a toolkit for understanding how well the objectives have been met and sheds lights on areas of performance so far not sufficiently explored.

This volume would not have been possible without the contribution of the World Trade Institute (WTI) and a number of outstanding people. We wish to thank the WTI and the NCCR Trade Regulation for financial support and hosting the World Trade Forum conference that provided the basis for this book. We further wish to thank Susan Kaplan, Morven McLean and Rebecca Gilgen from the WTI for their editorial support, and Kim Hughes from Cambridge University Press for her excellent guidance throughout the entire process and her continued support for the World Trade Forum Series.

ABBREVIATIONS

AB	Appellate Body
ACP Group of States	African, Caribbean and Pacific Group of States
AD	anti-dumping
AD Agreement	Anti-dumping Agreement
AoA	Agreement on Agriculture
BITs	bilateral investment treaties
BTN	Brussels tariff nomenclature
CAFTA–DR	Dominican Republic–Central America Free Trade Agreement
DESTA	Design of Trade Agreements
DSB	WTO Dispute Settlement Body
DSU	WTO Dispute Settlement Understanding
EEC	European Economic Community
EFTA	European Free Trade Association
EU	European Union
FIEs	foreign-invested enterprises
GATS	General Agreement on Trade in Services
GATT	General Agreement on Tariffs and Trade
GPA	Government Procurement Agreement
GVCs	global value chains
HS	Harmonized Commodity Description and Coding System
ICC	International Chamber of Commerce
ICJ	International Court of Justice
ICSID	International Centre for Settlement of Investment Disputes
IIT	intra-industry trade
INR	Initial Negotiating Rights
IO	International Organisation
ISDS	Investor-State Dispute Settlement
ITO	International Trade Organization
JPC	Joint Plant Committee
MAS	Mutually Agreed Solution
MFN	most-favoured nation
NAFTA	North American Free Trade Agreement
NGOs	non-governmental organisations

NME	non-market economy
NTMs	non-tariff measures
OECD	Organisation of Economic Co-operation and Development
PTA	preferential trade agreements
RTA	regional trading agreement
SCM Agreement	WTO Agreement on Subsidies and Countervailing Measures
SDF	Steel Development Fund
SOCB	state-owned commercial banks
SOE	state-owned enterprise
SPS	sanitary and phytosanitary measures
TBT Agreement	Agreement on Technical Barriers to Trade
TBTs	technical barriers to trade
TRIMs	Agreement on Trade-Related Investment Measures
TRIPS	Agreement on Trade-Related Aspects of Intellectual Property Rights
TTBs	temporary trade barriers
TTIP	Transatlantic Trade and Investment Partnership
UN	United Nations
US	United States of America
WDI	World Development Indicators
WHO	World Health Organization
WIOD	World Input-Output Database
WIPO	World Intellectual Property Organization
WTO	World Trade Organization

PART I

Introduction and Setting the Stage

1

Introduction

MANFRED ELSIG, BERNARD HOEKMAN AND JOOST PAUWELYN

The Rationale for the Volume

The World Trade Organization (WTO) has recently celebrated 20 years of existence. Although two decades is a relatively short period for an international organisation (IO), the WTO has established itself as the multilateral anchor of global trade politics and law. Its development has certainly been helped by the achievements of its forerunner treaty, the General Agreement on Tariffs and Trade (GATT), yet, the decision to create a new IO in the early 1990s was a landmark decision transforming trade politics for years to come. The timing was prompted by a so-called 'constitutional moment' at the end of the Cold War and the development of a broad consensus among leading industrialised countries on the need to create a more legalised system expanding commitments to new areas (such as services) in order to reflect the growing economic interdependence among nations and firms. In addition, many saw the development of new multilateral rules and a more judicialised system as an attempt to tame US incentives to go 'unilateral' in trade policy. In retrospect, the creation of the WTO and the new legal commitments was an important achievement.

The early history of the WTO is one of an ascending organisation that, in the 1990s, attracted considerable attention from the public at large. More and more states accelerated or started the process of gaining WTO accession (including China and Russia). Most notably, the dispute settlement arm of the organisation swiftly established itself as an authoritative voice by providing guidance as to how to interpret the thousands of new legal obligations when put into practice. It did so not with a rod of iron, but through persistent legal interpretation to foster a rules-based system and the development of case law. The first group of Appellate Body (AB) Members were aware that the 'young plant' needed to be tended and nurtured with a calm, but steady hand.

Towards the end of the 1990s, many WTO Members expressed the opinion that some rules needed to be updated and new agreements needed to be explored through a new trade round that would go beyond increased liberalisation in services and in agriculture (built-in agenda from the Uruguay Round). The failure of launching a new round in 1999 at the Ministerial Conference in Seattle exposed the difficulties in setting joint objectives for new rules in a growing organisation. Different expectations about the new round's mandate reflected important divergences of interests among WTO Members. In addition, the perceived strong dispute settlement arm (unintentionally) hampered efforts to quickly conclude new arrangements. The imbalance between the judicial and the legislative arm became all too obvious. Notwithstanding the successful start of a trade round in Doha in 2001, the organisation has not been able to formally update existing rules (either substantial or procedural). The growing network of bilateral and plurilateral agreements, including new mega-regionals, is partly a result of stagnation in the WTO and the difficulties of making new rules.

The objective of this volume is not to investigate further the root causes of this development (see e.g. Hoekman 2014; Francois and Hoekman 2015), but rather to take stock of what the WTO has achieved. The rhetoric of a 'deadlocked' organisation does not do justice to the WTO's continuing role as the multilateral anchor of trade relations. New Members join the organisation, multiple WTO committees monitor implementation and address trade concerns, WTO jurisprudence further evolves and the dialectical relationship between preferential agreements and the WTO inspires the daily work of the organisation on all levels. The WTO continues to provide transparency about its Members' trade policies and offers technical assistance and capacity building to the weaker actors, encouraging them to participate fully in the deliberations and negotiations (including dispute settlement procedures).

There are twenty years of WTO history providing fertile ground for inquiry into how well the WTO has performed. The collection of work presented in this volume is the result of the World Trade Forum 2015 conference where scholars representing various academic disciplines and traditions gathered to present their analyses of the WTO. The scholars who contributed to this book have closely observed and critically accompanied many of the steps the WTO has taken, from its pre-existence reflected in the nascent ideas formulated in the Uruguayan seaside resort of Punta del Este, to the most recent attempts to continue the journey at the 2015 Ministerial Conference in Nairobi. Contributors to this volume have different stories to tell, grounded in the theoretical and empirical traditions of their respective disciplines. Their analyses come to different conclusions, but, in the end, the collected work in this volume shows that the impact of the WTO might be much more positive than we are led to believe by the media and news on the current stage of the trade negotiations in a failed Doha Development Round.

Overview of the Contributions

This volume features fourteen substantive chapters that cover extensive ground. Reflecting the importance of dispute settlement, six of the contributions analyse the WTO's allegedly successful system. The other contributions focus on various issues ranging from the origins of the multilateral system, the accession process, the interaction between preferentialism and multilateralism, the prevalence of WTO-type provisions in preferential trade agreements (PTAs) and the interaction with other international organisations. The selection of these topics was inspired on the one hand by new findings and intriguing insights that have been largely overlooked in the past and on the other hand by the desire to reflect on important lessons drawn from twenty years of scholarship on trade policy and the WTO. We have chosen not to focus on governance in rule-making in the narrow sense as a recent volume in the World Trade Forum Series analysed the trends in and limits of decision-making in considerable depth (Cottier and Elsig 2011; see also Elsig 2016).

Below, we summarise the key findings of each of the chapters and how they relate to thinking about the achievements of the global trading system with the WTO at its centre. Chapter 2, 'Thinking About the Performance of the World Trade Organization: A Discussion Across Disciplines' by Manfred Elsig, Bernard Hoekman and Joost Pauwelyn, draws on the concept of performance and discusses different narratives from three disciplines: international relations, economics and law. The authors posit that these debates have often occurred in isolation, although they have considerable common ground. An important objective of this chapter is to summarise key contributions in the three disciplines and to encourage further cross-fertilisation across disciplines. What the chapter further shows is that, depending on the performance matrix used, the assessment of how the WTO matters (performance) can vary significantly (the 'eye of the beholder' effect). This has implications not just for research and future research programmes, but is important from an accountability and 'ownership' perspective. Governments find it increasingly challenging to explain why they negotiate trade agreements and what the impacts of trade agreements have been.

Chapters 3 and 4 offer new and intriguing insights into the early days of the multilateral system. Chad P. Bown and Douglas A. Irwin in their contribution 'The GATT's Starting Point: Tariff Levels Circa 1947', provide a new estimation approach for establishing the average tariff level when GATT participants began tariff negotiations after World War II. They find that starting tariffs were significantly lower than general wisdom has assumed (22 per cent rather than 40 per cent). These results help us reconsider the true success of the first rounds of trade negotiations. The GATT has still performed remarkably in terms of tariff reduction, but less so than the established trade community has suggested. This also shows other outcomes in an even more favourable light, such as binding the agreed tariff reductions, establishing the concept of non-discrimination through most-favoured nation (MFN) treatment and national treatment, ensuring increased transparency of trade policy measures, paving the way for future negotiations, and for establishing a system for long-term peaceful resolution of bilateral disputes.

Judith L. Goldstein and Robert Gulotty in their contribution 'Negotiating in the Early GATT: Norms, Rules and the US Tariff Schedule', provide a historical analysis of the success of the early regime in terms of trade negotiations. They offer new evidence based on archival data on how the early GATT negotiation rounds functioned. They analyse in detail how tariff reduction swaps took place, in order to gain a better understanding of when and why nations were able to conclude bargains. They show that the success of the organisation in its early years was less in the creation of strict rules to regularise trade, and more in accommodation of the domestic constraints faced by those who came to Geneva to negotiate tariffs. These lessons are interesting against the background of the current deadlock in WTO negotiations.

Part II is devoted to general trends and patterns in WTO dispute settlement. Frieder Roessler in Chapter 5, 'Dispute Settlement in the WTO: From a Deliberately Designed to a Spontaneously Grown Order', discusses how different practices affect the direction of the legal order. Roessler sees two types of order that have guided expectations in the field of dispute settlement in the GATT and the WTO: spontaneous orders, which grew out of practices, and directed orders, which were deliberately created by agreement. The dispute settlement order of the GATT grew spontaneously out of an accumulation of practices that the contracting parties to the GATT agreed to codify and refine. The dispute settlement order of the WTO, originally purposefully created by agreement, is turning into an order in which the expectations of Members are less and less based on the agreed provisions and more and more on practices that the disputant parties and the judicial organs of the WTO are adapting *praeter* or *contra legem*. This chapter nicely contrasts the different evolutionary pathways legal order can take.

In Chapter 6, Dirk De Bièvre, Arlo Poletti and Aydin Yildirim survey the literature that focuses on the important question of what explains the launching and resolution of disputes in the WTO. In 'About the Melting of Icebergs: Political and Economic Determinants of Dispute Initiation and Resolution in the WTO', they explore in particular how actual disputes relate to potential cases, i.e. WTO dispute settlement cases that could have been brought, but were not. In addition, the authors review possible political and economic determinants of dispute resolution. In doing so, they map out the universe of potential WTO disputes and then shed light on some of the political and economic factors that can explain under what conditions government representatives select the foreign trade barriers they want to target through WTO litigation. The challenge of analysing the submerged part of the iceberg remains in identifying the universe of potential WTO cases that government representatives can act upon and in assessing the relative weight of, and the relationships between, possible political determinants. In other words, without knowing how much of the iceberg is under the water, a systematic analysis of the functioning of dispute settlement can only be partial.

Chapter 7, 'The WTO Dispute Settlement System: Consolidating Success and Confronting New Challenges', takes stock of the operation of both panels and the Appellate Body. In this chapter, Giorgio Sacerdoti, a former Member of the Appellate Body, critically reviews the overall performance to date before going on to discuss a number of problems that have emerged in the dispute settlement process and the challenges that will confront WTO Members in the future. This chapter puts forward concrete proposals for dealing with both immediate constraints, and the longer-term challenges of ensuring the sustainability of the dispute settlement system, such as procedures for appointment and reappointment of Members of the Appellate Body.

The final chapter in Part III, 'Does Trade Comply?: The Economic Effect(iveness) of the WTO Dispute Settlement Process', analyses the performance of the WTO dispute settlement process by focusing on the effects on trade flows between disputing parties. Tobias Hofmann and

Soo Yeon Kim offer an important test for whether the dispute settlement mechanism works in the way it was intended to by the designers of the system. In their empirical analysis they find little support for such an assertion. The chapter focuses on two particular questions. First, does WTO dispute settlement matter? And, second, why do trade flows not necessarily resume following dispute settlement of compliance cases? The results show that trade 'does not comply'. The empirical analysis investigates the effects of tariffs and trade remedy investigations on trade between parties. The authors advance a new explanation that relies on trade policy substitutes that enable respondents to achieve non-compliance by other means. This is another form of unintended consequences.

Part IV focuses on specific debates. In Chapter 9, 'Twenty Years of Third-Party Participation at the WTO: What Have We Learned?', Krzysztof J. Pelc discusses the effects of opening up the WTO's litigation process, partly in an attempt to increase the transparency of dispute settlement, to third parties. Through this mechanism, countries that are not party to the dispute can be present in the room during otherwise private consultations, and their views are recorded as an integral part of the final report of the panel and the AB. The chapter addresses questions such as: how has the function of third parties and their views evolved since 1995?; how have litigants' attitudes to third-party participation changed?; and, finally, is third-party participation a net good, by making litigation more open, or a net bad, by making settlements more difficult? The most important finding is that third-party participation reduces the possibilities of settlement, which goes against a fundamental objective of the dispute settlement system. At the same time, when settlements are reached, they are less likely to be discriminatory.

Julia Qin's contribution focuses on the accession protocols and relationship with the WTO Agreement, an area that has been largely overlooked when focusing on WTO dispute settlement. In Chapter 10, 'Mind the Gap: Navigating Between the WTO Agreement and Its Accession Protocols', she re-examines the legal basis for member-specific rule-making, assesses relevant WTO jurisprudence and proposes a new approach to navigating such a relationship. Further, she addresses four specific interpretive issues arising from such a relationship: how to determine the availability of general exceptions of WTO Agreements to member-specific obligations; how to determine the scope of derogation from WTO provisions by the member-specific rules; the relevance of accession protocols to the interpretation of WTO multilateral agreements; and the relevance of the accession protocol of one Member to the interpretation of the accession protocol of another. These interpretive issues have arisen in one form or another in WTO disputes, but not all of them have been properly resolved and some have not even attracted much attention.

Luca Rubini's contribution in Chapter 11, 'The Age of Innocence: The Evolution of the Case Law of the WTO Dispute Settlement: Subsidies as a Case Study', provides an analysis of the work of both panels and the AB in this important area of WTO jurisprudence. Against a paradigmatically unclear regulatory framework, he examines the attitude of the panels and the AB during the first twenty years of the WTO by asking the following questions: Was the first phase one of simple discovery? Has this progressively given way to a more active approach towards the law, which could be – and has been – tagged 'activism'? Using representative examples of decisions on subsidies by panels and the AB, this chapter argues that the panels are on the whole more deferential than the AB. The latter is, in Rubini's view, adopting increasingly innovative decisions, which either raise serious doubts about their correctness or should be assessed as seriously wrong. The author advocates that WTO adjudicating bodies should pay more attention to the 'negotiated balance' and the 'point of balance' of the various disciplines and that, in this respect, a stronger use of the negotiating history is necessary

Finally, Part V looks at interactions within and across regimes. In Chapter 12, 'The Presence of the World Trade Organization Within Preferential Trade Agreements', Todd Allee and Manfred Elsig question the conventional wisdom that PTAs are at odds with the multilateral trading system and that they present a major challenge to the WTO's pre-eminence. They analyse the texts of hundreds of PTAs in two novel ways to see how compatible they are with WTO rules. First, for ten notable issues typically found in PTAs, they tally the number and prominence of references to the applicable GATT or WTO Agreement. Second, they calculate the percentage of text in a given PTA Article that is copied from the analogous GATT or WTO Agreement. Perhaps surprisingly, they find that many PTAs take the majority of their language from WTO Agreements and that across several notable trade issues PTAs defer heavily to the WTO. These unique findings illustrate an underappreciated role played by the WTO and suggest that perceived tensions between PTAs and the WTO are somewhat overstated, and that in assessing the true performance of the WTO one also needs to address the export of legal texts to the world of PTAs.

Chapter 13 focuses on the dialectical relationship between the multilateral system and PTAs. In 'The WTO and Regional Trading Agreements: Is It All Over for Multilateralism?', Alan Winters sets out the WTO's scorecard on regionalism starting with the inheritance it received in this respect from the GATT. He suggests that the WTO has been able to do very little about the march of PTAs and that we cannot expect very much more from it in the future. He discusses the argument that by avoiding the issue, the WTO has preserved itself and its other functions and has thus made the best of a very bad hand in maintaining multilateralism. He also suggests, however, that if we are to bequeath an effective multilateral system to the next generation, we will need to engineer a significant change in the hand that the WTO is dealt. These are important lessons for the potential future performance of the WTO.

Chapter 14, by Cédric Dupont and Manfred Elsig, addresses the question of the relationship of the WTO with other IOs. In 'Performance and International Organisations' Borders: The Case of the World Trade Organization', they argue that the international relations literature has paid little attention to questions related to boundaries between IOs. An analysis of the performance of the WTO, however, is not complete without an understanding of these politics at the border. This chapter aims to contribute to the literature by providing a framework of analysis. After conceptualising various border dynamics and outcomes, the chapter outlines conditioning factors and links these through a series of bivariate relationships with outcomes at the border. The analytical relevance of the framework is discussed with cases from the WTO and its border relations with other IOs, and a future research agenda on border politics is sketched out.

The final chapter, by Joseph Michael Finger, 'The GATT/WTO System and National Trade Policies: Which Comes First?', discusses the interrelationship between the WTO and national policy formation on the basis of case studies of Peru, Argentina and the United States. Finger argues that it is incorrect and misleading to regard the WTO as a 'top down' institution that imposes binding constraints on governments. Much depends on the preferences of national governments and how they respond to domestic political economy pressures. The case of Peru and the US illustrate how governments can use the WTO productively to manage such pressures; the case of Argentina in contrast illustrates how WTO rules can be circumvented for long periods of time, notwithstanding the DSU.

References

Cottier, Thomas and Elsig, Manfred (eds.). 2011. *Governing the World Trade Organization: Past, Present and Beyond Doha*. Cambridge: Cambridge University Press.

Elsig, Manfred. 2016. *The Functioning of the WTO: Options for Reform and Enhanced Performance*. Policy Option Paper, E15-Initiative, Geneva: ICTSD.

Francois, Joseph and Hoekman, Bernard (eds.). 2015. 'Structural Issues at the WTO'. *World Trade Review*, 14(1): 1–5.

Hoekman, Bernard. 2014. 'Sustaining Multilateral Trade Cooperation in a Multipolar World Economy'. *Review of International Organizations* 9(2): 241–260.

2

Thinking About the Performance of the World Trade Organization

A Discussion Across Disciplines

MANFRED ELSIG, BERNARD HOEKMAN AND JOOST PAUWELYN

A Introduction

The World Trade Organization (WTO) officially opened its doors in 1995 on the shores of Lake Geneva. Although it is one of the youngest major international governmental organisations, the WTO is built upon customs, principles and rules that developed over nearly half a century under the loosely institutionalised platform of the General Agreement on Tariffs and Trade (GATT). Notwithstanding its short history, in the past twenty years the organisation has drawn significant attention from various segments of society in both developed and developing countries and has attracted thirty-three new members, transforming it into a nearly universal organisation. It has also become the focus of extensive academic research spanning a number of disciplines, most notably international economics, international law and international relations (IR). While most experts would argue that the WTO matters, and research has focused on a variety of WTO-related achievements, there are conceptual and empirical holes in WTO scholarship. In particular, significant scope exists to extend interdisciplinary research – much of the scholarly literature is limited to specific disciplinary 'silos'. Consequently, the questions that are analysed by economists, legal scholars and political scientists differ significantly. While this makes research on the WTO complementary, it also implies that there are unexploited opportunities for synergies.

This chapter focuses on WTO outputs and outcomes by drawing on concepts that measure the performance of the organisation, providing different disciplinary narratives from IR, economics and law. A key objective of this chapter is to explore further cross-fertilisation across disciplines. What we find is that, depending on the performance matrix used (the 'eye of the beholder'), the assessment of how the WTO matters (performance) can vary significantly. This has implications not just for future research and research programmes, but is also important from an accountability and 'ownership' perspective. Governments have found it increasingly difficult to explain why they negotiate trade agreements and what the impacts of trade agreements have been. This is a challenge that applies to both preferential and multilateral trade agreements (the WTO) – indeed, one consequence of the 'lack of coherence' in approaches to assessing the impacts of trade agreements is that it makes it more difficult to understand the rationales for, and effects of, different types of trade agreements that are pursued by WTO Members. This challenge also applies to answering the critical policy questions: where does the WTO have a comparative advantage or can add most value in the pursuit of a given objective?

B How to Think About Performance

In basic terms, one could define performance as achieving agreed-upon objectives (Gutner and Thompson 2010). In this context three key questions arise.

First, what goal is to be achieved? Gutner and Thompson (2010) differentiate between macro objectives (which are ambitious goals), intermediate outcomes and narrower or process-related tasks within international organisations (IOs). As we move from specific tasks to high-impact objectives, reaching the set baseline becomes more difficult. Also, in reality, set goals might be imprecise or worse – ambiguous. Therefore, how well-defined the objectives are affects the overall analysis. An important qualification here is that members of IOs might disagree on the purpose and therefore on the tasks they expect to be performed. This has been described as an 'eye of the beholder problem'. While trade liberalisation might be a key objective for one WTO Member, another might push for constraining the ability of a large player like the United States to use trade policy instruments unilaterally or might seek to protect specific industries from global competition. Therefore, performance assessment might vary across states and across key constituencies.

Second, given the benchmark or baseline, the next question is how well the defined objective or task is achieved. To answer this question, we need to focus on the sources of performance. Gutner and Thompson (2010) differentiate between factors that are internal and those that are external to the organisation and social versus material factors. Internal factors relate to the delegated means (material) or the bureaucratic culture (social) prevalent in the organisation. External factors relate to the degree to which there are shared norms (social) or power politics (material) shaping trade policy. These factors all directly or indirectly affect overall performance.

Third, an important question is how good the performance would have been in the absence of certain institutional features and arrangements. Establishing counterfactuals often poses a methodological challenge to studies on performance (see also Elsig and Cottier 2011). In the past, research has mainly relied on a comparative case study design to analyse the institutional effects. A prominent example is the analysis of how the WTO dispute settlement system and its forerunner institution (the GATT) dealt with similarly tricky cases (Zangl 2008). A special test of the impact of institutions is how they perform in hard times. In the case of external shocks, such as economic and financial crises, it is important to understand how existing institutions buffer against demands for increased protectionism.

To sum up, measuring performance is far from trivial. It is composed of an analysis that first establishes the various baselines before mapping and tracing the key sources of performance in order to understand causal mechanisms. Finally, it often has to deal with methodological challenges in establishing causality, speaking to the need to think carefully about counterfactuals. In the following sections we examine three different angles of performance rooted in IR, economics and legal scholarship.

C An International Relations Angle

Most scholars in the mainstream IR tradition consider the role of IOs to be rather limited. However, institutions created in the trading system have been acknowledged to be more influential than institutions in many other policy fields. The seminal work of Keohane (1984) attributed to the GATT an important function in overcoming states' reluctance to cooperate, by providing information and helping induce compliance. Later, the WTO was excluded explicitly from realist-type scepticism that IOs without enforcement mechanisms are inconsequential (Downs et al. 1996). Most realist writings clearly stated that the WTO mattered as an institution as it was able to modify its Members' behaviour. The realist contributions focused more on the questions of who designed the rules and who controls the organisation (Gruber 2000). In addition, some work has suggested that increased legalisation could hurt weaker states (Drezner 2007). In particular, overlaps in new legal obligations create a fragmented system that allows larger states to strategically engage in forum-shopping of legal institutions. Power arguments were also tested in relation to weak states' (lack of) participation in the WTO dispute settlement system (Sattler and Bernauer 2011; Elsig and Stucki 2012).

I *So, What Needs to Be Achieved?*

In order to discuss the performance of the WTO, we need to start by asking: what is its purpose? While there are formal objectives listed in the treaties (e.g. in the preamble), these are often not suitable baselines for assessment because they are too ambitious or difficult to operationalise for the purpose of measurement (Elsig 2010). Also, some objectives are subject to significant change over time and actors' support for them can weaken or strengthen. For example, the original 1947 GATT agreement did not explicitly mention development (e.g. poverty reduction) as a goal to be achieved, and environmental concerns were absent as demonstrated by the objective of 'developing the full use of the resources of the world'. Notwithstanding differences with regard to the objectives and what importance they have, the multilateral trading system was created to help increase exchanges of goods (and later services) based on the general assumption that the lowering of barriers to trade increases overall welfare. While the economics literature (see below) has focused on this question, the IR literature has paid more attention to how the GATT/WTO institutions have served various political objectives. Below we distinguish between macro objectives and micro objectives.

A group of general objectives that are not core trade objectives, but that are important for the stability of the system, can be labelled macro goals. These goals are as follows:

First, international institutions are purposely designed to uphold the 'rule of law', which is reflected in rules that serve to protect in particular the weaker states and to control the abuse of power (Grant and Keohane 2005). This is particularly true for the WTO and its dispute settlement system. One of the main incentives for negotiating a highly legalised system to support the implementation of new sets of rules was to tame US unilateralism (Elsig and Eckhardt 2015; Pelc 2010). Therefore, a baseline objective can be derived around a shared objective held by a large group of contracting parties to constrain US unilateralism and to demand that the US uses the dispute settlement tools offered by the WTO.

Second, another potential objective is the ability of multilateral organisations to accommodate new powerful states. In the same way as some earlier GATT trade rounds were designed to integrate the EC and the emerging economies (e.g. Brazil and India) into the multilateral system, the WTO helps to manage the changing trade power dynamics driven by China's sustained high growth rates. China joined the WTO in 2001 after going through the accession procedure. More recently, WTO Members and Russia agreed on the terms of Russia's membership. Integrating these states into the existing system could certainly be seen as a major objective for international cooperation. The baseline here could be defined as the new entrants constructively playing the game (following the rules and rulings, providing leadership in ongoing negotiations).

Third, good international institutions are those that also work well in times of stress. Or put differently, an organisation's contribution to problem-solving could prove particularly important in times of crises. In the context of the GATT/WTO system, one can consider the economic and financial crises, which led to calls by domestic actors for protection of national markets, as a particular challenge. This raises the question of whether the WTO can mitigate the negative effects of increasing protectionism.

Fourth, focusing on the weakest members of the system, another potential baseline is the integration of least-developed countries (LDCs) into the system and providing them with support in negotiations, dispute settlement or implementation-related matters. For the legitimacy of the WTO (Elsig 2007), it is important to allow for differentiated treatment with a view to generating benefits for all WTO Members. While in the past LDCs were mostly excluded from concessions, more recently LDCs have been called upon to engage and take on commitments. The baseline here would consist of measuring the success of such integration and moving from exclusion to increasing involvement.

While the above objectives are situated at the macro level and primarily define the success of IOs such as the WTO, one can also consider less ambitious, institutional and procedural goals and functions that support the realisation of the macro objectives. There are four 'services' or institutional platforms that stand out in the context of the WTO as explained below.

The first of these is the simple provision of a negotiation platform where WTO Members can regularly meet, exchange concessions and explore new regulatory solutions to ongoing challenges. Ultimately, the baseline is the amount of outputs generated through these negotiations that have notable effects on market liberalisation and in addressing 'disguised' protectionism. Currently, the assessment of the outcome of the negotiation platform is straightforward given the lack of real progress on new agreements, with very few exceptions (e.g. the expansion of the information technology agreements and the agreement on trade facilitation).

Second, the WTO has an important function relating to regime management activities. The organisation assists in the implementation of the agreements through peer reviews, discussion fora and the active use of transparency mechanisms. Certain tools stand out in this context. One is the 'member-driven' work in the various committees, which allows for clarification, tabling concerns and learning about best practice, and can potentially lead to the elaboration of new regulatory initiatives (Lang and Scott 2009). Another example is the Secretariat-driven assessment of national trade policies (e.g. Trade Policy Review Mechanism). This helps provide more information and would potentially allow naming and shaming. Overall, the question is how well the system supports the implementation of the obligations (first-order compliance) and how committees could contribute to designing new initiatives.

Third, the WTO supports its Members through its technical assistance and capacity building arm. This raises the question of whether we are witnessing an improvement in Members' capacity to participate in the system. This is closely connected with the integration of LDCs into the system (macro goal). However, assessing technical assistance work is far from straightforward and to our knowledge no field experiments have been conducted to isolate the potential impact of the WTO from the impact of other factors.[1]

A fourth function is the provision of 'affordable' and equal access to the dispute settlement mechanism. Can all Members launch legal proceedings given power asymmetry, lack of direct support by stakeholders or lack of legal capacity? The objective is to support weaker actors and help them integrate into the system. Some research has suggested a continued lack of legal capacity (Kim 2008; Busch et al. 2009) as well as

[1] It would be interesting to study the effects of participation in training activities by comparing groups that were exposed to this 'treatment' with groups that have not participated in training. A major challenge here is to control for other actors' influence on technical assistance and training, as the WTO is just one of many providers of such services.

power asymmetry which leads to weak states not launching many complaints against more influential states (Elsig and Stucki 2012; Sattler and Bernauer 2011).

II Sources of Performance

Whatever macro- or micro objective is to be studied, an important next step is to attempt to locate the key internal and external factors as well as the social and material factors that influence performance. Which of these factors are at play depends on the objective aspired to. More salient and politicised goals (or where disagreement among Members on the direction is significant) may be more likely to be affected by material interests and external factors, whereas less contentious objectives and procedural goals might be significantly shaped by the institutional set-up and social factors.[2]

To provide an example of how these factors come into play, let us focus on the stalled WTO negotiations. How important are the different factors for reaching the objective of concluding the Doha Round? A key external factor has been the emergence of a multi-polar trade world which creates a larger set of 'material' interests diverging over the outcome of the Doha Round. Increasingly competing interests translate into varying expectations about the content of the Round. In other words, while few would dispute the importance of wrapping up the round, the 'eye of the beholder' problem as to what should be in the package deal leads to hard bargaining. Internal institutional challenges make it harder to find mutually agreeable solutions. That the decision-making mode is largely based on consensus-decision making makes the increased heterogeneity of interests more visible and creates an internal collective action problem. This 'institutional milieu' of the WTO (Elsig 2010) is further complicated by a socially constructed internal understanding that this organisation does not vote, although the treaty would allow recourse to voting. Thus, in this example, external and material interests are key, but the lack of performance can only be fully understood when internal norms and rules are also taken into consideration.

Collective action problems might, however, loom less large in WTO activities where norms are shared and material interests less conflicting.

[2] However, we can we think of alternative interaction effects, for instance internal and material interests (e.g. the interest of IO staffers in maximising bureaucratic power) or external and social factors (e.g. Washington Consensus affecting the work of the WTO).

This might explain why WTO Members agreed on a deal on trade facilitation at the WTO Ministerial Conference in Bali. It might, however, also be a result of smart design from which both developed and developing countries expect to reap benefits.

III Assessment

Based on the above conceptualisation of performance, the question of whether micro goals have been achieved cannot be easily answered without more in-depth causal analysis. We certainly witness areas of non-performance in relation to the negotiation function of the organisation. Here the 'eye of the beholder' problem related to the content of treaty outcomes looms large. By contrast, we also observe progress in terms of dispute settlement. Few would have expected the WTO dispute settlement system to play such a prominent role when it was created (see also Section E below). As to other micro goals such as regime management, and technical assistance and capacity building, the assessment is generally positive, although there is room for improvement (e.g. using the true potential of committee work).

If we focus on macro goals, at first glance, most of them seem to have been achieved to a large degree. The United States has taken less recourse to unilateral action and has been an active user of the dispute settlement system. Overall there is little evidence that the system has not moved towards more law (and therefore towards constraining the abuse of power). The integration of China in terms of dispute settlement seems to have worked well in light of avoiding 'trade wars'; the leadership role in negotiations might be another story. For the integration of Russia, it is too early to tell. Finally, the system was not damaged during the financial and economic crises. Whether this was a result of careful restraint by WTO Members in not bringing many more new cases, or an actual protectionism-taming-effect of the WTO's legal system remains unclear (see Baccini and Kim 2012). A counterfactual method could be employed to study this particular situation.

D An Economics Angle

Economists approach the question of assessing the objectives and performance of the WTO in a variety of ways. Below we focus on two dominant viewpoints or approaches. The first centres on understanding the rationale for trade agreements – the incentives governments have to cooperate. The second is primarily empirical, the aim being to assess the effects of WTO membership on individual countries and the impact of the organisation as a whole. Research in this vein centres on the design and results of negotiations aimed at reducing trade-distorting policies. The focus is on performance in the sense of understanding the economic implications of both what is being (might be) negotiated – ex ante analysis – and what has been agreed – ex post analysis.

Empirical economists have assessed the impact ('performance') of the WTO using a range of metrics, including the volume (value) of total trade flows, the structure and composition of trade flows (e.g. changes in the variety of goods traded or increases in the number of trading partners) and economic welfare (real income). Such empirical research is both 'macro' in the sense that it does not consider the specifics of any of the rules but simply analyses whether a 'WTO effect' can be discerned in the data, and 'micro' in the sense that the focus of analysis is on a specific area or set of disciplines – anti-dumping, agriculture, intellectual property, services, safeguards, technical barriers to trade, trade facilitation or the Dispute Settlement Understanding, for example.[3] Whether 'macro' or 'micro', it is usually taken as given that WTO disciplines and commitments are (have been) implemented and analysis tends to abstract from implementation costs in the narrow sense (see e.g. Finger 2007).

I Objectives of WTO Members

There are two strands of theorising in the economics literature about the 'macro' goals of countries that engage in trade agreements. One revolves around the terms of trade: the premise is that countries negotiate so as to reduce the negative terms-of-trade effects generated by trade policies of partner countries (Johnson 1953–1954; Bagwell and Staiger 2002).[4] A consequence of this view of trade cooperation is that agreements will (need to) be among countries that can affect their terms of trade. Small countries will generally have much less power to affect their terms of

[3] There is a huge literature on the many different WTO agreements and the effects, both normative and positive, of the policy disciplines that are embodied in each agreement. See, for example, the twenty-one-volume series *Critical Perspectives on the Global Trading System and the WTO* (Edward Elgar) for a collection of what leading scholars regard as core contributions on each of the main WTO agreements and activities.

[4] As such negative externalities can be created by domestic policies as well, the terms of trade theory also offers guidance regarding what types of policies could be the subject of multilateral negotiations and cooperation.

trade, although if products are differentiated even a small state will have some power to influence them.[5]

The other strand of the economics literature (e.g. Finger 1979; Tumlir 1985; Maggi and Rodriguez-Clare 1998; Ethier 2007) argues that trade agreements permit governments to adopt welfare-enhancing policies that are not (politically) feasible otherwise. The premise here is that governments are conservative in the sense that they give greater weight to prospective losses for groups in society than to the expected gains from liberalisation. More generally, governments have incentives to impose or maintain protection because this raises the incomes of the groups from which they derive political support. By committing to certain rules that constrain policy space, a government can make its reforms more credible: officials can tell interest groups seeking the (re-)imposition of trade policies that doing so will violate the nation's WTO commitments and provoke retaliation by trading partners. Trade agreements 'work' because they change the domestic political economy of trade policy. The agreements mobilise export interests to oppose lobbying for protection by import-competing interests because they would then lose access to foreign markets. By affecting the balance of political support, a more liberal trade policy stance becomes optimal.

The terms-of-trade and commitment-cum-political economy approaches generate clear goalposts from a performance perspective: both imply that the outcome of cooperation is a mix of liberalisation (lower average trade barriers) and rules that constrain the ability to reimpose barriers. All the different theories also imply that one effect of the WTO will be to increase trade relative to a counterfactual where no agreement had occurred because of the reduction in barriers and other trade-distorting policies and the uncertainty surrounding reduction in policy.

Views differ on how strong the evidence is for the presumed underlying rationale for trade cooperation. This is an active area of research. However, given that both theories imply that an outcome of cooperation is trade liberalisation and policy bindings that reduce uncertainty for traders, common measures of WTO 'performance' include:

[5] Bagwell and Staiger (2011). Of course, governments of small countries that cannot affect the terms of trade still have an interest in being members of the WTO because exporters will benefit from the tariffs that larger countries negotiate reciprocally with one another and then extend to all members under the most-favoured nation rule.

(i) progress in further reducing trade barriers and agreeing to new policy disciplines;
(ii) the extent to which domestic political economy pressures to reimpose protection were contained in times of stress and in response to shocks; and, more generally,
(iii) trade effects – whether the disciplines and operation of the WTO are associated with changes in trade and specialisation.

II Goals and Performance of the WTO: Three Metrics

1 Reducing trade barriers and agreeing to new policy disciplines

The basic stylised fact here is well known: to date the WTO's performance in delivering new policy commitments has been very weak. This does not require economic analysis because no new market access agreements were negotiated between 1995 and 2015. The Doha Development Agenda (DDA) has been moribund since 2008 and the large players that historically have been the mainstays of multilateral trade cooperation (the US and the EU) have shifted their main focus to the conclusion of so-called mega-regional agreements (namely, TPP and TTIP). Indeed, there has been a general shift towards preferential trade agreements (PTAs): some 400 PTAs have been notified to the WTO in the past twenty years. Much of the liberalisation that has occurred since 1995 has been associated with either unilateral reforms or the implementation of PTAs.

An interesting question is: to what extent are these reforms and agreements consistent with the 'macro' goal of reducing barriers to trade? Given that average levels of protection have continued to fall throughout the post-1995 period, and that the WTO explicitly allows for members to negotiate PTAs, it is not as clear as is often argued that the WTO has failed to deliver. It has not proved possible to conclude the Doha Round and agree to new rules in areas such as agricultural subsidies, but at the same time governments have signed numerous PTAs and reduced average levels of protection. Moreover, in key areas that economic research suggests will deliver large gains for developing countries – most notably trade facilitation (where estimated potential gains exceed what was proposed in Doha for reducing tariffs – e.g. Hoekman and Nicita 2011) – WTO Members did conclude an agreement.

2 Managing political economy pressures and preventing backsliding

Does the WTO improve national trade policy processes and outcomes? Here the answer is largely positive, although there is no consensus. At the national level there is evidence of a positive effect of the WTO on the 'quality' of trade policy. Although numerous, there are far fewer trade disputes than would be predicted based on the number of bilateral interactions between countries (Horn et al. 1999; Sattler and Bernauer 2011). In part this has been demonstrated by case studies of specific countries. Examples include the work of Finger and co-authors (Baracat et al. 2013; Finger and Nogues 2006) showing how WTO disciplines can be and have been used to manage and deflect pressures exerted by powerful interest groups for increased protection.

One measure of performance on this front is what happened (did not happen) following the 2008 financial crisis in the United States and the European Union. In contrast to the late 1970s and early 1980s – which are the most recent occasions when a major shock (Organization of the Petroleum Exporting Countries (OPEC) price rise) sent the global economy into a tailspin – when governments imposed a plethora of trade restrictions, including quotas and 'voluntary' export restrictions, there was no significant rise in average levels of protection post-2008.[6] In their study, Gawande, Hoekman and Cui (2015) find that WTO disciplines were a factor, although they also point to changes in the incentives to use trade policy: once countries are tightly integrated into international production networks they will not benefit from trade protection. But insofar as the rise of global value chains was a factor in restraining protectionism, to a significant extent this can also be attributed to the WTO: the open, rules-based multilateral trading system underpinned the shift by companies towards greater specialisation, cross-border investment and international production networks. Another measure of the performance of the WTO in this area is the absence of a large-scale increase in disputes alleging violations of WTO commitments following the 2008 crisis (see also Section E below). As discussed subsequently, some of the micro functions that played a supporting role in this regard are the WTO's various transparency mechanisms.

[6] While views on this differ – e.g. Evenett and Fritz (2015) argue there has been a significant increase in the use of trade-distorting policies – the majority view among economists is that average levels of protection did not increase significantly. See e.g. the contributions in Hoekman (2015).

3 Trade effects of the WTO

As noted previously, one measure of the attainment of both of the broad macro goals of the WTO that are distinguished in the economics literature is whether the WTO has an effect on countries' trade patterns and performance. The most straightforward measure of this is whether the WTO overall, or membership of a country in the WTO, increases trade volumes and the structure of trade (lower barriers and less uncertainty should increase investment in tradables and allow exploitation of comparative advantages that will be reflected in changes in specialisation).

The best evidence from a statistical perspective – in terms of identifying a 'WTO effect' – comes from studies of the effects of WTO accession. Countries that acceded to the WTO after 1995 differ from 'original' WTO Members in that they were forced to go through a rigorous and demanding process of review and scrutiny, and were required to do much more to bolster and reform their trade policy institutions than GATT incumbents. Rose (2005), Subramanian and Wei (2007) and Tang and Wei (2009) find a positive impact on trade for countries that joined the WTO after 1995. Tang and Wei (2009) attribute this positive effect to improved economic governance and argue that WTO accession acts as a partial cure for weaknesses in the investment climate in many acceding countries. The mechanisms at play here span various elements of the WTO, including greater policy certainty associated with bindings and transparency. Reducing uncertainty is an important dimension of the WTO and of trade agreements more generally (see, Francois 1997; Francois and Martin 2004; Handley 2014; Limão and Tovar 2011).

There has been debate in the economics literature as to whether positive trade effects apply more generally. Most notably, Rose (2004) undertook a gravity model analysis of the determinants of bilateral trade flows of GATT/WTO Members over a fifty -year period and failed to find a distinct impact associated with GATT/WTO membership. However, Subramanian and Wei (2007) find that the WTO does increase trade – by some 40 per cent on average – but only for those countries that participated in the process of reciprocal exchange of trade policy commitments. They do not find such a positive trade effect for most developing country members of the GATT. They attribute this to the pursuit of special and differential treatment, which implied that most of these countries did not make changes to their trade regimes. Similarly accounting for this selection bias, Liu (2009) and Dutt et al. (2013) find a strong role for the WTO in increasing the extensive margin of trade and conclude that WTO membership increases the extensive margin by 30 to 40 per cent.

Another example of a WTO agreement that should allow for clear identification of impacts is the Agreement on Government Procurement (GPA). This agreement applies to only a subset of WTO Members, thus permitting comparisons between signatories and non-signatories. No effects on the import behaviour of participating governments have been found. Shingal (2015) analyses procurement sourcing over time in Japan and Switzerland, and finds that GPA membership has no independent effect. Shingal (2011) concludes that the share of services contracts awarded to foreigners by these two countries, declined over time rather than rising. Rickard and Kono (2014) assess the effects of the GPA and forty-three PTAs that cover procurement and conclude that the agreements have no impact on foreign sourcing. However, here again there may be country-specificity at work. Fronk (2014), looking only at agreements negotiated by the United States, finds a statistically significant positive effect of bilateral procurement agreements on procurement behaviour. Thus, while the WTO overall has had the expected positive trade impact, this is not the case across the board.

III Sources of Performance

The determinants of the performance of the WTO in achieving the broad 'macro' goals that are the focus of economics research are varied. External events – not just events such as the 2008 crisis and recession or the 1998 East Asian financial meltdown, but also major structural changes such as the rapid growth experienced by China that led to a major rebalancing of the world economy – are clearly factors, as are decisions by WTO Members on whether and how to employ outside options to pursue macro goals. The extent to which WTO Members have used PTAs increased in the WTO's first twenty years and it is likely that this trend will continue. It is important to bear in mind that the WTO makes explicit provisions for the negotiation of PTAs between its Members. The WTO membership has a choice as to where and how to pursue trade cooperation. The revealed preference has been to pursue parallel tracks: the Doha negotiations and plurilateral initiatives as well as PTAs. Has a proliferation of PTAs led to significant trade diversion and negative spillovers for non-members? While the jury is still out on this question, empirical economic research suggests that PTAs have had nowhere near the negative effects they might have had and that on balance they have been associated with a general trend towards greater openness to trade globally.[7]

PTAs do not address many of the core issues that are of concern to the majority of the WTO membership and that are on the table in the DDA – most notably trade-distorting agricultural policies and subsidies. They are not a substitute for a comprehensive multilateral agreement that goes beyond what was negotiated in the 1990s in the Uruguay Round. An internal factor that many argue plays a role in limiting the achievements in new rule-making in the WTO is how the negotiating agenda is determined and the limited scope for adjusting it over time. Numerous economic analyses suggest that the 'landing zone' associated with the DDA is small and, perhaps more important, that the distribution of associated economic benefits and losses is quite asymmetric (Decreux and Fontagné 2015; Laborde and Martin 2015; Martin and Messerlin 2007). These are issues where there is substantial scope to apply both quantitative modelling and analysis used in other areas of economics (e.g. the theory of clubs and fiscal federalism), as well as a clear need for multidisciplinary research strategies to identify areas of complementarity between PTAs, small-group cooperation in the WTO and universal membership agreements.

One way in which the WTO has been able to sustain cooperation, prevent backsliding and avoid disputes, is through its various transparency mechanisms. These played a positive role in the post-2008 period in raising external visibility of national trade policy measures and signalling that the actions of governments would be scrutinised. Of course, the extent to which this led to fewer actions being taken is difficult to determine – there is no clear counterfactual. This is one aspect that requires a multidisciplinary analysis, e.g. detailed case studies of deliberation within governments and in parliaments. The same is true for assessments of the role that WTO commitments and disciplines play in determining how governments respond to pressures from domestic constituencies for economic assistance.

WTO rules, processes and interactions are just one mechanism through which government policy is affected. The economic research on the trade and growth effects of the WTO demonstrates that these

[7] In a survey of the empirical literature, Freund and Ornelas (2010) conclude that overall, PTAs have not had the adverse effects that many had expected, such as significant trade-diverting effects, because they were associated with a period in which countries liberalised more generally. Estevadeordal, Freund and Ornelas (2008) conclude that recent vintage PTAs have been accompanied by a reduction in MFN barriers to trade.

effects may be indirect as well as direct. The indirect channel may well be more important, but is difficult to identify. Thus, engagement in the WTO may help to stimulate a focus on improving the business environment and the investment climate more generally. The need to develop the capacity to implement agreements and to participate in dispute settlement may have spillover effects in other areas – e.g. the negotiation of investment agreements, or a reconsideration of approaches towards non-trade economic regulation. The WTO cooperates and interacts more closely with a large number of international agencies and organisations than the GATT did. One example is the work on 'aid for trade' which has brought the WTO into the ambit of the development community and raised awareness of trade capacity needs in the developing world. This may well have had significant payoffs in terms of attaining 'macro' goals. Documenting what achievements should be attributed to the operation of the WTO is a difficult challenge.

IV Assessment

Space constraints have limited this section to a very selective and partial discussion of the economic literature that is relevant to an assessment of the performance of the WTO. However, on balance this literature suggests that if the focus is on the three objectives identified above, the organisation has performed relatively well. The evidence indicates that the WTO has generated lower barriers to trade, sustained these in times of stress, and generated more trade. Insofar as greater trade is associated with higher incomes and a reduction in poverty, the WTO has increased world welfare – which is of course the primary high-level goal identified in the WTO Preamble. Clearly there are serious attribution problems associated with any empirical estimates of how much the WTO has contributed to global welfare (see e.g. Anderson 2014), and matters are complicated by the fact that the WTO builds on an acquis that was negotiated over a long period of time, including the GATT years. It is clear that future assessments of performance will depend on whether and how WTO Members are able to multilateralise what they achieve through PTAs and their willingness to do so.

E An International Law Angle

In legal scholarship, performance studies have focused on the effectiveness of international courts and tribunals or the dispute settlement mechanism set up in the context of certain IOs. With the considerable increase in the creation of international courts and tribunals, especially since the 1990s, the question of how these international adjudicators have performed has attracted significant attention. The puzzle of how international adjudicators can be effective without genuine policing or enforcement powers remains central. In the WTO, this has led to a focus on the performance of the dispute settlement system.

The predominant approach to assessing the performance of WTO dispute settlement is less than satisfactory. Most legal scholars and WTO insiders, be it from the WTO secretariat or the diplomatic missions of WTO Members, have focused on either usage rates, that is, how many disputes have been filed at the WTO, or compliance with adverse rulings issued by WTO panels or the Appellate Body (Wilson 2007; Davey 2009; Hughes 2012).

That usage rates or compliance with court judgments are at best limited proxies for performance should, however, be obvious. Indeed, in their annual updates on WTO dispute settlement, chairs of the WTO Dispute Settlement Body have referred to both low- and high usage rates as evidence of success.[8] When usage rates are *low*, the message is that WTO countries comply with WTO rules and jurisprudence, so there are no disputes and thus the system works. When usage rates are *high*, insiders congratulate themselves by stating that a high number of disputes demonstrates trust in, and effectiveness of, WTO dispute settlement. Either of these views can be correct (low usage rates, for example, can, indeed, be evidence of high levels of compliance, or of the complete ineffectiveness or unattractiveness of the system) but the two explanations cannot both be correct at the same time.

Similarly, there is no doubt that the rate of compliance with adverse WTO rulings by panels and the Appellate Body is impressively high (more than 80 per cent, Davey 2009; and, according to the WTO website, 'around 90 per cent', WTO 2015). Still, this alone tells us little, if anything, about overall compliance with WTO rules (the WTO disputes actually filed and ruled upon may only be the relatively uncontroversial tip of the iceberg of the total number of violations out there), nor even

[8] See Reflections from Outgoing Chairs on DSB Developments, 2010–2014, available at www.wto.org/english/tratop_e/dispu_e/dispu_e.htm#dsb. See also WTO Director-General Azevedo's statement in response to WTO disputes reaching the 500 mark: 'This shows that the WTO's dispute settlement system enjoys tremendous confidence among the membership, who value it as a fair, effective and efficient mechanism to solve trade problems' (WTO 2015).

about the actual compliance pull of WTO rulings. WTO rulings may be complied with because they impose relatively low burdens, since losing states see it as being in their own interests to do so, or for reasons external to the WTO such as unilateral threats to pull back development aid. As Shany puts it, 'a *low-aiming* court, issuing minimalist remedies, may generate a high level of compliance but have little impact on the state of the world' (Shany 2012: 227). The European Court of Human Rights, for example, boasted until recently that it had an almost perfect compliance rate. However, once the remedies called for became more intrusive – not just declaratory statements that a violation had occurred or relatively conservative monetary compensation, but also orders to reopen faulty legal proceedings or to adopt broad legal or policy reforms – compliance rates significantly declined (Shany 2012). Similarly, high rates of compliance with WTO judgments may be related to the relatively limited remedies provided: only prospective compliance in the individual case and no retroactive damages for past harm caused or obligation to reform vis-à-vis all WTO Members. Conversely, a certain degree of non-compliance with WTO judgments does not necessarily reflect badly on WTO performance. As Raustiala points out, international rules or rulings 'can be effective even if compliance with them is low. If a legal standard is quite demanding, even widespread failure to meet it may still correlate with observable, desired changes in behavior' (Raustiala 2000: 394). Also, less than perfect compliance may be good rather than bad for the WTO system: It provides an escape valve or limited 'exit option' for countries to accommodate exceptionally strong political or economic interests. This 'exit option' in the face of exceptional circumstances may, indeed, explain why WTO Members were able to sign onto the more legalised WTO dispute settlement system in the first place. Without it, they may also be less willing to consent to new agreements (Pauwelyn 2005). From this viewpoint, attempting to ratchet up compliance levels with WTO rulings to 100 per cent may backfire and harm the system (e.g. certain countries may leave the WTO) rather than enhance its performance.

I Performance: A New Approach

Non–WTO-specific studies on the performance of international courts and tribunals take a more structured approach, along the lines we suggest in Section B (establishing the benchmark, isolating key sources of performance and thinking hard about potential counterfactuals).

Rather than focusing on 'outputs' such as number of disputes filed or rulings issued, Shany (2012) proposes a 'goal-based approach' – focusing on 'outcomes' rather than 'outputs' – to assess the performance of international courts. '[I]n order to measure the effectiveness of an international court using this approach, one has to identify the court's aims or goals – that is, the desired outcomes that it ought to generate – and ascertain a reasonable time frame for meeting some or all of these goals' (Shany 2012: 225). At a minimum, this approach involves 'goal identification, outcome assessment and establishing causation'. A more comprehensive analysis would 'also refer to structural and procedural indicators in order the gauge outcomes better and to diagnose root causes for underperformance' as well as 'the cost-effectiveness and efficiency of specific goal-attainment strategies' (Shany 2012: 254–255). Shany notes that an international tribunal may have different goals and distinguishes between them on the basis of their source (goals set by external constituencies versus actors within the system), hierarchical level (ultimate ends versus intermediate goals) and method of articulation (goals explicitly identified versus implicit or unstated goals). He also identifies four generic goals that most international courts are encouraged to achieve:

(i) 'promoting compliance with the governing international norms (primary norm compliance)', that is, in the WTO context, the enforcement of WTO commitments or seeking compliance by WTO Members with WTO norms, not only through disputes filed but also by means of changing or influencing state behaviour 'in the shadow of the law',
(ii) 'resolving international disputes and specific problems (dispute resolution or problem solving)', in the WTO sphere, avoiding escalating trade wars or settling trade disputes between two specific WTO Members,
(iii) 'contributing to the operation of related institutional and normative regimes (regime support)', in the WTO, for example, contributing to the WTO's overall goal of trade liberalisation and
(iv) 'legitimizing associated international norms and institutions (regime legitimization)', in the WTO context, conferring legitimacy on, for example, the states and government officials that established the WTO or, more broadly, advancing the rule of law in IR.

Along similar lines, Helfer (2014) identifies four different dimensions of performance of international tribunals:

(i) 'case-specific effectiveness', a measure closely linked to the level of compliance with court rulings,
(ii) '*erga omnes* effectiveness' or the effect of court rulings on the behaviour of all states subject to the court's jurisdiction (not just the disputing parties),
(iii) 'embeddedness effectiveness' or 'the extent to which [international courts] anchor their judgments in domestic legal orders, enabling national actors to remedy potential treaty violations at home and avoid the need for international litigation' and
(iv) 'effectiveness in developing international law' or 'norm-development effectiveness', that is, how court rulings 'contribute to building a body of international jurisprudence' (Helfer 2014: 466).

Applying these insights to an assessment of the performance of WTO dispute settlement, five steps can be envisaged: (i) goal identification, (ii) measurement, (iii) establishing causation, (iv) assessing cost-effectiveness and (v) considering explanations or indicators of good or bad performance (leading to both diagnosis and cure).

1 Identification

It is clear that, for different people, the DSU may have different goals. For trade diplomats, the main goal may be the avoidance of escalating trade wars and the settlement of trade disputes based on rules rather than economic power (Shany's 'dispute resolution or problem solving' function; Helfer's 'case-specific effectiveness'). For private traders, the core goal may be to enhance market access in foreign countries by efficiently removing WTO-inconsistent trade barriers (Shany's 'primary norm compliance' and 'regime support' functions). For academics and international law practitioners, the main benchmark may be the quality of legal or economic reasoning of WTO rulings or the system's contribution to world trade law or, more broadly, public international law (Helfer's 'norm-development effectiveness'). Depending on the goal identified, the WTO dispute settlement system may thus be highly successful (e.g. in avoiding escalating trade wars, achieving compliance with actual court rulings or developing a stable jurisprudence), or deeply disappointing (e.g. in swiftly opening foreign markets for private traders, significantly reducing the total pool of trade protectionist measures or basing WTO rulings on solid economic evidence or reasoning).

As noted earlier, high levels of compliance with court rulings ('case-specific effectiveness') does not necessarily equate with high overall levels of norm compliance ('primary norm compliance'), see also Elsig 2015. In the WTO, for example, during the first twenty years (1995–2014), 488 requests for consultations were filed, leading to 154 panel reports and ninety-six Appellate Body reports. Since the majority of disputes were settled or not proceeded with, there were only eighteen disputes where the remedy of retaliation was authorised and close to 90 per cent compliance with court rulings. Yet, the distribution of cases across the different WTO agreements is very uneven: of 488 requests, 387 invoked GATT, 107 the Anti-Dumping Agreement and 104 the Subsidies Agreement; only 23 the GATS and 34 the TRIPS Agreement.[9] Low rates for GATS and TRIPS may indicate high levels of compliance with these agreements; they may also reflect ineffectiveness of the system in those sectors, or reluctance by WTO Members to enforce commitments in these areas. In any event, the end result is that WTO jurisprudence is highly developed in some areas (for example, national treatment and trade remedies) but underdeveloped or non-existent in others (for example, large parts of GATS and TRIPS, and GATT Article XXIV on regional trade agreements). The absence of disputes or jurisprudence under GATT Article XXIV is certainly not explained by the absence of free trade agreements. It may be explained by compliance by Members with the conditions under Article XXIV or, more likely, the adage that 'people who live in glass houses shouldn't throw stones', that is, many WTO Members may violate GATT Article XXIV; hence, they are unlikely to sue another country for doing so for fear of a ruling backfiring against themselves. WTO dispute settlement may thus perform better in some functions than in others (e.g. more 'case-specific effectiveness' than 'primary norm compliance'). Similarly, for one and the same function ('norm-development effectiveness'), it may perform better in some fields (national treatment) than others (GATT Article XXIV).

When it comes to Helfer's 'embeddedness effectiveness', for example, there can be little doubt that WTO dispute settlement has (predictably) performed rather badly: for lack of direct effect of WTO law in the national legal systems of the major trading nations and the absence of any requirement to exhaust domestic remedies before resorting to WTO dispute settlement, domestic courts have played almost no role in interpreting and enforcing the WTO treaty. Conversely, to the surprise of some, WTO dispute settlement, and especially the WTO Appellate Body, has played a major role in the elaboration and development not only of

[9] DSU Statistics made available by the WTO Legal Affairs Division.

WTO law but also of general principles of public international law (e.g. rules on treaty interpretation, burden of proof or good faith), thereby performing well in terms of 'norm-development effectiveness'.

It is also crucial to bear in mind that performance assessed as bad or good against a particular benchmark is not by definition bad or good normatively speaking. For many WTO insiders or diplomats, for example, neither 'embeddedness' nor 'norm-development' effectiveness is particularly desirable. Rather than delegating power to domestic courts or WTO panels and the Appellate Body, they may want to keep enforcement and lawmaking powers in their own hands. What is admirable norm-development for one person is unacceptable judicial activism for another. For some the DSU is there to boost and facilitate the enforcement of WTO commitments, whereas for others it is there to limit and control enforcement, especially unilateral enforcement by the most powerful countries e.g. by putting a cap on authorised retaliation.

2 Measurement and causation

Once goals and benchmarks have been identified and unpacked (step 1), as complex as this may be, the second and third steps of measurement and causation are arguably even more difficult. Measuring 'primary norm compliance' is particularly daunting: how many violations of WTO law are out there and how many would there have been but for WTO dispute settlement? Past research has worked with proxies to get an approximate measure of primary norm compliance, usually not going beyond single-country studies (e.g. Davis 2012 on the United States). These studies rely on government reports that list questionable import and behind-the-border measures imposed by trading partners (see Elsig 2015).[10] Gauging 'case-specific effectiveness' may be easier: of all trade disputes raised, how many are effectively resolved thanks to WTO dispute settlement? However, even in this case causation may be problematic: how does one demonstrate that a country withdrew its trade restriction, settled a case or complied with a WTO ruling because of WTO dispute settlement and not because of factors external to the WTO such as a change of government in the defendant country or military or development aid threats made by the complainant? Comparisons between WTO dispute settlement and its predecessor under the GATT or other international tribunals can be useful but have their limits (see Zangl 2008). Pointing out that more cases have been filed to the WTO than the GATT (500

[10] See also De Bièvre et al. (this volume).

requests for consultations in the WTO in little more than twenty years compared to 300 disputes over a period of forty-seven years of GATT, WTO 2015) does not necessarily mean that the WTO has performed better. As discussed earlier, there may be more cases because there are more norm violations (hence a lower level of 'primary norm compliance'). The WTO may also have more cases than the GATT or the International Court of Justice because more countries fall under its compulsory jurisdiction or because the WTO covers a broader set of issues.

3 Cost-effectiveness

Step 4 (cost-effectiveness) is particularly important but often overlooked. It may well be that WTO dispute settlement is effective in settling trade disputes or maybe even in substantially moving state behaviour away from trade protectionism. However, is WTO dispute settlement a more cost-effective means to achieve whatever results than, for example, peer review monitoring or softer, more collaborative mechanisms of ensuring implementation? The 'cost' related to WTO dispute settlement not only consists of time, human resources and money spent on channelling a case through the increasingly complex stages of the system (time, resources and money that cannot therefore be spent elsewhere). Other costs may be trade or broader political frictions or stalemates created by 'legalising' trade disputes with a binary win or lose outcome, or the fact that a compulsory and automatic DSU has made it more difficult to conclude new trade-liberalising agreements since the DSU's creation in 1995. If so, the benefits of enhanced enforcement of (some parts of) the 1995 Uruguay Round agreements thanks to the DSU must be weighed against the costs of legalisation including that of not seeing any substantial new trade liberalisation at the WTO since the WTO's creation. Crucially, this cost–benefit analysis may be positive or in favour of the DSU for some agreements or some types of norms (say, national treatment) but negative for others (e.g. trade facilitation commitments where breaches occur, less because of strategic defection than because of a lack of resources, so that collaborative methods may be more cost-effective than legal enforcement backed up by trade retaliation).

4 Indicators for (good or bad) performance

Finally, step 5 goes beyond the descriptive stages of measuring the effect and comparing the costs and benefits of WTO dispute settlement. Taking a more normative turn, step 5 considers explanations or indicators of good or bad performance under one or more goals for one or more agreements or rules. This can lead to both a diagnosis of existing problems and suggestions for reform. Shany lists both 'structural indicators' and 'processes employed by international courts' that may be outcome predictors for a court's performance (Shany 2012). These are mostly internal material factors and include legal powers, personnel capacity, resources and structural independence. Relevant process features are access to justice, participation of stakeholders, transparency and costs.

Judicial independence as a driver of court effectiveness has been particularly controversial. Posner and Yoo (2005) argue that 'independence prevents international tribunals from being effective' as they 'can render decisions that conflict with the interests of state parties' and make states 'reluctant to use international tribunals unless they have control over the judges'. Helfer and Slaughter (1997), in contrast, argue that the most effective tribunals are independent ones. The truth is probably somewhere in between and depends on the particular benchmark or court function looked at. Especially if one defines independent tribunals, as Posner and Yoo do, as tribunals where 'the judges are appointed in advance of any particular dispute and serve fixed terms' (think of the International Court of Justice, International Criminal Court or the WTO Appellate Body) – as opposed to dependent tribunals which have judges who 'are appointed by the state parties for the purpose of resolving a particular dispute' (such as the Iran–US Claims Tribunal, investor–state arbitration tribunals or GATT/WTO panelists) – independent tribunals are more likely to perform well in terms of 'norm-development effectiveness' and 'regime legitimization'; dependent tribunals may perform better in terms of resolving specific disputes between two parties ('case-specific effectiveness'). Since party-appointed adjudicators deciding one specific dispute (dependent tribunals) may be more closely attuned to the interests of the disputing parties, untroubled by broader systemic concerns, they may, indeed, be better situated to facilitate a judicial outcome that is palatable to the parties in dispute. However, 'case-specific effectiveness' may then be achieved at the expense of other court functions or goals. It all depends, once again, on goal identification.

Beyond independence, Helfer and Slaughter (1997) list another twelve material and social factors that, in their view, enhance the performance of supranational adjudication, distinguishing between factors within the control of states (such as the composition of the tribunal or functional or fact-finding capacity of the court), factors within the control of judges themselves (such as awareness of audience, incrementalism and quality of legal reasoning) and factors outside the control of either states or judges (such as relative cultural and political homogeneity of states subject to the court).

II Assessment

Legal scholarship on WTO performance has focused on WTO dispute settlement. Too often, however, commentators have wrongly fixated on usage rates (500 requests for consultations in little more than twenty years; it is hard to say whether this is high or low without knowing the total number of WTO violations that have taken place) or compliance with WTO panel or Appellate Body rulings (at around 90 per cent, very high, but this tells us little about causation or primary norm compliance). A better approach consists of: (i) goal identification, (ii) measurement, (iii) establishing causation, (iv) assessing cost-effectiveness and (v) considering explanations or indicators of good or bad performance. In this light, the WTO has performed better with some goals (resolving specific disputes, developing case law) than others (primary norm compliance, promptly offering market access to traders). In addition, the jury remains out on whether these achievements are cost-effective or could have been reached by other means (e.g. transparency, peer review or more collaborative methods) at lower cost. Finally, the WTO's good performance against some benchmarks is probably partly explained by the 'dependence' of WTO panels and the Appellate Body on WTO Members, the fact that WTO adjudicators are jointly appointed by WTO Members and the close interaction between WTO dispute settlement and WTO membership control.

F Discussion and Conclusion

This chapter discusses the performance of the WTO as an organisation from different disciplinary perspectives. In Table 2.1 we summarise the key WTO objectives that we focus on. What we observe is that the eye of the beholder problem is further accentuated as the baselines vary across disciplines. However, some objectives, such as the performance during crises, are of interest to both economists and IR scholars. These two fields also share an interest in the operation of specific 'micro goals' or functions of the WTO. One example is the impact of the various transparency mechanisms that have been established by the WTO membership and specific transparency-related functions that have been delegated to the

Table 2.1 *Disciplinary Objectives*

Discipline	Key Objectives
IR	Rule of law against abuse of power
IR	Integrating emerging powers
IR	Performance in times of distress
IR	LDC integration
Economics	Reducing trade barriers and agreeing to policy disciplines
Economics	Avoiding protectionism during economic crises
Economics	Increasing trade volumes and specialisation
IL	Case-specific compliance
IL	Primary norm compliance
IL	Embeddedness effectiveness – direct effect
IL	Norm development

Source: Created by the authors.
IR, international relations; IL, international law; LDC, least-developed country.
Note: Objectives that overlap are shaded grey.

Secretariat. All three disciplines have an interest in the operation of the dispute settlement system – perhaps the only function of the WTO where this is clearly the case.

Two important take-home points can be distilled: first, the literature in all three fields is vibrant. A variety of objectives are discussed and many conceptual and methodological tools offered to study WTO performance. International law mainly focuses on the degree of compliance with legal norms or dispute rulings, the way these can be applied domestically and how the case law develops in ways that are consistent with building a body of law. Research so far has not sufficiently engaged with social scientific ways to measure performance or effectiveness more systematically. International relations pays most attention to how the institution (understood broadly) facilitates international cooperation and constrains powerful actors. There is an often implicit underlying assumption that for a system to work it has to contain incentives for unilateral action against trading partners and help to integrate weaker states. Finally, and not surprisingly, the economic literature has focused most directly on the economic impacts of the WTO. While some of the economics literature has centred on big conceptual questions about why trade agreements exist in the first place, there is an extensive literature that seeks to gauge both 'macro' goals and 'micro' objectives and functions.[11]

Second, different discursive tools have developed within the three disciplines. While similar phenomena are captured and assumptions shared, these concepts might work with very different connotations and labels. This at times makes cross-disciplinary debate less efficient and may sometimes prohibit it altogether. However, it also offers the potential for cross-fertilisation: it may support the legal field to further embrace empirical analysis and assist economics to broaden its (sometimes) narrow focus on welfare-enhancing performance indicators. Finally, IR may serve, more than in the past, to perform a bridging function between international law and economics, bringing the politics to the forefront of international cooperation.

To conclude, overall the WTO's performance cannot be reduced to single indicators. A more holistic approach allows an understanding of the multitude of objectives an organisation such as the WTO can serve and also sends a warning signal against having unrealistic expectations about the role of international institutions. At the same time, sources of good or bad performance need to be exposed. Such an approach might be particularly helpful to policy-makers trying to better understand the limited effects of the organisations they create.

References

Anderson, Kym. 2014. 'Contributions of the GATT/WTO to Global Economic Welfare: Empirical Evidence', *ANU Working Paper* 2014/15.

Baccini, Leonardo and Kim, Soo Yeon. 2012. 'Preventing Protectionism: International Institutions and Trade Policy', *Review of International Organizations* 7(4):369–398.

Bagwell, Kyle and Staiger, Robert. 2002. *The Economics of the World Trading System*. Cambridge, MA: MIT Press.

Bagwell, Kyle and Staiger, Robert. 2011. 'What Do Trade Negotiators Negotiate About? Empirical Evidence from the WTO', *American Economic Review* 101 (4): 1238–1273.

[11] As mentioned earlier, a discussion of the extensive economics literature dealing with the effects of specific WTO agreements and disciplines was beyond the scope of this chapter.

Baracat, Elías A., Finger, J. Michael, Thorne, Raúl León and Nogués, Julio. 2013. *Sustaining Trade Reform: Institutional Lessons from Peru and Argentina*. Washington, DC: World Bank.

Busch, Marc L., Reinhardt, Eric and Shaffer, Gregory. 2009. 'Does Legal Capacity Matter? A Survey of WTO Members', *World Trade Review* 8 (4): 559–577.

Davey, William. 2009. 'Compliance Problems in WTO Dispute Settlement', *Cornell International Law Journal* 42 (1): 119–128.

Davis, Christina L. 2012. *Why Adjudicate? Enforcing Trade Rules in the WTO*. Princeton, NJ: Princeton University Press.

Decreux, Yvan and Fontagné, Lionel. 2015. 'What Next for Multilateral Trade Talks? Quantifying the Role of Negotiation Modalities', *World Trade Review* 14 (1): 29–43.

Downs, George W., Rocke, David M. and Barsoom, Peter N. 1996. 'Is the Good News about Compliance Good News about Cooperation?' *International Organization* 50 (3): 379–406.

Drezner, Daniel. 2007. *All Politics Is Global: Explaining International Regulatory Regimes*. Princeton, NJ: Princeton University Press.

Dutt, Pushan, Mihov, Ilian and Van Zandt, Timothy. 2013. 'The Impact of the WTO on the Intensive and the Extensive Margins of Trade', *Journal of International Economics* 91 (2): 204–219.

Elsig, Manfred. 2007. 'The World Trade Organization's Legitimacy Crisis: What Does the Beast Look Like?' *Journal of World Trade* 41(1):75–98.

Elsig, Manfred. 2010. 'The World Trade Organization at Work: Performance in a Member-driven Milieu', *Review of International Organizations* 5 (3): 345–363.

Elsig, Manfred. 2015. 'WTO Dispute Settlement and the Study of Compliance', *Journal of International Trade Law and Policy* 14(3):112–115.

Elsig, Manfred and Cottier, Thomas. 2011. 'Reforming the WTO: The Decision-making Triangle Revisited'. In *Governing the World Trade Organization: Past, Present and Beyond Doha*, edited by Thomas Cottier and Manfred Elsig. Cambridge: Cambridge University Press.

Elsig, Manfred and Eckhardt, Jappe. 2015. 'The Creation of the Multilateral Trade Court: Design and Experiential Learning', *World Trade Review* 14 (S1): 13–32.

Elsig, Manfred and Stucki, Philipp. 2012. 'Low-Income Developing Countries and WTO Litigation: Why Wake Up the Sleeping Dog?' *Review of International Political Economy* 19 (2): 292–316.

Estevadeordal, Antoni, Freund, Caroline and Ornelas, Emanuel. 2008. 'Does Regionalism Affect Trade Liberalization toward Non-Members?' *Quarterly Journal of Economics* 123 (4): 1531–1575.

Ethier, Wilfred. 2007. 'The Theory of Trade Policy and Trade Agreements: A Critique', *European Journal of Political Economy* 23:605–623.

Evenett, Simon and Fritz, Johannes. 2015. *The Tide Turns? Trade, Protectionism, and Slowing Global Growth*. CEPR: Global Trade Alert.

Finger, J. Michael. 1979. 'Trade Liberalization: A Public Choice Perspective'. In *Challenges to a Liberal International Economic Order*, edited by Ryan Amacher, Gottfried Haberler, and Thomas Willett. Washington, DC: American Enterprise Institute.

Finger, J. Michael. 2007. 'Implementation and Imbalance: Dealing with the Hangover from the Uruguay Round', *Oxford Review of Economic Policy* 23 (3): 440–460.

Finger, J. Michael and Nogués, Julio. 2006. *Safeguards and Antidumping in Latin American Trade Liberalization: Fighting Fire with Fire*. Washington, DC: World Bank.

Francois, Joseph. 1997. 'External Bindings and the Credibility of Reform'. In *Regional Partners in Global Markets*, edited by Ahmed Galal and Bernard Hoekman. London: Centre for Economic Policy Research.

Francois, Joseph and Martin, William. 2004. 'Commercial Policy, Bindings and Market Access', *European Economic Review* 48: 665–679.

Freund, Caroline and Ornelas, Emanuel. 2010. 'Regional Trade Agreements', *Annual Review of Economics* 2 (1): 139–166.

Fronk, Jared. 2014. 'Do Procurement Agreements Work?' Georgetown University. http://www.freit.org/WorkingPapers/Papers/PoliticalEconomy/FREIT793.pdf

Gawande, Kishore, Hoekman, Bernard and Cui, Yue. 2015. 'Global Supply Chains and Trade Policy Responses to the 2008 Financial Crisis', *World Bank Economic Review* 29 (1): 102–128.

Gutner, Tamar and Thompson, Alexander. 2010. 'The Politics of IO Performance: a Framework', *Review of International Organizations* 5 (3): 227–248.

Grant, Ruth and Keohane, Robert. 2005. 'Accountability and Abuses of Power in World Politics', *American Political Science Review* 99 (1): 29–43.

Gruber, Lloyd. 2000. *Ruling the World: Power Politics and the Rise of Supranational Institutions*. Princeton, NJ: Princeton University Press.

Handley, Kyle. 2014. 'Exporting under Trade Policy Uncertainty: Theory and Evidence', *Journal of International Economics* 94 (1): 50–66.

Helfer, Laurence. 2014. 'The Effectiveness of International Adjudicators'. In *Oxford Handbook of International Adjudication*, edited by Karen Alter, Cesare Romano, and Yuval Shany. Oxford: Oxford University Press, pp. 464–482.

Helfer, Laurence and Slaughter, Anne Marie. 1997. 'Toward a Theory of Effective Supranational Adjudication', *Yale Law Journal* 107: 273–392.

Hoekman, Bernard. (ed.). 2015. *The Global Trade Slowdown: A New Normal?* London: CEPR Press.

Hoekman, Bernard and Nicita, Alessandro. 2011. 'Trade Policy, Trade Costs and Developing Country Trade', *World Development* 39 (12): 2069–2079.

Horn, Henrik, Nordström, Håkan and Mavroidis, Petros C. 1999. 'Is the Use of the WTO Dispute Settlement System Biased?' *CEPR Discussion Paper* 2340.

Hughes, Valerie. 2012. 'Why Is the WTO Dispute Settlement System So Successful?' Video lecture. http://mdsweb.vuw.ac.nz/Mediasite/Viewer/Viewers/Viewer320TL.aspx?mode=Default&peid=375b3db3-0b6d-4d8e-b3b0-7d45a9d2d904&pid=3daf095e-e1a8-4f1f-8ec2-0abfd39640be&playerType=SL1, accessed 21 February 2016.

Johnson, Harry. 1953–54. 'Optimum Tariffs and Retaliation', *Review of Economic Studies* 21 (2): 142–153.

Keohane, Robert. 1984. *After Hegemony: Cooperation and Discord in the World Political Economy*. Princeton, NJ: Princeton University Press.

Kim, Moonhawk. 2008. 'Costly Procedures: Divergent Effects of Legalization in the GATT/WTO Dispute Settlement Procedures', *International Studies Quarterly* 52 (3): 657–686.

Laborde, David and Martin, William. 2015. 'Formulas for Failure? Were the Doha Tariff Formulas too Ambitious for Success?' *World Trade Review* 14 (1): 45–65.

Lang, Andrew and Scott, Joanne. 2009. 'The Hidden World of WTO Governance', *European Journal of International Law* 20 (3): 575–614.

Limão, Nuno and Tovar, Patricia. 2011. 'Policy Choice: Theory and Evidence from Commitment via International Trade Agreements', *Journal of International Economics* 85 (2): 186–205.

Liu, Xuepeng. 2009. 'GATT/WTO Promotes Trade Strongly: Sample Selection and Model Specification', *Review of International Economics* 17 (3): 428–446.

Maggi, Giovanni and Rodriguez-Clare, Andres. 1998. 'The Value of Trade Agreements in the Presence of Political Pressures', *Journal of Political Economy* 106 (3): 574–601.

Martin, Will and Messerlin, Patrick. 2007. 'Why Is It So Difficult? Trade Liberalization Under the Doha Agenda', *Oxford Review of Economic Policy* 23 (3): 347–366.

Pauwelyn, Joost. 2005. 'The Transformation of World Trade', *Michigan Law Review* 104: 1–70.

Pelc, Krzysztof. 2010. 'Constraining Coercion? Legitimacy and Its Role in US Trade Policy, 1975–2000', *International Organization* 64 (1): 65–96.

Posner, Eric and Yoo, John. 2005. 'Judicial Independence in International Tribunals', *California Law Review* 93 (1).

Raustiala, Kal. 2000. 'Compliance and Effectiveness in International Regulatory Cooperation', *Case Western Reserve Journal of International Law* 32: 387–440.

Rickard, Stephanie and Kono, Daniel. 2014. 'Think Globally, Buy Locally: International Agreements and Government Procurement', *Review of International Organizations* 9 (3): 333–352.

Rose, Andrew. 2004. 'Do We Really Know That the WTO Increases Trade?' *American Economic Review* 94 (1): 98–114.

Rose, Andrew. 2005. 'Which International Institutions Promote International Trade?' *Review of International Economics* 13 (4): 682–698.

Sattler, Thomas and Bernauer, Thomas. 2011. 'Gravitation or Discrimination? Determinants of Litigation in the World Trade Organization', *European Journal of Political Research* 50 (2): 143–167.

Shany, Yuval. 2012. 'Assessing the Effectiveness of International Courts: A Goal-Based Approach', *American Journal of International Law* 106 (2): 225–270.

Shingal, Anirudh. 2011. 'Services Procurement under the WTO's Agreement on Government Procurement: Whither Market Access?' *World Trade Review* 10 (4): 527–549.

Shingal, Anirudh. 2015. 'Econometric Analyses of Home Bias in Government Procurement', *Review of International Economics* 23:188–219.

Subramanian, Arvind and Wei, Shang-Jin. 2007. 'The WTO Promotes Trade, Strongly but Unevenly', *Journal of International Economics* 72 (1): 151–175.

Tang, Man-Keung and Wei, Shang-Jin. 2009. 'The Value of Making Commitments Externally: Evidence from WTO Accessions', *Journal of International Economics* 78 (2): 216–229.

Tumlir, Jan. 1985. *Protectionism: Trade Policy in Democratic Societies.* Washington, DC: American Enterprise Institute.

Wilson, Bruce. 2007. 'Compliance by WTO Members with Adverse WTO Dispute Settlement Rulings: The Record to Date', *Journal of International Economic Law* 10 (2): 397–403.

WTO. 2015. 'WTO disputes reach 500 mark', News Item, 10 November 2015 (www.wto.org/english/news_e/news15_e/ds500rfc_10nov15_e.htm, accessed 21 February 2016).

Zangl, Bernhard. 2008. 'Judicialization Matters! A Comparison of Dispute Settlement under GATT and the WTO', *International Studies Quarterly* 52 (4): 825–854.

PART II

New Insight from the Early Times

3

The GATT's Starting Point

Tariff Levels Circa 1947

CHAD P. BOWN AND DOUGLAS A. IRWIN

A Introduction

The General Agreement on Tariffs and Trade (GATT) is usually given substantial credit for the liberalisation of world trade that took place after World War II. At the time it was formed in 1947, barriers to world trade were considerable. The Great Depression of the 1930s saw the imposition of higher tariffs, tighter import quotas, foreign exchange controls and discriminatory trade arrangements around the world (Irwin 2012). World War II brought additional governmental controls on foreign trade. Had they remained in place, these restrictions would have stifled the growth of world trade in the post-war period, and presumably slowed the economic recovery from the war.

Of course, as is well known, leading countries met in Geneva in 1947 to address this state of affairs. They negotiated tariff reductions and reached an agreement regulating the use of trade policies. Three subsequent negotiating rounds expanded the number of GATT participants (notably adding Germany and Japan) and reduced tariffs further. By the start of the Kennedy Round in 1964, average tariffs for the major players in the GATT – the United States, the European Economic Community (EEC), Japan, and the United Kingdom – were about 15 per cent.

For useful comments, we thank Michael Finger, Judith Goldstein, Bernard Hoekman, Manfred Elsig, Carlos Primo Braga, Alan Winters, Alejandro Jara, Frieder Roessler, Michele Ruta, Robert Staiger, and participants at the World Trade Forum 2015 in Bern. Semira Ahdiyyih and Taylor Ng provided outstanding research assistance. Research for this paper has been supported in part by the World Bank's Multidonor Trust Fund for Trade and Development Strategic Research Partnership on Economic Development. Any opinions expressed in this paper are the authors' and should not be attributed to the World Bank. All remaining errors are our own.

But what were the average tariff levels immediately prior to the establishment of the GATT on the eve of the Geneva conference in 1947? Because tariff compilations from this period do not exist, the starting point of the GATT has never really been determined. A frequently cited figure is that average tariffs in 1947 were 40 per cent; this figure can be traced back as far as the World Bank's flagship *World Development Report* for 1987, which stated:

> From the end of World War II until 1974, protectionism seemed to be in decline. Successive rounds of negotiations in the GATT had cut tariffs on trade in manufactures – from an average level of 40 per cent in 1947 to between 6 and 8 per cent for most of the industrial countries – even before the last round of multilateral trade negotiations (the Tokyo Round, 1974–79) had taken place. (World Bank 1987: 134–135)

This figure was widely accepted and frequently mentioned by policymakers and international organisations in the 1990s.[1]

A figure of 40 per cent for average tariffs in 1947 would imply that the first fifteen years of GATT made enormous progress in reducing applied tariffs. Unfortunately, although this figure has been widely cited, no source was provided and it has never been verified. By contrast, the World Trade Organization (WTO) (2007: 207) later suggested that average tariffs at the time of the GATT's founding were 'situated in a range between 20 and 30 per cent', implying that early reductions in applied tariffs were more modest.

The initial level of the average applied tariff matters for how we assess the GATT's early success in reducing tariffs. Going from 40 per cent in 1947 to 15 per cent in 1964 is quite different from going from 20 per cent to 15 per cent in the same period.

Determining the GATT's actual starting point is also relevant to a growing body of contemporary research, both theoretical and empirical, that seeks to provide conceptual foundations for the role and impact of the GATT and the WTO, as well as to provide empirically based estimates of this impact.[2] First, such pre-GATT tariff estimates may be a useful benchmark to compare against the non-cooperative Nash tariff that one might calculate in a computational model as the outcome of a multi-country 'trade war'. For example, Ossa (2014: 4122) finds in his

[1] See the references in Bown and Irwin (2015). The first mention of the 40 per cent figure that we were able to find was in a *New York Times* article in September 1986 at the launch of the Uruguay Round.

[2] Recent surveys include those of Bagwell, Bown and Staiger (2016) and Anderson (2016).

seven-country computational model that the 'median Nash tariff across all countries is 58.1 per cent which is remarkably close to the average tariff of 50 per cent typically reported for the trade war following the Smoot-Hawley Tariff Act of 1930'. Second, such estimates are important for understanding and contextualising the outcomes of negotiations under the early GATT Rounds, the micro-level bargaining analysis of which is subject to research informed by the newly available declassified data (for the Torquay Round of 1951, see Bagwell, Staiger and Yurukoglu 2015).

In this chapter we review the scattered and incomplete evidence on tariff levels circa 1947 in an attempt to pin down the GATT's starting point in terms of tariff levels. We provide some new evidence on tariff levels and perform some new calculations (such as backcasting tariff rates from the 1960s) to shed light on the likely height of tariff barriers in place at this time. Our results indicate that average tariff levels for the major GATT participants were about 22 per cent, much lower than the oft-cited 40 per cent figure. This leads us to the conclusion that the tariff reductions negotiated in the initial GATT rounds had a modest impact on average tariff levels. We also provide statistical evidence on whether the early GATT participants experienced noticeable reductions in their average tariffs as a result of the first negotiating rounds. Here we find some evidence of lower tariffs resulting for the GATT core countries of the United States, United Kingdom, Canada and Australia, relative to other contracting parties and non-GATT participants.

Finally, and although we find that the reduction in the average applied tariff before the Kennedy Round was apparently modest, this does not lead us to conclude that the GATT's early contribution to trade liberalisation was unimportant. For in addition to facilitating applied tariff reductions, the early GATT accomplished many things, most of which are arguably much more difficult to measure than tariffs and thus to capture empirically in summary statistics. These would include binding the negotiated tariff reductions for an extended period (made more permanent in 1955), establishing the generality of non-discrimination through most-favoured nation (MFN) treatment and national treatment, ensuring increased transparency of trade policy measures, and providing a forum for future negotiations and for the peaceful resolution of bilateral disputes. All of these elements contributed to the rationalisation of trade policy and to the reduction of trade barriers and policy uncertainty. The focus of this chapter is simply on one element of the GATT's contribution, the reduction in average applied tariff levels.

B Methods for Measuring Average Tariff Levels

Before presenting data on tariff levels for the period under study, the term 'average tariffs' deserves discussion. There is no unique way of measuring the level of a country's tariffs or comparing tariff levels between countries. In this section we therefore introduce the predominant approaches and discuss the trade-offs associated with each.

I Trade-Weighted Average Tariffs

The easiest method for calculating average tariffs is simply to use the weighted average tariff, where the weights are the value of imports. This average tariff measure is straightforward to construct because it can readily be calculated from only two pieces of aggregate-level data for a country: it is defined as the value of a country's total customs revenue divided by the value of its total imports. Because data on these two components are frequently available, this measure can be calculated even without access to the individual, product-specific rates of duty in the country's tariff code. For the United States, for example, data are reported on both the trade-weighted average tariff on total imports and the trade-weighted average tariff on dutiable imports.[3]

The most important problem with the import-weighted average tariff measure is its downward bias. Because imports of goods subject to high duties will be very small, those duties will receive low weights in the index and prohibitive duties will receive no weight in the calculation at all. An alternative approach to trade-weighting would be to use the imports of 'someone else' (e.g. the rest of the world) as opposed to the importing country itself, in order to construct the weights used in the measure. Of course, the major problem introduced by such an approach is that the measure is then no longer easily calculable from the readily available, aggregate-level customs revenue and total import value data. That is, such an approach would require detailed information on product-level tariff rates and product-level imports (of the 'someone else') and this would also require that the products be categorised under the same classification scheme across countries. As we describe in more detail below, achieving a product-level classification scheme consistently

[3] These two measures often diverge substantially because many imports are given duty-free status in the tariff code. Unfortunately, other countries do not report the average tariff on dutiable imports, which might be a more accurate indication of a country's protective duties on imported manufactures. Lloyd (2008) reports such data for Australia.

defined across countries is a relatively recent (late twentieth-century) historical phenomenon.

Second, in comparing the tariff levels of two countries, a higher trade-weighted average tariff does not necessarily mean that trade is more restricted or that it imposes a greater welfare cost than a lower tariff. The Anderson and Neary (2005) 'trade restrictiveness index' is an alternative method, albeit a fairly complicated and computationally challenging one, that attempts to deal with these problems in order to draw economic inference from measures of import protection.[4]

Third, for the inter-temporal assessment of tariff policy changes, another problem with relying on trade-weighted averaging is that the weights (imports) may change from year to year for reasons that are completely independent of *policy* changes. For example, a negative supply shock abroad (e.g. a drought or a flood) could lead to a severe decline in quantities of imports of certain products that will affect the relative weighting. This could similarly result from product- or industry-specific (positive or negative) demand shocks at home. For this reason, it is often difficult to interpret changes in the import-weighted average tariff as necessarily reflecting a change in commercial policy that would arise through changes to the official tariff rates.

II Simple Average Tariffs

A second approach is simply to take an unweighted average of all tariff rates across all products within a country. However, unlike the trade-weighted average, which can be calculated solely from data on customs revenue and the total value of imports, calculation of even the simple average requires much additional information. Furthermore, even if the problems of obtaining such additional information can be overcome (so that the measure can be constructed), there are still difficulties in drawing inference from cross-country and inter-temporal comparisons of simple average tariffs.

The first requirement for construction of a simple average tariff is the conversion of all non-*ad valorem* tariffs – e.g. specific duties and compound rates – into *ad valorem* equivalent rates. This requires, at a minimum, additional information on import prices.

[4] Literature on empirical applications and estimating such trade restrictiveness indices on contemporary tariff data includes the studies by Kee, Nicita and Olarreaga (2008, 2009) and Kee, Neagu and Nicita (2013) and on US historical tariff data by Irwin (2010).

The second requirement is for access to detailed, consistently-defined, product-level tariff rates listed in the tariff code. If the unweighted average is simply an arithmetic average of the duties in the individual lines in the tariff code, the calculation is potentially misleading if there are many rates for a small number of imports and few rates for the broadest base of imports.[5] Thus it may be difficult make comparisons between countries if the countries being compared do not use the same nomenclature for defining the scope of products and tariff lines. The Brussels tariff nomenclature (BTN) was not established by the Customs Co-operation Council until December 1950 and slowly came into use during that decade. It is only after this time that disaggregated tariff averages could be usefully compared between countries. The lack of any comparable system during the early post-war era is likely to severely hamper any 'bottom up' effort to generate average tariff measures that would build from the product level. And, of course, the United States never adopted the BTN.

The concerns associated with this second requirement are particularly relevant for trade policy analysis even as late as 1988, the point at which the major trading economies finally introduced and adopted the common Harmonized Commodity Description and Coding System (HS) for product-level tariff classification.[6] One of the resulting benefits has been to make such accounting exercises for constructing measures of average tariffs potentially more meaningful across countries and over time; however, it is important to note that this innovation did not occur until relatively late in the twentieth century.

Finally, in addition to there being no ideal weighting scheme in creating a tariff index or tariff average, even basic information on tariffs was not readily available in the 1930s and 1940s.[7] While the United States was transparent about its tariff code, this was not the case for most other countries. And, for the tariff schedules of the leading countries that may

[5] To take an extreme example, if a country has only two tariff lines and two rates of duties, 100 per cent on imported rhinoceroses and 0 per cent on everything else, the average duty is 50 per cent because every duty gets a weight of $1/n$ in the calculation where n is simply the number of tariff lines.

[6] Since 1988, the Harmonized System has adopted a definition of roughly 5,200 products that are common at the six-digit level across all countries. The products at the six-digit level are also consistently defined over time, subject to revisions – such as those taking place in 1996, 2002, 2007, and 2012 – that have changed the definition of about 200 products at each revision.

[7] The League of Nations (1927) presented some tariff index numbers in preparation for the 1927 World Economic Conference.

have existed, no government or international organisation made the effort to compile the rates so as to make them comparable across countries. Not until the Kennedy Round in the 1960s did GATT negotiators have access to detailed figures on average tariffs using various weighting schemes. We will show later how the different calculations under these schemes affect the reported tariff averages.

C Initial Evidence Based on Trade-Weighted and Simple Average Tariffs

Unlike today, there was no GATT or WTO secretariat in 1947 that could present compilations and summary statistics on the tariff codes of the participating governments. In addition, it is only recently that official, declassified documents have begun to be made publicly available so as to give researchers the opportunity to judge the results of the first few GATT rounds.[8] Thus this section describes some sources that we can use to fill in the gaps in our knowledge until such time as the tariff schedules of different countries can be analysed in greater detail.

I Trade-Weighted Average Tariffs in 1947 and Peak Tariffs from 1929–1947

Table 3.1 presents the first body of evidence, which is based on the import-weighted average tariffs for 1947 and other selected years over the 1929–1964 period for the main GATT participants as well as a number of other major economies for which data are available.[9]

The column for 1947 (Geneva) lists the average tariff in that year and indicates relatively low tariffs of under 10 per cent for most of the countries. By this measure, India and Canada had tariffs of about 11 per cent, New Zealand about 20 per cent, Australia nearly 30 per cent, and the United Kingdom more than 40 per cent.

[8] The results of the first bilateral negotiations have recently been posted on the WTO website: www.wto.org/english/docs_e/gattbilaterals_e/indexbyround_e.htm. Nevertheless, even eventual analysis of detailed tariff schedules in place at that time will still run into the averaging problems described in the previous section that are associated with inconsistent product nomenclature across countries and over time.

[9] The average tariff is calculated as the value of customs revenue divided by the value of imports. Like Clemens and Williamson (2004), our source is *International Historical Statistics* (Palgrave Macmillan, 2013) originally compiled by Brian Mitchell and now edited and updated by Palgrave Macmillan.

Table 3.1 *Weighted-Average Tariff Levels 1929–1964, Selected Years*

				Customs Revenue/Total Value of Imports						
	GATT CP year	Peak year, 1929–1947	Peak level, 1929–1947	1939	1947 (Geneva)	1949 (Annecy)	1951 (Torquay)	1956 (Geneva)	1960 (Dillon)	1964 (Kennedy)
GATT 1947 Contracting Parties (CPs)										
Australia	1947	1932	41.2	31.0	27.9	18.8	15.4	8.4	10.6*	9.5*
Belgium	1947	1934	10.7	7.3	4.3	4.1	3.1	–	–	–
Brazil	1947	1933	35.0	20.6	8.2	–	–	–	–	–
Canada	1947	1931	16.6	13.8	11.4	8.2	8.5	9.6	9.1	8.3
Chile	1947	1933	6.2	5.7	4.7	7.5	9.4	–	–	–
France	1947	1935	29.4	23.3	9.3	10.9	12.6	20.0	22.6	22.1
India	1947	1933	40.0	25.8	11.7	19.1	23.9	21.1	18.0	29.8
Netherlands	1947	1935	9.1	7.9	1.6	4.8	4.2	5.1	5.6	6.1
New Zealand	1947	1946	46.1	20.2	20.9	23.3	14.1	10.8	–	11.8*
Norway	1947	1940	15.8	11.3	5.7	3.6	2.8	3.8	4.2	3.7
United Kingdom	1947	1946	47.7	29.6	44.0	35.7	25.6	30.7	32.4	36.5
United States	1947	1932	24.4	13.3	8.2	5.5	5.5	5.3	6.6	5.3
Other countries										
Argentina	1967	1932	28.8	22.5*	9.7	–	–	–	–	–
Austria	1951	1963	–	–	–	–		4.3*	8.2	8.3
Denmark	1950	1935	8.2	7.1	3.3	3.0	–	–	–	–

Finland	1950	1931	32.7	20.6	9.7	18.8	10.0	20.5	13.5	–
Italy	1950	1933	25.2	11.2	–	–	4.2	6.7	6.3	6.0
Japan	1955	1931	6.8	3.6	0.0	0.4	1.6	4.0	6.8	7.7
Mexico	1986	1943	34.5	29.7	14.9	25.0	19.6	19.1	20.8	17.6
Peru	1951	1933	28.0	19.5	26.1	12.6	26.8	–	–	–
Portugal	1962	1935	50.7	37.1	16.1	17.3	20.5	19.2	20.1	17.0
Spain	1963	1946	26.9	10.0*	18.5	14.4	23.8	23.8	13.9	10.4
Sweden	1950	1932	11.9	8.3	5.7	5.6	4.0	4.9	5.4	4.8
Switzerland	1966	1935	23.3	17.5	9.1	10.2	8.4	9.7	11.1	10.9
Turkey	1951	1945	24.6	–	16.6	14.8	17.1	30.1	–	–
West Germany	1951	1938	33.4	32.6	–	–	6.8	7.1	7.0	5.1

Source: Compiled by the authors with data from Palgrave Macmillan (2013). Data not available for 1947 GATT Contracting Parties Burma (Myanmar), Ceylon (Sri Lanka), China, Cuba, Czechoslovakia, Lebanon, Luxembourg, Pakistan, South Africa, Southern Rhodesia (Zimbabwe) and Syria.

* Indicates data replaced with those from a nearby year, i.e. Argentina: 1939 is 1938; Australia: 1960 is 1959 and 1964 is 1965; Austria 1956 is 1955; New Zealand: 1964 is 1965; and Spain: 1939 is 1940.

The average tariff levels were lower in 1947 (even before the first GATT tariff reductions had been negotiated and implemented) than in 1939 for all countries for which figures are reported, with the exception of New Zealand, Peru, Spain and the United Kingdom. Thus, in terms of tariffs, the situation appears to have improved in the immediate post-war period relative to the pre-war period. The lower post-war duties may be a result of inflation and specific duties; this is certainly the case for the United States, but the degree to which other countries used specific duties is not as well known. Of the exceptions, the substantially higher average tariffs for the United Kingdom may be due to fiscal reasons. However, and with the exception of the United Kingdom, the data presented in Table 3.1 do not suggest that the average tariffs in 1947 were close to 40 per cent for any of these countries.

Another possibility is that countries had already reduced their average tariffs substantially by 1947, and so scholarly reference to 'pre-GATT' tariffs at rates of 40 per cent or more had in mind the peak levels that were reached either during, or in the aftermath of, the Great Depression. We examine this possibility as Table 3.1 also reports the peak level for the trade-weighted average tariff by country over the 1929–1947 period. However, while the peak levels were significantly higher than 1947 (or even 1939) levels for almost all countries, in only five (Australia, India, New Zealand, Portugal and the UK) of the 25 countries in Table 3.1 did the peak average tariff even reach 40 per cent.

For the United States, the average import-weighted tariff on total imports was 8.2 per cent in 1947 and the peak trade-weighted tariff in the United States over the 1929–1947 period reached 24.4 per cent in 1932. One partial explanation as to why the US average tariff in 1947 was so low is because 61 per cent of imports (by value) at that time were duty free (US International Trade Commission 2014). The US International Trade Commission also reports the average tariff on dutiable imports, which is calculated as collected duties divided by dutiable imports. The US average tariff on dutiable imports alone in 1947 was 20.1 per cent,[10] and this measure of tariffs for the US peaked at 59.1 per cent in 1932. While this particular data series is not, to our knowledge, systematically

[10] The US International Trade Commission (2014, Table 1) reports values for the trade-weighted average tariff data that are slightly different from those reported in the International Historical Statistics and which we report in Table 3.1. In particular, they find the US trade-weighted average tariff was 7.9 per cent as opposed to 8.2 per cent in 1947.

available for all GATT countries for this time period, it is possible that scholars could be making reference to this series (at least for the United States) when they are describing pre-GATT average tariffs at 40 per cent or above.

Of course, as already noted, the import-weighted average tariff may also be downward biased. Data on tariff levels presented below will allow us to assess the extent of that potential bias.

II *Later Evidence: Simple Average Tariffs*

While the trade-weighted average tariff data contained in Table 3.1 are the only broad tariff measures that exist, to our knowledge, for the period just prior to the first GATT negotiations in 1947, the discussions that eventually led to the European Common Market meant that more attention was paid to European tariff levels throughout the 1950s. As a result, published reports of tariff averages started to become available, although still relatively infrequently.

One of the first compilations was made by Woytinsky and Woytinsky (1955), which is presented in Table 3.2 as an unweighted tariff average for 1949 (after the first Geneva Round but before the second Annecy

Table 3.2 *European Tariff Levels in 1949 (%)*

	Unweighted Average	Agricultural Products	Industrial Products
Denmark	2	0.7	3.4
Sweden	7	4.6	8.5
Benelux	9	7.1	11.2
Norway	9	7.8	10.8
United Kingdom	16	9.3	23.3
France	22	26.5	17.9
Italy	23	21.6	25.3
Germany	27	26.7	26.4
Austria	27	36.3	18.0
Portugal	30	41.5	18.0
Greece	42	44.8	39.0

Source: Woytinsky and Woytinsky (1955: 284–285).

Round).[11] While Benelux and Scandinavian countries have low tariffs at under 10 per cent, the larger continental European countries of France, Germany and Italy as well as the United Kingdom have higher tariffs ranging from 16 to 27 per cent.[12] Furthermore, a comparison of these simple averages in Table 3.2 with the 1949 trade-weighted averages reported in Table 3.1 reveals mixed results – for Denmark, Sweden and the United Kingdom the simple average is lower, whereas for Benelux, Norway, France and Portugal the simple average is substantially higher.

Table 3.3 presents two sources of data on tariff levels in 1952 and 1955. The 1952 data originally appeared in a 1953 GATT report, although unfortunately the report provides no details on how they were calculated.

Table 3.3 *Tariff Levels in 1952 and 1955 (%)*

		1955	
	1952	Unweighted Average	Weighted Average
France	19	18.1	5.1
Germany	16	15.5	5.6
Italy	24	17.3	7.1
Belgium–Luxembourg	–	9.5	4.3
Netherlands	–	9.5	5.5
United Kingdom	17	–	–
United States	16	–	–

Source: 1952 data from GATT (1953a: 62); 1955 data from Balassa (1961: 46).

[11] The source for the data used by Woytinsky is given as Groupe d'Études pour l'Union Douanière Européenne, Comité Spécial Restreint de la Nomenclature, *Average Rates of Duty* dated 31 August 1949 and *Draft Revised Tariff Nomenclature* in two volumes published in Brussels in 1950.

[12] However, the WTO (2007: 206) reports: 'A recalculation of the Woytinski results showed several inaccuracies. For some of the low rate countries errors in the averaging calculations were found which imply that the, relatively low, average rate for Denmark and Norway had been actually somewhat higher than reported. For Austria, Germany and Greece, however, the estimates are upward biased, as the underlying trade flows (and prices) refer not to 1950 but to pre-World War II imports with their much lower average prices. Therefore the actual average tariff rates of Austria and Germany (both not yet Contracting Parties in 1950) had been far less above the country group average than indicated by Woytinski and Woytinski (1955).'

The 1955 data are from two German publications as reported by Balassa (1961) and show the difference between the import-weighted average and the unweighted average. The difference in levels between these two figures indicates that the 1952 tariffs reported by the GATT are unweighted averages. These sources also indicate that the average tariff across Western Europe was about 16 per cent in the early 1950s.

Table 3.4 presents disaggregated tariff data (based on the Brussels product classification) compiled by the GATT in 1953 for use in future tariff negotiations. This table reveals that the unweighted average of tariffs was about 12–13 per cent for Germany and France and 7–8 per cent for Benelux countries, Canada and the United States.

This exhausts our findings for tariff averages that were compiled for the late 1940s and early 1950s. The general conclusion that emerges is that European tariff levels were in the 15–20 per cent range during this period, although Benelux and the Scandinavian countries had lower tariffs than the larger continental European countries and the United Kingdom.

Once we move into the late 1950s and especially the early 1960s, published data on average tariff levels are more readily available.[13] In 1958, the EEC was formed with its common external tariff, which required extensive tariff harmonisation among the six European participants. In addition, the United States was preparing to launch the Kennedy Round, whose purpose was to reduce the external tariff of the EEC and hence the margin of preference for intra-EEC trade. Tables 3.5, 3.6 and 3.7 present average tariffs for the late 1950s and early 1960s prior to the Kennedy Round negotiations. Table 3.5 shows the average US and EEC tariff before the 1961–1962 Dillon Round. This table also reveals the bias of import-weighted versus unweighted tariff averages. In both the United States and the EEC, the import-weighted tariff is about 8 per cent whereas the unweighted tariff is about 14 per cent. Therefore, the unweighted average tariff is about double the weighted average tariff.

Tables 3.6 and 3.7 show the pre-Kennedy Round average tariffs that are, once again, in the low teens. However, these tariffs are for dutiable imports, meaning that duty free imports were not included in the calculation. Still, the unweighted tariffs are in the mid-teens for both the US and the EEC; the weighting scheme seems to be much less important when considering only dutiable imports.

[13] For a look at European tariff levels pre-EEC, but unfortunately highly disaggregated without import weights, see Political and Economic Planning (1959).

Table 3.4 *Weighted Average Tariffs by Country and Sector, 1953 (%)*

	Austria	Benelux	Canada	Denmark	France	Germany	Italy	Norway	Sweden	United States
Primary products, food	30	1	4	1	11	11	27	2	5	2
Manufactured food	21	5	7	1	9	21	23	3	3	10
Fish and fish products	1	14	9	0	9	15	19	1	2	6
Raw materials, including petroleum	1	0	2	0	2	2	2	1	0	4
Products of chemical and allied industries	9	4	7	1	17	15	20	6	3	6
Leather and products of leather, fur skins, rubber, wood, cork, paper and printed matter	10	10	11	4	15	14	21	8	5	2
Textile products and clothing	21	13	14	4	18	18	22	13	6	18
Base metals and manufactures	11	4	10	1	6	10	22	3	3	6
Machinery, electric and transport equipment	23	10	9	4	16	12	23	6	10	6
Miscellaneous manufactures	11	9	11	5	14	8	20	13	6	16
Average of above (unweighted)	**14**	**7**	**8**	**2**	**12**	**13**	**20**	**6**	**4**	**8**

Source: GATT (1953b: 22).

Table 3.5 *Pre-Dillon Round (pre-1960) Tariff Levels (%)*

		Weighted	
	Unweighted	By own imports	By combined imports
United States	14.0	7.6	8.1
EEC	14.8	8.3	10.2

Source: Committee for Economic Development (1964: 70–71).

Table 3.6 *Tariff Averages, Pre- and Post-Kennedy Round, Dutiable Nonagricultural Imports (%)*

	Total		Manufactures	
	Before	After	Before	After
United States	13.5	9.6	14.3	9.9
EEC	12.8	8.1	13.5	8.6
United Kingdom	16.6	10.6	17.8	10.8
Japan	15.5	9.5	17.6	10.7

Source: Preeg (1970: 208–211).

Table 3.7 *Pre-Kennedy Round Average Tariff, by Weighting Scheme, Dutiable Nonagricultural Products (other than mineral fuels) (%)*

		Weighted by	
	Unweighted tariff	Own imports	World imports
United States	16.5	13.5	14.5
EEC	13.1	12.8	13.4
United Kingdom	18.2	16.7	17.0
Japan	18.0	15.5	19.0

Source: Preeg (1970: 277–278).

To sum up, from the evidence that we have been able to compile, the average tariff in the mid-1950s for the major players in the GATT was about 15 per cent.

D United States: Evidence on Levels and Cuts

This section provides additional information on the tariff level and reductions in US tariffs during this period. As the World Trade Organization (2007: 205) reports: 'To our knowledge the only comprehensive estimate concerning the average tariff reduction rate in the first GATT Round of tariff negotiations is provided by the United States Tariff Commission for US tariffs.'

The United States is the most transparent country in terms of its tariff policy, and also the country with the best information on its average tariff. In 1947, the average US tariff on total imports was 7.9 per cent and the average tariff on dutiable imports was 20.1 per cent. This had already come down sharply from pre-war levels; the rates were 14.4 per cent and 37.3 per cent, respectively, in 1939. As Irwin (1998) points out, this decline is mainly a result of the impact of higher inflation during and after the war in reducing the *ad valorem* equivalent of the many specific duties in the tariff code.[14] Throughout the 1950s, the average tariff on imports was about 6 per cent and the average tariff on dutiable imports was about 12 per cent; neither of these figures changed much over the course of the decade.

The US Tariff Commission (1948) also presented clear details on the degree to which US tariffs were reduced in the reciprocal trade agreements reached in the 1930s as well as the 1947 Geneva negotiations. Table 3.8 reports the average pre-agreement rates (those established in the Tariff Act of 1930, the infamous Smoot-Hawley Tariff), those that prevailed in 1947 prior to the Geneva conference and those implemented in 1948, the year after the GATT was created. As Table 3.8 shows, the average tariff on goods (subject to negotiated rate changes) was 32 per cent in 1947 and 25 per cent in 1948, an average reduction associated with the timing of the Geneva Round of 21 per cent.

Furthermore, Table 3.8 also suggests that while the average pre-agreement tariff for the US was 48 per cent, the bilateral agreements under the Reciprocal Trade Agreements Act of 1934 reduced those tariffs by a third, cutting them to 32 per cent by 1947. These tariff changes are based on fixed

[14] See also Crucini (1994).

Table 3.8 *Imports of Commodities Subject to Rates of Duty Reduced by Trade Agreements, by Tariff Schedule*[a]

		Proportion Subject to Reduced Rates Equivalent *ad valorem* on Imports Subject to Reduced Rates (%)			Average Reduction in Rates (%)		
Tariff schedule	Value of dutiable imports, 1939 (US$ millions)	Pre-agreement rates	As of 1947 (pre-Geneva)	As of 1 January 1948 (post-Geneva)	Pre-agreement to pre-Geneva	Pre-agreement to post-Geneva	Pre-Geneva to post-Geneva
1. Chemicals, oils and paints	56.6	37.2	31.5	30.4	15	18	3
2. Earths, earthenwares and glassware	25.4	43.0	40.3	34.9	6	19	13
3. Metals and manufactures of	89.7	40.3	27.7	21.4	31	47	23
4. Wood and manufactures of	17.0	16.8	10.6	7.0	37	58	34
5. Sugar, molasses and manufactures of	90.5	69.4	35.2	24.4	49	65	31

Table 3.8 (*cont.*)

Tariff schedule	Value of dutiable imports, 1939 (US$ millions)	Proportion Subject to Reduced Rates Equivalent *ad valorem* on Imports Subject to Reduced Rates (%)			Average Reduction in Rates (%)		
		Pre-agreement rates	As of 1947 (pre-Geneva)	As of 1 January 1948 (post-Geneva)	Pre-agreement to pre-Geneva	Pre-agreement to post-Geneva	Pre-Geneva to post-Geneva
6. Tobacco and manufactures of	36.0	77.5	58.6	55.2	24	29	6
7. Agricultural products and provisions	173.8	36.8	23.1	21.3	37	42	8
8. Spirits, wines and other beverages	59.1	109.8	56.0	34.7	49	68	38
9. Cotton manufactures	27.3	38.3	33.8	28.9	12	25	14
10. Flax, hemp, jute and manufactures of	54.8	24.7	18.5	9.8	25	60	47
11. Wool manufactures	49.3	76.3	60.8	47.7	20	37	22

12 & 13. Silk manufactures and rayon and synthetics	15.5	37.6	35.2	28.5	6	24	19
14. Paper and books	11.5	21.8	17.3	14.3	21	34	17
15. Sundries	133.3	28.8	24.3	19.2	16	33	21
Free list subject to excise tax on importation	38.1	31.3	21.1	16.7	33	47	21
Total	877.7	48.2	32.2	25.4	33	47	21

[a] Based on reductions in effect 1 January 1948.

Source: US Tariff Commission, Operation of the Trade Agreements Program, June 1934 to April 1948, Part III. Trade-Agreement Concessions Granted by the United States, Report No. 160 (Washington, DC: GPO, 1948): 37.

weights (imports in 1939) and therefore focus exclusively on change in tariff rates as a result of trade negotiations. The calculation does not take into account the impact of higher import prices or changing import composition on the import-weighted average tariff during this period.

Finally, Table 3.8 also provides useful information on the variation in tariff reductions across different tariff schedule categories for the United States during this period. Some schedules saw large reductions (duties on flax, hemp and jute manufactures were cut by 47 per cent), while others were cut very little (chemicals and oils were cut by only 3 per cent) in the first round.

E Backcasting to 1947

Given the lack of any official information on tariff levels circa 1947, one way to ascertain those levels is to take later tariff levels known with confidence and to 'backcast' (as opposed to forecast) the 1947 tariff levels based on the tariff reductions that are thought to have taken place.

As we have seen, the earliest, most solid estimates of the post-war average tariff come from calculations done during the Kennedy Round. Around 1964, before the Kennedy Round tariff cuts had been negotiated, the average combined tariff for the United States, European Economic Community (EEC-6), the United Kingdom and Japan – the four major players – was 14 per cent. This figure is based on the import-weighted average of tariff rates in each of the four. The country tariff averages are from Preeg (1970: 208–211), also presented here as column 1 of Table 3.6 and column 2 of Table 3.7. These are combined together in one figure by weighting the four tariffs by the region's value of imports in 1964; these weights are 0.4 for the EEC, 0.3 for the United States, 0.175 for the United Kingdom, and 0.125 for Japan (WTO 2007: 208).

Table 3.7 reveals two main results. First, the average tariffs were roughly comparable across countries, ranging from 12.8 for the EEC to 16.6 for the United Kingdom. Second, the weighting scheme (whether unweighted or weighted by world imports or the country's imports) does not make much difference to these country averages.

If we therefore accept that the average tariff was about 14 per cent before the Kennedy Round – something that Table 3.7 seems to confirm – what does this imply about the average tariff prior to the 1947 Geneva Round? Fortunately, the percentage average tariff reduction – but not the average tariff level – in each of the previous GATT rounds is widely reported. As

Table 3.9 shows, the average tariff reduction in the first Geneva Round was estimated to be 26 per cent, followed by 3 per cent in the Annecy Round, 4 per cent in the Torquay Round, 3 per cent in the Geneva Round, and then 4 per cent in the Dillon Round. This amounts to a cumulative tariff reduction of 36 per cent. Where do the figures on the tariff cuts by round come from? These figures are based on the concessions made by the United States, the country with the most transparent trade policy at the time, and reported by the Tariff Commission.[15]

If the United States made the most significant tariff reductions during this period, as is commonly thought, applying these cuts to other countries should give us an upper bound of the level of the tariff in 1947. Thus, applying these tariff reductions to the 14 per cent pre–Kennedy Round average tariff implies that the average tariff was 21.8 per cent in 1947, which fell to 16.8 per cent following the first Geneva conference.[16] This is depicted in Figure 3.1, which shows two paths for average tariffs, one starting at 40 per cent and the other at 21.8 per cent. If tariffs had in fact been at 40 per cent in 1947, the average tariff level would have been subject to enormous cuts prior

Table 3.9 *GATT Tariff Reductions*

Implementation Period	Round Covered	Weighted Tariff Reduction (%)	Weights Based on MFN Imports (year)
1948	Geneva (1947)	−26	1939
1950	Annecy (1949)	−3	1947
1952	Torquay (1950–51)	−4	1949
1956–58	Geneva (1955–56)	−3	1954
1962–64	Dillon Round (1961–62)	−4	1960
1968–72	Kennedy Round (1964–67)	−38	1964
1980–87	Tokyo Round (1973–79)	−33	1976/77
1995–99	Uruguay Round (1986–94)	−38	1988/1989

Source: WTO (2007: 207).

[15] See Finger (1979, Tables 1 and 10) for a discussion of the tariff reductions and information on the Tariff Commission reports.

[16] The formula for the backcast is $\tau_{1947} \cdot (1 - \Delta\tau) = \tau_{1964}$, or $\tau_{1947} = \tau_{1964}/(1 - \Delta\tau)$, where τ_{1947} is the average tariff in 1947 (pre-GATT), τ_{1964} is the average tariff in 1964 (pre-Kennedy Round), and $\Delta\tau$ is the percentage change in the tariff between these two periods, i.e., $(1 - \Delta\tau) \equiv (1 - \Delta\tau_{Dillon})(1 - \Delta\tau_{Geneva})(1 - \Delta\tau_{Torquay})(1 - \Delta\tau_{Annecy})(1 - \Delta\tau_{Geneva})$. Hence, $0.218 = 0.14/(1 - 0.36)$.

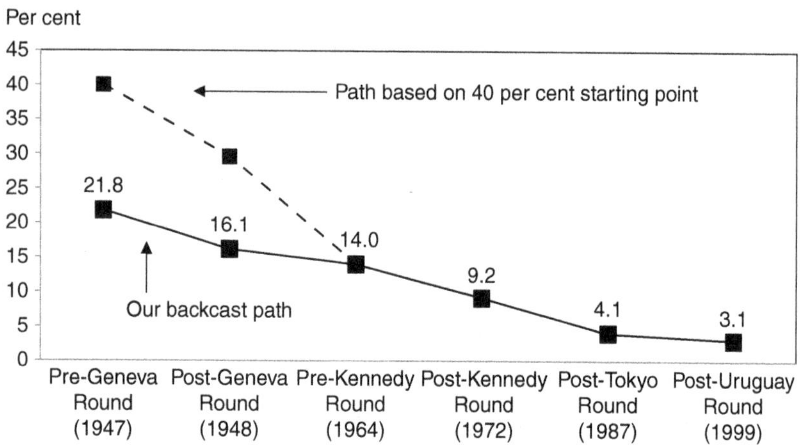

Figure 3.1. Path of average tariffs: pre-Geneva to post-Uruguay Round.
Source: Constructed by the authors, based on average tariff levels for United States, European Community/Union and Japan. See text for discussion. Backcast estimate of pre-GATT 1947 average tariff level of 21.8 per cent based on upper bound assumption of 26 per cent tariff cut in the first (Geneva) Round. Assuming a 21 per cent tariff cut in the first (Geneva) Round would imply a backcast estimate of pre-GATT 1947 average tariff level of 20.3 per cent.

to the Kennedy Round. If the tariff at the beginning of the 1947 GATT negotiations was 40 per cent, then given the degree of tariff cutting that took place, the average tariff should have been about 26 per cent prior to the Kennedy Round instead of the actual figure of 14 per cent. The calculation presented here, in which the average tariff was about 22 per cent in 1947, shows that the downward path of average tariffs was slower but smoother.

One way to verify this calculation is to take the GATT's calculated average tariffs for 1952, presented in Table 3.5, and see if they match what emerges from the backcast. The average shown in Table 3.3 is 18.4 per cent for 1952; the average is about 15.3 per cent after the Torquay Round (not weighted across countries). According to our backcasting exercise, the average tariff should have been 15.0 per cent after the Torquay Round, suggesting that this approach is reasonably accurate.

This exercise was based on a 26 per cent tariff cut in the first round. However, this is likely an upper bound because the United States was thought to have made most of the concessions in the first negotiating round.[17] In addition, the 26 per cent average reduction excludes agricultural

[17] As the WTO (2007: 181) notes: 'We lack appropriate data to gauge the precise extent of the tariff cuts. Only for the United States is a detailed analysis available. However, it is generally

tariffs; for all products, as we have seen, the average US tariff reduction was 21 per cent (Table 3.8, last column). If we assume that all countries cut their tariffs by 21 per cent, then the cumulative tariff reduction was 31 per cent and the backcast average tariff in 1947 becomes 20.3 per cent.

We can also backcast the average tariffs for the United States, EEC and Japan for 1947. Using the 26 per cent cut for the first round, the backcast 1947 tariff would be 21 per cent for the United States, 20 per cent for the EEC and 23 per cent for Japan. (The figures would be slightly lower taking the first round cut as 21 per cent; in this case, the results would be 20 per cent for the US, 19 per cent for the EEC and 21 per cent for Japan.) The one check that we can do on this result is for the United States where, in 1947, the average (import-weighted) tariff on dutiable imports was 20 per cent, essentially the same as our backcast result for that year.

F Assessing the Average Tariff Data: Is the Time Path Meaningful?

Having established the average unweighted level of the tariff in 1947 at about 22 per cent, we next return to our data on the import-weighted tariff average in order to examine empirically whether there are discernible reductions in this particular measure of tariffs following the initial GATT negotiating rounds. One way to assess whether the data on trade-weighted average tariffs presented in Table 3.1 are at all informative, for example, is to examine whether the data are at least consistent with other accounts of the results of the GATT tariff negotiations taking place at the time. It is worth recalling our discussion in Section B, however, where it was noted that these particular tariff measures are probably inferior to the unweighted tariff averages. They are downward biased. Changes in these particular tariff measures may reflect factors other than changes in official tariff rates. These other factors include import prices and the composition of imports, both of which were changing rapidly in the immediate post-war period. Nevertheless, the advantage of these measures is that

recognized that the United States made the most generous tariff concessions reflecting its strong economic situation and relatively high level of tariff protection.' The WTO (2007: 206) also states: 'For France and the United Kingdom, no average rate of reduction has been provided in the various government reports dealing with the results of these negotiations. The tariffs of the Benelux countries at the time had been recognized to be well below the average prevailing in the other industrial countries and therefore these countries made concessions principally by binding most of their tariffs at the already low levels. It is therefore plausible to assume that the average tariff reduction on industrial products of all industrial countries achieved in 1947 was somewhat less than the reduction observed for the United States.'

they are available on an annual basis; thus we examine whether they reveal evidence on the tariff reductions undertaken during this period.

We perform a set of difference-in-difference regressions to help assess whether the inter-temporal patterns in the import-weighted average tariff data over the 1944–1959 period of the first few GATT Rounds provide useful information. In particular, we examine whether the average tariffs for the active GATT participants at its inception in 1947 – what we refer to as the 'core' GATT Contracting Parties of Australia, Canada, the United Kingdom and the United States – had larger subsequent reductions in their average tariffs during the initial rounds than 'other' (comparison group) countries. We consider two definitions for the set of other comparison group countries: the first includes all other countries listed in Table 3.1, a mix of initial GATT 1947 Contracting Parties and countries that only joined later; the second comprises only the eight other initial GATT 1947 Contracting Parties listed in Table 3.1 (Belgium, Brazil, Chile, France, India, Netherlands, New Zealand and Norway).

Table 3.10 presents our regression estimates on average tariff data covering the years 1944–1959. The data are in 'long-differences' in which the dependent variable is defined as the three-year difference in trade-weighted average tariffs.[18] The two main sets of regressors are dummy variables for the years (1947, 1950, 1953, 1956 and 1959) and year dummies *interacted* with an indicator for the importer being one of the four 'core' GATT Contracting Parties. In columns (1) and (2), the comparison group of countries includes all of the other countries listed in Table 3.1 for which data are available, and in columns (3) and (4) the comparison set of countries is only the other initial (non-core) GATT 1947 Contracting Parties. In columns (1) and (3), the annual percentage change in average tariffs is constructed using conventional methods, whereas the robustness checks provided in columns (2) and (4) use log differences in trade-weighted average tariffs.

Columns (1) and (2) of Table 3.10 suggest that, when looking at three-year differences in tariffs, there is no (robust) statistically significant change in average tariffs across the full sample of countries in 1947, 1950, 1953, 1956 or 1959. For the smaller sample of GATT 1947 Contracting Parties only (columns 3 and 4), there is evidence of a

[18] This is opposed to a regression framework analysing annual changes in tariffs, which yields qualitatively similar results. Focusing on three-year changes may better reflect the cumulative effect of a given tariff cut over a couple of years. Finally, while the data used cover 1944–1959, because the regressions examine three-year changes in average tariffs, the regressions ultimately cover changes in tariffs over the 1947–1959 period.

Table 3.10 *Three-Year Tariff Differences Across Countries, 1947–1959*

	Dependent Variable: Long Difference (3-year change) in Customs Revenue/Imports			
Explanatory variables	Baseline (1)	Use log differences (2)	GATT CPs only (3)	GATT CPs and log differences (4)
Year = 1947	−0.04	−0.07	−0.03	−0.06
	(0.06)	(0.06)	(0.11)	(0.10)
1950	**0.29****	0.17	0.39	0.19
	(0.15)	(0.11)	(0.29)	(0.21)
1953	0.33	0.11	**0.20***	**0.16***
	(0.31)	(0.13)	**(0.10)**	**(0.08)**
1956	0.12	0.06	−0.12	−0.17
	(0.10)	(0.08)	(0.10)	(0.12)
1959	0.10	0.03	0.20	0.15
	(0.09)	(0.11)	(0.13)	(0.11)
GATT core x 1947	**1.29*****	**0.84*****	**1.28*****	**0.83*****
	(0.42)	**(0.18)**	**(0.46)**	**(0.21)**
GATT core x 1950	**−0.55*****	**−0.48*****	**−0.65****	**−0.49****
	(0.16)	**(0.13)**	**(0.30)**	**(0.23)**
GATT core x 1953	−0.33	−0.11	**−0.20***	**−0.17***
	(0.31)	(0.13)	**(0.11)**	**(0.09)**
GATT core x 1956	−0.30	−0.32	−0.05	−0.09
	(0.19)	(0.24)	(0.20)	(0.27)
GATT core x 1959	0.02	0.08	−0.09	−0.05
	(0.11)	(0.13)	(0.15)	(0.13)
Observations	96	96	51	51
R-squared	0.19	0.20	0.46	0.40

Source: Created by the authors.
Notes: Model estimated without a constant term. Robust standard errors in parentheses, with ***, ** and * indicating estimates statistically different from zero at the 1, 5, and 10 per cent level, respectively. Definition of dependent variable in (1) and (3) is (X_t-X_t-3)/X_t-3 and in (2) and (4) it is ln(X_t)-ln(X_t-3), where X is the ratio of customs revenue to imports. Years are 1947–1959, and the full sample of 25 countries includes 12 of the original GATT Contracting Parties ('GATT CPs') of Australia, Belgium, Brazil, Canada, Chile, France, India, Netherlands, New Zealand, Norway, United Kingdom, United States and 13 of the non-original GATT Contracting Parties of Argentina, Denmark, Finland, Italy, Japan, Mexico, Peru, Portugal, Spain, Sweden, Switzerland, Turkey and West Germany. The core GATT countries defined as Australia, Canada, United Kingdom and United States. Columns (3) and (4) drop all countries that were not original 1947 GATT Contracting Parties.

statistically significant *increase* in average tariffs across those countries in 1953 relative to their levels in 1950.

The main result of interest in Table 3.10 is seen in the bottom set of rows, which presents estimates of the *interaction* of the year dummies with an indicator for whether the country was one of the core GATT 1947 Contracting Parties – Australia, Canada, the United Kingdom and the United States. Indeed, relative to the full sample of countries (columns 1 and 2), there is a negative and statistically significant differential estimate (−0.55 and −0.48, respectively) for the changes in the average tariffs for those four countries in 1950 relative to their average tariff levels in 1947. In particular, whereas the average tariff across the entire sample of countries was 29 per cent higher in 1950 than in 1947, the statistically significant differential estimate in column (1) implies that the average tariff was 26 per cent lower (= 0.29 – 0.55) for the four core GATT Contracting Parties in 1950 relative to 1947. This statistically significant differential for these four countries is robust across model specifications of Table 3.10, and the estimates are of a cumulative average tariff reduction from 1947 to 1950 for the four countries ranging between 26 and 31 per cent.

Furthermore, for the regressions on the subsample of GATT 1947 Contracting Parties only (columns 3 and 4), a second result is that average tariffs increased across the sample by an average of 16–20 per cent between 1950 and 1953. However, relative to only these other GATT 1947 Contracting Parties, average tariff changes for the four core GATT Contracting Parties were statistically different from the sample average in columns (3) and (4), with differential estimates of −0.65 and −0.49, respectively. Overall, despite tariffs for the GATT Contracting Parties increasing on average between 1950 and 1953, average tariffs for Australia, Canada, the United Kingdom and the United States managed to remain flat between 1950 and 1953.

When combined, the estimates for the changes in 1950 and 1953 reflect the *cumulative* effect of tariff liberalisation *differentials* arising for these four countries (relative to the other GATT 1947 Contracting Parties) after the Geneva (1947), Annecy (1949) and Torquay (1951) rounds of GATT negotiations. Thus we conclude that, relative to other 1947 GATT Contracting Parties as well as a wider sample of countries, average tariffs for the four core GATT Contracting Parties were significantly lower by 1953 than they had been in 1947.

Finally, it is also worth noting for the core countries that, relative to the average across both the full sample of countries (columns 1 and 2) and the smaller sample of GATT 1947 Contracting Parties (columns 3 and 4), their pre-GATT 'starting point' trade-weighted tariffs were significantly higher in 1947 than they had been three years earlier (in 1944). In particular, the column (1) estimate indicates that average tariffs for Australia, Canada, the United Kingdom and the United States were 129 per cent higher in 1947 than in 1944.[19] Nevertheless, it is extremely doubtful that these tariff increases reflected changes in applied tariff *rates* as opposed to changes in the composition of trade as a result of the end of World War II. For example, Canada did not change the rates in its tariff code during this period (Hart 2003).

G Conclusion

This paper has attempted to shed light on the height of tariff barriers on the eve of the 1947 Geneva conference that established the GATT and negotiated the first post-war tariff reductions. We find that the average tariff among the key GATT participants – the United States, Western Europe and Japan – was about 22 per cent at the time of the first Geneva conference, significantly lower than the oft-reported 40 per cent figure (World Bank 1987). This figure refers to the unweighted tariff average; the import-weighted tariff average would be much lower than this. In addition, we report limited econometric evidence of significant tariff reductions by the key early GATT participants – the core of the United States, United Kingdom, Canada and Australia – but not for others in the late 1940s and early 1950s.

While it is beyond the scope of this chapter to determine the economic effect of these tariff reductions, we should point out that the early tariff reductions were thought to have a muted impact on world trade flows, largely due to the presence of other non-tariff barriers at the time. In particular, the coexistence of import quotas and foreign exchange controls (European currencies were not fully convertible into dollars until 1958) meant that tariff reductions by themselves may have had little impact on trade.[20] Nevertheless, Goldstein, Rivers and Tomz (2007) use

[19] Between 1944 and 1947, trade-weighted average tariffs in Australia increased from 8.6 to 27.9 per cent, in Canada from 6.5 to 11.4 per cent, and in the United Kingdom from 24.5 to 44.0 per cent. Among the core countries, only in the United States did the tariffs fall between 1944 and 1947, from 10.6 to 8.2 per cent. Lloyd (2008) advises strong caution in interpreting the tariff figures for Australia during this period.

[20] As Curzon (1965: 80–81) notes: 'It must also be remembered that principally only in the United States (and Canada) were tariff cuts effective during the 1950s. In other countries

a gravity equation and provide some evidence that the early GATT had a positive and significant effect on world trade. Pinning down exactly how the GATT boosted early post-war trade is thus an important topic for further research.

References

Anderson, James and Neary, J. Peter. 2005. *Measuring the Restrictiveness of Trade Policy*. Cambridge, MA: The MIT Press.

Anderson, Kym. 2016. 'Contributions of the GATT/WTO to Global Economic Welfare: Empirical Evidence'. *Journal of Economic Surveys* 30 (1): 56–92.

Bagwell, Kyle, Bown, Chad P. and Staiger, Robert W. 2016. 'Is the WTO Passé?' *Journal of Economic Literature* 54 (4): 1125–1231.

Bagwell, Kyle, Staiger, Robert W. and Yurukoglu, Ali. 2015. 'Multilateral Trade Bargaining: A First Look at the GATT Bargaining Records'. *NBER Working Paper*, No. 21488, August.

Balassa, Bela. 1961. *The Theory of Economic Integration*. Homewood, IL: Irwin.

Bown, Chad P. and Irwin, Douglas A. 2015. 'The Urban Legend: Pre-GATT Tariffs of 40%'. VoxEU, 19 December. www.voxeu.org/article/myth-40-pre-gatt-tariffs

Brusse, Wendy A. 1997. *Tariffs, Trade, and European Integration, 1947–1957*. New York: St. Martin's Press.

Clemens, Michael A. and Williamson, Jeffrey G. 2004. 'Why Did the Tariff-Growth Correlation Change after 1950?' *Journal of Economic Growth* 9 (1): 5–46.

Committee for Economic Development. 1964. *Trade Negotiations for a Better Free World Economy*. New York: CED.

Crucini, Mario J. 1994. 'Sources of Variation in Real Tariff Rates: The United States, 1900–1940'. *American Economic Review* 84 (3): 732–743.

Curzon, Gerard. 1965. *Multilateral Commercial Diplomacy: The General Agreement on Tariffs and Trade and Its Impact on National Commercial Policies and Techniques*. London: Michael Joseph.

Finger, Joseph M. 1979. 'Trade Liberalization: A Public Choice Perspective'. In *Challenges to a Liberal International Economic Order*, edited by R. C. Amacher, G. Haberler, and T. Willett. Washington, DC: American Enterprise Institute.

quotas and exchange controls interfered sufficiently with the trade flow to make any measurement meaningless.' And Brusse (1997) adds: 'While the average depth of the tariff cuts negotiated in 1947 stands out quite favorably compared to those of the subsequent rounds, the reductions themselves hardly affected levels of protection. Many rates contained "extra margins" that could easily be cut without changing effective protection levels.'

General Agreement on Tariffs and Trade. 1953a. *International Trade, 1952.* Geneva: GATT.

General Agreement on Tariffs and Trade. 1953b. *Report of the Intersessional Working Party on the Reduction of Tariff Levels.* G/53, October 9, https://gatt.stanford.edu/bin/detail?fileID=17024479, accessed 17 March 2016.

Goldstein, Judith, Rivers, Douglas and Tomz, Michael. 2007. 'Institutions in International Relations: Understanding the Effects of the GATT and the WTO on World Trade'. *International Organization* 61 (1): 37–67.

Hart, Michael. 2003. *A Trading Nation: Canadian Trade Policy from Colonialism to Globalization.* Toronto: UBC Press.

Irwin, Douglas A. 1998. 'Changes in U.S. Tariffs: The Role of Import Prices and Commercial Policies'. *American Economic Review* 88 (4): 1015–1026.

Irwin, Douglas A. 2010. 'Trade Restrictiveness and Deadweight Losses from US Tariffs'. *American Economic Journal: Economic Policy* 2 (3): 111–133.

Irwin, Douglas A. 2012. *Trade Policy Disaster: Lessons from the 1930s.* Cambridge, MA: MIT Press.

Kee, Hiau, Neagu, C. and Nicita, Alessandro. 2013. 'Is Protectionism on the Rise? Assessing National Trade Policies during the Crisis of 2008'. *Review of Economics and Statistics* 95 (1): 342–346.

Kee, Hiau, Nicita, Alessandro and Olarreaga, Marcelo. 2008. 'Import Demand Elasticities and Trade Distortions'. *Review of Economics and Statistics* 90 (4): 666–682.

Kee, Hiau, Nicita, Alessandro and Olarreaga, Marcelo. 2009. 'Estimating Trade Restrictiveness Indices'. *Economic Journal* 119 (1): 172–199.

League of Nations. 1927. *Tariff Level Indices.* Geneva: League of Nations.

Lloyd, Peter. 2008. '100 Years of Tariff Protection in Australia'. *Australian Economic History Review* 48 (2): 99–145.

Ossa, Ralph. 2014. 'Trade Wars and Trade Talks with Data'. *American Economic Review* 104 (12): 4104–4146.

Palgrave Macmillan (ed.). 2013. *International Historical Statistics,* http://www.palgraveconnect.com/pc/doifinder/10.1057/9781137305688.0216, accessed 17 September 2015.

Political and Economic Planning. 1959. *Tariffs and Trade in Western Europe.* London: George Allen & Unwin.

Preeg, E. H. 1970. *Traders and Diplomats: An Analysis of the Kennedy Round of Negotiations under the General Agreement on Tariffs and Trade.* Washington, DC: Brookings Institution.

United States International Trade Commission. 2014. *U.S. imports for consumption, duties collected, and ratio of duties to value, 1891–2013.* Office of Analysis and Research Services, Office of Operations, https://dataweb.usitc.gov/scripts/AVE_table_1891-2013.pdf, accessed 17 March 2016.

US Tariff Commission. 1948. *Operation of the Trade Agreements Program, June 1934-April 1948, Part III. Trade-Agreement Concessions Granted by the United States*, Report No. 160. Washington, DC: GPO.

World Bank. 1987. *World Development Report, 1987*. Washington, DC: World Bank.

World Trade Organization. 2007. *World Trade Report: Six Decades of Multilateral Cooperation, What Have We Learnt?* Geneva: WTO.

Woytinsky, Wladimir S. and Woytinsky, Emma S. 1955. *World Commerce and Governments*. New York: Twentieth Century Fund.

4

Negotiating in the Early GATT

Norms, Rules and the US Tariff Schedule

JUDITH L. GOLDSTEIN AND ROBERT GULOTTY[1]

A Introduction

How important was the General Agreement on Tariffs and Trade (GATT) to the liberalisation of world trade after World War II? In the halls of the World Trade Organization (WTO) today, few question the value of the early regime as a critical predecessor of the current WTO. But, among scholars of international organisations there has been less certainty and a lively debate has developed, even among those using similar methods of assessing trade flows.[2] Longitudinal aggregate analyses of trade flows pre- and post-accession to the GATT, however, may be the wrong way to examine the function of the early organisation. The role of the international trade regime has changed over time; its purposes today, and certainly its scope, is far different from that imagined by the founders. In fact, in the early years, the GATT was little more than a forum for swaps with a 'thin' set of rules on how to rebalance concessions if nations reneged on an agreement. The organisation was small and truly member-driven.

Below we look more carefully at the early GATT so as to better understand how it functioned and why it was deemed successful. In particular, we focus on the details of tariff reduction swaps to gain a better understanding of when and why nations were able to conclude bargains. We will argue that the success of the organisation in its early years was less in the creation of strict rules to regularise trade, but rather,

[1] We would like to thank Rafael Ramos and Sung Mi Kim for their able research assistance as well as the comments from both panelists and attendees at the 2015 World Trade Forum conference.

[2] For example see Rose (2004) on the negative side and Goldstein et al. (2007) for the more positive case for the role of the WTO.

in an accommodation for the domestic constraints faced by those who came to Geneva to negotiate tariffs.

Our focus is the first Round of trade talks, the GATT47, and its effects on the United States tariff schedule. We begin agnostic on the economic purposes of trade treaties; earlier economic work has shown convincingly that unless a country is able to set an 'optimal tariff', nations should be able to obtain the same utility from moving unilaterally as from going through an arduous negotiation. Yet, trade liberalisation rarely takes place in the absence of some formal agreement. For a better understanding of why we see so many treaties, we turn to scholars of politics who offer two different explanations for the prevalence of these treaties. On one side are those that suggest that the treaty is a commitment device, and has resulted in considerable empirical work on compliance. Alternatively, many scholars argue that treaties are focused on a domestic audience, and in particular, that the agreement motivates exporters or other beneficiaries of the treaty to organise themselves to gain access to foreign markets. While both approaches provide insight into the incentives that may propel a nation to the bargaining table, neither focuses attention on the choice of instruments found in the treaty that lead to specific changes in market access.

What does explain which particular products see a reduction in protection within a negotiation and the overall success of a Round? Again, looking at the political economy literature, the prevailing explanations for product choice focus on the mobilisation of producer 'power' in each of the two parties to the agreement (Schattschneider 1935; Grossman and Helpman 1994; Irwin and Krosner 1996; Gilligan 1997). While a good starting point, we know that treaties reflect an interactive process; products are cut because a trading partner makes a request. To explain outcomes, we need to pay attention to both why a nation is willing or unwilling to lower rates on particular products and to why those products are sought after by others. Finally, to explain how these interests translate into tariff reductions, we must explicate the exact negotiating rules on product reductions.

To explain the national demand for tariff reductions from others, the willingness to reduce one's own rates and then the structure of the interaction between the two, we expand upon work associated with Bagwell and Staiger (2002), Jones (1969) and Johnson (1953–1954) who argue that governments, even those motivated just to increase national income, need treaties so as to undo or limit restrictions in trade volume that arise when governments use trade policy to change the terms of trade. Why? A national-income-maximising politician in a market large enough to influence the price of traded goods has an incentive to charge an 'optimal' tariff and improve their nation's terms of trade. Whereas in a small country the burden of a tariff is borne by domestic consumers, in a large country, foreign exporters internalise the tariff cost, which allows the home government to shift the burden of tariff revenue onto foreign exporters. If all large nations pursue such a policy, however, the result will be suboptimal trade volumes. In order to mutually disarm, treaties are negotiated – states swap reductions to ratchet down barriers in a way that avoids harm to their terms of trade. Thus treaties, according to Bagwell and Staiger (2002), internalise a terms-of-trade externality between countries. And consistent with this logic, trade treaties ameliorate an incentive structure akin to a prisoner's dilemma through a set of rules that prioritise reciprocity and non-discrimination.[3]

Even if we acknowledge that rules are made to 'mutually disarm', uncertainty remains about the exact nature of the rules. What rules are in the interest of large states? And once written, are they uniformly adhered to? What if a nation is large but has tariffs that are not oriented towards taking advantage of terms-of-trade externalities, or they have chosen to impose a high rate to garner favour from a powerful interest group? What rules would they advocate? Answering these questions requires that we examine the political incentives, and constraints, of that income-maximising politician.

From a political perspective, it is logical to assume that treaty rules and negotiation procedures were written to increase aggregate trade *and* in response to some domestic constraint facing the negotiator. Let us assume that a central decision-maker recognises the value of trade liberalisation and concludes some treaty. In most nations, that leader would still need to worry about groups that could potentially block passage of his agreement, even if that treaty is Pareto improving. The rational decision-maker must consider the size of his or her pro-trade coalition or the goal of increased trade and greater welfare would not be met. Rules must be flexible so as not to undermine his coalition. Consistent with his needs to create a pro-trade coalition, we can imagine that some negotiation policies would be aimed at the reduction of

[3] Why do small nations sign trade treaties? If a nation is economically small, there is not much that a politician can do to change foreign prices, and so their partners have little to gain from constraining their own policy. However, a treaty may be valuable to small states in that they stipulate common rules that lower the costs of exporting. In terms of bargaining with others, however, small nations have limited power to stipulate rules of their choosing, given limited market size.

optimal and/or high tariffs. Others, however, could well reflect more particularistic goals.

Given these political constraints, we can assume that trade agreements reflect some trade-off between domestic constituent pressures and international economic opportunities. The key function of a trade treaty is to set expectations for signatories. Treaties specify which industries will face market forces and under what conditions. It is in equal parts a domestic political device allowing leaders to assure a pro-trade coalition and an economic innovation, providing transparency and predictability for those involved in commerce. Successful trade treaties are able to satisfy domestic pressures while increasing trade volume.

Below, we use data from the first GATT Round to illustrate how the initial GATT satisfied both these demands in the case of US tariff reductions. We focus on the format of the tariff negotiations and the importance of the structure of interaction that was imposed on the participants. Foreshadowing the data, we find that the negotiating strategy of the partner with the United States was an important determinant of success. Specifically, when countries came to the table with open-ended or under-specified requests for tariff reductions, they were more successful than if they came with particularistic requests for a cut. An open-ended request allowed the US negotiator to pick products based on the changing nature of the pro-trade coalition back home. A strategy that focused on particular products and deeper cuts often failed to materialise because of lack of attention to US domestic constraints. Consistent with Bagwell et al. (2015), we find that bargaining to obtain reciprocal benefits was far more difficult on the intensive margin (the level of tariff cut offered) and more successful on the extensive margin (which products were to be included in the bargain). We believe that this pattern reflects domestic political constraints, that is, the fact that bargaining occurred in the shadow of a congressional veto. Final cuts in the US tariff schedule reveal that constraint, as well as an Executive Office interest in negotiating increased volume via a reduction of high tariffs. Presidents were always anticipating the coalition patterns that would be affected by changing trade flows and they agreed to the tariff cuts that were most convenient (Goldstein and Gulotty 2014).

B GATT 1947: Norms and Rules

We begin with a query about the origin of the 'rules of the game'. As with many accounts of US trade liberalisation post–World War II, we begin with the implications of passage of the Smoot-Hawley Tariff in 1930. That tariff raised US tariffs to their twentieth century pinnacle and was followed by the onset of the Great Depression. As a result of economic hard times, the Democratic Party won control of government. In order to undercut legislative log rolling on individual products, thought to be a cause of the tariff and thus the depression, Congress delegated authority to the Executive Office to set tariff rates.[4]

The new Democratic majority, long advocates of lower tariffs, could have, but did not grant powers to the Executive office without constraint. Rather, Congress's role remained central, with the legislature setting tariff reduction procedures and forcing the Executive to return regularly to Congress to renew authority to continue to negotiate trade treaties. In particular, as well as specifying administrative guidelines for tariff negotiations, Congress specified a rule, MFN, and a norm, reciprocity, to guide negotiations. Legislation was oriented towards the protection of constituent interests. Any product subject to negotiation had to be authorised prior to negotiations, those negotiations had to be focused on the principal supplier of the good and reductions could not exceed a specified amount.[5]

With congressional approval, but with these constraints, the president negotiated a set of bilateral agreements with major trading partners up to the beginning of World War II. After the war, the United States once again initiated tariff talks, spurred by the impending expiration of the

[4] Congress continued to legislate lowered rates for particular products at the end of the tariff schedule. The 1930 tariff act was the last complete overhaul by Congress of rates that, for the most part, increased rates over their prior amount.

[5] The principal supplier rule maintained support for trade liberalisation, first, because it provided information to representatives about whether or not producers in their district were likely to be cut in a particular dyadic treaty, and second, because it gave the president information about which members of Congress would potentially resist an agreement. The principal supplier rule was offered as a compromise by then Secretary of State Hull to Congress to assure continued support of MFN inclusion in the treaties. While Hull did get agreement to universalise agreements by including MFN language, the compromise actually undermined his intent by protecting many highly tariffed products. The reason was that many producers were excluded from the liberalisation forces simply because the principal supplier and often tertiary suppliers were from nations with which the United States did not enact a trade treaty. For example, in 1934, a large number of highly protected products came from Germany, a country conveniently ignored as a potential treaty partner in the bilateral years and in the early GATT. The result of the omission was that a significant number of highly protected products were untouched until the 1960s. While this may seem counter-intuitive given the administration's support for widespread trade liberalisation, the absence of these products in tariff 'bundles' actually facilitated programme support by dampening interest group mobilisation.

president's negotiation authority and the upcoming debate on its renewal. Anticipating this debate in 1948, the United States pushed for the creation of an Interim Tariff Committee at the International Trade Organization (ITO)'s London Conference to allow early negotiations. In effect, it was the timing of US legislation that would ultimately separate tariff reduction policy in Geneva from deliberations on the more general rules of commerce. And with the failure to create the ITO, the rules appended to the tariff schedule reductions in 1947 became the backbone of the trade organisation until the WTO's creation.

None of these events was truly exogenous. The Great Depression was exacerbated by US tariff policy, which itself was a product of uneven growth after World War I. The Depression brought in a Democratic Party majority that decided to delegate to the president because he was a member of their party. But given the uncertainty of party control, they sunsetted delegation; and since the tariff legislation was up for renewal in 1948, the United States could not wait for passage of the ITO treaty.

While acknowledging endogeneity, we focus on the fact that congressional legislation specified *reciprocal, MFN* treaties with nations which were the *principal importer* of a particular product. This trifecta of policy guidelines served multiple purposes. The principal supplier rule, that is, the specification of negotiations with the low cost producer, provided information to legislators on whether or not products in his district could be in the reciprocal bundle. MFN merged America's multilateral aspirations with the principal supplier rule that focused on trading dyads. The reciprocity rule assured equity and motivated exporters to become politically active.[6]

[6] The 1934 Act and subsequent renewals stipulated very clear procedures for vetting potential product cuts. According to legislation, the President needed to seek advice from the Tariff Commission, the departments of State, Agriculture and Commerce and from all other appropriate sources before lowering a tariff. To accommodate this mandate a series of committees, the Trade Agreements Committee, country-specific committees and the Committee for Reciprocity Information, were assembled to give interested parties the opportunity to present views. They took briefs and held public hearings. Until 1937, a formal announcement of intent to negotiate was accompanied by a list of the principal producers who could potentially get a tariff cut; this was later replaced by the 'public' list, which signalled all items that were under consideration in any negotiation. The 1934 Act also dictated the form of tariff setting. All agreements were bilateral with some foreign government and although treaties had only two signatories, their effect extended beyond the two nations. After 1923, the US was bound by Executive Order to grant MFN privileges to its trading partners. Also, the Executive was bound by law to negotiate *reciprocal* agreements, extending to parties withdrawing from the treaty.

The early documents from the wartime conferences on the future of global trade outlined a negotiation process akin to that found in US legislation (Chapter III of the First Session and Chapter IV of the Preparatory Committee's second session report). Joining the ITO would mean that nations were committed to a substantial reduction of their tariffs and other charges on imports and exports, as well as the elimination of preferences. This reduction was to be reciprocal and mutually advantageous. MFN was to be applied to both reductions in general and reductions in preferential rates. In no circumstance could a rate be increased as a result of negotiations; bindings, as well as previous reductions via trade treaties, could be counted as part of a reciprocal deal. Excepted from these rules were previous preference agreements – they did not have to be granted MFN privileges. These included not only the British Imperial system but also Cuban–American preferences.

While the general structure of negotiations was set pre-GATT, the application of principles evolved over the course of the trade talks. The process was ultimately organised into three stages. First, nations simultaneously conveyed to every other participant a list of products they wanted to negotiate over and a preferred reduction amount. These lists varied dramatically in number, product content and level of demand. They were not made public. Some nations, such as France and England, specified products but not reductions; the United States, in comparison, had a much more detailed request list of desired cuts. Looking back, we see that France and England focused on the extensive margin, that is, the number of products; others, such as the United States, focused on the intensive margin or the depth of a cut in a particular product. Reciprocity did not mandate one or the other. Small reductions in a larger number of products were no different than large reductions in fewer products.

After receiving the product list from each nation, countries responded with a list of bilateral offers. These were available to all the participant nations but not to the general public. Offers were followed by bilateral negotiations. The offers were not binding in any respect and a review of the negotiations reveals that counter-offers were changed substantially, both up and down. In principal, they could have also been supplemented by offers on new items but in practice that almost never occurred. We return to this observation below and suggest that for the United States, change on the extensive margin was difficult because of administrative and political constraints. More often, offers were withdrawn.

Overall, the negotiation stage was messy and the Secretariat laboured to get nations not only to meet but simply to report at least twice a month on the status of talks and what products were still open for possible cuts. The target date for completion of this process was 15 August 1947; the first negotiations began on 23 April. It went slowly. By mid-June 1947, 298 meetings had been held by the ninety-three pairs of countries that entered negotiations.[7] Some countries met often (five pairs met more than ten times) but most met only sporadically. By the close of the negotiations, however, almost all dyads did conclude an agreement. The exceptions for sovereign states all involved Cuba: Benelux and Cuba, France and Cuba, and the UK and Cuba.[8] The GATT Contracting Parties accounted for three-quarters of global international trade in 1938 (US Department of State 1947).

Of course, not all dyads of negotiations were equally important. If we use trade volume in 1938 to organise the group, twenty-five dyads accounted for 87 per cent of all trade of the group. Canada–US trade alone was about 11 per cent; UK–US trade was another 10 per cent. The next seven were either among UK and current or ex-colonies or between European nations. The volume of US trade with Europe was small – US–Benelux trade was about 3.6 per cent of total trade among all the negotiating countries, although Benelux had more US trade than any other European partner. Progress towards agreement was not necessarily associated with the amount of trade. The first completed negotiation was between Canada and Norway, which ranked fifty-fifth in trade importance. Every other set of talks dragged on. Still, the US footprint at the talks was significant, with a bilateral trade proportion of almost 39 per cent.

Looking at the US dyads, there was considerable variation in both the scope and outcome of talks. The United States' two top trading partners, Canada and the United Kingdom, had previous bilateral deals that had reduced many of the easy tariffs. Talks were now more difficult and occurred in the shadow of the UK's preference system. Talks with Australia were difficult not only because of the interaction with UK preferences but also because of US duties on wool products, butter and beef. Australia's original offers were taken off the table owing to the perception that the US was unwilling to reduce rates. Talks with the

[7] The twenty-three countries finishing the negotiations were Australia, the Belgium-Netherlands-Luxembourg Customs Union, Brazil, Burma, Canada, Ceylon, Chile, China, Cuba, Czechoslovakia, France, India, the Customs Union of Lebanon and Syria, New Zealand, Norway, Pakistan, Southern Rhodesia, the Union of South Africa, the United Kingdom and the United States (US Department of State 1947).

[8] Some of the UK colonies participated in the early stages and did not complete negotiations.

Benelux countries were easier for the US although the depths of cuts were less than in the Australia case. US talks with Latin American nations were also completed early on with little fanfare.

C GATT 47: Outcomes

The bargaining 'rules' in the early GATT Rounds were set before nations arrived in Geneva. The structure of the talks forced nations to make decisions about requests with limited knowledge of the politics of their trading partner; nations needed to request reductions knowing that they would have to respond in a reciprocal manner. Nations that were unable or unwilling to open their own market were limited in what they could demand of others. Unsurprisingly, the aggregate data reveals marked differences in participant behaviour. Some nations asked for specific reductions and others for just the deepest cut possible. Participant requests varied both in the number of items specified and in the nature of the reduction request. Some nations asked for bindings, others for sharp reductions, others listed a small group of products and some nations listed almost the entire US tariff schedule.

The purpose of a request to reduce an American tariff is to either enable a new foreign exporter to enter the US market, or to enhance the market position of existing exporters. Insofar as tariffs are a binding constraint on exporter activity, we would expect that governments would aim to lower tariffs to the greatest extent possible, but value any concession. If, however, the tariff is not a binding constraint, and even a marginally lower tariff would not enable export, we would expect governments to only value concessions large enough to enable entry. Governments so constrained may have an interest in signalling that constraint through the negotiating strategy.

The review of *requests* provides information both about the interests of exporters and the perception of government leaders of exactly how import competing interests would respond to a concession. A nation requesting a reduction from the United States would have been wise to consider the congressional charge to American negotiators. According to the 1934 legislation that allowed the US president to negotiate reductions, products needed to be vetted by a series of domestic committees and industries were given time to respond to their being considered as part of a tariff reduction bundle. Given that constraint, an unconstrained rational decision-maker would include as many products on the request list as possible. Of course, reciprocity precluded that strategy.

What was offered and what were the responses? Table 4.1 lists the US bargains with other GATT participants, organised by how much GATT trade was contributed by the United States and the other nation. Viewed this way, Canadian trade was most important to the United States, representing about 11 per cent of all its GATT trade. Canada asked the United States for concessions on 686 products and the United States responded positively to 263 of those requests. This was not Canada's first bilateral trade negotiation with the United States – they had an existing bilateral arrangement that was concluded before the war. Trade dependence alone cannot explain the pattern of requests and concessions. For example, France asked for the most products, 1194, from the United States yet that dyad was only 2.9 per cent of GATT trade. Likewise, if trade flows alone explained the pattern, France would not have received as many concessions as it did.

Table 4.1 *Requests and Concessions by Percentage of All GATT Trade by US and Partner Nation, GATT 47*[a]

No. of Requests to US	No. of Concessions Granted by US	Partner Nation	Percentage of Total GATT Trade (1938)
686	263	Canada	11.4
442	559	United Kingdom	10.0
212	156	Benelux	3.6
1194	148	France	2.9
NA	44	Cuba	2.8
153	34	Brazil	2.5
NA	119	China	1.5
36	24	India	1.4
29	4	South Africa	1.3
48	18	Australia	1.3
30	15	Chile	0.9
218	31	Czechoslovakia	0.8
30	17	Norway	0.6
47	9	New Zealand	0.5
NA	6	Lebanon/Syria	0.1

Source: Created by the authors.

[a] Cuba and Lebanon's request schedules are unavailable in the archive documents.

Countries' strategies at the bargaining table varied on another dimension. Some nations sought security in current rates, focusing more on the threat that the United States could potentially raise rates in the future. Others focused on market access. Some nations focused on their major trading partners; others had a less specific policy.

Table 4.2 provides data on the variation in requests and outcome with the United States and compares that with other negotiating partners. The first column of Table 4.2, *Total Asks*, sums the total listed requested tariff changes by country of all other countries in the first round of negotiation. The second column, *Average Ask*, suggests that the average requests varied across dyads, with states concentrating their effort on particular countries. The third column, *Total US*, lists the number of tariff line changes asked of the United States. The next column, *US Ask (%)*, computes the percentage of all the requests to the United States that the dyad request represents. This is a measure of how focused a nation was on the US market. Some countries were completely focused on the United States, such as Chile, and some countries were focused elsewhere,

Table 4.2 *Requests and Outcomes, GATT 47*

Country	Total Asks	Average Ask	Total US	US Ask (%)	Ratio of Average Asks
Australia	105	26.25	48	46	1.83
Benelux	567	189.00	212	37	1.12
Brazil	290	20.71	153	53	7.39
British colonies	28	28.00	28	100	1.00
Canada	1,030	44.78	686	67	15.32
Ceylon	49	9.80	12	24	1.22
Chile	30	30.00	30	100	1.00
Czechoslovakia	430	35.83	218	51	6.08
France	1,506	251.00	1194	79	4.76
India	85	17.00	36	42	2.12
Lebanon/Syria	25	12.50	18	72	1.44
New Zealand	384	29.54	47	12	1.59
Norway	108	12.00	30	28	2.50
South Africa	90	18.00	29	32	1.61
United Kingdom	759	189.75	442	58	2.33

Source: Created by the authors.

like Norway. The final column, *Ratio of Average Asks*, is the ratio of the requests of the United States to the average request, showing that some countries demanded much more of the United States than of other countries, such as Canada, and some countries demanded the same amount, such as Benelux.

In Table 4.3 we also see that there was variation in the form of concession the United States granted, with far more bindings than reductions.

Table 4.3 *US Concessions by Country, GATT 47*

Country	Bind (%)	Reduce (%)	No. of Products
Czechoslovakia	87	13	31
Belgium	84	16	70
Lebanon	83	17	6
France	82	18	148
China	79	21	119
Cuba	77	23	44
United Kingdom	72	28	559
Netherlands	69	31	86
Norway	59	41	17
Canada	57	43	263
South Africa	50	50	4
India	46	54	24
Australia	44	56	18
New Zealand	44	56	9
Brazil	38	6	34
Chile	27	73	15

Source: Created by the authors.

Finally, Table 4.4 illustrates that there was considerable variation in the type and number of concessions the United States granted across product groupings. The first column indicates the percentage of requests that were refused, the second the number of products in that category that were bound and the third, the number reduced. The number of possible products that were requested by group is listed in the last column. The United States refused a significant percentage of requests. In particular, almost three-quarters of the requests in non-metallic minerals were rejected and almost half of those in chemicals. There is similarly

Table 4.4 *Specific US Cuts by Product Category*

	No Cut (%)	Bind (%)	Reduce (%)	No. of Products
Animals and animal products	24	49	27	533
Vegetable food products and beverages	40	43	17	386
Vegetable products	44	23	34	231
Textile fibres and manufactures	15	72	13	288
Wood and paper	32	46	22	161
Non-metallic minerals	72	13	15	54
Metals and manufactures	37	49	15	189
Machinery and vehicles	27	56	16	128
Chemicals and related products	49	25	26	265
Miscellaneous	48	41	11	214

Source: Created by the authors.

significant variation in whether or not the outcome was a reduction of a binding. Textile products were bound but not cut; the largest number of cuts was in animal products and the highest percentage of cuts was in vegetable products. Overall, primary products were more often in the final tariff bundle than were final goods.

What explains this pattern of US responses? We consider a range of possible explanations rooted in the negotiation process.

D Negotiations

Were outcomes related to requests? And if so, was there an interaction between the specificity of the 'ask' by the other nation in the dyad and the ability of the United States to respond? We examine the relationship of requests and offers in the following three figures. Figure 4.1 illustrates the relationship between asks and results for all US dyads; Figure 4.2 depicts trade flows and Figure 4.3 the variation in types of requests and success.

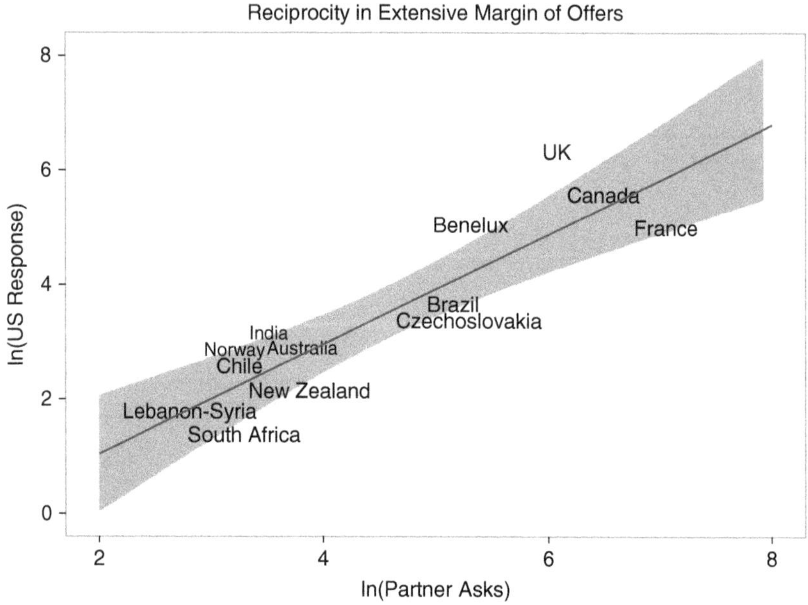

Figure 4.1. Reciprocity in extensive margin of offers.
Source: Computed and created by the authors.

Beginning with Figure 4.1, we see the relationship between the number of products on the 'ask' list and the US response by nation. The x-axis is the natural log of the number of US tariff line changes that were asked of the US; the y-axis is the number of US tariff lines commitments the United States made in response to those requests. The plot indicates that the more products the US partner asked for, the higher, in general, was the concession that the United States gave. France underperformed on this front, and the United Kingdom overperformed.

The next figure, Figure 4.2, depicts the ratio of US concessions to the partner requests as a function of the type of requests that were made. Here we organise request type by *complexity*, that is, did a country ask for specific reductions as a strategy in all their relationships with other nations in 1947 or were they more likely simply to provide a long list of products and a general request for a reduction. The former we coded as a complex request strategy and the other as an open-ended strategy. In this figure, the x-axis is a measure along the complexity continuum and the y-axis is a ratio of how many concessions were granted, given the demands of the other nation. A high ratio indicates that the United States gave

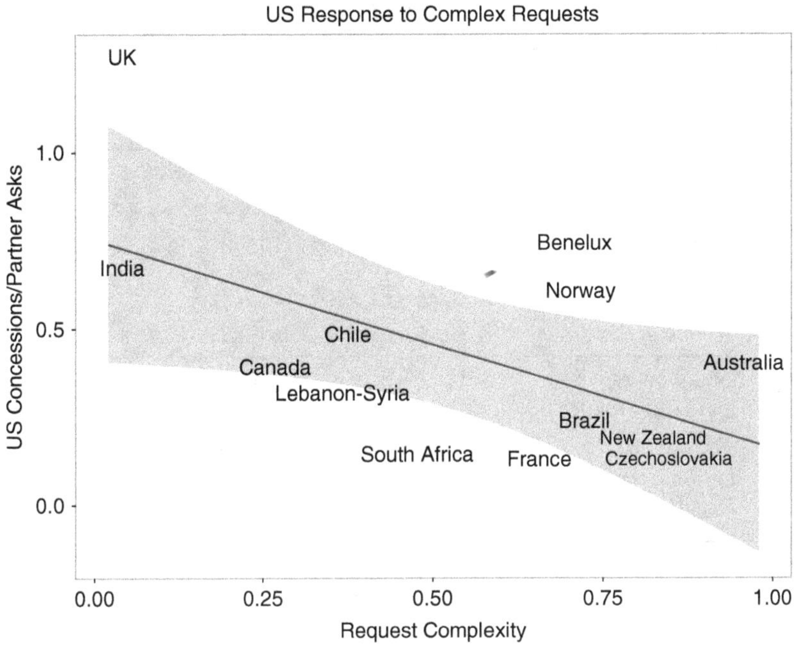

Figure 4.2. US response to complex requests.
Source: Computed and created by the authors.

more products than the partner asked for, a low ratio indicates that the United States gave less than the partner asked for. The plot shows that the more complex the request, the less the United States conceded. Combined with the figure above, it appears that the US schedule changed most often when countries listed many products without specifying a variety of different reduction requests.

Finally we consider whether or not the relationship we see above is simply a function of trade flows. To do that, Figure 4.3 provides the natural log of the percentage of US trade taken by each country, and the natural log of the number of products reduced by the United States. As we can see, US negotiations did focus on its principal trading partners although that does not explain all the variation we see above.

When we interact complexity and trade in Table 4.5, we find that the ratio of the number of concessions granted versus those asked for is higher for countries with either complex requests, a high proportion of trade with the United States, or both.

Table 4.5 *Complexity, Trade and Concessions, GATT 47*

	Concessions/Requests	
	(1)	(2)
Complexity	−0.60*	−0.46
	(0.27)	(0.34)
Per cent trade		0.02
		(0.03)
Constant	0.80***	0.65**
	(0.17)	(0.26)
Observations	11	11
R2	0.35	0.39
Adjusted R2	0.28	0.24
Residual standard error	0.29 (df = 9)	0.29 (df = 8)
F statistic	4.81* (df = 1; 9)	2.56 (df = 2; 8)

Source: Created by the authors.
Note: * $p < 0.1$; ** $p < 0.05$; *** $p < 0.01$

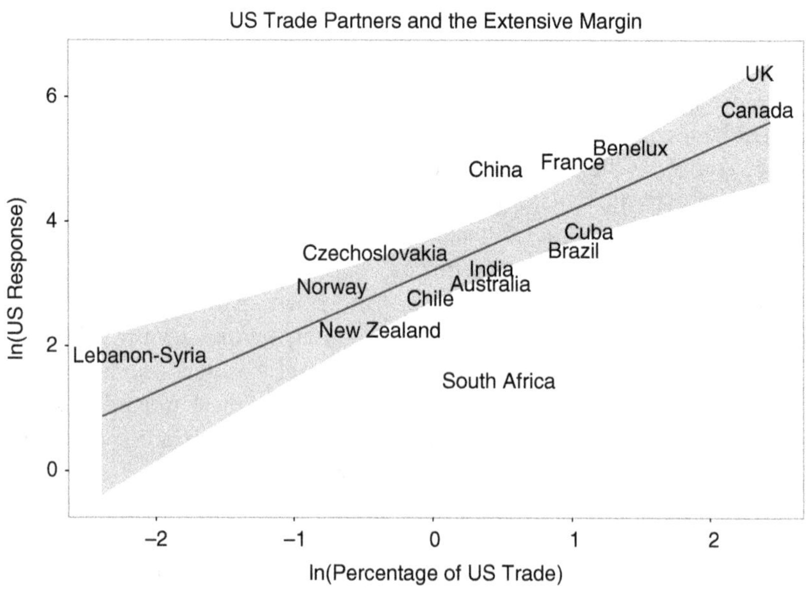

Figure 4.3. US trade partners and the extensive margin.
Source: Computed and created by the authors.

E Discussion

Our data provide some novel insights into the importance of the early GATT in explaining variation in US tariff levels. In previous work we argued against the view that liberalisation occurred in the United States because the president was able to bypass traditional congressional pressure politics. Instead we argued that the choice of how to open the US market was, in fact, significantly influenced by Congress, even after the president was granted negotiating authority in 1934. In fact, we suggest that the 'shadow of Congress' is influential because presidents have always needed congressional approval to renew any trade agreement (Goldstein and Gulotty 2014). In this chapter we add a set of new variables to explain US behaviour, focusing on the negotiation process itself. Uniquely, our dataset uses US initial negotiating rights (INRs) to measure what commitments were made by the United States and to whom during the Round.

Incorporating data on requests from nations to the United States in the Geneva Round with US responses leads to some general conclusions. First, looking more closely at the GATT47 results, we found that trade flows alone did not predict either the number of concessions or the number of product requests. However, we did find that nations with larger flows that focused on the extensive margin were more successful than those that asked for specific requests on the intensive margin and/or were not large trade partners. More important was variation in national strategies adopted in the GATT47 negotiations. Variation was not only on the expected emphasis on particular markets but more importantly, on what we call the complexity of their request. Some nations asked for a large number of products but without specific reductions while others targeted specific products and amounts of reductions. The more successful strategy from the perspective of having the most products either bound or reduced in negotiations with the United States was the former.

Second, we found that the most likely outcome of negotiations with the United States was a binding. The vast majority of US concessions were not cuts in a tariff but the promise of security of not raising a rate in the future. In terms of product category, the greatest number of successful reductions/bindings was in animals and animal products; the most asymmetric outcome where bindings dominated was in the textile fibres and textile-manufacturing category.

Are there general insights from these specific findings? We suggest four that help to explain the success of the early GATT. First, the principal supplier rule constrained outcomes in a positive way. In intent, the rule was thought of as a means to abrogate free-riding by producers who were not the low-cost importer. But the rule had a political function as well – it provided information to Congress about the products in a potential trade bundle. Representatives were well aware of producer interests in their districts and supported those interests for many reasons, spanning from fundraising to assuring local economic growth. It is interesting, then, that Bagwell et al. (2015), found that reductions in a subsequent Round were less likely to be a result of a concession to the low-cost importer. Why the difference? It is possible that the variance is a function of data collection. We organised concessions by INRs and not who was the principal supplier of that product in 1947.[9] But, to get the INR, the nation needed to list the product on their request list and the US negotiator had to have the ability to make the offer. Our guess is that the difference is associated with a small rule change. In GATT47, all parties to the talks knew all offers. In fact, the United States used one collated schedule for all participating parties. This allowed negotiators to adhere to the reciprocity rule more easily by moving around concessions without violating the overall intent of the principal supplier rule. Given this structure, and the rarity of adding products onto an offer list after the negotiations had begun, we believe that most products bound and/or reduced had a significant presence in the US market.

Second, the US system of pre-vetting products made it difficult to expand new offers to nations. And when nations had fewer requests because of less trade with the United States, negotiators could not offer a deeper reduction, given the specified upper limits of reductions in the legislation. Given these constraints, the best strategy for a nation was to list every product it imported and ask for the deepest cut possible. In fact, this was the form taken by Canada's request list. Canada's success is also more remarkable given that this was their third treaty with the United States and the 'easier' tariffs had already been lowered. While overall, those with bilateral treaties did not appear to do better than nations that were negotiating with the United States for the first time, it seems that both Canada and Great Britain were able to leverage their understanding of US politics to their own advantage in the Round.

[9] We chose to collect data on principle suppliers of the highly protected products in 1931, before any formal treaties. We were unsure of the effect of the treaties, since they were not with all trading partners, so we used a common base year. In fact, we believe that Congress also used the 1931 data in their deliberations.

Third, as in the Torquay Round (Bagwell et al. 2015), when bargaining occurred, the United States usually altered its offers but rarely changed its requests; bargaining on the intensive margin was of a take it or leave it nature and the United States was more likely to engage in offers and counter-offers on the extensive margin. Why? Because of the process of vetting imported products and the lack of organisational capacity of exporters, it is not surprising that the United States would not change its requests during the negotiation process. Further, once a product had been vetted and cleared in the United States for a specific reduction, negotiators would feel free to move around offers from this product list but feel constrained in offering deeper reductions.

Returning to our original questions, that is, what explains the success of the early GATT, the data point to an unexpected role for the GATT. The GATT was less a means to solve a 'defection' problem and more a tool, providing transparency and predictability in trade, so as to facilitate signatories' ability to support open borders. The agreement increased volume by creating big and flexible 'bundles' of reductions. The system of requests and responses allowed political leaders to pick and choose among producer groups while establishing a majority coalition in support of the overall agreement. Reciprocity kept exporters interested but it was never the constraint envisioned in a prisoner's dilemma situation and alone, a reciprocity principle would have predicted far more and more even cuts among the GATT47 parties than occurred. This is not to argue that the strategic environment was unimportant. Rather, the more important element of the strategic environment was that requests came prior to offers. Nations were both first and second movers in the decision on what would be in the reciprocal bundle. Reciprocity worked because the process provided enough information to facilitate multiple possible bundles, allowing leaders to pick only those that were politically convenient.

Bibliography

Bagwell, Kyle and Staiger, Robert W. 2002. *The Economics of the World Trading System*. Cambridge, MA: MIT Press.

Bagwell, Kyle and Staiger, Robert W. 2011. 'What Do Trade Negotiators Negotiate About? Empirical Evidence from the World Trade Organization'. *American Economic Review*, American Economic Association, 101 (4): 1238–1273.

Bagwell, Kyle, Staiger, Robert and Yurukoglu, Ali. 2015. Multilateral trade bargaining: a first look at the GATT bargaining records. MS (unpublished document).

Baldwin, Richard. 1987. 'Politically Realistic Objective Functions and Trade Policy'. *Economic Letters* 24:287–90.

Bailey, Michael, Goldstein, Judith and Weingast, Barry R. 1997. 'The Institutional Roots of American Trade Policy: Politics, Coalitions, and International Trade'. *World Politics* 49(3):309–338.

Bidwell, P.W. 1944. 'A Postwar Commercial Policy for the United States'. *American Economic Review* 34 (1): 340–453.

Broda, Christian, Limão, Nuno and Weinstein, David E. 2008. 'Optimal Tariffs and Market Power: The Evidence'. *American Economic Review* 98 (5): 2032–65.

Brown, William Adams Jr. 1950. *The United States and the Restoration of World Trade*. Washington, DC: Brookings Institution.

Diebold Jr. W. 1941. *New Directions in Our Trade Policy*. New York: Council on Foreign Relations.

Eckes, Alfred E. 1999. *America's Market: U.S. Foreign Trade Policy Since 1776*. Chapel Hill, NC: University of North Carolina Press.

Gilligan, Michael J. 1997. *Empowering Exporters*. Michigan Studies in International Political Economy, Michigan: University of Michigan Press.

Goldstein, Judith and Gulotty, Robert. 2014. 'American and Trade Liberalization: The Limits of Institutional Reform'. *International Organization* 68 (2): 263–295.

Goldstein, Judith and Gulotty, Robert. 2015. 'Weighing Economic Ideology: The Role of Economic Ideas in American Trade Policymaking'. Working paper, Stanford University.

Goldstein, Judith, Rivers, Doug and Tomz, Michael. 2007. 'Institutions in International Relations: Understanding the Effects of the GATT and WTO on World Trade'. *International Organization* 61(1):37–67.

Grossman, Gene and Helpman, Elhanan. 1994. 'Protection for Sale'. *American Economic Review* 84: 833–850.

Hawkins, Harry C. 1951. *Commercial Treaties and Agreements, Principles and Practice*. New York: Rinehart.

Hiscox, Michael J. 1999. 'The Magic Bullet? The RTAA, Institutional Reform, and Trade Liberalization'. *International Organization* 53 (4):669–698.

Irwin, Douglas A. 1998. 'Changes in U.S. Tariffs: The Role of Import Prices and Commercial Policies'. *American Economic Review*, 88: 1015–26.

Irwin, Douglas A. 2002. *Free Trade Under Fire*. Princeton, NJ: Princeton University Press.

Irwin, Douglas A. 2011. *Peddling Protectionism*. Princeton, NJ: Princeton University Press.

Irwin, Douglas A. and Krosner, Randall S. 1996. 'Log-Rolling and Economic Interests in the Passage of the Smoot-Hawley Tariff'. *Carnegie-Rochester Conference Series on Public Policy* 45 (December 1996) 173–200.

Irwin, Douglas, Mavroidis, Petros and Sykes, Alan. 2008. *The Genesis of the GATT*. New York: Cambridge University Press.

Johnson, Harry G. 1953–54. 'Optimum Tariffs and Retaliation'. *Review of Economic Studies* 21 (2):142–153.

Jones, Ronald W. 1969. 'Tariffs and Trade in General Equilibrium: Comment'. *American Economic Review* 59: 418–424.

Regan, Donald H. 2006. 'What Are Trade Agreements For? Two Conflicting Stories Told by Economists, with a Lesson for Lawyers'. *Journal of International Economic Law* 9: 951–988.

Rose Andrew. 2004. 'Do We Really Know That the WTO Increased Trade?' *The American Economic Review* 94(1): 98–114

Schattschneider, E. E. 1935. *Politics, Pressures, and the Tariff.* New York: Prentice Hall.

Swift, Elaine K., Brookshire, Robert G., Canon, David T., Fink, Evelyn C., Hibbing, John R., Humes, Brian D., Malbin, Michael J. and Martis, Kenneth C. 2009. 'Database of [United States] Congressional historical statistics 1789–1989'. Computer file ICPSR03371-v2.

US Government. 1932–1933. *Economic Analysis of Foreign Trade of the United States in Relation to the Tariff.* S. Res. 325, 72nd Congress, 2nd session.

US Government. 1961. *Historical Statistics of the United States: Colonial Times to 1957.* Washington, DC: US Department of Commerce, Bureau of Census, *series U 15–20*, p. 539.

US Department of State. 1947. *Analysis of General Agreement on Tariffs and Trade.* Washington, DC. US Department of State.

United States Tariff Commission. 1940. *Pre-agreement and post-agreement trade of the United States with the principal countries with which trade agreements were made before 1937.* Washington, DC.

United States Tariff Commission. 1945. *Trade agreements a miscellany of information.* Washington, DC.

ANNEX 1

Data Collection

The history of the negotiations of the 1947 GATT has recently become declassified. The new public record includes all offers, responses and final concessions. The product lists are Tagged Image File Format (TIFF) documents and not searchable in their current form. For this project we hand-coded the initial requests, the counter-offers for all parties and the final concessions by the US.

Requests: All the bilateral requests to parties to the GATT 47 were coded by product, request type and request amount. Benelux countries were coded separately, but for most of the analysis they were merged into one negotiating unit. In total, 16 countries' offers to each other are included in the dataset.

Offers: All bilateral offers were coded by product, offer type (reduction or binding) and amount, of the nations coded for requests.

US Tariff Schedule

The US tariff schedule post-GATT (the US Protocol that was published after the tariff talks ended) was coded by INRs from the Round. This includes all products that were negotiated during the GATT 49 Round and which subsequently became available to nations with MFN benefits.

A separate tariff schedule was compiled of all products that had a 50 per cent ad valorem tariff in 1929–1930. This tariff schedule included reductions from the bilateral treaties in effect before GATT as well as the GATT reductions. INRs, or the negotiating nation that led to the lowered rate was coded along with the amount of reduction. See Goldstein and Gulotty (2014) for a further explanation of the coding rules.

PART III

General Trends and Patterns in WTO Dispute Settlement

5

Dispute Settlement in the WTO

From a Deliberately Designed to a Spontaneously Grown Order

FRIEDER ROESSLER

A Introduction

While Article XXIII of the General Agreement on Tariffs and Trade (GATT) defines in the broadest possible terms the claims that can be submitted for adjudication, it does not establish a judicial body to examine such claims nor a procedural framework for the conduct of such an examination. During the first three decades of its existence, the GATT experimented with rulings of chairpersons, working parties that drafted their reports with the parties to the dispute and panels composed of delegates from countries not involved in the dispute. Each of these bodies established its own working procedures. There were no written rules, and there was no formal obligation to cooperate. Each step in the dispute settlement process – the establishment of the panel, the determination of the mandate and composition of the panel and the adoption of its report – required the consent of the parties to the dispute. In a Darwinistic process of selection among methods to settle disputes, panels and the working procedures customarily followed by them have survived as the fittest (Hudec 1975).

This period of experimentation ended in 1979 when the contracting parties adopted an 'Understanding' with an agreed description of practices that had been followed during the previous 32 years and an agreement to continue to follow them.[1] Following the adoption of this Understanding, the diplomatic, consensual elements in the GATT's

[1] *Understanding on Notification, Consultation, Dispute Settlement and Surveillance of 28 November 1979*, GATT, Basic Instruments and Selected Documents (BISD) 26th Supplement p. 210.

dispute settlement practices receded. Legal considerations gradually became the only basis on which panels were expected to make their recommendations. GATT practices moved from conciliation to adjudication (Roessler 2015). Blocking the establishment of a panel, insisting on self-serving limitations to the mandate of the panel and frustrating the composition of a panel became less and less acceptable. In 1989, the GATT decided to make the best practices that had emerged under this new approach legally binding: the complainant was accorded a right to the establishment of a panel, standard terms of reference were to apply unless otherwise agreed, and upon request, the Director-General of the GATT could determine the composition of the panel.[2] The only step in the dispute settlement process that still required the consent of the parties to the dispute was the formal endorsement of the panel's rulings and recommendations.

The drafters of the WTO Dispute Settlement Understanding (DSU) set out to create a dispute settlement order based on that of the GATT but without its last remaining consensual element. From the perspective of the complainant, the main shortcoming of the GATT procedures was that the adoption of the panel reports required the consent of the respondent. From the perspective of the respondent, the major deficiency was the lack of a possibility to submit the panel's legal reasoning to appellate review. The drafters concluded that, under the new WTO dispute settlement procedures, if the parties to a dispute are dissatisfied with a panel report, they should have the right to have their objections examined by a standing Appellate Body but – once that examination has taken place – they should be obliged to accept the result of the dispute settlement proceedings as binding. Articles 17 to 23 of the DSU realised these objectives: they established the Appellate Body and the so-called 'negative consensus' rule for the adoption of panel and Appellate Body reports and authorisations to retaliate, a rule that makes it impossible for the respondent to block decisions on these matters.

As will be shown below, the DSU has not operated as its drafters had anticipated. Some of the newly negotiated provisions turned out to be unworkable. Some of the provisions inspired by GATT practices turned out to be inappropriate or incomplete in the context of compulsory adjudication. In a system of voluntary dispute settlement and in a system of compulsory adjudication, the parties to the dispute and the

[2] *Decision of 12 April 1989 on Improvements to the GATT Dispute Settlement Rules and Procedures*, BISD 36th Supplement p. 61.

judicial organs respond to completely different incentives and constraints. Procedural rules that were adequate and sufficient in the GATT's voluntary system therefore had unintended consequences and revealed lacunae when transposed to the WTO's system of compulsory adjudication.

The drafters of the DSU recognised that it was an experiment with uncertain results. The Ministers who signed the Agreement Establishing the WTO, therefore invited the WTO Ministerial Conference to complete a full review of the DSU within four years and to decide 'whether to continue, modify or terminate' the new rules and procedures.[3] That review took place but produced no results. Also, subsequent reviews conducted in a Special Session of the Ministerial Conference produced no agreement on any amendment of the DSU. In these reviews, the negotiators were close to a consensus on a number of changes to the DSU but never achieved unanimous agreement.[4]

An amendment of the DSU can only be adopted if no Member present at the meeting of the Ministerial Conference formally objects to the decision when the amendment is voted on.[5] Under the GATT there was a possibility to adopt rules and procedures for dispute settlement by a majority vote if no consensus could be reached. That option is not available in the WTO. This effectively accords each of the 164 Members a right to veto any amendment. Consequently each Member has the possibility to 'sell' its consent to any amendment, and, unfortunately, Members have not always resisted the temptation to exact 'payments', even for their consent to amendments they agreed with. In certain cases, so it is said, Members have even linked their consent to a DSU amendment they agreed with to the grant of market access rights and other matters not relevant to dispute settlement. More than two decades of failed reform efforts have shown that changes to the DSU are well-nigh impossible as long as each Member can individually block any reform and the *do ut des* of trade negotiations dominates the discussion on all reforms.

[3] *Decision on the Application and Review of the Understanding on Rules and Procedures Governing the Settlement of Disputes*, adopted by the Trade Negotiations Committee on 15 December 1993.

[4] See the Report by the Chairman of the Special Session of the Dispute Settlement Body (TN/DS/27, 6 August 2015) for a long list of amendment proposals that Members discussed fruitlessly, in large part for a period of more than two decades.

[5] Footnote 1 to Article IX and Article 10:8 of the Marrakesh Agreement Establishing the World Trade Organization.

This has meant that the text of the DSU could not be modified to respond to unexpected consequences of its provisions, the discovery of drafting mistakes and lacunae, the emergence of unforeseen problems or changes in preferences and concerns. As a result, the gap between what is prescribed by the DSU and what the disputant parties, panels and the Appellate Body perceive as necessary and appropriate has continually widened. The pressure to close that gap has gradually led to the modification of the dispute settlement order by other means, in particular by agreements between disputant parties and by practices of the judicial organs of the WTO.

This chapter analyses and evaluates the shift from designed to grown norms in WTO dispute settlement. It describes the emergence of agreements between disputant parties and judicial practices that supplement or supersede the provisions of the DSU and examines the causes and consequences of this trend. The chapter concludes that the spontaneous growth of norms has improved the process of dispute settlement in the WTO by making it more responsive to the needs of the disputant parties and the constraints faced by the judicial organs, but that a system of checks and balances is needed that enables the membership to supplement, clarify and, if necessary, control the practices adopted by the disputant parties and the judicial organs.

B The Spontaneous Growth of Norms in WTO Dispute Settlement

I Voluntary Arrangements

1 Sequencing agreements

A number of the problems to which the DSU gave rise have been resolved through voluntary arrangements between Members. One of these problems is the so-called 'sequencing problem'. If a complainant considers that the respondent has not withdrawn a measure found to be inconsistent with a WTO agreement, it may ask for an authorisation to retaliate. That authorisation must be requested within thirty days of the expiry of the implementation period accorded to the respondent.[6] If the respondent considers that it has withdrawn the contested measure, it may submit the disagreement to the panel that made the ruling, which then has to submit its report within 90 days.[7] The DSU thus requires the

6 Article 22:6 of the DSU.
7 Article 21:5 of the DSU.

complainant to request the right to retaliate well before the panel has resolved the disagreement on the implementation. In practice this problem has been overcome by 'sequencing agreements' between the disputants that preserve the right of the complainant to request retaliation until the dispute on the implementation has been resolved.[8]

2 Agreements on non-violation complaints

Another problem that was resolved by agreements among the Member was the resort to so-called 'non-violation complaints' under the Agreement on Trade-Related Aspects of Intellectual Property Rights (TRIPS Agreement).

The causes of action under the WTO dispute settlement procedures are defined in Article XXIII of GATT. This provision permits any Member of the WTO to bring a complaint when it considers that

> any benefit accruing to it directly or indirectly under this Agreement is nullified or impaired ... as a result of
>
> (a) the failure of another Member of the WTO to carry out its obligations under this Agreement,
> (b) the application by another Member of the WTO of any measure, whether or not it conflicts with the provisions of this Agreement, or
> (c) the existence of any other situation.[9]

Taken literally, the provision implies that an illegal measure is neither sufficient nor necessary to bring a successful complaint. The key concept of Article XXIII is that of nullification and impairment. Any measure, whether legal or illegal, that nullifies or impairs any benefit accruing under any WTO agreement and any situation that does so, can be the basis of a complaint under the DSU.

Article XXIII was inspired by the consultation clauses contained in trade agreements concluded by the United States in the 1930s and 1940s.

[8] For a recent example see the 'Understanding between the European Union and the United States Regarding Procedures under Article 21 and 22 of the DSU', Document WT/DS353/14 of 27 April 2012.

[9] According to Article 26:2 of the DSU, the adoption of reports on situation complaints must be done in accordance with the procedures set out in the GATT Dispute Settlement Understanding, hence with the consent of the parties to the dispute. The resolution of problems arising from situations must therefore effectively be negotiated and the reports of the panel and the Appellate Body could at best serve as an input in these negotiations. Some situation complaints were initiated in the early days of the GATT but none was pursued (See GATT, Analytical Index, Vol. 2: 668–671). Paragraph 1(c) of Article XXIII has never been invoked in the WTO.

These agreements had to be renewed every few years and any consultations on the operation of the agreement were therefore effectively also consultations about the continuation of the agreement. The decision whether or not to continue the agreement could be affected not only by violations of the agreement but also by a legal measure or a change in circumstances that adversely affected the trade between the parties. The consultation clauses in those agreements therefore covered nullification or impairment in all three cases (Hudec 1975: 19–21).

The drafters of the GATT conceived the concept of nullification or impairment as a benchmark for multilateral decision-making and negotiations (Hudec 1975: 33–42). The administrators of the GATT used the concept in the context of dispute settlement procedures under which each contracting party had the possibility to block the adoption of a finding that a measure consistent with an obligation had impaired benefits accruing under that obligation. Under the WTO Agreement, however, the determination of the benefits that accrue to the complainant under a provision in addition to the benefit of its observation by the respondent is done by judicial organs whose decisions must be unconditionally accepted. The drafters of the DSU thus decided to define the mandate of independent judicial organs with a legal concept that was originally used to define the scope of the consultation obligation under bilateral trade agreements.

In respect of legal measures covered by Article XXIII:1(b) of the GATT, the concept of nullification and impairment has in the past been invoked only in respect of benefits expected as a result of a tariff concession set out in a schedule annexed to the GATT.[10] In the light of this experience, the drafters of the General Agreement on Trade in Services (GATS) decided to permit non-violation complaints only in respect of benefits accruing under the specific commitments contained in the schedules annexed to the GATS.[11] However, given the broad sweep of Article XXIII:1(b) and the references to it in most of the WTO agreements, this provision could theoretically also be invoked in respect of benefits accruing under other obligations. The consequences of such an extension of the application of Article XXIII:1(b) would be significant. The respondent may react to

[10] For a review of the application of Article XXIII: 1(b) see Gappa and Roessler (2005).

[11] Article XXIII: 3 of the GATS. Both the GATT and the GATS are framework agreements designed to permit the exchange of market access commitments. In the absence of a tariff concession for a particular product or a specific commitment in a particular services sector, they do not provide the basis for a legitimate expectation of market access. This explains the limitation of non-violation complaints to scheduled commitments.

a finding that a tariff concession or a specific commitment under the GATS has been impaired by a legal measure either by withdrawing that measure or by renegotiating its scheduled obligation. The WTO Member concerned may therefore reassess the advantages of adhering to the scheduled obligations and, if necessary, return to the *status quo ante*. It is for this reason that the concept of nullification and impairment, when applied to the renegotiable obligations set out in GATT or GATS schedules, operates like a *clausula rebus sic stantibus*.

Obligations under WTO agreements other than the scheduled tariff concessions and specific commitments may not be individually renegotiated. A Member that wishes to maintain a legal measure found to have impaired benefits accruing under a non-renegotiable obligation under a WTO agreement therefore may not return to the *status quo ante* except by withdrawing from the WTO Agreement. As long as it remains a Member of the WTO, it is subject to the same sanctions that apply in the case of a violation. These sanctions would effectively force the WTO Member to accord to other Members not only the benefit of a performance of its obligations in good faith but also any additional benefit that the panel or Appellate Body found to accrue under that obligation.

There is no common understanding among WTO Members on the benefits generated by the general policy obligations set out in the WTO agreements beyond their performance in good faith. For instance, there is no understanding among Members on the benefits that might accrue to a Member under the TRIPS Agreement beyond the performance of the obligations under that Agreement by the other Members. If the judicial organs were to create such benefits, they would be acting in a complete normative void and hence contrary to the principle that their rulings 'cannot add to or diminish the rights and obligations provided in the covered agreements'.[12]

The issue was inconclusively debated by the drafters of the TRIPS Agreement. The compromise reached was to suspend the right to bring non-violation complaints for a period of five years and to further examine the matter in the interim.[13] Since that period came to an end, the suspension has been extended from one ministerial conference to the next through decisions under which Members agree not to initiate non-violation complaints under the TRIPS Agreement.[14] The dispute

[12] Article 3:2 of the DSU.

[13] Article 64 of the TRIPS Agreement.

[14] See the Ministerial Decision adopted on 19 December 2015 on 'TRIPS Non-violation and Situation Complaints' (WT/MIN (15) 41 and WT/L976).

settlement procedures of the TRIPS Agreement have thus been modified not through an amendment, but through an agreement among Members cast in the form of a decision of the Ministerial Conference.

3 Agreements to open proceedings to the public

According to Article 17:10 of the DSU 'the proceedings of the Appellate Body shall be confidential'. Under the GATT, panels kept their proceedings confidential because they were expected to act not only as adjudicators but also as conciliators. The process of conciliation – by its very nature – must be confidential. A remnant of that practice can be found in Article 11 of the DSU, according to which panels 'should consult regularly with the parties to the dispute and give them adequate opportunity to develop a mutually satisfactory solution'. However, WTO panels perceive adjudication to be their only function. The admonition to regularly consult with the parties on the possibilities of a mutually satisfactory solution is therefore ignored in practice. With this change in the perception of the role of the judicial organs, the confidentiality principle has lost its original rationale.

Numerous third parties now regularly participate in the panel proceedings, be it to defend trade or systemic interests or simply to familiarise themselves with the complexities of the WTO dispute settlement process. Given that any of the WTO's 164 Members has a right which is, in practice, unchallengeable, to satisfy its curiosity about an Appellate Body proceeding simply by raising its flag in a meeting of the Dispute Settlement Body (DSB) to reserve its third-party rights, it is difficult to see what the confidentiality requirement governing such proceedings could effectively achieve. In the GATT, the legitimacy of the panel rulings rested primarily on their formal acceptance by all contracting parties. In the WTO, the legitimacy of the rulings rests primarily on an impeccable observation of sound legal principles in the proceedings. Legal proceedings behind closed doors are considered to be contrary to sound legal principles in many countries. The lack of transparency deprives the rulings emerging from such proceedings of their political acceptability in those countries and therefore renders their implementation difficult.

Against this background, the Appellate Body ruled that the parties to the dispute have the right to agree to open the hearings to the public.[15] Members are increasingly making use of this possibility and the most

[15] See Appellate Body, Annual Report for 2013: 23–24.

frequent users of the DSU, in particular the United States and the European Union, do so regularly. The requirement of confidentiality is gradually being modified by agreements between the disputant parties.

4 Agreements on other matters

The possibilities for streamlining and improving the dispute settlement procedures consensually are far from exhausted. Here are some examples of further possibilities:

- The DSU permits the respondent to block the establishment of a panel at the first DSB meeting at which the matter is considered but not at the second.[16] This rule emerged one night in December 1989 from a meeting of the Trade Negotiations Committee when it was agreed that the complainant should have a right to the establishment of a panel. To placate those who had opposed the creation of that right, the possibility to object to the establishment at the first meeting was accorded to the respondent. In the context of the WTO's system of compulsory adjudication, the compromise reached in 1989 does not perform a constructive function and needlessly prolongs the dispute settlement process. Members could agree to forego their right to block the establishment of a panel at the first meeting in all disputes with one another.
- Agreements between or among Members could also shorten the period within which an appeal may be initiated.
- Agreements between Members could provide for streamlined and simplified panel procedures in cases in which the Appellate Body could not complete the analysis for lack of facts.
- A list of persons that would be eligible to be proposed as panelists could be established by agreement. This would facilitate the, often protracted, panel composition process and the reappointment of persons with experience.

It would be unfortunate if such agreements were concluded only between pairs of Members to resolve specific issues in cases that have already arisen, such as the sequencing agreements. Ideally, a group of Members would draft an agreement that improves proceedings in many areas in all future disputes between the Members of the group. If Members could freely opt in and out of such an agreement, they would be less hesitant to engage in experiments with new procedures and it would be easier to

[16] Article 6:1 of the DSU.

modify the agreement in the light of experience. If such an arrangement operates satisfactorily over many years, the membership as a whole may be willing to make its provisions part of the DSU. In this manner, the WTO could, just like the GATT in its early days, first experiment with new procedures in the framework of voluntary cooperation and then codify the results of experiments that have proven to be successful.

In the context of the cases that are typically brought to the WTO, a substantial amount of cooperation can be expected. In most of these cases, the measure at issue is an economically costly, non-transparent or inefficient restrictive measure protecting a specific import-competing industry or a discriminatory measure raising the cost of imports by denying market access to efficient suppliers. The removal of such measures benefits both the complainant and the respondent; in the end, the economic welfare of both parties to the dispute is likely to increase. The fundamental purpose of the rulings of the WTO's judicial organs in such cases is not to allocate funds, territories or other resources claimed by both parties but to provide the respondent with the means to overcome the political factors that prevent it from acting in its own economic interests.[17] These considerations suggest that a wide range of issues could be successfully resolved through voluntary arrangements among Members.

II Norms That Emerged from Panel Practices

1 Grant of enhanced third-party rights

The DSU knows multiple complainants but not multiple respondents. A Member wishing to support the respondent's position can do so only as a third party. But in panel proceedings, the rights of participation of third parties are strictly limited: according to Article 10:3 of the DSU, third parties receive only the parties' submissions made at the first meeting of the panel. They are not entitled to the parties' rebuttal submissions, any questions of the panel to the parties and any replies to them. Neither do they have the right to participate in the panel's meetings with the parties. Article 10:3 is an operationally awkward compromise between those who consider third-party participation to be an unwelcome interference in the process of settling a dispute between two Members and those who consider that, given the multilateral nature of the obligations under the

[17] This is more systematically analysed in Roessler (1991).

WTO Agreement, all Members should have the right to participate in the process of interpreting and applying these obligations.

If the measure at issue in a DSU proceeding is designed to favour a third party, such as preferential tariff treatment accorded in the framework of a free trade agreement or the Generalised System of Preferences, the favoured third party may be as interested in the proceeding as the respondent. This can also be the case if a third party maintains a measure similar to the measure at issue in the proceedings. In such circumstances panels have accorded third parties so-called 'enhanced third-party rights' going beyond the limitations set out in Article 11 of the DSU. Thus, they have accorded them the right to receive all submissions of the parties and to participate in all meetings of the panel.[18] The grant of additional rights of participation in those circumstances has become so common that Members in such circumstances consider themselves to be entitled to them. Custom has replaced the provisions of Article 11.

2 Nullification and impairment in the case of violation complaints

As pointed out above, according to the wording of Article XXIII:1 of the GATT, a panel cannot simply find a measure to be inconsistent with a WTO agreement and recommend that it be brought into conformity with that agreement; it must also find that the measure nullified or impaired a benefit accruing to the complainant under that agreement. From the early days of the GATT onward, violations of GATT provisions have been presumed to nullify or impair the benefits accruing under them[19] and no respondent, either under the GATT or the WTO, has ever been allowed to rebut that presumption. The creation of the presumption of nullification or impairment and the irrefutability of that presumption have rendered a central concept of Article XXIII inutile in violation cases.

What prompted this panel practice? Under both the GATT and the WTO jurisprudence, the benefit accruing under the basic provisions of

[18] The Appellate Body did not interpret Article 10:3 as a provision protecting the parties against interference by third parties but as a provision setting out minimum rights for third parties. It ruled: '. . . the rights of third parties in panel proceedings are limited to the rights granted under Article 10 . . . Beyond those minimum guarantees, panels enjoy a discretion to grant additional participatory rights to third parties in particular cases, as long as such "enhanced" rights are consistent with the provisions of the DSU and the principles of due process.' Appellate Body Report, United States – Tax Treatment for 'Foreign Sales Corporations' – Recourse to Article 21.5 of the DSU by the European Communities (US – FSC (Article 21.5 – EC)), WT/DS108/AB/RW, paragraph 777.

[19] According to Article 3.8 of the DSU this principle now applies to all WTO agreements.

the GATT, the legitimate expectations they create, is the maintenance of the conditions of competition prescribed by them, not the protection of expected trade flows. As one GATT panel noted, the 'Contracting Parties have consistently interpreted the basic provisions of the General Agreement as provisions establishing conditions of competition. Thus, they have found that an import quota constitutes an import restriction within the meaning of Article XI:1 whether or not it actually impeded imports.'[20] The Appellate Body continued this jurisprudence (Van den Bossche and Zdouc 2013: 353, 484–485). Once the judicial organs had defined the benefit accruing under the market access provisions of the GATT as the maintenance of the conditions of competition prescribed by them and not the maintenance of expected trade flows, they could logically no longer accept a respondent's claim that its failure to maintain the prescribed conditions of competition provision did not cause impairment because it did not reduce the complainant's exports.

Once it had been recognised that the multilateral trade order does not guarantee trade results but trade opportunities, the requirement imposed on the complainant to show adverse trade impact and the possibility accorded to the respondent to show that its failure to accord trade opportunities consistently with its obligations did not have an adverse impact on the complainant had lost their rationale. By creating an irrefutable presumption of nullification or impairment, the judicial organs adapted the application of Article XXIII to the *ratio legis* of the provisions on which the market access claims before them are generally based.

3 Timeframe for panel proceedings

The DSU obliges panels to complete their work within short periods of time. Panels shall, 'as a general rule', submit their report within a period of six months and shall inform the DSB if they are unable to do so. In cases of urgency, panels shall 'aim to' submit their report within three months. In no case, 'should' the period exceed nine months. In the case of disputes relating to prohibited subsidies, the Agreement on Subsidies and Countervailing Measures (SCM Agreement) imposes an even shorter deadline: panels 'shall' circulate their report within 90 days. In the case of prohibited subsidies the maximum period is 60 days.[21]

[20] See the discussion of the scope of the GATT Panel on *European Community – Payments and Subsidies Paid to Processors and Producers of Oilseeds and Related Animal-Feed Proteins* (BISD 37th Supplement p. 86).

[21] Articles 12:8 and 12:9 of the DSU.

The drafters setting the time frames for panel proceedings based them partly on the experience under the GATT. However, the disputes under the GATT were in general much simpler than the disputes under WTO agreements. WTO panels must examine more complex facts, longer submissions and more legal claims, and all this in the light of a much more complex legal framework and an increasingly sophisticated Appellate Body jurisprudence. It is often impossible for them to proceed as quickly as GATT panels would have done. As a result, virtually all WTO panels have exceeded the six-month limit that they should 'as a general rule' observe. At the beginning of the proceedings they typically establish a calendar providing for a submission of their report within nine months, but then usually delay the submission of their report beyond the self-imposed deadline. There is virtually no panel that has observed the maximum period allowed under the SCM Agreement.

There is no longer any link between the prescriptions of the DSU and the SCM Agreement as to the length of proceedings and the constraints that the judicial organs of the WTO are facing. It is not the provisions of the DSU but the deviating practices of the judicial organs that now guide expectations. The DSU prescriptions have therefore lost their normative force.

III Norms that Emerged from Appellate Body Practices

1 Completing the panel's legal analysis

The Appellate Body's mandate according to Article 17 of the DSU is to address those 'issues of law covered in the panel report and legal interpretations developed by the panel' that have been raised in the appeal. There were cases in which the panel had examined the matter under one provision but the Appellate Body considered another closely related provision to be applicable to the measure. Since the closely related provision does not form part of the issues of law and legal interpretation set out in the panel report, it falls outside the mandate of the Appellate Body. If the Appellate Body had been given the right to remand the case to the panel, a strict application of Article 17 would not be a problem. However, the DSU does not provide for remands. If the Appellate Body does not rule on the related provisions, the parties' only option is therefore to return to square one and initiate a new proceeding on the unresolved issue.

For these reasons, the Appellate Body developed the practice of what it calls 'completing the panel's analysis' and examines provisions closely related to those examined by the panel when the facts established by the panel permit it to do so. The Appellate Body did not invoke a provision of the DSU or a principle of interpretation to justify the completion of the analysis; it simply stated that it would be 'remiss' in not completing the panel's analysis (Van den Bossche and Zdouc 2013: 242). The Appellate Body's completion of the analysis is now an established and undisputed practice and is invoked by appellants as a matter of entitlement.

2 Exercise of judicial economy

Article 17 of the DSU provides that the Appellate Body 'shall address each of the issues raised' in the appeal and authorises the Appellate Body to 'uphold, modify or reverse' the panel's legal findings and conclusions. These definitions of the Appellate Body's mandate gave rise to problems in cases in which the panel made rulings that the Appellate Body considered unnecessary to resolve the dispute. If those rulings are appealed, according to Article 17, the Appellate Body must address them and either uphold, modify or reverse the ruling; it may not simply declare the panel's findings and conclusions to be unnecessary. However, the Appellate Body repeatedly ruled that the requirement to address all legal issues appealed does not prevent it from declaring panel rulings it considers unnecessary to be 'moot and without legal effect' (Van den Bossche and Zdouc 2013: 241).[22] It is difficult to reconcile this practice with the provisions of Article 17 but, taking into account that the judicial organs of the WTO are to clarify the law not in the abstract but only for the purpose of resolving the dispute before them, the practice seems more reasonable than the requirements set out in those provisions. Also this practice is now established and undisputed.

3 Timeframe for Appellate Body proceedings

According to Article 17:5 of the DSU, the Appellate Body shall 'as a general rule' circulate its reports within 60 days of the appeal and 'in no case shall the proceedings exceed 90 days'.[23] Initially the Appellate Body was able to meet the deadlines imposed by the DSU in most cases.

[22] The author believes that underlying the Appellate Body's practice may be the reasoning 'that expressly exercising judicial economy with regard to an issue (as opposed to remaining silent on that issue) is considered to amount to "addressing" the issue'. However, the requirement to address *all* issues appealed might have arisen from the concern that a panel ruling, even if declared to be unnecessary to resolve the specific case, might still guide decisions in future cases.

[23] Article 17:5 of the DSU.

However, its reports were short and, in some cases, the reasoning supporting its interpretations was very brief.

As appeals became more complex and more frequent and its own jurisprudence more refined, the Appellate Body was often unable to submit its report within 90 days. At first, it sought the agreement of the parties to the dispute to the extension of the proceedings, apparently for fear that they could otherwise argue that the delayed report is not the report they are obliged to accept according to Article 17:14 of the DSU. When several notices of appeal were submitted at the same time and the resulting workload exceeded its capacities, the Appellate Body met with the parties concerned, urging them to withdraw their notices and to agree on a staggered resubmission at later dates.

The DSU does not provide for delays in Appellate Body proceedings with the consent of the parties, and whether the parties' consent to the Appellate Body's timing proposals lent these arrangements legitimacy is doubtful given the parties' dependency on the Appellate Body. In any case, *ultra posse nemo obligatur*. Why therefore should a court seek the disputant parties' consent to unavoidable delays? More recently the Appellate Body has ceased to resolve its timing problems in cooperation with the parties to the dispute; like panels, it simply exceeds the maximum period when this is unavoidable.

For these reasons, the DSU provisions setting out timeframes for Appellate Body proceedings have lost their normative force. Of course, delay can drain Appellate Body rulings of their value because the withdrawal of the measure found to be illegal is the only remedy available to the complainant under the WTO dispute settlement proceedings. However, hastily drafted rulings can also have reduced value for the WTO membership. The timeframes actually observed by the Appellate Body are adapted to the particular constraints it faces in each case and therefore constitute a better compromise between speed and quality than the maximum period prescribed by the DSU across the board.

C Evaluation of the Spontaneous Growth of Norms in WTO Dispute Settlement

I Advantages of Grown Over Designed Norms

There can be little doubt that the new norms created by agreements between disputant parties and by the judicial organs of the WTO are superior to the negotiated provisions that they have replaced.

The sequencing agreements correct a drafting mistake. Non-violation complaints should never have been made possible under the TRIPS Agreement. The agreements not to bring such complaints resolve this issue. The confidentiality principle followed by GATT panels should never have been made part of the compulsory system of adjudication of the WTO. The agreements between parties to open proceedings to the public are welcome improvements to the WTO's dispute settlement practices. This applies also to the practices of panels and the Appellate Body that supplement or supersede DSU provisions. The grant of enhanced third-party rights by panels, the irrefutability of the presumption of nullification or impairment, the completion of the panel's analysis by the Appellate Body, its exercise of judicial economy and the conduct of proceedings within timeframes that permit a thorough examination of the case are all substantial improvements to the dispute settlement order set out in the DSU. It is therefore not surprising that, in general, the Members have not opposed any of these changes to the dispute settlement order that they had negotiated.

The advantage of grown norms is that they tend to reflect the experience of many decision-makers in many cases. They emerge as solutions to issues that actually arise in concrete cases. Their authority rests on their practicability and their acceptance *hic et nunc*. By contrast, negotiated norms can only be based on the limited knowledge of the drafters. The normative force of negotiated provisions rests primarily on their prior formal acceptance. Grown norms are backed by what the German lawyer Georg Jellinek called 'the normative force of the factual'.

If the task of drafting dispute settlement rules is assigned to a body composed of representatives of Members, practicality, coherence and clarity can suffer as a result of the need to forge compromises, a lack of legal expertise and negotiating linkages to issues outside the field of dispute settlement. The maximum time periods imposed by the DSU illustrate this phenomenon. The time required by a panel or the Appellate Body to examine a case is not shorter in the case of export subsidies than in the case of restrictive trade measures. The DSU nevertheless imposes shorter time limits for disputes on subsidies as a result of a negotiating compromise under which weaker substantive rules on subsidies were exchanged against stronger enforcement rules. Whether a case concerns perishable or other products, the time required to resolve it will be the same. The DSU nevertheless requires panels to treat cases involving perishable products more urgently because this requirement placated those who would have preferred interim measures in such instances. Each of the timing requirements set out in the DSU was thus negotiated in the light of considerations extraneous to the fundamental objectives of the DSU.

II *Advantages of Designed Over Grown Norms*

The norms that emerge from agreements between the disputant parties are legally unstable. The sequencing agreements are not agreements covered by the DSU and it is therefore not possible to enforce them through the DSU procedures. Neither could such an agreement be invoked before the DSB as a legal basis for declining an authorisation to retaliate. The legal status of the decisions of the Ministerial Conference recording the Members' agreement not to bring non-violation complaints under the TRIPS Agreement is highly uncertain. Are these agreements, by virtue of their incorporation into a decision taken under Article IX of the WTO Agreement, part of the WTO Agreement and hence part of a covered agreement? Do these agreements constitute renunciations of rights that a panel would have to take into account in determining its jurisdiction?

There is no jurisprudence clarifying these issues. The agreements on sequencing and non-violation complaints have certainly resolved problems, but they are far from being perfect substitutes for an amendment of the DSU addressing these problems. Moreover, their existence creates a moral hazard: because they largely resolve the problems *de facto*, they reduce the incentive to resolve them *de jure*. The spread of such agreements runs counter to the basic objective of the drafters of the DSU to move from a consensual to an automatic dispute settlement system creating more predictability for Members.

Panel and Appellate Body practices are also not perfect substitutes for negotiated norms. Reasoned decisions resolving particular disputes, even if repeated in many cases, can never provide the same legal certainty as an abstract rule. What turns a ruling into a precedent is its rationale and what turns the precedents into a new norm is the frequent repetition of the same rationale. However, since the rulings are made by different persons in different cases, the rationale is likely to be expressed differently in different cases. Thus, the grant of enhanced third-party rights is an established practice, but panels have applied this newly created legal institution differently in different cases. Members expect that the Appellate Body will complete the panel's analysis; however, they do not know precisely under what circumstances the Appellate Body will do so. It is clear that the Appellate Body will exercise judicial economy, but it is difficult to determine on the basis of its jurisprudence in which cases it will do so. We know that panels will not observe the time limits set out in the DSU but we do not know how long individual proceedings will last.

If the grown norms deviate from the agreed norms, conflicting signals are sent to the membership. This not only creates confusion but also encourages further departures from the agreed norms and undermines the respect of disputant parties and the judicial organs for such norms. For these reasons, grown norms deviating from the prescriptions of the DSU should be codified and clarified by agreement. The following case illustrates how the advantages of grown norms can be combined with those of designed norms through codification and clarification.

In the *EU – Sardines* dispute, the Appellate Body permitted the EU to withdraw its notice of appeal and replace it with a revised notice because the EU had not done so abusively.[24] The Appellate Body thereby created a new procedural step with undefined contours that was contemplated neither in the DSU nor in the Appellate Body's working procedures. While the revision of the notice may have been a reasonable and practical solution in the circumstances of the case, it remained unclear under what circumstance and within what timeframe the new right to amend the notice of appeal could be exercised and how the interests of the other participants in the appeal in a fair and orderly proceeding would be taken into account. The Appellate Body therefore subsequently inserted Rule 23bis into its working procedures, which defines precisely the conditions that a Member wishing to revise its notice of appeal must fulfil and what the rights of other participants are. In this case, a new norm emerged spontaneously in the practices of the Appellate Body. That norm was not based on the DSU and was unclear. Its incorporation into the Appellate Body's working procedures gave it a legal status and clear contours.

D Conclusions

The above review of the evolution of the dispute settlement orders of the GATT and the WTO shows that there are two types of norms that have guided the expectations in the field of dispute settlement: (a) norms that emerged spontaneously from the practices and (b) norms that were deliberately created through negotiations.[25] The dispute settlement

[24] European Communities – Trade Description of Sardines, WT/DS231/AB/R, para. 151.

[25] See on the distinction between these two types of norms: Hayek (1979: 35–54). On use of these two types of norms by international organisations see: Frieder Roessler (1978: 27–59).

order of the GATT initially consisted almost entirely of practices. At the end of a long period of experimentation, the GATT contracting parties agreed to codify those practices and to adopt a number of improvements. The WTO began with a deliberately created, novel order of compulsory adjudication with new bodies, new procedures and new obligations. Since the establishment of that order, new practices of the disputant parties and judicial organs of the WTO spontaneously emerged that supplemented or superseded the agreed order. While the GATT moved from spontaneously emerged to deliberately created norms, the reverse is taking place in the WTO.

The norms that grew spontaneously in the WTO took the form of agreements between Members and decisions of the judicial organs. The norms that emerged in this manner corrected drafting mistakes, dealt with unanticipated problems and permitted the observation of sound legal principles in the proceedings and have served the membership well. These norms have never been formally endorsed by the WTO's Members but in practice are accepted by them. Fettered by veto rights and reciprocity demands, the membership effectively delegated its legislative function to the disputant parties and the judicial organs. This suggests that the Members themselves consider that the institutional and procedural framework for DSU amendments is inimical to the creation of a coherent, workable and up-to-date dispute settlement order and that they therefore have no option but to leave the performance of their legislative functions in this area to others.

In the field of dispute settlement procedures, the delegation of legislative functions to judicial organs is very common. Thus, the rules of procedures of the European Court of Justice were drafted by the Court itself.[26] Similarly, the WTO Appellate Body was authorised to draw up its own working procedures in consultation with the Chairman of the DSB and the Director-General.[27] The working procedures of the Appellate Body are professionally drafted, clearly set out what the party must and the Appellate Body will do and have been adapted when new problems arose. At the panel stage, no standing body to which legislative functions could be entrusted exists. Unlike the Appellate Body, panels cannot draft norms applicable in all future cases. They can only create new norms through a lengthy accumulation of consistent practices and they have done so with the implicit

[26] See Official Journal of the European Union, L265, Volume 55, 25 September 2012.

[27] Article 17:9 of the DSU.

endorsement of the membership. In the case of the Appellate Body, the membership has formally transferred legislative functions; in the case of panels, it has done so by default.

This does not mean that the membership should completely abdicate its legislative function in the field of dispute settlement. The range of issues that can be resolved through voluntary arrangements between disputant parties is limited. If, in more and more situations, a reasonable, workable solution can only be adopted if the parties to the dispute agree, the WTO would gradually move back to a consensus-based dispute settlement order. Norms that emerge from judicial practices tend to be imprecise and therefore need to be supplemented by legislated or agreed norms regulating details. Furthermore, there are matters – such as new institutional arrangements – that require a legislative act. Most importantly, the spontaneous growth of norms can lead to undesirable results and consequently cannot be left completely uncontrolled. The delegation of legislative functions therefore has to be combined with a system of checks and balances that permits the WTO's legislative branch to supplement and, if necessary, correct the spontaneous growth of norms in its judicial branch.

The Members of the WTO clung to their right to veto DSU amendments to protect their sovereignty, but it is that very right that now prevents them from exercising their sovereignty. The Members no longer want the dispute settlement order they negotiated but are unable to negotiate the order they do want. The numerous provisions of the DSU that have been overridden by grown norms show that a dispute settlement order on which representatives of WTO Members are able to agree after long negotiations is unlikely to be the order that the same Members want to apply in practice. When reviewing the DSU, the Members should therefore cease to discuss competing proposals to improve the dispute settlement order and examine instead the institutional and procedural framework for the adoption of such improvements.

References

Gappah, Petina and Roessler, Frieder. 2005. 'A Re-appraisal of Non-Violation Complaints under the WTO Dispute Settlement Procedures'. In *The World Trade Organization: Legal, Economic and Political Analysis*, Volume 1, edited by Arthur E. Appleton, and Michael G. Plummer. New York: Springer, 1371–1387.

Hayek, Friedrich A. 1979. *Law, Legislation and Liberty*, Volume 1: Rules and Order. London: Routledge & Kegan Paul, 35–54.

Hudec, Robert E. 1975. *The GATT Legal System and World Trade Diplomacy*. New York: Praeger, 59–190.

Roessler, Frieder. 1978. 'Law, De Facto Agreements and Declarations of Principle in International Economic Relations'. *German Yearbook of International Law* 21: 27–59.

Roessler, Frieder. 1991. 'The Constitutional Function of the Multilateral Trade Order'. In *National Constitutions and International Economic Law*, edited by M. Hilf and E.U. Petersmann. Deventer: Kluwer, 52–62.

Roessler, Frieder. 2015. 'The Rule of Law in International Trade Relations and the Establishment of the Legal Affairs Division of the GATT'. In *A History of Law and Lawyers in the GATT/WTO*, edited by Gabrielle Marceau. Cambridge: Cambridge University Press, 161–181.

Van den Bossche, Peter and Zdouc, Werner. 2013. *The Law and Policy of the World Trade Organization*, 3rd edn. Cambridge: Cambridge University Press, 353, 484–485.

6

About the Melting of Icebergs

Political and Economic Determinants of Dispute Initiation and Resolution in the WTO

DIRK DE BIÈVRE, ARLO POLETTI
AND AYDIN YILDIRIM*

A Introduction

What do we know about, and how can we improve our understanding of, the performance of the enforcement mechanism of World Trade Organization (WTO) norms and rules? Such performance can be thought of as a function of the degree and speed with which it incentivises WTO Members' first- and second-order compliance with WTO rules. First-order compliance can be conceived as the extent to which WTO Members conduct trade policies that are in line with their international commitments under WTO law. Second-order compliance grasps whether states bring their policies into line with recommendations of the WTO Dispute Settlement Body. In this case the question is how WTO Members react to trade partner's demands when these partners raise complaints with the adjudicative body of the WTO.

The literature on the institutional foundations of international cooperation has long taught us that the existence of mechanisms for the credible enforcement of agreed upon rules is key to overcoming problems of cooperation that are typical of international trade relations (Mayer 1981; Keohane 1984; Martin 1992; Bagwell and Staiger 2001). Any cooperative equilibrium in the form of agreements on the

* We are grateful to the organisers of the World Trade Forum at the World Trade Institute 2015, as well as to Chad Bown, Manfred Elsig, Judith Goldstein, and Krzysztof Pelc for comments on an earlier draft of this literature review with research outlook. We also gratefully acknowledge funding by the Research Foundation Flanders FWO and the Research Council of the University of Antwerp.

liberalisation of trade can be expected to remain unstable unless robust and effective enforcement mechanisms are put in place. This is because states face ever-present powerful incentives to renege on their trade liberalisation commitments, either by failing to implement the rules they have negotiated and eventually raising new trade barriers in contravention of the rules they have agreed upon, or by failing to correct their misbehaviour. Theory thus suggests that a quasi-judicialised system of enforcement such as the WTO Dispute Settlement Mechanism (DSM) should be capable of preventing both first order and second order compliance problems by creating disincentives for policies incompatible with WTO rules being adopted in the first place, and compelling WTO Members to bring their policies back into compliance with WTO rules whenever their wrongdoing is ascertained.

But has the empirical record of enforcement of rules in the WTO met these theoretical expectations? Do WTO Members live up to their obligations or do they pursue policies and actions that are in conflict with these commitments? And, do WTO Members bring their policies back into compliance swiftly when they are found to be in violation of their commitments, or are they impermeable to such pressures?

In this chapter, we review the state of the art of existing theory-driven empirical research on economic and political determinants with regard to both dimensions of the performance of the WTO's DSM and suggest possible avenues for pushing this research agenda forward. To gain relevant insights on first-order compliance, we argue in favour of a shift of empirical focus from formalised observable trade disputes to potential ones. Through an exclusively empirical focus on actual trade disputes we can infer very little about the degree of first order compliance with WTO rules. Observing that in some instances the policy-makers of some WTO Members decide to act upon the requests of domestic organised groups to seek the removal of WTO-incompatible trade barriers abroad by filing a formal complaint tells us only that some WTO-inconsistent policies were challenged, not that all such WTO-inconsistent policies were targeted. In fact, the literature shows that trade policy officials in WTO Members decided to act upon a small fraction of the demands made by domestic exporters seeking the removal of policies allegedly in violation of WTO agreements through the DSM. The greatest challenge for empirical research on first-order compliance is therefore to set the benchmark of how many cases *could* have been filed, that is to define the universe of potential cases out of which governments select topics that lead to the filing of WTO disputes. Doing so enables one to overcome the methodological problem of selection bias by which inferences about first-order compliance are developed on the basis of few actual and observable WTO disputes and, in a second stage, to shed light on some of the political and economic factors that might explain the conditions under which government representatives select the foreign trade barriers they target in WTO litigation.

While empirical research on potential disputes can improve our understanding of the overall record of first-order compliance with WTO rules, an important component of the performance of WTO enforcement institutions concerns the extent to which they incentivise compliance once the adjudicative body of the WTO is formally activated. For this purpose, we first review a series of theoretically possible political and economic determinants of dispute resolution, i.e. systematic explanations for defendants' responses to actual WTO dispute settlement complaints. In our view, the challenge in analysing this tip of the iceberg of actual WTO disputes lies in assessing the relative weight of, and the relationship between possible political determinants of compliance and timely resolution of disputes. The existing literature on WTO dispute settlement has already shed light on numerous important aspects of the political economy of second-order compliance in the WTO (Bernauer, Elsig and Pauwelyn 2014; De Bièvre and Poletti 2015). These include: strategic behaviour by dispute settlement panels (Kelemen 2001; Garrett and Smith 2002; Busch and Pelc 2010), the choice of institutional venue for resolving trade disputes (Busch 2007; Davis and Shirato 2007), why disputes escalate (Busch 2000; Guzman and Simmons 2002; Davis 2012), whether the DSM enforces or informs (Sattler, Spilker and Bernauer 2014), how litigation affects the domestic balance of trade-related interest groups (Goldstein and Martin 2000; Goldstein and Steinberg 2008; Poletti 2010; Poletti 2011; Poletti and De Bièvre 2016), under what conditions parties comply with decisions adopted through third-party review (Bown 2004a; Davis 2008; Young 2010; Poletti and De Bièvre 2014) and the effects of judicialisation on interest mobilisation (Poletti, De Bièvre and Hanegraaff 2015; De Bièvre et al. 2016). Despite the growing quantity and quality of this literature, we contend that the question of how to define second-order compliance conceptually and measure it empirically remains problematic, and suggest possible ways to overcome these problems.

Assessing the performance of the enforcement mechanisms of the WTO has never been more relevant than it is now. The financial crisis of 2007–2008 and the ensuing sovereign debt crises of the Eurozone created social and economic havoc that have led to sustained demands for protectionism. In addition, the global economy is undergoing rapid changes, not least due to the rise of so-called emerging economies, which promise to transform economic power structures in international trade relations. Also, the impasse and then meagre results of the Doha Round negotiations have further increased the importance of the WTO's judicial arm as a tool for maintaining a liberal trade regime. These systemic transformations can be expected to have significant effects on the performance of multilateral institutions such as the WTO, which regulates more than €23 trillion in trade in goods and services on the basis of formal treaty agreements every year. Existing research suggests that the WTO has performed quite well so far with respect to both first and second order compliance (Allee 2005; Wilson 2007; Irwin and Mavroidis 2008; Zangl 2008; Zangl et al. 2012; Baccini and Kim 2012). In this chapter we argue in favour of more scholarly work to acquire a deeper understanding of whether, and if so under what conditions, the WTO has performed well in terms of fostering greater compliance with multilateral trade rules.

B Melting the Bottom of the Iceberg: Which Potential Disputes Never Materialise?

When it comes to assessing first-order compliance with WTO rules, political scientists and political economists have extensively analysed WTO dispute settlement, focusing mainly on actual and often on highly visible trade disputes. However, actual disputes are only the tip of the iceberg. When governments initiate trade disputes in the WTO, they tend to do so in response to pressures from domestic producers who may have been negatively affected by the existence of certain policies or by the imposition of new ones in other WTO Members. Such exporters may be negatively affected either because such policies restrict their export opportunities in third markets (e.g. disputes over export subsidies) or because they confront exporters with allegedly WTO-inconsistent import restrictions in the defendant's market (Bown and Reynolds 2014).

A number of studies on WTO Members' policies and actions potentially in conflict with WTO laws concur with the opinion that only a small fraction of such policies brought to the attention of policy-makers in (potential) complainants end up being litigated at the WTO (Davis and Shirato 2007; Kim 2008; Young 2009; Davis 2012). Most of the WTO-incompatible trade barriers simply do not come to the surface because governments do not always respond by launching a WTO complaint in response to pressures emanating from mobilised domestic groups. This may be because producers and exporters do not report these trade barriers to their public authorities, or because nobody actually ever noticed that some measures are non-WTO-conforming.

One of the key challenges in the study of the disputes that have been filed at the WTO is therefore to set the benchmark in terms of how many and what types of cases could have been filed, but were not. What is the universe of potential cases from which governments select topics that lead to the filing of a case before the WTO DSM? And which types of trade barriers are more likely to be signalled by domestic constituencies? Difficulties in clearly defining the potential universe of cases, the so called 'iceberg' issue, raises the question of selection bias in trade dispute research in general and in the empirical assessment of first-order compliance in particular. Scholars are well aware of the selection problem in studying litigation outcomes in domestic legal settings (Priest and Klein 1984). The same problems exist at the international level and it has been convincingly argued that problems of selection plague the empirical analysis of WTO dispute settlement (Kim 2008). Two key problems arise from failing to recognise that trade disputes are only a small fraction of the total number of policies in violation of WTO agreements. First, observers risk drawing incorrect inferences about first order compliance, depicting trade interactions as conflictive when they may in fact be quite cooperative, or vice versa. For instance, high profile WTO disputes initiated by the United States against the European Union (EU)'s bans on imports of hormone-treated beef and on genetically modified (GM) crops have led some commentators to portray the EU as a WTO Member with structural problems of first order compliance in the areas of consumer and health safety regulation (Davis 2003; Young 2004). However, these are the only two WTO disputes that emerged out of nearly 3,000 notifications these two WTO Members brought to the attention of the Sanitary and Phytosanitary Standards (SPS) and Technical Barriers to Trade (TBT) WTO Committees in the period from 1995–2009 (Young 2009).

Second, scholarly research has so far been largely unable to develop systematic explanations for how governments choose whether or not to file a dispute with the WTO DSM. This is an important research question that connects the question of first-order compliance to the question of second order compliance. Assessing the WTO's performance in terms of incentivising first order compliance is important not only in itself, but also because it helps establish a better empirical grounding for the analysis of second-order compliance. Indeed, understanding the politics of dispute initiation is crucial to shed light on the missing link between research on first- and second-order compliance. Once the overall degree of (dis)respect for WTO rules is known, and before addressing the question of compliance with the adjudicative body of the WTO, we need to understand whether, and eventually how, access to WTO adjudication is hampered in systematic ways. In principle, any move towards a rule-based system can be expected to provide an essential public good: levelling the playing field to make sure that all stakeholders (e.g. WTO Members and different actors within WTO Members) are not systematically denied the opportunity to see their rights enforced through legal means. However, in practice, several factors can hinder the capacity of the WTO DSM to contribute to the attainment of this essential public good. For instance, weak states might not be able to bring legal claims to challenge violations of their rights, or they might face constraints in doing so against powerful countries. A closely related question concerns whether the WTO's DSM is activated to challenge WTO-illegal policies that affect only a narrow subset of WTO Members or policies that have negative effects for the majority of WTO Members. An additional problem concerns the potential bias in the representation of different constituencies within WTO Members, rather than across them. For instance, the WTO's DSM could be used to defend a restricted set of domestic constituencies representing concentrated and narrow interests, leading to the underrepresentation of other important but more diffuse interests. To sum up, while in principle a move towards a rule-based system should be expected to provide the public good of equitable access to enforcement, in practice such a move may simply reinforce existing power asymmetries and political biases that lead to the systematic exclusion of some sets of actors from the scope of WTO's ability to incentivise second-order compliance.

More generally, a number of striking regularities remain largely unexplained because of the tendency not to systematically analyse non-cases in WTO dispute settlement. For instance, the EU and the United States have never initiated complaints against least developed countries (LDCs) (Horn, Johannesson and Mavroidis 2011); LDCs tend to prefer to participate as third parties in WTO dispute settlement rather than as complainants (Elsig and Stucki 2012); there has been only one dispute settlement ruling on whether a bilateral or regional preferential trade agreement (PTA) conforms to WTO rules (Mavroidis 2006), and WTO agreements covering a broad range of regulatory policies such as the Agreement on Trade-Related Aspects of Intellectual Property Rights (TRIPS) and the General Agreement on Trade in Services (GATS) only rarely prompt dispute settlement cases (Pauwelyn 2010).

I Identifying the Universe of Potential Cases in WTO Dispute Settlement

The challenge in providing a more reliable empirical assessment of the WTO's ability to incentivise first-order compliance with its rules, as well as in gaining a comprehensive understanding of the degree to which trade-related actors can take the opportunity to compel others into second-order compliance through the adjudicative institutions of the WTO, is to identify the universe of measures and policies that are in potential conflict with WTO commitments. But how can we collect systematic information on such potential WTO disputes? Acknowledging that it is virtually impossible to collect data on all policies or measures potentially in conflict with WTO law in all WTO Members, the question is how best to obtain a representative sample of the universe of potential WTO disputes. Some studies have defined the universe of potential trade disputes by way of an estimation based on trade flows between pairs of trade partners, making the assumption that the number of potential disputable issues should increase with greater trade (Sattler and Bernauer 2011). While in the absence of viable alternatives estimation can certainly help in identifying a benchmark for the potential for trade disputes, it necessarily remains an imprecise guess that again risks leading to partial inferences in the best case scenario, or to entirely incorrect ones in the worst case scenario.

A number of alternatives are available in the field of WTO dispute settlement research. Although clearly more time consuming, in our view a more interesting route is to actually try and empirically trace potential WTO disputes. Some studies have adopted this approach focusing on temporary trade barriers (TTBs) such as anti-dumping measures and countervailing duties (Allee 2005; Bown 2005; Kim 2008). While this approach offers the considerable advantage of allowing for the identification of the full sample of potentially WTO-incompatible trade measures, i.e. we can identify all the TTBs that have been put in place, it does not allow for generalisations beyond this particular set of trade measures.

Another approach is to rely on WTO Members' notifications or measures raised as specific concerns to WTO technical committees (Young 2009). This approach also seems problematic for a number of reasons. Notifications are made by national administrations, and it is clear from patterns of self-reporting that not all WTO Members comply with their notification obligations. Specific concerns raised to WTO technical committees are also problematic in that they may already represent a subset of politically relevant potential trade barriers as a result of the gatekeeping power trade policy officials exercise in selecting issues to be brought to the attention of such committees. More generally, these data are only available with respect to two sets of WTO commitments, SPS and TBT, and it is therefore difficult to advance generalisable arguments.

In our view, the most promising way to acquire reliable and comprehensive evidence on first order compliance is to concentrate on potentially WTO-inconsistent policies and measures abroad that are brought to the attention of WTO Members' policy officials by domestic exporters. Our point of reference here is the impressive study conducted by Christina Davis (2012) on the determinants of dispute initiation in the United States and Japan in which she systematically collected data on such potentially WTO-inconsistent policies and measures by relying on the *National Trade Estimate Report on Foreign Trade Barriers* and on the *Report on Compliance by Major Trading Partners with Trade Agreements* both published annually by the US Trade Representative and the Japanese Government respectively. Such an approach offers a number of advantages. For one, it allows the focus to be put on potentially WTO-inconsistent policies that are politically relevant, namely those that are relevant enough to have engendered organised groups within (potential) WTO complainants to mobilise and ask their government to act on their behalf. Moreover, these reports include all kinds of potentially WTO-inconsistent policies and measures, and are therefore not restricted to any particular WTO commitment. One of the drawbacks of such an analysis is that it covers a limited time-span, i.e. 1995–2004, and is limited to only two WTO Members.

This pioneering work could fruitfully be expanded in both respects. Since such reports, as well as data on economic indicators, are now available up to 2015, it would be possible to cover a period of two decades (1995–2015), a period long enough to also understand in a systematic way the effects of the 2007–2008 financial crisis on first order compliance in the WTO. A greater challenge is to expand the analysis to a much larger set of WTO Members, as the vast majority of them do not have at their disposal formalised mechanisms for market access investigations as the United States and Japan do. Some other important WTO Members, however, do have such mechanisms. For instance, since 2009, the European Commission has published an annual *Trade and Investment Barriers Report*. Data on barriers to trade and investment faced by EU exporters prior to 2009 can be retrieved from the *Market Access Database* of the European Commission. This is a publicly available computer database on export formalities, WTO bound tariff levels and existing barriers to trade. This database forms the informational backbone of the EU's litigation strategies in the WTO since it establishes a systematic and centralised source of information on market access difficulties encountered by EU industry. Similar data will soon be available for South Korea, as the South Korea Ministry of Trade, Industry and Energy (MOTIE) and the Ministry of Foreign Affairs and Trade (MOFAT) initiated a jointly published *National Report on Foreign Trade Environment* in 2013. While to our knowledge these are the only WTO Members that have equipped themselves with formalised mechanisms for market access investigations, other Members organisations representing sectoral interests do produce annual reports. For instance, while Brazil is still in the process of developing its formal institutional mechanisms, business organisations representing various industry sectors produce informal lists of foreign trade barriers they would like to see their government act upon through WTO litigation. Such data are broadly comparable with previous government-based data as in both cases reports collect complaints about potentially WTO-incompatible policies and measures by organised non-state actors.

II Potential Determinants of Dispute Initiation in the WTO

So far, we have assessed possible empirical strategies to confront the challenges of understanding first-order compliance. Once such WTO-incompatible policies and measures have been identified, the next logical step is to investigate what drives policy-makers' choice to use WTO adjudication. The degree of second-order compliance is crucial in assessing the performance of the WTO's enforcement capacity, but, logically, before the question of compliance with WTO DSM rulings can be answered, it is necessary to address the issue of access to adjudication. Neither practitioners nor scholars have been at all short of ideas as to the possible sources of dispute initiation. We review some these ideas here and suggest possible ways to expand the scope of these analyses.

To account for differences in dispute initiation *across* countries, some authors have concentrated on WTO Members' legal capacity (Kim 2008;

Busch, Reinhardt and Shaffer 2009). Taking legal action in the WTO can be very costly because it requires continuous monitoring of other countries' trade policies and import restrictions, collection of evidence on policies and practices that violate international trade law, and, most importantly, hiring legal staff for disputes that often last for some years. Following through with a WTO dispute thus requires that WTO Members have the capacity to meet the administrative and expertise requirements for preparing and following WTO proceedings. Given the high costs associated with WTO litigation, poor countries that have less financial and human resources may find it harder to resort to WTO litigation than rich ones. While previous experiences of WTO litigation can help poor countries overcome some of these problems (Davis and Bermeo 2009), overall, poor countries can be expected both to initiate fewer disputes than rich ones, and to be more likely to participate in WTO dispute settlement as third parties (Elsig and Stucki 2012).

Legal capacity, however, can tell us little about how the logic of dispute initiation may vary *within* WTO Members. Drawing on the work of Sattler and Bernauer (2011), a number of interesting hypotheses on how policy-makers choose their targets in WTO litigation can be identified. For instance, dispute initiation can be thought of as a function of power asymmetries between WTO Members. The logic of this argument is that if the potential complainant is much more powerful, i.e. has a larger market size than the potential defendant, it is more likely to get what it wants, i.e. the removal of trade barriers, through bilateral interactions before a dispute is initiated because it can threaten to impose greater costs on the target with limited harm to its own economy (Guzman and Simmons 2005). The probability of an out-of-court settlement thus increases with larger power asymmetries since more powerful complainant countries are more likely to succeed in getting the potentially disputed trade restrictions lifted without resorting to WTO proceedings.

As Sattler and Bernauer (2011) point out, dispute initiation can also be affected by a gravitational logic driven both by economic size and trade volumes. This line of argument essentially applies gravity models of inter-state conflict to trade disputes (Horn, Mavroidis and Nordström 1999) by arguing that large economies attract a disproportionate amount of disputes. This may be so for two reasons. For one, large economies are particularly attractive targets for potential complainants because of their large market size, which ultimately affects the economic stakes of a case (Allee 2005; Guzman and Simmons 2005). If the WTO rules in favour of the complainant, exporters from the complainant country can gain more when the destination market is larger. The incentive to take legal action can therefore be expected to be particularly strong when suspected violations of international trade law occur in a large economy. Large trade volumes increase these incentives for the simple reason that a large exporting country will be more likely encounter disputable trade restrictions in some other country. In other words, large volumes and a wide diversity of trade flows existing between two large and interdependent trade partners increase the probability that one of these trade partners will be negatively affected by an import-restricting measure and decide to challenge this measure at the WTO.

These arguments do not systematically take into account the domestic politics of trade policy-making, however. Davis (2012) suggests that this gap can be addressed by conceiving of dispute initiation as a function of the political pressure exerted on WTO Members' policy-makers by powerful exporting constituencies. This pressure argument builds on classical political economy approaches that see government choices of economic policies as a function of political pressures exerted by key economic interest groups within society (Frieden 1991). According to this perspective, governments use WTO litigation to target those trade barriers that impose costs on exporters that can affect their chances of re-election or re-appointment. This perspective suggests that public policy-makers will be more responsive to demands being pushed by domestic interests groups who have a strong capacity to mobilise politically and exert pressure on them, offering resources that are key for policy-makers in exchange for policies that they desire. One of the main challenges here is to devise empirical strategies to conduct meaningful comparisons between WTO Members. Davis (2012) analyses governmental choices on dispute initiation in the United States and Japan by measuring interest groups' lobbying in terms of political contributions. This approach can be problematic when it comes to testing the same hypothesis in other WTO Members. For instance, data on interest group spending may not be systematically collected, or direct campaign contributions by firms can be forbidden, as in the case of the EU and most of its Member States. The challenge here is to identify measures that can grasp the logic underlying the pressure politics hypothesis while allowing for meaningful comparisons across WTO Members. One possibility could be to rely on the Herfindahl–Hirschman Index (HHI), which measures the size of firms in relation to the industry size and indicates the level of competition among them, thus directly speaking to theories of collective action, which suggest that highly concentrated sectors should find it easier to mobilise politically.

In our view, looking at an additional set of hypotheses could usefully expand upon this important work. For instance, it would be interesting to subject to empirical scrutiny the argument that the domestic political logic driving dispute initiation may be affected by the extent to which WTO dyads are engaged in intra-industry trade (IIT). This hypothesis posits that IIT, i.e. trade of varieties of the same product between countries with similar factor endowments, makes collective action easier because it makes firms or agglomerations of firms leading actors in their market niche. While on the one hand, IIT reduces the costs of trade relative to inter-industry trade, on the other hand, it significantly reduces collective action costs. The costs of adjusting to IIT may be lower, and yet they are not concentrated in a single social class or in a single industry. Rather, a small set of hyper-specialised producers, or even a single firm carry the burden. Because IIT leads firms to act more individually or in small groups (rather than collectively within or across sectors), trade policy lobbying is likely to be easier to organise effectively. Since firms consider the expected benefits and costs of lobbying, as well as the likelihood that their individual and joint efforts will have an impact on policy outcomes (Olson 1965), IIT can be expected to ease political mobilisation (Gilligan 1997). By extension, one can hypothesise that high levels of IIT generated between two WTO Members may increase the ability of organised exporters to successfully pressure their government into WTO litigation.

Another important factor influencing WTO Members' choice as to dispute initiation may be related to the type of policy measures that can be targeted through WTO litigation. In their impressive analysis of WTO disputes, Bown and Reynolds (2014) show that some policies targeted through WTO disputes are 'partial' – i.e. they affect only the complainant or a small subset of actors – while others are 'global' – i.e. they negatively affect all trading partners. Examples of the former type of WTO disputes are those that question the WTO-compatibility of anti-dumping measures or other safeguard measures, while examples of the latter include WTO-inconsistent applications of an internal tax, subsidy or regulation imposed on a most-favoured-nation (MFN) conforming basis. This means that some trade disputes generate benefits that are appropriated by one or a small subset of WTO Members, while others promise to generate benefits that can be appropriated by WTO Members more widely. It is quite plausible to hypothesise that there is a lower probability of initiation of 'global' WTO disputes given the incentives for free-riding that might arise when such challengeable policy measures are at stake.

Finally, it might be worthwhile exploring whether the probability of dispute initiation decreases when the two potential disputants are partners in a preferential trade agreement (PTA) with a highly legalised dispute settlement mechanism. This alternative forum hypothesis holds that the availability of alternative fora for discussion about the elimination of trade barriers makes WTO litigation less likely (Busch 2007). The number of PTAs has skyrocketed in the past two decades and recent research has shown that one of the most striking features of the current wave of regionalism is the increasing presence of enforcement mechanisms in such PTAs (Dür and Elsig 2014). Other things being equal, it is just plausible that the likelihood of dispute initiation in the WTO is lower when the two potential complainants have an alternative forum at their disposal, i.e. a dispute settlement mechanism in the PTA to which both are signatories, to settle the controversy.

C Melting the Tip of the Iceberg: What Favours Timely Resolution of Actual WTO Disputes?

Having addressed the issue of first-order compliance and dispute initiation, we now turn to the question of second-order compliance. Scholarly literature by political scientists has put forward a series of theoretical explanations for Members' behaviour in WTO litigation and (non)compliance in the tradition of institutionalist international relations. Although compliance is an essentially contested concept, this literature generally understands compliance to mean bringing rules and practices in line with WTO law once they have been found to pursue WTO-inconsistent policies by the WTO adjudicative body, and meeting the complainants' demands (for an elaboration on the second aspect, see more below). One of the reasons why compliance according to the first meaning of the word is bound to remain elusive to any analysis, is that information on early settlements in the form of mutually agreed solutions most often remains private to the disputing parties and the extent to which settlements actually result in compliance with WTO law remains unclear (De Bièvre and Poletti 2015; Mavroidis 2015). Nevertheless, this literature on possible political determinants of compliance has focused on two broad sets of explanatory factors. First, some scholars have proposed that states' propensity to comply with their international trade commitments can be explained by either the normative pressure applied by the international community that challenges the reputation of a state (Keohane 1984; Zangl 2008) or the pressure exerted by the retaliatory capacity of trade partners (Bown 2004). A second strand of the literature makes the alternative suggestion that political traits of states themselves can account for the variation in second-order compliance. Such traits include the defendant's political regime and the presence of democratic institutions (Slaughter 1995) as well as the number of domestic veto players whose consent is necessary to secure domestic policy change (Young 2010; Poletti and De Bièvre 2014).

Scholars who focused on the impact of external pressures firstly argued that the normative power of a dispute settlement panel ruling – and the panel's legally binding recommendations – compels states to comply, as rule abidance becomes a norm that the world trade community members are expected to follow (Busch and Reinhardt 2000). Secondly, some further argued that domestic reputational concerns arise if states decide to renege on their international commitments, mainly in the form of audience costs that may damage states' reputation globally. Domestic audience costs may arise since citizens tend to care about their country's international reputation as well as the reputation of a leader in global fora (Tomz 2007). Thus, the potential for damage to a state's reputation on the international scene may well restrain states from ignoring their commitments, and induce to them to follow through on their promises (Fearon 1994). Furthermore, audience costs may also arise because of the presence of third parties at the WTO dispute settlement – effectively observers to the judicial proceedings – who may trigger additional concerns for defendants who would not want to risk their reputation in the eyes of those scrutinising their behaviour. Yet it has also been suggested that the presence of third parties prevents WTO Members from reaching a mutually agreed solution through the WTO DSM by increasing bargaining costs and thus lowering the prospects of settlement (Busch and Reinhardt 2006; Johns and Pelc 2014). At the same time, more egregious violations of WTO law may well attract more third parties to want to attend the proceedings, challenging the basis for causal inferences about this alleged detrimental effect of third-party presence on compliance.

Apart from reputational concerns that may prevent states from reneging on their international commitments, scholars also argued that complainants' retaliatory capacity induces compliance with the WTO DSM. While some argued that the threat of authorised trade sanctions put pressure upon defendant states to ensure compliance to avoid economic costs of reneging (Bown 2004; Bown and Pauwelyn 2010), others emphasised that the threat of retaliation creates an incentive for the domestic pro-trade groups to overcome their collective action problems and mobilise in favour of compliance and trade liberalisation (Goldstein and Martin 2000; Goldstein and Steinberg 2008). Others have also argued that the threat of retaliation can be especially effective in promoting compliance where the disputing parties have large power asymmetries, i.e. where a more powerful complainant could impose its will upon a weaker defendant (Guzman and Simmons 2005).

Two additional sources of compliance may well warrant attention, but have not been subjected to precise empirical scrutiny so far. Firstly, based on a general conjecture on interdependence, *the dyadic trade relationship* between a complainant and a defendant may have the potential to affect a dispute's timely and effective resolution. We can reasonably expect disputes to be resolved faster and more effectively if the defendant and the complainant engage in extensive bilateral trade, because they are likely to be willing to avoid any disruption to their trade relationship (Bown 2009). Secondly, compliance at the WTO could also be more likely if the complainant and the defendant are part of a military pact or, even more plausibly, a trade alliance in the form of a PTA, since such partnerships may induce states to avoid conflict with their exclusive partners.

An alternative strand of the literature has argued that a state's rule abidance record is affected by factors particular to that state. As international institutions are designed to affect the behaviour of governments (Kennedy and Southwick 2002), the domestic actors to which the governments are accountable may play the most decisive role in determining the government's behaviour. Two arguments have been put forward in this regard. The first posits that more democratic states are more likely to comply with their international commitments, and the second argues that the higher the number of legislative veto players whose consent is necessary to bring about policy change, the more difficult it is for states to comply – especially within democracies.

The assertion that international commitments are more likely to be honoured by democratic states constitutes an extension of theories of the so-called democratic peace. However, they locate the cause of this pressure in the properties of democracies or the activities of constituencies within these states, rather than the mere interaction between states at the international level (Dixon 1993; Milner and Moravcsik 2009). The underlying reasoning rests on the supposed dedication of democratic states to the rule of law and their tendency towards abidance with international rules stemming from local democratic values (Slaughter 1995). Others have suggested that democracies are more compliant because democratic systems are accountable to their domestic constituencies (Mansfield, Milner and Rosendorff 2002). Therefore, if a democratic state made an international commitment – supposedly in the interests of its domestic audience(s) – it is reasonable to expect it to follow through on its promise and satisfy the demand of those domestic constituencies.

However, some have argued instead that the notion of accountability is exactly why second order compliance following WTO disputes may be difficult. If policy-makers are assumed to be accountable to their domestic constituencies, they would be susceptible to the pressure of domestic mobilised actors who may or may not be in favour of compliance. By conceiving governments as gatekeepers in trade disputes, some have argued that policy-makers attempt to steer a course between two balancing pressures from domestic mobilised actors – e.g. economic sectors – in bringing compliance following WTO disputes (Spilker 2012). For instance, in response to an adverse panel ruling, a defendant's domestic sectors characterised with high import-dependence would be in favour of compliance and ask to remove trade barriers to access cheaper imports. In contrast, import-competing sectors affected by such disputes would instead press for protection in order to continue being shielded from foreign competition. Yet, only a small proportion of WTO dispute settlement cases lends itself to such a reading, as most tend to be resolved at an early stage.

Similarly, there have also been suggestions that regardless of the democratic nature of the state parties, and beyond the preferences of domestic actors, the number of veto players whose consent is necessary to enact policy change co-determines states' capacity for compliance (Young 2010; Poletti and De Bièvre 2014). In this vein, it is argued that the variation in responses to WTO litigation depends on the number of veto players in the defendant – highlighting that a high number of domestic veto players can significantly hamper WTO Members' ability to comply with WTO rules, even when policy-makers are willing to do so.

I *Current Challenges and Ways Forward*

These plausible explanations have greatly advanced our understanding of second-order compliance with the WTO DSM. Yet the literature on compliance published so far has empirical and conceptual shortcomings. In their empirical approach, the most prominent works have often focused on small-*n* samples or high-profile non-compliance cases, mainly transatlantic disputes (Busch and Reinhardt 2003b; Zangl 2008), comparative case studies (Young 2004; Busch, Reinhardt et al. 2009; Young 2010; Young 2011; Poletti and De Bièvre 2014) or have limited their study to a particular time period or subject matter of a dispute (Spilker 2011). Where an attempt has been made to identify a relationship between the aforementioned explanations and states' record of abidance with the rulings of the WTO, it has remained somewhat puzzling that many of the most active users of the system consistently resist compliance (Pauwelyn 2000; Davey 2007). In particular, the hypotheses following in the tradition of democratic peace theory do not withstand rigorous testing, as numerous democratic WTO Members, such as Norway, Canada, the United States and Australia have compliance problems, while their authoritarian counterparts, for example China, have shown willingness to comply (Harpaz 2010).

Moreover, the exact conceptualisation and the empirical measurement of compliance with the WTO DSM remains somewhat problematic. Whereas a large majority of scholars follow Hudec (1992) in measuring second-order compliance by looking at the policy change in a defendant state following a WTO panel ruling (Busch 2000; Guzman and Simmons 2002; Busch and Reinhardt 2003a; Petersmann and Pollack 2003; Young 2004; Busch and Reinhardt 2006; Zangl 2008; Young 2010), this approach does not provide a comprehensive evaluation of the performance of the WTO DSM in bringing about the swift resolution of disputes. Yet the inherent instability of the seemingly obvious concept of compliance with WTO law can be overcome by conceptualising compliance pragmatically as a defendant *meeting a complainant's demands*. This opens up the possibility to investigate how long complainants viewed defendants as being in violation of their WTO commitments before the defendant enacted (or revised) its policy. Existing studies have thus often overlooked an important variation in the time it takes for defendants to bring their policies into line with their WTO commitments. Even though the large majority of WTO disputes do indeed result in compliance, such rule abidance might actually come about after a consistent violation for a long period of time – as in the case of the EU's bananas dispute with Latin American countries or the United States' upland cotton dispute with Brazil.

To account for these challenges, we offer empirical and conceptual alternatives. From an empirical standpoint, it may prove useful to assess whether a delay in compliance with WTO rulings may be explained by factors that the political economy of trade literature has paid great attention to in recent years, yet surprisingly little with regard to WTO dispute settlement. Indeed, considerable variation in trade policy preferences, political mobilisation and trade policy outcomes may be attributable to the extent to which sectors (and firms) are active in so-called global value chains (GVCs), which are networks characterised by internationalisation and vertical integration of production processes. Thus, the degree to which firms and sectors in a complainant and a defendant Member are involved in a WTO bilateral dispute may well affect timeliness of compliance. Firms and sectors embedded in GVCs have been demonstrated to press for PTAs (Manger 2012) and have been found to be associated with significantly lower demand for trade protection (Dür, Baccini and Elsig 2014). Since it is likely that GVC integration stimulates bilateral trade liberalisation (Antràs and Staiger 2012; Orefice and Rocha 2014) as it activates political mobilisation by import-dependent firms and sectors, different degrees of GVC integration might well shape domestic firms' and sectors' preferences towards (not) liberalising and (not) complying with WTO rulings. The level of integration of domestic actors into GVCs could constitute a more parsimonious and simpler explanation of states' compliance with the international trade agreements of the WTO.

At the same time, the very rise of GVCs may be just as likely to reduce the incentives for governments and domestic interests to put into place or maintain trade barriers that are not in conformity with one or more of the WTO's agreements. Those same pressures that may favour more timely compliance with WTO rulings should logically work just as well under the mere threat of WTO litigation, or should even make the very emergence of such trade barriers less likely in sectors characterised by a high degree of integration into GVCs. However, in order to advance and test such propositions, different degrees of integration into GVCs would need to be operationalised and rigorously measured to pave the way to understanding the changing nature of conflict and cooperation in the international trade regime.

Two sources of evidence could be very helpful in this regard. Firstly, researchers can now use the European Commission sponsored *World Input–Output Database* (WIOD), which has sector-level trade data on almost all OECD countries for the past twenty years and provides a number of GVC indicators, the most important being the level of value added trade and the intermediate consumption of every sector (Timmer et al. 2015). Scholars can use this dataset to gauge the level of import dependence of sectors by calculating the ratio of intermediate consumption to the whole sector's output. They can also use it to gauge sector productivity by calculating each sector's value added trade as a ratio of its total output. Secondly, as already mentioned, the World Bank-sponsored *Trade Flows and Trade Disputes* database, compiled by Bown and Reynolds (2014), offers impressive trade data about every WTO dispute. Beyond descriptive data on all (more than 400) disputes brought to the WTO, such as dispute initiation and the DS number of the disputes, allowing for inferences on the entire population of actual WTO disputes, the database includes trade volumes between defendants and complainants (from two years before dispute initiation until a year after dispute resolution), the six-digit Harmonized System (HS) codes for products associated with each dispute, and a dichotomous measure of whether the allegedly inconsistent policy is a global or a partial one – i.e. a policy imposed on a subset of the defendant's trade partners. The dataset thus allows one to operationalise a defendant's level of vulnerability towards its trade partners by looking at the level of imports and exports at the six-digit HS level, and perhaps to observe the change in trade volumes between a defendant and a complainant before and after a dispute is resolved.

The empirical opportunities brought about by the construction of this database could thus be fruitfully accompanied by conceptual clarification on definition and measurement of compliance. Indeed, one way to remedy some of the above-mentioned problems with the literature is to measure compliance with the WTO DSM by looking at *how long* it takes for defendants to meet their international obligations, and conceptually equate compliance with *meeting a trade partner's demands*. In our view, measuring compliance by considering the aspect of *timeliness* provides the best alternative because it allows researchers to observe for how long the defendants resist compliance before satisfying complainants' demands and then to look for factors to account for this variation. Moreover, instead of attempting to assess whether a defendant's enacted (or revised) policy after an adverse panel ruling is consistent with WTO law, conceptualising compliance as meeting a trade partner's demands would be more advantageous because a dispute is only taken off the agenda of the DSB when the complainant concerned is satisfied with the implementation of a ruling or there is a mutually agreed solution – except in *very* rare cases where a compliance panel disagrees with a complainant. Therefore, in most cases, even though the defendant may not necessarily be in strict 'compliance' with WTO law, the WTO DSB considers the case resolved and settled when a complainant is satisfied one way or another. In other words, since the reliable and comprehensive determination of (partial or full) compliance with WTO DSB rulings for the entire population of WTO dispute settlement cases may well be elusive, compliance might be more usefully conceptualised and investigated as the resolution and settlement of a dispute whenever a complainant is satisfied with the defendant's response.

Furthermore, for calculating the time it takes for defendants to meet their trade partner's demands, two options with different conceptual implications are available. Firstly, one can calculate the time from dispute initiation until dispute resolution – regardless of whether the dispute was resolved by early settlement or by domestic policy change after a panel ruling. The downside to this approach is that defendants are implicitly considered 'guilty' or unable to satisfy their trade partners' demands until there is a settlement (or a domestic policy change) that brings about compliance. Clearly, in certain cases, defendants may attempt to clarify the WTO-inconsistent policies by bringing disputes to the panels, or may attempt to prove that their policies are not in violation of any WTO law, which is admittedly very rare but occurs nevertheless – as with the asbestos dispute brought against the EU by Canada. To sum up, calculating the time it takes for defendants to meet their trade partners' demands, from dispute initiation until dispute resolution still has the advantage of offering a coherent and simple conceptualisation, while bearing in mind the underlying assumptions of such an approach.

An alternative approach would be to calculate timeliness separately for disputes that were settled and for disputes that were empanelled. For the disputes that resulted in a mutually agreed solution, one could calculate the time from the initiation of the dispute until the date of its settlement. This would reveal how long it takes a defendant to satisfy its trade partner by offering a settlement. For the empanelled disputes, one option would be to calculate the time it takes a defendant to implement a panel ruling after the adoption of a final panel report, which would reveal the time it takes for a defendant to change its domestic policies to meet its trade partner's demands. The advantage of this approach is that it takes into account the certainty of violation from a defendant's perspective. In other words, taking this approach, defendants would clearly know which parts of their allegedly inconsistent policies need to be corrected – if any.

However, this would also mean that any examination that uses this approach separates compliance with panel rulings from compliance in the form of settlement. This in turn would mean neglecting the variation in the defendant behaviour towards prolonging a dispute. The defendants at the WTO DSM may very well be prolonging disputes, either because they are unable to meet their trade partners' demands – e.g. because domestic veto players inhibit states' ability to enact new policies – or because they want to appease their domestic pro-protectionist constituencies by signalling commitment to their interests in the form of non-compliance.

D Conclusion

In this chapter, we have presented an overview of existing arguments and research on the performance of the WTO in inducing first and second order compliance with WTO law. A comprehensive understanding of the performance of the WTO DSM in inducing compliance has to come to terms with both the degree to which WTO Members conduct trade policies that are in line with their commitments under WTO law and the degree to which Members bring their policies into line after they have been challenged by a trade partner and/or ruled upon by the WTO DSB. In this literature review with a research outlook, we have sketched the state-of-the-art of the political science and political economy literature on this topic of great importance to the stability and predictability of the world trading regime, while highlighting some of the challenges ahead.

For one, the identification of economic and political sources of dispute initiation at the WTO has to confront the tip-of-the-iceberg issue. This refers to the question of which potential disputes might never come to the water's surface, and which subset of those surface as the tip of the iceberg, i.e. which cases WTO Members actually table as disputes in Geneva. Whereas identifying such a universe of potential cases is inherently difficult and incomplete, a feasible and reliable empirically grounded way of approximating this universe is to rely on evidence collected by WTO Members on trade barriers and impediments abroad. This should inform us on the systematic causes of initiation and non-initiation of WTO disputes.

Second, there is the question of compliance in actual dispute settlement cases, i.e. whether or not Members bring their policies into line with complainants' demands and/or the rulings of the DSB and is thus concerned with the melting of the tip of the iceberg, i.e. the actual dispute settlement cases. While compliance is an essentially contested concept with an inherently unstable meaning, we have argued that for empirical research purposes it is very useful to conceptualise it simply as meeting a complainant's demands, and to gauge the potential causes for swift resolution of disputes at the WTO.

While we have restricted our coverage of existing literature and our speculation about possible ways forward, the results coming out of this rich literature should also be able to inform us about the performance of compliance and enforcement institutions in PTAs. Increasingly being part of such agreements, but as yet attracting relatively few formal dispute settlement cases, the judicial institutions being put into place in PTAs might well be understood and explained with the help of the conjectures and findings that research on WTO dispute settlement has already generated.

References

Allee, Todd. 2005. *The 'Hidden' Impact of the World Trade Organization on the Reduction of Trade Conflict. 2005 Midwest Political Science Association Conference.* Chicago, Illinois.

Antràs, Pol and Staiger, Robert W. 2012. 'Offshoring and the Role of Trade Agreements'. *American Economic Review* 102(7): 3140–3183.

Baccini, Leonardo and Kim, Soo Yeon. 2012. 'Preventing Protectionism: International Institutions and Trade Policy'. *Review of International Organizations* 7 (4): 369–398.

Bagwell, Kyle and Staiger, Robert W. 2001. 'The WTO as a Mechanism for Securing Market Access Property Rights: Implications for Global Labor and Environmental Issues'. *Journal of Economic Perspectives* 15(3): 69–88.

Bernauer, Thomas, Elsig, Manfred and Pauwelyn, Joost. 2014. 'Dispute Settlement Mechanism: Analysis and Problems'. In *The Oxford Handbook on The World Trade Organization*, edited by M. Daunton, A. Narlikar and R. M. Stern, 485–506. Oxford: Oxford University Press.

Bown, Chad. 2004a. 'On the Economic Success of GATT/WTO Dispute Settlement'. *Review of Economics and Statistics* 86 (3): 811–823.

Bown, Chad. 2004b. 'Trade Disputes and the Implementation of Protection under the GATT: An Empirical Assessment'. *Journal of International Economics* 62 (2): 263–294.

Bown, Chad. 2005. 'Trade Remedies and World Trade Organization Dispute Settlement: Why Are so Few Challenged?' *Journal of Legal Studies* 34 (2): 515–555.

Bown, Chad. 2009. *Self-enforcing Trade*. Washington, DC: Brookings.

Bown, Chad and Pauwelyn, Joost. 2010. *The Law, Economics and Politics of Retaliation in WTO Dispute Settlement*. Cambridge, UK: Cambridge University Press.

Bown, Chad and Reynolds, Kara M. 2014. 'Trade Flows and Trade Disputes'. *World Bank Policy Research working paper* (WPS 6979).

Busch, Marc L. 2000. 'Democracy, Consultation, and the Paneling of Disputes under GATT'. *Journal of Conflict Resolution* 44(4): 425–446.

Busch, Marc L. 2007. 'Overlapping Institutions, Forum Shopping, and Dispute Settlement in International Trade'. *International Organization* 61 (4): 735–761.

Busch, Marc L. and Pelc, Krzysztof J. 2010. 'The Politics of Judicial Economy at the World Trade Organization'. *International Organization* 64 (2): 257–279.

Busch, Marc L. and Reinhardt, Eric. 2000. 'Bargaining in the Shadow of the Law: Early Settlement in GATT/WTO Disputes'. *Fordham International Law Journal* 24 (1): 158–172.

Busch, Marc L. and Reinhardt, Eric. 2003a. 'Developing Countries and GATT/ WTO Dispute Settlement'. *Journal of World Trade* 37 (4): 719–735.

Busch, Marc L. and Reinhardt, Eric. 2003b. 'Transatlantic Trade Conflicts and GATT/WTO Dispute Settlement'. In *Transatlantic Economic Disputes: The EU, The US, and the WTO*, edited by Ernst-Ulrich Petersmann and Marc A. Pollack. Oxford: Oxford University Press, 465–485.

Busch, Marc L. and Reinhardt, Eric. 2006. 'Three's a Crowd: Third Parties and WTO Dispute Settlement'. *World Politics* 58 (3): 446–477.

Busch, Marc L., Reinhardt, Eric and Shaffer, Gregory. 2009. 'Does Legal Capacity Matter? A Survey of WTO Members'. *World Trade Review* 8 (4): 559–577.

Davey, William J. 2007. 'Implementation in WTO Dispute Settlement: An Introduction to the Problems and Possible Solutions'. *Illinois Public Law Research Paper* 05–16.

Davis, Christina L. 2003. *Food Fights over Free Trade: How International Institutions and Issue Linkage Promote Agricultural Trade Liberalization*. Princeton: Princeton University Press.

Davis, Christina L. 2008. *The Effectiveness of WTO Dispute Settlement: An Evaluation of Negotiations versus Adjudication Strategies. Annual Meeting of the American Political Science Association*. Boston.

Davis, Christina L. 2012. *Why Adjudicate? Enforcing Trade Rules in the WTO*. Princeton, NJ: Princeton University Press.

Davis, Christina L. and Bermeo, Sarah B. 2009. 'Who Files? Developing Country Participation in GATT/WTO Adjudication'. *Journal of Politics* 71 (3): 1033–1049.

Davis, Christina L. and Shirato, Yuki. 2007. 'Firms, Governments, and WTO Adjudication: Japan's Selection of WTO Disputes'. *World Politics* 59 (2): 274–313.

De Bièvre, Dirk and Poletti, Arlo. 2015. 'Judicial Politics in International Trade Relations: Introduction to the Special Issue'. *World Trade Review* 14 (SupplementS1): S1–S11.

De Bièvre, Dirk, Poletti, Arlo, Hanegraaff, Marcel and Beyers, Jan. 2016. 'International Institutions and Interest Mobilization. The WTO and Lobbying in EU and US Trade Policy'. *Journal of World Trade* 50 (2): 289–312.

Dixon, William J. 1993. 'Democracy and the Management of International Conflict'. *Journal of Conflict Resolution* 37 (1): 42–68.

Dür, Andreas, Baccini, Leonardo and Elsig, Manfred. 2014. 'The Design of International Trade Agreements: Introducing a New Dataset'. *Review of International Organizations* 9 (3): 353–375.

Dür, Andreas and Elsig, Manfred (eds.). 2014. *Trade Cooperation: The Purpose, Design and Effects of Preferential Trade Agreements*. Cambridge: Cambridge University Press.

Elsig, Manfred and Stucki, Philipp. 2012. 'Low-Income Developing Countries and WTO Litigation: Why Wake Up the Sleeping Dog?' *Review of International Political Economy* 19 (2): 292–316.

Fearon, James D. 1994. 'Domestic Political Audiences and the Escalation of International Disputes'. *American Political Science Review* 88 (3): 577–592.

Frieden, Jeffry. 1991. 'Invested Interests: The Politics of National Economic Policies in a World of Global Finance'. *International Organization* 45 (4): 425–451.

Garrett, Geoffrey and Smith, James M. 2002. 'The Politics of WTO Dispute Settlement'. *UCLA Occasional Papers Series.*

Gilligan, M.J. 1997. 'Lobbying as a Private Good with IIT'. *International Studies Quarterly* 41 (3): 455–474.

Goldstein, Judith L. and Martin, Lisa L. 2000. 'Legalization, Trade Liberalization, and Domestic Politics: A Cautionary Note'. *International Organization* 54 (3): 603–632.

Goldstein, Judith L. and Steinberg, Richard H. 2008. 'Negotiate or Litigate? Effects of WTO Judicial Delegation on US Trade Politics'. *Law and Contemporary Problems* 71(1): 257–282.

Guzman, Andrew T. and Simmons, Beth A. 2002. 'To Settle or Empanel? An Empirical Analysis of Litigation and Settlement at the WTO'. *Journal of Legal Studies* 31 (1): 205–227.

Guzman, Andrew T. and Simmons, Beth A. 2005. 'Power Plays and Capacity Constraints: The Selection of Defendants in World Trade Organization Disputes'. *Journal of Legal Studies* 34 (2): 557–598.

Harpaz, Marcia. 2010. 'Sense and Sensibilities of China and WTO Dispute Settlement'. *Journal of World Trade* 44 (6): 1155–1186.

Horn, Henrik, Johannesson, Louise and Mavroidis, Petros C. 2011. 'The WTO Dispute Settlement System 1995–2010'. *Journal of World Trade* 45 (6): 1107–1138.

Horn, Henrik, Mavroidis, Petros C. and Nordström, Håkan. 1999. 'Is the Use of the WTO Dispute Settlement System Biased?' *Discussion paper 2340*. London: CEPR.

Hudec, Robert E. 1992. *Enforcing International Trade Law: The Evolution of the Modern GATT Legal System*. Salem: Butterworth.

Irwin, Douglas A. and Mavroidis, Petros C. 2008. 'The WTO's Difficulties in Light of the GATT's History'. *Vox*. http://voxeu.org/article/wto-failure-light-gatt-s-historys.

Johns, Leslie and Pelc, Krzysztof J. 2014. 'Who Gets to Be in the Room? Manipulating Participation in WTO Disputes'. *International Organization* 68 (03): 663–699.

Kelemen, R. Daniel 2001. 'The Limits of Judicial Power: Trade-Environment Disputes in the GATT/WTO and the EU'. *Comparative Political Studies* 34 (6): 622–650.

Kennedy, Daniel L.M. and Southwick, James D. 2002. *The Political Economy of International Trade Law. Essays in Honor of Robert E. Hudec*. Cambridge: Cambridge University Press.

Keohane, Robert. 1984. *After Hegemony: Cooperation and Discord in the World Political Economy*. Princeton, NJ: Princeton University Press.

Kim, Moonhawk. 2008. 'Costly Procedures: Divergent Effects of Legalization in the GATT/WTO Dispute Settlement Procedures'. *International Studies Quarterly* 52 (3): 657–686.

Manger, Mark S. 2012. 'Vertical Trade Specialization and the Formation of North-South PTAs'. *World Politics* 64 (4): 622–658.

Mansfield, Edward D., Milner, Helen V. and Rosendorff, B. Peter. 2002. 'Why Democracies Cooperate More: Electoral Control and International Trade Agreements'. *International Organization* 56 (3): 477–513.

Martin, Lisa L. 1992. 'Interests, Power, and Multilateralism'. *International Organization* 46 (4): 765–792.

Mavroidis, Petros C. 2006. 'If I Don't Do It, Somebody Else Will (or Won't)'. *Journal of World Trade* 40 (1): 187–214.

Mavroidis, Petros C. 2015. 'Dealing with PTAs in the WTO: Falling Through the Cracks Between "Judicialization" and "Legalization"'. *World Trade Review* 14 (SupplementS1): S107–S121.

Mayer, Wolfgang. 1981. 'Theoretical Considerations on Negotiated Tariff Adjustments'. *Oxford Economic Papers* 33 (1): 135–153.

Milner, Helen and Moravcsik, Andrew (eds.). 2009. *Power, Interdependence, and Nonstate Actors in World Politics*. Princeton, NJ: Princeton University Press.

Olson, Mancur. 1965. *The Logic of Collective Action. Public Goods and the Theory of Groups*. Cambridge, MA: Harvard University Press.

Orefice, Gianluca and Rocha, Nadia. 2014. 'Deep Integration and Production Networks: An Empirical Analysis'. *The World Economy* 37 (1): 106–136.

Pauwelyn, Joost. 2000. 'Enforcement and Countermeasures in the WTO: Rules Are Rules – Toward a More Collective Approach'. *American Journal of International Law* 94: 335–347.

Pauwelyn, Joost. 2010. 'The Dog that Barked but Didn't Bite: 15 Years of Intellectual Property Disputes at the WTO'. *Journal of International Dispute Settlement* 1(2): 389–429.

Petersmann, Ernst-Ulrich and Pollack, Mark A. (eds.). 2003. *Transatlantic Economic Disputes: The EU, the US, and the WTO*. Oxford: Oxford University Press.

Poletti, Arlo. 2010. 'Drowning Protection in the Multilateral Bath: WTO Judicialisation and European Agriculture in the Doha Round'. *British Journal of Politics & International Relations* 12 (4): 615–633.

Poletti, Arlo. 2011. 'World Trade Organization Judicialization and Preference Convergence in EU Trade Policy: Making the Agent's Life Easier'. *Journal of European Public Policy* 18 (3): 361–382.

Poletti, Arlo and De Bièvre, Dirk. 2014. 'Political Mobilization, Veto Players, and WTO Litigation: Explaining European Union Responses in Trade Disputes'. *Journal of European Public Policy* 21 (8): 1181–1198.

Poletti, Arlo and De Bièvre, Dirk. 2016. *Judicial Politics and International Cooperation: From Disputes to Deal Making at the WTO*. Colchester: ECPR Press.

Poletti, Arlo, De Bièvre, Dirk and Hanegraaff, Marcel. 2015. 'WTO Judicial Politics and EU Trade Policy: Business Associations as Vessels of Special Interest?' *The British Journal of Politics & International Relations*. doi: 10.1111/1467-856X.12071.

Priest, George and Klein, Benjamin. 1984. 'The Selection of Disputes for Litigation'. *Journal of Legal Studies* 13 (1): 1–55.

Sattler, Thomas and Bernauer, Thomas. 2011. 'Gravitation or Discrimination? Determinants of Litigation in the World Trade Organisation'. *European Journal of Political Research* 50 (2): 143–167.

Sattler, Thomas, Spilker, Gabriele and Bernauer, Thomas. 2014. 'Does WTO Dispute Settlement Enforce or Inform?' *British Journal of Political Science* 44 (4): 877–902.

Slaughter, Anne-Marie. 1995. 'International Law in a World of Liberal States'. *European Journal of International Law* 6 (1): 503–538.

Spilker, Gabriele. 2011. 'Compliance with WTO Dispute Rulings'. *NCCR Trade Working Paper* 2011/25.

Spilker, Gabriele. 2012. 'Helpful Organizations: Membership in Inter-Governmental Organizations and Environmental Quality in Developing Countries'. *British Journal of Political Science* 42 (2): 345–370.

Timmer, Marcel P., Dietzenbacher, Erik, Los, Bart, Stehrer, Robert and de Vries, Gaaitzen J. 2015. 'An Illustrated User Guide to the World

Input–Output Database: The Case of Global Automotive Production'. *Review of International Economics* 23 (3): 575–605.

Tomz, Michael R. 2007. 'Domestic Audience Costs in International Relations: An Experimental Approach'. *International Organization* 61 (4): 821–840.

Wilson, Bruce. 2007. 'Compliance by WTO Members with Adverse WTO Dispute Settlement Rulings: The Record to Date'. *Journal of International Economic Law* 10 (2): 397–403.

Young, Alasdair R. 2004. 'The Incidental Fortress: The Single European Market and World Trade'. *Journal of Common Market Studies* 42 (2): 393–414.

Young, Alasdair R. 2009. 'Confounding Conventional Wisdom: Political Not Principled Differences in the Transatlantic Regulatory Relationship'. *British Journal of Politics and International Relations* 11 (4): 666–689.

Young, Alasdair R. 2010. 'Effective Multilateralism on Trial: EU Compliance with WTO Law'. In *The EU's Presence in International Organisations*, edited by S. Blavoukos and D. Bourantonis. Abingdon: Routledge, 114–131.

Young, Alasdair R. 2011. 'Of Executive Preferences and Societal Constraints: The Domestic Politics of the Transatlantic GMO Dispute'. *Review of International Political Economy* 18 (4): 506–529.

Zangl, Bernhard. 2008. 'Judicialization Matters! A Comparison of Dispute Settlement Under GATT and the WTO'. *International Studies Quarterly* 52(4): 825–854.

Zangl, Bernhard, Helmedach, Achim, Mondré, Aletta, Kocks, Alexander, Neubauer, Gerald and Blome, Kerstin. 2012. 'Between Law and Politics: Explaining International Dispute Settlement Behavior'. *European Journal of International Relations* 18(2): 369–401.

7

The WTO Dispute Settlement System

Consolidating Success and Confronting New Challenges

GIORGIO SACERDOTI

A Introduction

On reaching its twentieth anniversary, the Dispute Settlement System (DSS) of the World Trade Organization (WTO) continues to be considered a success story, and rightly so. The mechanism has been defined by a former Director General as the 'jewel in the crown' of the WTO, a statement which is even more justified in light of the failure of the WTO Members to conclude the Doha Development Round (started in 2001), notwithstanding the limited success of the Bali (2013) and Nairobi (2015) Ministerial Conferences and to reinforce other non-judicial mechanisms within the WTO. The DSS, specifically the Appellate Body (AB), is now taken as a model for 'judicialising' other fields, an example being the recent European Union (EU) proposal to replace investor–state arbitration (ISDS) with a two-level international tribunal in the Transatlantic Trade and Investment Partnership (TTIP).[1] At its beginning, however, the DSS was criticised both by some WTO Members[2] and by non-governmental organisations (NGOs) for allegedly devolving to unrepresentative international 'faceless judges' – accused moreover of

The author is grateful for the reflections shared with him by Members of the WTO Secretariat, AB Members and delegates who agreed to be informally interviewed in Geneva and Brussels while he was preparing this chapter. A slightly shorter version of this text has been published as Chapter 4 of 'The Future of the Global Trade Order' (Carlos Braga and Bernard Hoekman eds.), IMD/EUI 2016 under the title 'The Future of the WTO Dispute Settlement System: Consolidating a Success Story'.

[1] See the full text at http://trade.ec.europa.eu/doclib/docs/2015/november/tradoc_153955.pdf. A two-level, permanent bilateral Investment Court, replacing Investor-State traditional dispute settlement arbitration, has been introduced in the final revised text of the Canada-EU Trade and Investment Agreement (CETA) at the beginning of 2016, see EU Commission, trade doc. 154329 (February 2016) and at www.international.gc.ca, Final CETA text.

[2] Notably by members of the US Congress.

indulging in 'judicial activism' – disputes also affecting non-trade interest and individual governments' regulatory powers.

The shift to a more positive evaluation is based on:

The high number of cases introduced (the 500 mark was reached in November 2015) and the very high proportion of cases resolved effectively by the removal of measures found to be in breach of WTO obligations (some 90 per cent of those brought to adjudication).

The effective functioning of its multistage procedure (from consultation to implementation, through a double-stage adjudication phase), which is meant to solve specific, mostly bilateral disputes, but at the same time to give guidance to all the interested members and to take into account the multilateral dimension of the trading system.

The participation of both major trading powers and small developing countries (signalling the importance of the DSS also for small players and developing economies to ensure access for their products to the larger economies' markets).

The development of a balanced and consistent case law, sensitive to non-trade concerns such as environment protection and health, which recognises on one hand the need to uphold market access obligations, and on the other hand the existence of evolving non-trade values and policies – domestic and international – that need to be safeguarded as part of the domestic policy space of WTO Members.

This has afforded 'stability and predictability' to the system (as set forth in Article 3.2 of the Dispute Settlement Understanding, or DSU), also in the recent times of financial crisis and economic slowdown. According to official documentation, opportunistic resort to protectionist measures (such as anti-dumping, subsidies, and safeguard actions) has been contained, although independent research tends to challenge this claim and has a more pessimistic, especially once more 'murky' measures are taken into account.[3]

On the other hand, the system shows signs of stress (as a victim of its own success, mainly due to the increase in the number of disputes and their complexity), while multilateral negotiations in the Doha Round are lagging. The following major issues have emerged which threaten its

[3] For a relatively positive view, see the various reports submitted by the WTO to the G20 meetings pursuant to the latter's request and the related data available at http://tmdb.wto.org. For a more critical assessment, see the reports of the Global Trade Alert at www.globaltradealert.org.

effectiveness and may thus diminish the trust in, and recourse to, the system:

1. The increasing number of cases brought to panels and the increasing complexity of disputes and sophistication of arguments made is extending the length of proceedings beyond reasonableness, especially at the panel stage, and is putting strain on the limited resources of the Secretariat.
2. The willingness of losing respondents to promptly comply with the decisions appears to be decreasing, in that effective implementation, while usually performed, requires on average more time. Alternatives to compliance (such as compensation), which appear to be on the rise, may tilt the system towards the protection of the interests of major trading nations, who may be able to pay off weaker Members while maintaining their import restrictions.
3. WTO Members appear to be unable to agree on further liberalisation (notably in services) and on adding new rules to the multilateral system to face new issues (such as the green economy, environmental subsidies or electronic commerce). This leads to a possibly problematic role of 'gap-filling' and 'law-making' for the DSS, which was not intended.
4. The parallel massive increase of regional trade agreements (RTAs), to which WTO Members are increasingly turning (including 'mega-RTAs' such as the TPP and the TTIP), risks reducing the relevance of the WTO and therefore possibly of its DSS, which moreover might find competitors in the dispute settlement mechanisms of RTAs.[4]

This chapter addresses these issues and points to possible solutions, several of which have already been aired in various circles in the past. These proposals fall into two groups. The first group is meant to address the most pressing problem at present, which has been raised more than once by countries concerned at the Dispute Settlement Body (DSB), namely, delays in the process at the panel stage due to the lack of legal resources in the Secretariat to staff the many panels that are being established.[5]

[4] It has been noted that RTAs have practically never been challenged in the WTO DSS. This could be due to the fact that they are considered by and large to be compliant with WTO obligations. Alternatively, it is possible that participants in RTAs refrain from challenging other RTAs in order to avoid provoking challenges to their own (the compliance of any RTA with all WTO requirements being doubtful).

[5] A forceful complaint was that by Korea at the DSB of 31 August 2015. Korea complained that in DSS 488, where Korea challenged US anti-dumping measures, the Secretariat had notified Korea that the panel established on 25 March 2015 would not begin its work until the end of 2016 at the earliest, a date some 15 months from the time Korea had been

The second set of proposals centres on broader changes to remedy structural problems which involve changes to the DSU that can be adopted within the current framework.

B Achievements

On November 10, 2015, the WTO website featured as a news item a statement by Director-General (DG) Roberto Azevêdo celebrating the receipt of the 500th trade dispute for settlement. He argued that this showed 'that the WTO's dispute settlement system enjoys tremendous confidence among the membership, who value it as fair, effective and efficient mechanism to solve trade problems'. The 500th dispute was submitted on 10 November 2015, when Pakistan filed a request for consultations with South Africa regarding the latter's provisional anti-dumping duty on cement from Pakistan. The parties involved and the subject matter of the dispute are also significant, because they show that developing countries use the system both as complainants and respondents in South-South relations, and that trade remedy measures feature importantly in matters brought to the WTO.

The news item included comments and data that are the starting point of our analysis, taking stock of the achievements of the DSS as an introduction for addressing the current issues in a system that has been, and is, successful in offering an orderly rule-based solution to trade frictions, but that shows signs of stress (in part due to its own success). The success is evidenced by the fact that resort to the DSS has become a normal feature in the operating of the multilateral trading system, displacing resort to unilateral measures. Practice has confirmed what had been set forth in Article 3.10 DSU, namely that 'requests for conciliation and the use of the dispute settlement procedures should not be intended or considered as contentious acts'. This setting distinguishes the WTO from other international fora, where respondents often raise lack of jurisdiction as a preliminary objection to escape the process. It makes it more businesslike, as is the case in the national context.

Of the 500 disputes notified to the WTO, only 282 have been brought to litigation. Resolution through bilateral negotiations, including formal

notified of the delay, not because the panelists were unavailable, but due to the constraints affecting the Secretariat. Korea pointed out that this 'remarkable, extraordinary, unreasonable delay' in light of both the DSU provisions and the economic reality, just for the case to get started 'was almost twice as long as the period foreseen by Art. 12.9 DSU between the establishment of the panel and the circulation of the report'.

withdrawal of the request, has been notified to the WTO in 110 of the cases, while the parties have not informed the WTO of the status of the other 108 (which must be considered dormant or de facto settled).[6] As of the end of 2014, 201 panel reports had been issued, of which 136 had been appealed (68 per cent of the total, on average). In 2014, thirteen panel requests were appealed, while the AB issued eight reports concerning five matters.[7] In 2015, by the end of November four panel reports had been issued covering five disputes and eleven had been adopted by the DSB, while the AB had issued appellate reports in four disputes on different subject matters.[8]

Another measure of success is the broad participation of WTO Members in the DSS. As of November 2015, some two-thirds of the Members (102) had participated in dispute settlement proceedings, either as parties (claimants and/or respondents) or as third parties (35 Members as third parties only). Looking at the consultation requests, developing and developed countries are equally represented as complainants, while complaints are mostly directed towards developed countries.

As can be expected, the largest economies are both the most frequent initiators of cases (with the United States leading with 108, followed by the European Union, Canada, Brazil, Mexico, India, Japan and Argentina all above the twenty mark) and the most frequent defenders (with the United States again leading with 124, followed by the European Union, China, India and Argentina). Finally, the compliance mark is said to be about 90 per cent. Countermeasures in the form of withdrawal of benefits, i.e. imposition of selective additional duties, have been imposed only

[6] This lack of information signals the need to strengthen the obligation of Members to notify the WTO in a timely manner of the status and outcome of all disputes that have been formally filed.

[7] The data provided are drawn from those provided, mostly in the form of tables, by the DG in his statement to the DSB of 22 October 2015, those annexed to the AB Report for 2014 and those included in the news item of 12 November 2015 on the 500 mark. Some data are not easy to compare, especially since there is a difference with regards to the relevant year between panel and AB reports *issued* and *adopted* by the DSB. Moreover, some proceedings concern several disputes brought by different claimants against the same measure of the respondent State that are examined together by a single panel. On the other hand some appeals are formally separate (and counted individually) because the claimants are different but are dealt with in a single report.

[8] The exact numbers do not always match because of the different practice of the panels and the AB in calculating as single or separate disputes those in which different claimants challenge the same measures of the respondent state, the same panel being appointed to hear all the challenges.

in a handful of cases, while no Member has ever denied responsibility to comply with an unfavourable final decision.

Of course the number of disputes is not by itself a sign of a healthy system; what matters is the ability to process them on a timely basis and according to the rules.[9] Notwithstanding some delays in full compliance, there is no sentiment that WTO Members have become less inclined to respect the rules. On the other hand, a certain surge of national antidumping measures, as monitored by the AD Committee, could be a sign of increased pressure on export markets at a time of economic slowdown, to the point of being a sign of resort to unfair competition.[10] This is possibly a cyclical phenomenon, rather than a structural disregard for the rules.

In fact, Article 3.7 of the DSU would discourage Members from bringing disputes which might be resolved amicably without even resorting to the system, stating that '[b]efore bringing a case a Member shall exercise its judgment as to whether action under these procedures would be fruitful' and that '[a] solution mutually acceptable to the parties to the dispute and consistent with the covered agreement is clearly to be preferred'. In the same spirit of not considering the starting of a case to be an unfriendly act and encouraging at the same time parties to exercise some kind of self-restraint when considering bringing a case, Article 3.10 states in its final sentence that '[i]t is also understood that complaints and counter-complaints in regard to distinct matters should not be linked'.

This notwithstanding, on several recent occasions the initiation of a case by a country against another country has been immediately followed by the initiation of a separate case by the respondent in the previous case against the first country (notably between the United States and China and between Argentina and the United States and the European Union). Although there is no evidence that the second case was a kind of tit-for-tat response to the first one, this belief has been informally expressed as a sign of an abuse or political strategic use of the DSS contrary to its purpose.[11]

[9] According to the AB Report for 2014, p. 3, 'In its first 16 years the DSB has handled disputes spanning over USD 1 trillion in trade flows'.

[10] This could be the situation in the steel market, where sources indicate overproduction in the face of a decrease in demand (see https://www.steelorbis.com/steel-news/latest-news/oecd-steel-committee-calls-for-immediate-action-to-address-excess-capacity-909449.htm).

[11] See Robert Feinberg and Kara Reynolds, 'The Spread of Anti-Dumping Regimes and the Role of Retaliation in Filings', Southern Economic J., 72, 2006, 877–890; European Commission, Press Release (IP/13/772), European Union requests WTO Panel on Chinese Anti-Dumping duties on Steel Tubes, 16 August 2013, available at http://europa.eu/rapid/press-release-IP-13–772 en.htm

Finally, the smooth functioning of the DSS and the accumulation of consistent interpretations of key provisions of the WTO agreements, while not discouraging the bringing of new disputes, has made reliance on those provisions more firm. Outcomes are more foreseeable, thanks to the role of the AB in providing consistent case law on which panels in turn can rely. The overall role of the DSS has been expanded by the lack of action by Members in other capacities. Authoritative interpretations by the General Council acting under Article IX of the WTO Agreement have never been issued and other quasi-legislative action by Members, such as within WTO specialised committees, has been scant. Thus the DSS has remained the only source of authoritative guidance for the multilateral system at large.

C Current Problems

Panel proceedings should in theory not take more than six months (Article 12.9 DSU). Until recently, in practice panels tended to take around one-and-a-half years in 'normal' cases. Today, however, cases can take between two or three years from the formal establishment of the panel by the DSB to the circulation of their report. Panel reports are thereafter subject to appeal, where the Appellate Body faces increasing difficulties in respecting the short ninety-day period prescribed for issuing its own reports, not to speak of the further possible proceedings before full implementation by the losing party.[12] These time lags undermine the value of any favourable decision for obtaining effective redress against domestic measures in breach of WTO commitments, which is

[12] As an example, at a recent DSB meeting in 2015 Canada complained that four-and-a-half years after the establishment of the panel, the COOL dispute with the United States was still far from being settled. After the panel report and the appeal, there occurred the fixing by an arbitrator of a reasonable period of time for the United States to comply (which was not respected) and a compliance panel (Art. 21.5 DSU) ruling against the United States for Canada and Mexico (the other complainant), where the panel and the Appellate Body found that the measure taken by the United States had not brought compliance (but possibly even worsened the breach). The arbitration panel (Article 22.6 DSU) was just starting its work to establish whether the countermeasures announced by Canada and Mexico were excessive in comparison with the trade loss caused to them by the COOL measure, as submitted by the United States. President Obama announced the repeal of the relevant US provisions on 18 December 2015, just a few days after the arbitration panel had concluded its work, determining the level of retaliation that Canada and Mexico could put in place to offset the adverse effect of COOL on their exports. For a realistic view, see *The Economist* (2015).

especially damaging in respect of temporary measures such as anti-dumping duties.

More broadly, this dysfunctional dimension of the operation of the DSS, in disregard of one of its basic tenets and praised features, namely its speed, may undermine the whole operation of the system and recourse to it as the key instrument for ensuring respect of trade-opening commitments. As stated by Korea at the DSB meeting of 31 August 2015:

> WTO disputes are not about abstract disagreements. Real world economic interests underlay every dispute. There were real people suffering while a dispute was pending ... The problem would get worse if left unaddressed. Long delays created perverse incentive by lowering the cost of adopting and maintaining WTO-inconsistent measures, insisting, rightly, that they would not be subject to review by the WTO for years. Members could therefore expect more protectionist measures and more, not less disputes being brought to the WTO. These in turn, would cause further delays, prompting a vicious, never-ending cycle. It was in the interest of everyone, the parties, the wider membership and the Secretariat not to let this happen.[13]

It is curious, however, that Korea itself, followed by other speakers, did not ask for more effective remedies beyond increased transparency and

[13] Doc. WT/DSB/M/ 367, pp. 22–29. The concerns of Korea were shared at the meeting by a number of countries, starting with Guatemala whose delegate stated aptly, '[t]he WTO dispute settlement system was one of the most effective and prompt international systems of adjudication. Victim of its own success, the system faces the risk of becoming slower. If no effective action were taken to address this unfortunate situation, the principle of "prompt settlement of disputes" in art. 3.3. DSU would become a mere "best effort" provision, not more than an illusionary aspiration . . . long delays in the DSS mechanism may create perverse incentives for the adopting political motivated WTO-inconsistent measures.' Other interventions came from (in order) Chile, China ('this unprecedented situation would seriously undermine the effectiveness and credibility of the WTO DSS'), Australia ('willing to consider any option that might help alleviate the current situation and improve the system over the long term. This included ensuring that the Secretariat had the resources needed to service disputes in a timely manner and also exploring ways for the Membership to reduce the burden on the system in terms of the length and complexity of disputes'), Russia, Mexico, Pakistan, Japan, Brazil, Canada, India, ('the credibility of the system was at stake'), the European Union ('manage the situation at hand' and 'find solutions to the mid and long-term situation against the background of ever increasing pressures in the WTO DSS'), Argentina, Chinese Taipei and Norway. In contrast with the serious concerns voiced by most other countries, the United States was more restrained, stating briefly that 'Korea has raised an important systemic issue . . . This raised some significant concerns, particularly in light of the fact that the WTO DSS had, for many years, operated with admirable concern. The US shared the view that Members needed a better understanding of the causes behind delays so that they could develop and consider appropriate solutions.'

information from the Secretariat as to the reasons for the 'queue', where cases stand in the queue and the outlook for 'their' case being decided. The same attitude prevailed in the discussion that followed the DG's lengthy and detailed statement at the DSB of 28 October 2015 (see below), where he made the point that the problems would not be resolved solely through administrative measures and shifting resources within the Secretariat. Several Members acknowledged this issue and decried the negative consequences of the current set on the effectiveness of the DSS, but abstained from launching any ideas for tackling the problems more seriously.[14]

I The Increased Number and Complexity of Disputes

In his statement at the DSB on 28 October 2015, the DG provided information on the increased use of the DSS and the increased complexity of cases that are putting a strain on the resources and generate delays. The DG pointed to the number of active panels that are operating at the same time, which reached thirty as of September 2015 (compared with 29 in 2014,[15] and an average of twenty between 2000 and 2013). The number of new panels established by the DSB had increased from six in 2010, to nine in 2011, to eleven in 2012, to thirteen in 2014 and finally to fifteen by September 2015.[16] Disputes have also become more complex in that more domestic measures of the respondent country are being challenged – currently each dispute involves an average of twenty-eight measures and 180 claims. The evidentiary burden before panels is also more demanding – one ongoing dispute (and not one of the two massive Boeing-Airbus aircraft disputes, which are still before the panels under Article 21.5 at the compliance stage) has reached more than 1,700 exhibits just at the initial stage. 'On average, there are three times as many exhibits per panel now than in early WTO days', noted the DG.

14 See the minutes of the meeting at WT/DSB/M/369 of January 20th, 2016, p. 20. Deputy-Director General Brauner has been entrusted by the DG to follow up with the Members on these issues.

15 Nineteen panels in operation (12 in trade remedies and seven in other areas), 11 in composition, besides three appeals and two arbitrations on the reasonable period of time pending.

16 The issue of delays at the panel level caused by resource constraints in the Secretariat had been already raised at the DSB in 2014, and the DG explained the shifts and increase in legal resources he had undertaken in a statement at the DSB meeting of September 26th, 2014. This statement and the data provided are to be found in the AB report for 2014, 93 ff.

Another complexity relates to the requests by parties for preliminary procedural rulings (for example, to declare some claims inadmissible because they were not included in the initial request for consultations), which has become almost a standard feature in panel proceedings, adding submissions or exhibits, and therefore requiring more time of the Secretariat and the panelists.[17] This is a typical lawyers' trick that shows how much the system has tilted – as have other arbitral *fora* – towards judicialisation, when a more conciliatory approach originally prevailed and was assumed.

The increase in the number of disputes brought to the WTO has led to the delay in the effective initiation of the DS process, once the DSB formally has established a panel at the second meeting in which a Member has requested this, pursuant to Article 6.1 DSU. The DSU envisages in Article 8.7 that a panel be composed – that is, the panelists be appointed – 20 days thereafter, if the parties agree on the names suggested by the Secretariat (Article 8.6), or within an additional 10-day period if the DG appoints them due to lack of agreement. Recently, however, the practice has been for several months to elapse between establishment and composition or between composition and initiation of the panel process. This is not due to procedurally difficulties but is a deliberate, inevitable choice by the Secretariat because of a lack of resources to staff the panels. The difficulty of finding suitable panelists due to the high demand caused by the number of panels operating at the same time adds an increased layer of difficulty and possibility for delay.[18] It must be said that the situation of an adjudicating body (to which a dispute has been submitted) not even starting to examine the matter for several months is not unprecedented at the international level, where various courts and their member states strive to find solutions to the increasing recourse to adjudication.[19] This is however not a justification for the WTO not to stick

[17] The high number of third parties in many proceedings (up to 36 in a recent case) adds also complexity in the handling of cases by panels.

[18] Besides the 15-month delay complained about by Korea at the DSB of August 31st, 2015 referred to above, the most recent document on the issue is telling. On 6 October 2015 the chairman of the panel in a case between the European Union and Brazil (joined to one on the same issue initiated by Brazil against Japan, DS 472 and 497) informed that the panel established on 17 December 2014 and composed more than three months later on 17 March 2015 expected to issue its report by the end of 2016, more than two years after the European Union had obtained the institution of the panel in order to obtain the withdrawal of the measures by Brazil that it had challenged.

[19] In the European Union it was decided in 2015 to double from the numbers of the judges of the first level tribunal (the General Court) from 28 to 56. At the European Court of Human Rights, various procedural devices have been introduced through the years (such as increasing the possibility of summarily dismissing petitions for manifest inadmissibility) to cope with the explosion of recourses (which, however, are predominantly from private parties in both *fora*).

to its short deadlines which are one of the most distinctive and positive features of its dispute settlement system.

In his statement to the DSB on 28 October 2015, following that of 26 September 2014 on the same issues,[20] the DG presented various measures he had put in place to add resources to the Secretariat to address the most pressing problems, and to bolster the capacity to manage the dispute settlement case load.[21] The DG underlined that the measures he was taking to reinforce the human/legal resources available to panels and reorganise the cooperation between the Legal and Rules Divisions would not resolve the structural problems or prevent an increase of the backlog[22] and warned the Members that more is needed. The DG invoked the cooperation of the Members, specifically of the disputing parties, to 'alleviate the pressure on the system' and to avoid a collective failure. In this respect, he alluded to 'Member-driven, demand-side solutions', without indicating specific initiatives, which might be beyond his powers. He launched, procedurally, a cautious consultation process with Members within the WTO to devise solutions that could be implemented by best practices without implying DSU amendments (such as limiting the number of pages of briefs or the number of exhibits).

However, the unconcerned attitude of most WTO Members as to these issues, at least until recently (they see the problems but prefer to leave any solution to the DG, though conscious of its limited capabilities to resolve them), does not bode well for any effective solution. On the contrary, the DSS not being too efficient and allowing delays in implementation and

[20] His first intervention on the subject was at a DSB in September 2014, when he announced the creation of 15 new lawyer posts in the three dispute settlement divisions: Legal Affairs, Rules, and the AB. However, the organisation had difficulties in filling these. In his address to the DSB on 28 October 2015 the DG explained in detail the further steps he had taken and was taking to mitigate delays, consisting mostly of reallocating of personnel; hiring new legal staff; adjusting the grades and salaries to the competence of the lawyers, taking into account the competition by law firms; increasing internal mobility; and pooling junior lawyers of both divisions assisting panels. This should result in more efficiency and has already nearly doubled the relevant positions – from thirty to fifty-seven – since 2013.

[21] An important initiative of the Legal Affairs Division has been the launch of the WTO Digital Dispute Settlement Registry, which will allow electronic filing of submissions and secure access to briefs and documents by the parties, besides serving as an electronic repository of all panel and AB records and providing easy online access to non-confidential information on cases to the public.

[22] The merging of the two divisions could also be envisaged, fully pooling the resources devoted to the DSS while maintaining the distinct expertise of the Rule Division in trade remedy disputes.

political twisting may even accommodate some frequent users of the DSS. They may view themselves more as defendants and thus not in a hurry to implement changes through politically difficult domestic processes of compliance, rather than as successful claimants eager to obtain as promptly as possible the other party's due market opening to the benefit of its producers and exporters.

It is unlikely that the tendency to have recourse to the DSS will slow down, in view of the increased favour for litigation at the international level, the increase of instances where trade obligations collide with the exercise of domestic regulatory powers and the increase in WTO Members that are actively engaged in international trade matters.

D Proposals

While the practical measures at the administrative level implemented by the DG are steps in the right direction, a focus on increasing human resources – i.e. competent lawyers – in the WTO's Legal Affairs Division and the Rule Division (the units in the WTO that service panels) does not seem sufficient to fix the problem. Other solutions may be called for that go beyond the decisions that can be taken by the DG. Accordingly, the proposals discussed in what follows are more far reaching and forward looking, as they are meant to address the long-term sustainability of the DSS with regards to effectiveness and outputs. While these proposals do not require any overhaul of the current system, and do not affect the basic tenets of the original WTO DSS, their adoption (as would any other proposal to this effect) would require a broad consensus of the membership. This is currently lacking, and not just in relation to these issues.

More substantial reforms to resolve the issue at the *panel level* requires considering more far-reaching options, such as:

1. Discouraging the bringing of complaints to the panel stage by making the initial phase (consultations) less of a mere formality, possibly with the engagement of the DG and resort to mediation and conciliation.
2. Putting more financial resources to the service of the legal Secretariat, overcoming the zero-growth budgetary constraint that tilts in favour of first shifting resources within the WTO Secretariat without the possibility of adding new resources from the legal market place.
3. Reorganising the legal Secretariat by merging the Legal Division with the Rule Division, a distinction that reflects a division of work from GATT times and which is not just any more.

4. Enlarging the available pool of panelists and the spread of nationalities (resorting also to non-governmental panelists from third parties in dispute); using more systematically available competent panelists (leading to the de facto creation of a pool of recurrent, semi-permanent panelists); and reducing procedural delays due to the 'interim report' and translation (the availability of a greater number of more devoted and competent panelists could in turn make it possible to rely more on them also for drafting, as is the practice in both international courts and investment or commercial arbitration).
5. Making the disputing parties pay a share of the costs of the proceedings, which are currently charged to the whole membership.

Other phases and aspects of the DSS also need interventions to make them more efficient. As to the *Appellate Body*, in view of the fact that the number of disputes brought to the panels is ever increasing, and thus will also lead to increasing cases going to the appellate stage, possible remedial solutions are:

1. Staffing the Appellate Body more adequately.
2. Increasing the number of Appellate Body Members from seven to nine.
3. Making their position permanent, a status that would also better ensure in the future the selection of competent, diverse and truly independent judges.
4. Replacing their four-year term, renewable once, with one non-renewable seven-year term, so to avoid any possible improper interference with their independence and impartiality by the WTO Members through the renewal process.

As to the implementation phase:

5. The monitoring role of the DSB should be made more effective in order to induce more prompt compliance.[23]

The procedure should be tightened so that the prospective nature of WTO remedies (the obligation to comply not being retroactive from the date of the breach but to be implemented only after a 'reasonable period of time' from the adoption of a panel or Appellate Body report) does not reward the losing party for dragging its feet with regards to compliance with adverse decisions.

[23] As advocated by Canadian Ambassador Jonathan Fried when he was chairman of the DSB in 2013.

Maintaining the efficiency of the DSS and its effectiveness in ensuring compliance with the WTO multilateral trade rules entails broader benefits beyond ensuring the effectiveness of expected trade openings from the commitments that WTO Members have undertaken, as important as these are.

It ensures at the same time the role of the WTO as the guardian of the multilateral trading system and the position of its multilateral rules as the accepted global framework within which interested countries may engage in regional trade agreements. RTAs should be the basis for extending international cooperation and trade liberalisation ('WTO-plus') without endangering the WTO acquis. They should represent building blocks, and not stumbling blocks, by establishing supplemental frameworks to further facilitate trade through coordinated regional action that should be supportive of the multilateral rules.

It must be recognised that the possible solutions to these current problems are not a quick fix that may be implemented without WTO Members engaging in the issues, evaluating the most appropriate remedies and being open to looking for shared improvements. That said, this is not an out-of-reach ambitious programme or an all-comprising shopping list. Rather, it is a realistic and modest agenda for fixing, within the existing framework, the current problems and enabling the DSS to go on serving the WTO Membership and complying with its objectives and purpose in the years to come. We do not propose to transform the panels to a first-instance tribunal, or to abolish the adoption of panel and AB reports or other similarly radical overhauls.

Moreover, there is a specific instrument for Members to discuss and elaborate the necessary amendments to the dispute settlement rules. This is the DSU review negotiation framework agreed by a Ministerial Declaration in 1994 and extended by the Doha Ministerial Declaration in 2001, under which amendments to the DSU may be agreed without having to activate the cumbersome WTO amendment process. This exercise should have been completed first by 1997/1999, and then by 2003, but it is still going on indefinitely at an almost standing pace.

I Remedies to Tackle the Root of the Problems

The inability of the current system to cope with the increase in litigation is due in great part to its structure, which at the panel and Secretariat levels is still basically patterned after the GATT model of panels. As is well known, these panels were made almost exclusively of governmental experts, picked *ad hoc* to resolve occasional specific disputes among trade diplomats in Geneva familiar with the system, reflecting the non-legal character of trade disputes in those days.[24] Even today, panelists are not professional judges or arbitrators – about half of them are trade diplomats based in Geneva who do not have a legal degree and normally work for their government. The rest is made of governmental experts. Academics are picked rarely to serve on the panels.

As a consequence, these panelists have to rely heavily on the lawyers of the Secretariat assigned to each panel (one senior and one junior, as a rule) to perform their job, from research, to organising hearings, to drafting. In the abstract, this approach appears contradictory in view of the professionalisation required and legalisation inserted in the system, but WTO Members are attached to the tradition of being judged by their peers and also value the assistance of the Secretariat as a guarantee of consistency.

Now that the flow of cases is constant and sustained, similar to or perhaps even more so than in a regular court, the system will be increasingly unable to perform its functions effectively unless (a) the Secretariat is expanded in consequence, including its budget; and/or (b) panelists are more devoted to the task and professional, that is, available on short notice to actively and exclusively perform their tasks and able to so more autonomously.[25]

This suggested configuration is found both in permanent international courts and within international commercial and investment arbitration under different models. At international courts, judges are mostly full time and are assisted by a centralised Secretariat and/or by one or two full-time individual clerks. The secretarial support is much less in international arbitration, even compared to the WTO – arbitrators are selected among recognised experts in the field who are able to research and draft by themselves, possibly with the support of personal assistants

[24] Small but important efficiency innovations could also affect the composition of panels, where parties often disregard the provision of Article 8.6 that '[t]he parties to the dispute shall not oppose nominations suggested by the Secretariat under the same provision except for *compelling reasons*', thus causing additional delays; and the suppression of the Interim Review Stage (Article 15), which has become redundant with the introduction of appeal.

[25] In December 2015 the General Council adopted a new fee pattern whereby non-governmental panelists now receive CHF (Swiss francs) 900 per day and government panelists 300.

from universities or their own law offices.[26] The support of the secretariat of the institution is limited to procedural matters and formal external review of the decision as autonomously prepared by the arbitrators themselves.

At the WTO such a development, that is, engaging more panelists while maintaining the unique role of the Secretariat, would in turn be facilitated by broadening the pool of potentially available panelists. The first easy change is to allow nationals of third parties to a dispute to be selected as panelists, provided they are non-governmental. Currently, nationals both of the litigating parties and of third parties can be appointed only with the consent of the parties (Article 8.3). Besides depriving the system of competent experts who could act as panelists[27] and thus relieving the shortage, this restriction leads to the panelists being chosen mostly from a small group of (small, mainly developing) countries that are rarely involved in disputes. This means that the representative character of the adjudicators is not in line with the geography of the litigants and the issues raised.[28]

Also, the procedure for selecting panelists, which is currently rather cumbersome and entails a delicate interaction between the Secretariat, the parties and the prospective panelists, should be streamlined so as to discourage parties from dragging their feet (Malacrida 2015). Transferred to the WTO, either model would require:

More financial resources to the legal Secretariat (Legal Affairs and Rule Divisions), also for compensating panelists;[29] adequate additional funding cannot be made available by just shifting funds within the budget, and a real increase of the budget and therefore of the Members' contribution would be required.

[26] The differences between the WTO DSS at the panel level and ISDS, especially as concerns origin, qualification and the role of the adjudicators, has been addressed recently in Pauwelyn (2015).

[27] This means that in practice, potential US, European, Japanese, Canadian, and Chinese panelists are hardly ever appointed, since the respective countries almost always participate as third parties to proceedings when they are not the main parties.

[28] Joost Pauwelyn has noted that by contrast, for investment disputes at ICSID, where most challenges involve developing countries, most arbitrators chosen are nationals of developed countries (Pauwelyn 2015).

[29] Governmental panelists currently work for free since they are supposed to act for the WTO during their working hours (the WTO pays a small sum to the Members that lend them); the others receive a small per diem, which does not reflect the engagement that should be required of them, even after a recent small increase. The issue has been recognised, and an increase was decided in December 2015, see note 24.

Having recourse to a (probably not so) *small group of recurrent panelists*, as is already de facto the case,[30] who should be able to ensure availability and capability of operating autonomously; they should therefore not be engaged currently in governmental work and be remunerated adequately.

Panels could thus operate somewhat like the AB, their members meeting for longer periods in Geneva during proceedings and immediately thereafter for the deliberation of their report. It would be for the Secretariat to go on giving support to the panelists in the form of research, previous case law and precedent, while active drafting could be more in the hands of the panelists or, in any case, of the chairman. The current role of the Secretariat would remain necessary in order to ensure that these ad hoc panels, composed of diverse members, do not endanger with their individual decision-making the consistency of case law (which is, in any case, subject to appellate review).

Such an evolution would not even require changes in the DSU provision. It would probably entail a change in the mix of panelists' backgrounds. There would be fewer active trade diplomats and more retired experts and persons with different backgrounds, such as academics and former officials from international organisations. Since high-quality reports are a must that is advocated by everybody concerned, it is difficult to see how this quality can be maintained without changes to the current system. The challenge is that the steady increase of complex disputes and sophisticated arguments (moreover increasingly exposed by expert lawyers from specialised resourceful law firms) require increasing the:

- legal competence of the adjudicators
- availability of legal support to them
- time they must be able to devote to each case
- remuneration of lawyers.

What this change requires is for guaranteed *additional financial resources*, whereas Members appear/like to believe that quick, high-quality and efficient justice may be obtained at no cost – an obvious impossibility. The mantra that Members are not ready to accept increases in the yearly budget ('zero-growth') of course renders a solution quite difficult. Hardly anybody has looked at *the costs of the DSS*, how it is financed and how it is apportioned among those who directly benefit

[30] Pauwelyn (2015) assessed that there are 15 panelists who have been appointed more than six times in recent years, and a high number of 'single shooters'.

from it. There is no accurate breakdown of the general costs of the WTO Secretariat and those pertaining to dispute settlement, because it appears that a consistent share of the latter (above the official figure of only 13 per cent of the total) is charged to general administrative costs. Looking at the official data on the WTO website, however, it appears that the services of the organisation cost little in absolute terms to the Members, and even less so the Dispute Settlement System.

The US contribution to the total WTO budget in 2015 is US$22 million, China pays US$16.8 million, Japan US$8.7 million, Brazil US$2.4 million, and the EU Members together (although they contribute individually) about US$75 million. Without commenting on the incredible imbalances that these figures reveal, especially considering the frequency of recourse to DSS by individual Members (such as Austria contributing almost as much as Australia, and Singapore almost twice that of Brazil), one is on the safe side submitting that just the costs of the lawyers engaged by either parties (including the lawyers of the industry concerned standing behind them) in the cases involving the United States are higher than the contribution of the United States to the whole WTO budget (and this is the same for any other country involved in disputes).[31] If the overall budget devoted to the DSS cannot be increased (some Members may even consider that this constraint is a way to put pressure on the DSS and its components by micromanaging any additional resource and their destination), one should reflect on an alternative solution – *making the users pay* for using the system (either through a fee system or having a separate budget for the DSS), as is the case in most courts and for the international secretariats administrating institutional arbitration, such as ICSID (International Centre for Settlement of Investment Disputes) or the ICC (International Chamber of Commerce).

A final item concerns the *demand side*. Is it possible to limit the number of cases brought to adjudication?

In this respect, it would be worth studying how to make the pre-adjudication phase (the *consultations*) more effective, possibly providing for the input of the Secretariat as legal-economic support (What is involved economically? What legal alternatives could be acceptable? What issues are in fact not in dispute?). Also recourse to 'good offices, conciliation and mediation' as envisaged in Article 5 as voluntary steps at any time during the dispute, for which the DG is available under

[31] By comparison, it has been stated that the legal costs of an average ICSID case are US$4 million.

Article 5.6, could be reinforced. They might be made compulsory as a preliminary stage for certain types of disputes.

Also related to the demand side is the frequency of compliance proceedings under Article 21.5 DSU. These are panel proceedings started by the original complainant who challenges the WTO consistency of the measures that the respondent has taken to comply with an unfavourable outcome. This entails the obligation to withdraw or amend appropriately the measure found inconsistent with the provisions invoked by the claimant (as per Articles 3.7 and 21). These disputes are heard by the original panel reconvened for this purpose, whose report may in turn be appealed. Article 21.5 claims are upheld in the DSS most of the time, signalling a lack of proper follow-up by respondents. At the same time, these proceedings consistently absorb resources of the system, especially considering that some of the most complex disputes have gone through this stage and thus appear almost never-ending (e.g. EC-Hormones; the two aircraft cases, Boeing /Airbus, US-COOL, just concluded after more than four years; US-Tuna II).[32] Some kind of simplified or accelerated proceedings should be devised for these cases, which are often the most complex. In these cases, the parties involved could be asked to assume the costs, which are currently charged to the whole membership.

II *Improving the Operation and Ensuring the Independence of the Appellate Body*

The problems faced by the panel stage and the Secretariat due to the increase in the number and complexity of disputes are now reaching the Appellate Body – lengthier panel reports,[33] more appeals pending at the same time, more complex cases with more issues appealed and more challenges raised.[34] Cross appeals have also become more frequent. This makes the issuance of shorter reports, as is also often advocated for panels, quite difficult.

[32] If the reports of the compliance panels in the two aircraft cases (DSB 316 and DSB 353) are issued as announced in mid-June 2016, this will be around four years after the two panels were composed in 2012. The *Australia Tobacco* dispute will also have lasted about four years at the panel stage if the report is issued as announced in mid-2016.

[33] The number of pages of 'average' panel reports has increased from forty-nine in 1996–2000 to 183 in 2010–2014, AB Report for 2014, at 94 (DG Statement of 26 September 2014).

[34] This evolution has been highlighted by the AB in a Communication of May 30th, 2013 ('The Workload of the Appellate Body').

This 'wave' may put additional pressure on the ability of the AB to perform its task in a timely manner while maintaining the high quality of its reports, for which it is generally praised and which represents a basis of the trust that the DSS inspires in Members and beneficiaries. The organisation of the AB under the relevant rules of the DSU (Article 17) leaves it little flexibility to cope with a regular higher number of cases; it is made of only seven Members, who decide in randomly composed divisions of three, and it must issue its reports within ninety days.

As to procedure, the AB has adopted in recent years several practical measures within its competence to establish its 'working procedures' (Article 17.9), including reducing the time framework in the initial phase of the process in order to have more time to examine the case and decide (in 2010), and asking the parties to supply summaries of their arguments, to be annexed to the AB report without need for the AB and its legal staff to perform this task directly (in 2014). In parallel with the increase of staff at the panel level, the legal staff of the AB – until recently a relatively small group of just ten lawyers – has also been marginally increased. The AB has lately suggested a limit to the volume of parties' submissions in a communication circulated in October 2015, in which the AB gave evidence of its workload and the size and complexity of the cases, with a view to stimulating the debate with interested WTO Members and in the hope of a positive response.

Dealing with the case load and the complexity of appeals is directly related to the issue of *respect of the ninety-day deadline*. The AB has tried its utmost to respect in all cases this deadline, to which Members attribute great importance, although a delay of a few days is irrelevant compared to the delays normally accumulated in the other phases of the proceedings, sometimes by decision of the parties themselves.

Going beyond this deadline is sometimes caused by the complexity of the case (such as in the aircraft cases), but recently it is more often caused by the overlapping of appeals that makes it impossible for the Members of the AB to attend to multiple disputes according to the standard time schedule. The issue has been that a few parties, especially the United States, insist that this should be made only with the consent of the parties to the dispute. The AB has recognised that involving the parties is appropriate and has done so, but does not want its hands tied and to subordinate the establishment of its agenda, as necessary in these formerly labelled 'exceptional cases', to the will of the litigants in any given case. The debate has been ongoing for some time, fuelled by criticism from some countries in the DSB when a deadline has been missed (although when this does occur it is usually just by a few days). The complaints have not been against extending the proceedings in case of objective impossibility of respecting the deadline, but focus on the lack of previous agreement with the parties (the United States) or the lack of full information on the reasons thereof from the AB (Japan).[35] Other countries (the European Union, India and Brazil) pushed back against Japan's request, saying that micromanaging the AB schedule would not help resolve the issue of delays. An alternative is to have a custom-made schedule, agreed to by the parties, for any case where it appears that the ninety-day deadline will not be met.

If the workload remains at the current level, relaxing the ninety-day deadline by a few days on a case-by-case basis, or even replacing the ninety days with 120 days, will not resolve the issue. *The number of the AB Members should be increased*, taking into account that when it was initially created with seven Members, the Membership of the WTO was more limited and important current players in the DSB, such as China and Russia, were not even Members. A suggested reasonable number of Members has been nine; new human resources would be added, reflecting geographically the expanded membership without diminishing the collegiality on which the consistency of the AB case law and its independence rests.

The AB would benefit from (modest) reforms limiting the *risk of a reduction of the authority of the AB* as a pivot of the stability and the predictability of the WTO system. First, since the AB Members are de facto engaged full time, it would be reasonable for the terms of their employment to reflect this situation. In case of full-time employment, a fixed monthly compensation might even be less onerous for the WTO budget than the current *per diem* arrangement.[36]

The increased tendency for AB Members to be chosen from trade diplomacy and national administration at the expense of academics and national judges (who are endowed with practical international experience as negotiators, arbitrators or administrators), risks diminishing the ability of the AB to reason and decide with full independence, impartiality and objectivity. This is irrespective of the personal integrity of all AB Members, who have never been criticised from this point of view.[37]

35 Most recently at the DSB meeting of 28 October 2015.

36 Making the position full time would also make potential candidates more aware of what the position entails and would thus encourage more competent candidates to come forward.

37 On these issues see Shaffer, Elsig and Puig (2016).

An appropriate mix of competences within the AB is key for it to operate at the highest qualitative level, irrespective of the ability of its dedicated legal staff. It is important that the AB be able to issue well-reasoned reports, based on a full knowledge of international law, that receive not only the approval of WTO Members, but also praise from the community of academics and other experts in the field.[38]

Second, and more crucially, the issue of the *modalities of the renewal* of their tenure after the first four-year term should be streamlined. This issue has become paramount since at the DSB of 23 May 2016 the United States blocked the reappointment for a second term of Seung Wha Chang, from Korea, based on his participation in appeals that resulted in reports that were objectionable to the United States in terms of both content and approach.

Until recently renewal was 'semi-automatic', and appropriately so, with the DSB extending any mandate as a matter of course if the AB Member concerned had expressed his willingness to renew. More recently, in 2015, under the impulse of the United States, the DSB has asked that the AB Members coming up for renewal meet the WTO Members and be available for questioning. The issue became sensitive, because one could foresee a situation in which countries would thereby interfere with pending cases and try to influence the judges, making the renewal of AB Members dependent upon their answers.[39]

The solution was finally found by holding an informal DSB meeting on November 12th, 2015, with this encounter taking place on the understanding that questions by delegations would be of a general and systemic nature only. In the subsequent, formal DSB meeting of November 25th, Singh Bathia from India and Thomas Graham from the United States were reappointed by consensus.

With the position taken by the United States at the DSB of 23 May 2016, after Mr Chang had been questioned by twenty-six

[38] See the piece by former AB Member David Unterhalter of South Africa (Unterhalter 2015).

[39] This process is reminiscent of the hearings by the US Congress for appointees to the US Supreme Court proposed by the president, but the setting, the position of the US Supreme Court and the individual role of its judges is quite different. On the other hand, one should not forget that the AB, however modest its name and institutional setting, is the only international court with compulsory jurisdiction (moreover in respect of broad sensitive matters) over states such as the United States, China and Russia, which usually accept to participate in international adjudication, if at all, only on an ad hoc, mostly ex post facto basis. Hence the keen interest of large economies in the selection of their future judges.

delegations at an informal meeting, a further big leap on this slippery road has been taken, notwithstanding the unanimous criticism expressed at the meeting by the thirty-one Members who took the floor, including all major users of the dispute settlement system and other parties whose voice is rarely heard. The United States stated that it had been 'troubled ... about the disregard for the proper role of the Appellate Body' by the Body itself, because in certain reports in which the United States was a party the 'report engaged in a lengthy abstract discussion' on non-appealed issues, as well as in *obiter dicta*.[40] The United States raised its 'concern with the Appellate Body's adjudicative approach in a number of appellate proceedings in which Mr. Chang was involved' and in addition criticised 'the manner in which he had conducted oral hearings'. The United States further took issue with a support letter circulated by all the other Members of the Appellate Body, defining it as 'unfortunate', noting that the decision on reappointment must be made by the DSB and not the Appellate Body, considering this 'to be another instance of Appellate Body members acting outside of the role assigned to them by the WTO members'.[41]

In an unprecedented letter to the DSB Chair, signed by all thirteen former Members of the Appellate Body on this issue (including the present writer) – and widely circulated soon thereafter – these former Members raised their concern on the threat that this attitude by any WTO Member would pose for the integrity of the DSS.

> [I]f, now, the fact that a Member of the Appellate Body joined in the consensus on the outcome on a particular legal issue or on a particular dispute becomes for the first time a factor in a decision on that Member's reappointment, all of the accomplishments of the past generation in

[40] To this criticism an obvious reply, which has been given by more than one commentator in the *International Economic Law and Policy Blog* of 23 May, is that, since *obiter dicta* by definition are irrelevant to decide a case and as guideline for the future, no WTO Member should be concerned by them.

[41] In this cautious letter, framed in general terms, the six Members recalled that 'our mandate states in Art. 3.2., 17 and 19.2 of the DSU that we are to adjudicate appeals and clarify existing provisions of the covered agreements without adding to or diminish the rights and obligations provided in those agreements'. The letter adds that 'With regard to risks for the trust that WTO place in the independence and impartiality of Appellate Body Members, we are concerned about the tying of an Appellate Body Member's reappointment to interpretations in specific cases, and even doing so publicly. The dispute settlement system depends upon the WTO Members trusting the independence and impartiality of Appellate Body Members. Linking the reappointment of a Member to specific cases could affect that trust.'

> establishing the credibility of the WTO dispute settlement system can be put in jeopardy. This raises the prospect of inappropriate pressures by participants in the WTO trading system. There must be no opening whatsoever to the prospect of political interference in what must remain impartial legal judgments in the WTO's rule-based system of adjudication.[42]

Already the current practice of active engagement of key WTO Members in the initial appointment process appears excessive; it gives the impression that some key WTO Members try to form an AB composed of Members who are responsive to their wishes with regards to their approach to interpretation and similar issues. The process has recently even entailed interviews in Washington and Brussels (a kind of roadshow to which candidates have had to submit lately) and the close scrutiny of their academic CVs and publications.[43] This resulted in a notable instance in 2014 when a qualified candidate who had accepted by all the membership was then vetoed by the United States, leading to the repetition of the selection process.

What happened in the failed reappointment of Mr. Chang risks to undermine the impartial independence of the Appellate Body, threatening the integrity not just of the Appellate Body and the DSS, but putting at risk the functioning of the entire WTO trading system.[44] In Sacerdoti (2016: 64), I conclude that 'The independence of the AB is fortunately assured by two factors. First, the collegial attitude of its members makes it impossible to single out an individual member's position on any specific issue from the outside. Second, the different, even opposing positions of WTO Members on these issues, as on many others, while paralysing even modest reforms, has the advantage of making it unlikely that initiatives to reduce the authority of the AB will succeed.' In light of the most recent

[42] The letter also points out that if WTO Members should ever conclude that the Appellate Body has erred when clarifying a WTO obligation in dispute settlement, the appropriate remedial action lies in applying Art. IX. 2 of the Marrakesh Agreement which provides the Ministerial Conference and the General Council with 'the exclusive authority to adopt [binding] interpretations of this Agreement and of the Multilateral Trade Agreements' by a three-fourths majority of the Members.

[43] Elsig and Pollack (2014) examined this issue through extensive interviews with former candidates.

[44] A first effect of this risk of politicisation manifested itself at the very same DSB meeting where none of the names suggested by the Selecting Committee to replace Yeujiao Zhang of China enjoyed the consensus of the entire membership, with Korea blocking the consensus.

unfortunate developments just described this cannot be taken for granted any more.

As suggested by many commentators, by some WTO Members at the DSB meeting mentioned above and in the letter quoted above, the most reasonable solution to help ensure the impartiality and independence of the Appellate Body is that the current system of reappointment be replaced by a single, longer term. It is however questionable whether those who are inclined to use the reappointment phase to control the Appellate Body share this objective. In fact such a suggestion made by several delegations at a special session of the DSB held on 26 October 2016 was rejected by the United States, which reiterated 'that it opposes the single term because reappointment provides a mechanism for accountability'. Shortly thereafter, following the recommendations of the Selecting Committee at its regular session of 23 November 2016, the DSB appointed Ms Zhao Hong and Mr Hyun Chong Kim – not unexpectedly nationals respectively of China and Korea as the two outgoing Members – to fill the two vacancies, thus concluding at least for the time being the 'saga' of Appellate Body Members' (re-)appointment.

III The Implementation Phase of the DSS

The DSS ultimately pursues a practical objective: maintaining the balance of rights and obligations, market access and liberalisation commitments agreed upon by the Members in the various WTO agreements, discouraging breaches and redressing them as promptly as possible. The *monitoring role of the DSB on implementation* is one of the features that makes the WTO DSS stand out in comparison to other international dispute settlement mechanisms, where implementation is ultimately left to the good will of the party concerned, under threat of diplomatic pressure or unilateral countermeasures.

Surveillance by the DSB should be made more effective, as advocated by the Canadian Ambassador Jonathan Fried when he was chairman of the DSB in 2013. It should not be just a formal exercise of registering statements or automatically authorising countermeasures in the form of suspension of concessions when an adjudicative body has confirmed non-compliance. Ways and means should be devised, based on twenty years of experience, to exercise collective pressure on a recalcitrant Member in order to *induce and facilitate prompter compliance.* One avenue might be to suggest ways to effect implementation, which is currently left completely to the party found in breach. This option is currently in the hands of panels and of the AB under Article 19.1 DSU, but they have generally refrained from using it. The reason is that there is the risk that these suggestions will not be followed (they are not binding), thus indirectly diminishing the authority of the underlying holdings contained in the panels and Appellate Body report. A commitment to the DSB by a party obliged to comply might stimulate more active domestic engagement by the competent national authorities to effect timely and complete implementation.

The implementation procedure should also be tightened to induce compliance by avoiding that the prospective nature of (future) WTO remedies, which already favours non-compliant respondents, rewards even more dragging of feet by the losing party in implementing adverse decisions.

One possible way to reinforce the compliance process might involve rethinking the relationship between the imposition of countermeasures and arbitration *ex* Article 22.6 when there is a dispute on the proportionality of the level of concessions that the winning party intends to put in place. Currently, the principle stated therein is that '[c]oncessions or other obligations shall not be suspended during the course of the arbitration'. As currently framed, this provision favours the party in breach, in that the application of trade sanctions against it is postponed. At the same time it protects that party from being subject to unilaterally determined excessive sanctions by prohibiting their application altogether. A more efficient compliance-inducing mechanism should be devised, for example providing for authorisation to apply trade sanctions at the initiation of the Art. 22.6 arbitration, subject to restitution with interest and possibly a penalty of sanctions applied in excess of the determination of the arbitrators.

E Concluding Remarks

I conclude with some remarks on the interplay between the broader evolution of international trade relations and the functioning of the DSS.

It has been submitted that the existence of an efficient DSS makes concluding the Doha Round less pressing, since its smooth functioning alleviates the need to address difficult negotiating issues. The most contentious issues, so runs the argument, may be left to be resolved by the panels and the AB. This argument does not stand in my view, because adjudicating disputes concerning existing agreements cannot be a replacement for the making of new agreements, whether within the Doha mandate or 'post-Doha', especially if negotiations are meant to cover 'new', hitherto unregulated areas. Nor can dispute settlement 'compensate' for the lack of further liberalisation of trade, be it in the form of negotiated reductions of tariffs on goods or new concessions on services. I do not believe that there is any evidence of the inverse either, namely that the efficiency of the DSS makes WTO Members vary of concluding new agreements; it would be always possible to carve out some agreements from the DSS jurisdiction should this be the problem.[45]

The greatest challenge to the WTO and the protection it affords to small economies comes rather from regional trade agreements, since difficult issues that are intractable at the global level may be agreed more easily between like-minded countries or countries with similar or complementary economies (but at the risk of being biased in favour of the major players). A multilateral response might be to resort to plurilateral agreements in which the WTO and its DSS maintain a role (Hoekman and Mavroidis 2015).The looming weakening of the effectiveness of the DSS in settling disputes highlighted above (delays at the panel stage, threats to the role of the Appellate Body), if not resolved, would be worrying for the whole multilateral system at the current juncture. This is because of the combination of the competition to the global system from the bilateral, regional or plurilateral approach and the need to address with appropriate new regulation the challenges posed by new economic, environmental, scientific developments.

References

The Economist. 2015. 'Torture by Tariff – Retaliating Against Unfair Trade Practices Is a Calculation in Cruelty'.

Elsig, Manfred and Pollack, Mark A. 2014 'Agents, Trustees, and International Courts: The Politics of Judicial Appointment at the World Trade Organization'. *European Journal of International Relations* 20 (2): 391–415.

Hoekman, Bernard and Mavroidis, Petros. 2015. 'WTO "à la carte" or "menu du jour"? Assessing the Case for More Plurilateral Agreements'. *European Journal of International Law* 26 (2): 319–343.

Malacrida, Reto. 2015. 'WTO Panel Composition: Searching Far and Wide for Administrators of World Trade Justice'. In *A History of Law and Lawyers in*

[45] Thus in the TPP certain 'SPS-plus' obligations have been excluded from the dispute settlement mechanism.

the GATT/WTO, edited by Gabrielle Marceau. Cambridge: Cambridge University Press.

Pauwelyn, Joost. 2015. 'The Rule of Law Without the Rule of Lawyers? Why Investment Arbitrators Are from Mars, Trade Adjudicators Are from Venus'. *The American Journal of International Law* 109 (4): 761–805.

Sacerdoti, Giorgio. 2016. 'The Future of the WTO Dispute Settlement System: Consolidating a Success Story'. In *The Future of the Global Trade Order*, edited by C. Braga and B. Hoekman. Florence: EUI.

Shaffer, Gregory, Elsig, Manfred and Puig, Sergio. 2016. 'The Extensive (but Fragile) Authority of the WTO Appellate Body'. *Law and Contemporary Problems* 79 (1): 237–273.

Unterhalter, David. 2015. '*The Authority of an Institution: The Appellate Body under Review*'. In *A History of Law and Lawyers in the GATT/WTO*, edited by Gabrielle Marceau. Cambridge: Cambridge University Press.

8

Does Trade Comply?

The Economic Effect(iveness) of the WTO Dispute Settlement Process

SOO YEON KIM AND TOBIAS HOFMANN

A Introduction

Studying the effects and effectiveness of international institutions has a long tradition in international relations and has sparked a number of debates over the past couple of decades. One prominent example is the 'enforcement versus management' exchange between Chayes and Chayes (1993) and Downs, Rocke, and Barsoom (1996) in the mid-1990s, which raised many of the questions that are still debated today: what can and should we expect international institutions to accomplish, who joins and what motivates countries to join international institutions, how can we measure and compare the effectiveness of diverse international institutions and what can we do to improve their effectiveness?

Since then, countless theoretical and empirical studies have investigated the effectiveness (or the lack thereof) of international institutions in specific issue areas or of individual international institutions. Mitchell (1994), Helm and Sprinz (2000), and many others have analysed whether and how international environmental regimes can protect or improve the environment. Studies have scrutinised the impact of human rights treaties on the protection of human rights (Neumayer 2005; Hollyer and Rosendorff 2011), preferential trade agreements on bilateral trade (Baier and Bergstrand 2007), and investment treaties on flows of foreign direct investment (Peinhardt and Allee 2012). Scholars have even studied the effects of international institutions across policy areas, such as the effects of preferential trade agreements on investment (Büthe and Milner 2008) or of trade agreements on human rights (Hafner-Burton 2005).

Not surprisingly, many studies have analysed the impact of the General Agreement on Tariffs and Trade (GATT) and the World Trade

Organization (WTO) on trade (cf. Gowa and Kim 2005; Rose 2004; Subramanian and Wei 2007). What is more surprising, however, is that these studies have primarily focused on whether the GATT/WTO as a whole matters or makes a difference (and for whom) and have not looked at what it is that drives the trade effects of the multilateral trade regime. With few exceptions (cf. Bown 2004; Bechtel and Sattler 2015; Kucik and Pelc 2016; Chaudoin, Kucik and Pelc 2016), GATT/WTO and trade scholars have taken a broad, macro perspective and failed to identify empirically what aspect of the rules and regulations promote or hinder the GATT/WTO's effectiveness. Looking at this issue from a slightly different perspective, it becomes obvious that – more than sixty years after the original signing of the GATT and twenty years after the establishment of the WTO – we still do not know much about the effects and effectiveness of specific aspects of the trade regime on trade.

We focus on the effectiveness of such a specific aspect by analysing the trade effects of one of the most prominent features of the WTO, namely the Understanding on Rules and Procedures Governing the Settlement of Disputes. The Dispute Settlement Understanding or DSU has been hailed as one of the main achievements of the Uruguay Round. It created a highly legalised institutional mechanism for the settling of trade disputes between members of the global trade regime (Guzman and Simmons 2002; Jackson 2001; Cameron and Campbell 1998). Various scholars have argued that the DSU has redressed many of the GATT's weaknesses in resolving trade disputes, most notably by providing for 'the guaranteed right to a panel' (Grinols and Perrelli 2002: 338). While any of the disputing parties could veto the formation of a dispute panel or the adoption of a panel report following arbitration under the GATT system, disputing parties now have the right to request a panel following the failure of consultations (Young 1995; Jackson 2000; Bello and Holmer 1998). As well as providing institutional arrangements for the arbitration of disputes, the DSU includes provisions for the monitoring of progress towards compliance with the terms of panel and Appellate Body reports adopted by the WTO's Dispute Settlement Body (DSB), which consists of all WTO Members.

We previously noted (cf. Hofmann and Kim 2010, 2011) that scholarship on the WTO's dispute settlement process has devoted much attention to its legal aspects, the (dis)advantages of developing countries utilising the mechanism and the political and economic factors associated with the initiation, escalation and the outcomes of WTO disputes. Studies on the initiation of WTO disputes, for example, have found strong support for prior experience in trade adjudication, whether as a complainant or respondent, as a determining factor (Davis and Bermeo 2009). At the same time, these studies have yielded divergent findings on the impact of power and capacity, centred on the effect of gross domestic product (GDP) per capita as the key indicator (Horn, Mavroidis and Nordström 1999; Reinhardt 2000; Guzman and Simmons 2005). Other studies focused on the factors affecting the 'early settlement' or escalation of disputes from initial consultations to the formal panel stage (Busch and Reinhardt 2001, 2002, 2003). More recently, Busch and Reinhardt (2006) found, for example, that the participation of third parties increases the likelihood that WTO disputes will escalate to the formal panel stage.

While Hofmann and Kim (2010) addressed the fact that surprisingly little attention had been directed to the compliance stage of the dispute settlement process, we are now interested in the under-studied economic effects of WTO disputes. Having previously analysed the reasons for compliance and found that compliance is a function of the political importance of the domestic economic sectors that are benefitting from continued infringements of the international rules of trade, we now investigate the consequences of compliance. Does compliance with WTO dispute panel and Appellate Body reports and establishing or restoring the WTO-consistency of national trade policies matter and make a measurable difference for international trade? Referencing the title of our chapter, we ask: does trade comply with DSU rulings?

The main contribution of this chapter is that it provides an explicit test of the economic effectiveness of the rule-making function of the WTO as exercised by its judicial arm – the DSU. The case histories that have accumulated since the establishment of the multilateral trade regime in 1995 are evidence of the activism of its judges, rightly or wrongly (Esserman and Howse 2003; Ragosta, Joneja and Zeldovich 2003). While much has been written about the legal strength and success of the WTO's DSU process, little attention has been given to whether this celebrated legal mechanism has the tangible benefit of increased trade flows once disputes are formally settled.

The present study builds on the existing scholarship in several ways. As do the studies subsequent to Bown (2004), we examine the WTO, the current multilateral trade regime characterised by a highly legalised dispute settlement process with high levels of obligation, precision and delegation (Abbott et al. 2000).[1] Our major point of departure from existing studies, however, is that we examine trade flows in the years following the uncontested compliance by the respondent country with panel and Appellate Body rulings.

We believe it is important to observe the effects of WTO rulings once the measure or measures in question have actually been removed by the respondent and this action goes uncontested by the complainant. The ruling itself may well generate an anticipatory trade surge in expectation of compliance by the respondent. This is certainly implied by findings of existing studies that analyse trade flows in the years immediately following the ruling stage (Bechtel and Sattler 2015). However, the question remains as to whether trade flows also respond to the institutional removal of trade barriers themselves when (and sometimes if) they do happen. Moreover, even if trade flows do increase as a response to the ruling (though it is unclear how this occurs when the offending trade barrier is still in place), this raises the question as to whether such short-term increases are sustainable and whether the removal of WTO-inconsistent trade barriers has a long-term positive effect on trade flows among disputing parties.

Focusing on the economic effects of compliance at the implementation stage, rather than at earlier stages of the dispute, contributes to the current scholarship in several ways. First, it takes into account that panel rulings are often appealed and subsequently turned over to the Appellate Body, which lengthens the dispute settlement process well beyond the time of the rulings and therefore delays formal resolution. Second, and more important, the implementation stage is also hotly contested, as complainants often assert that the respondent has not implemented panel rulings even if the respondent has reported to the DSB that it has done so. Such cases are then referred to a 'compliance panel' consisting of the original panel members, who make a ruling on whether the respondent has indeed implemented reforms. As illustrated in the long-standing cases on bananas and beef hormones that pitted the United States against the EU, disputes are thus likely to persist for more than the four years post-ruling stipulated by existing studies as adequate for observing changes in trade flows.

To answer these questions, we start out with a brief discussion of the compliance proceedings that are specified in the DSU and the existing literature on the effectiveness of WTO dispute settlement and dispute

[1] Indeed, Abbott et al. (2000) place the WTO's dispute settlement process at the highest level of legalisation, approaching what they term 'full legalization' (p. 405).

settlement's effects on trade flows. Following this discussion, we develop two lines of argument that not only provide a theoretical explanation for the direct trade effects of compliance with WTO dispute panel and Appellate Body reports for the countries involved in a trade dispute, but also for the effects of compliance on third parties and the unintended consequences of dispute settlement that tend to reduce or even undermine the broader effectiveness of the DSU. Specifically, we present hypotheses that we derive from the long-standing discussion on 'trade creation versus diversion' of preferential trade agreements and the existing literature on endogenous trade policy. In the empirical section, we test some of the observable implications of our theoretical arguments. We conclude with suggestions on avenues for future research on compliance and effectiveness in the context of the WTO and other international institutions.

B WTO Disputes and Compliance

Compliance involves behaviour that is consistent with provisions of an institutional agreement (Dai 2007; Young 1979; Fisher 1981; Mitchell 1994). Such provisions can take the form of procedural obligations, substantive obligations, or just the general spirit of an agreement (Weiss Brown and Jacobson 1998). In the WTO context, compliance encompasses all behaviour that is consistent with Members' obligations to adhere to the rules of trade that are enumerated in the GATT/WTO agreements. However, compliance really comes to the fore in the context of and towards the end of WTO disputes.

The WTO's official compliance proceedings are initiated under the DSU following the circulation and adoption of a dispute panel or Appellate Body report and the 'convicted' country expressing its intention to implement the recommendations of the adopted report in a statement to the DSB. If immediate compliance is not practicable, a 'reasonable period of time' can be designated, at the end of which the respondent must demonstrate that it has implemented the required changes so that the trade measures at issue in the dispute are now WTO-consistent. According to DSU Article 21.4, this reasonable period of time for implementation shall not exceed fifteen months beyond the adoption of the dispute panel or Appellate Body report and may be determined through a proposal by the respondent and agreement by the DSB, mutual agreement between the disputing parties or arbitration. The report that the respondent submits to the DSB at the end of the reasonable period of time contains detailed information on the changes to the particular policies, which have to be brought (back) into compliance with WTO provisions and the dates on which these changes were implemented.

Compliance is considered to be restored if the respondent's report is accepted by the complainant country. However, if the respondent fails to report compliance or if the report is contested, the compliance proceedings move on. The next step of the proceedings consists of negotiations for the compensation of the complainant. If the respondent fails to report compliance at the end of the reasonable period of time, DSU Article 22.2 provides for the respondent to enter into negotiations with the complainant to determine a mutually acceptable compensation, such as tariff reductions in a particular sector that is of interest to the complainant country. If the complainant contests the respondent's report, DSU Article 21.5 provides the complainant with the right to request that a compliance panel be formed. More specifically, the case may be referred to the original panel for the evaluation of the reported implementation of the recommendations by the adopted report dispute panel or Appellate Body report, i.e., for an assessment of the respondent's changes to the trade policy measures in question.

At this point, if compliance still fails to be established or if the disputing countries cannot mutually agree on the level of compensation for the complainant within twenty days, the complainant may request the DSB to authorise retaliatory measures. Under DSU Article 22, the DSB is required to authorise the complainant to suspend concessions or obligations equivalent to the amount of trade that is affected by the respondent's trade measures at issue within thirty days following the expiration of the reasonable period of time, unless opposed by consensus.

As in earlier stages of the WTO's dispute settlement process, compliance may be brought about during any part of the compliance stage through Mutually Agreed Solutions (MAS) between the dispute participants. That is, the disputing parties can agree at any step during the compliance proceedings to extend the reasonable period of time for the implementation of the recommendations of the dispute panel or Appellate Body report or to reduce the degree of change that satisfies the complainant that compliance is indeed established or restored.

C The Economic Effects of Compliance

While the WTO's elaborate compliance proceedings clearly indicate that compliance is important, it is important to remember that compliance is not an end in and of itself. Of course, an international institution that consistently fails to monitor and enforce compliance with its rules and regulations might lose its reputation, legitimacy and eventually collapse (cf. League of Nations). However, we care about the DSU and about compliance with dispute panel and Appellate Body reports because of the role they are intended to play within the larger WTO framework, because of the consequences that compliance has on the WTO's achievement of the overarching goals of liberalising and increasing global trade. So, what does the DSU contribute to the WTO's overall effectiveness? What do we know about the impact of dispute settlement and compliance on trade?

Few studies have examined the aftermath of dispute settlement. The ones that do exist have generally found that trade flows do increase as disputes are resolved. Among the earliest studies to examine the economic consequences of the multilateral regime's dispute settlement process is Bown (2004), which analysed changes in imports of the products at issue in a dispute after settlement. Settlement could take the form of the adoption of the panel/Appellate Body report or, in the absence of such a resolution, the last official communication between the disputing parties. The study conceptualised changes in trade flows in the aftermath of a dispute in terms of the broader GATT/WTO objective of trade liberalisation and whether the dispute settlement was successful in bringing about trade liberalisation by respondent countries that lost their cases. In an analysis of 174 dispute dyads in the years 1973–1998, Bown (2004) found that the retaliatory capacity of the complainant/plaintiff was a strong and robust predictor of trade liberalisation in the imports of defendant countries.

More recent studies have focused on actual trade flows following dispute settlement. Kucik and Pelc (2016) highlight the trade-off in the economic success of dispute settlement by drawing attention to the distributive consequences. Their study finds that the settlements that are inferred from the trade flows following settlement at the consultation stage are discriminatory in favour of the complainant. They argue that the private nature of the consultations gives rise to greater opportunism on the part of complainants. The authors note that settlements at the consultation stage are associated with greater economic gains for the complainant relative to other WTO Members. However, the discriminatory effects are redressed when third parties participate. The study concludes that while third parties may increase the chances of dispute 'escalation' through the formation of a panel, thus corroborating existing research on the role of third parties in WTO disputes (Busch and

Reinhardt 2006), their presence at the consultation stage is also associated with economic gains that are more equitably distributed between complainants and the rest of the WTO membership.

Bechtel and Sattler (2015) also analyse the economic effects of the WTO dispute settlement process in terms of the economic gains made by complainants and third parties. Using a host of matching techniques to correct for the non-random selection of WTO disputes that move on to the panel stage, they examine trade flows between complainants and third parties vis-à-vis respondents in cases where a panel ruling was delivered. They find that complainants do indeed gain when cases are paneled and a ruling is issued, as trade flows initially increase in the four years subsequent to the year of the ruling. However, the study also finds that complainants' exports to the respondent are not significantly different from those of third parties to the respondent. The study suggests that the WTO dispute settlement process may well generate positive externalities for paneled cases and increases the incentives for third parties to lobby for arbitration.

I *Does Arbitration Matter?*

This study focuses on two aspects of the question of whether arbitration of trade disputes through the WTO's DSU process is effective in bringing about the recovery of trade lost owing to the imposition of WTO-inconsistent trade barriers by the respondent. First, the analysis addresses whether legal compliance leads to economic compliance. That is, for WTO disputes that lead to a panel and/or Appellate Body ruling that produces recommendations for the respondent to follow and thus provide a legal basis for observing compliance, do trade flows similarly comply by responding positively to the removal of the WTO-inconsistent trade barriers that were at the heart of the dispute? The expectation is that trade would comply. In the dispute between Argentina and Chile (DS238), for example, in which Chile requested consultations and then a panel regarding Argentina's use of a safeguard measure applied to imports of preserved peaches, the panel's report found that Argentina acted inconsistently with several obligations under WTO agreements. At the end of the reasonable period of time designated for the implementation of the Panel Report, 31 December 2003, Argentina withdrew the safeguard measure and reported compliance to the WTO's DSB. Chile welcomed the removal of the measure, and the dispute was concluded at this point.

The Argentina–Chile case above illustrates what can be expected of trade flows in the post-dispute period. If WTO-inconsistent measures are successfully removed through the formal litigation process under the DSU, then one would expect that trade in relevant sectors would increase and return to the pre-dispute levels. However, recent studies such as the one by Bechtel and Sattler (2015) suggest otherwise. These studies suggest that trade flows are not affected by litigation, or are largely unaffected by moving through the WTO's dispute settlement process.

This chapter builds on these studies by separating out the trade effects of WTO disputes that undergo formal arbitration and the subsequent implementation and compliance stage. In doing so, the focus is on the most important aspect of the WTO dispute settlement process – the ability of the WTO's judicial arm to produce not only legal resolution of trade conflicts but also to affect trade flows between disputing parties. Where a panel or Appellate Body report issues recommendations for the removal of WTO-inconsistent trade barriers, and the respondent complies with the report by implementing the recommendations within the designated 'reasonable period of time', an increase in trade flows in the products identified in the dispute should be observed.

Compliance cases – those that involve implementation of panel/ Appellate Body recommendations – are especially important for their transparency and the degree to which the explicit rule-making function of the WTO's dispute settlement process yields tangible economic effects. Unlike disputes that are resolved through MASs that are negotiated privately, panel or Appellate Body reports on disputes include explicit findings of WTO-inconsistency and specific recommendations regarding the trade policies of respondents. Moreover, the transparency of dispute settlement extends to the implementation stage. The implementation/compliance process is transparent because the respondent must report to the DSB the state of implementation at the end of the reasonable period of time determined either by the Report or by arbitration specifically to determine the implementation period. Thus, our interest in the economic effects of the WTO's explicit rule-making function forms the basis of the first hypothesis examined in this chapter. We expect that if a respondent formally complies with the recommendations of a panel or Appellate Body report, its imports from the complainant in the sector involved in the dispute will increase in the post-dispute period.

II Why Doesn't Trade Comply? The Effects of Policy Substitutes

Second, this chapter also addresses the question of why, even with legal compliance with the recommendations of panel or Appellate Body reports, trade flows do not respond positively, especially as more time passes after implementation. The analysis focuses on the role of policy substitutes where the dispute settlement process does not subsequently yield the expected upsurge and recovery in trade. We rely on a political economy explanation for how dispute resolution affects the domestic politics of trade policy formation. The reduction or removal of WTO-inconsistent tariffs or non-tariff barriers increases the competitiveness of foreign companies vis-à-vis inefficient companies in the home country, and domestic consumers substitute foreign products for local ones and generally consume more of the now cheaper, imported goods and services. As a consequence, import-competing producers are faced with the new reality of tougher competition.

In an earlier paper (Hofmann and Kim 2010), we showed that delays in policy change towards WTO-consistent trade practices depend on the relative political weight of domestic special interests that are benefitting from continued non-compliance. Delays in the implementation of WTO-recommended policies are the battles that opportunistic governments fight for politically influential, import-competing sectors of the economy in an effort to maximise their political support function. If delays are a battle, compliance with dispute panel or Appellate Body report recommendations is the admittance of defeat. However, losing a battle is not the same as losing the war and unconditional surrender. Compliance does not make politicians less opportunistic and import-competing industries less vocal, influential and interested in protection.

In less cryptic terms, we can expect that compliance with a dispute panel or Appellate Body ruling increases the respondent's imports. Increasing imports, in turn, leads import-competing producers to demand relief and protection in the form of new tariff or non-tariff barriers. While painful structural reforms would probably be the wiser choice and open up new avenues towards long-term competitiveness, governments tend to find supporting non-competitive industries to be politically more expedient. So, in response to lobbying pressure from import-competing industries, myopic and re-election-minded governments supply new protectionist policies that undermine the very trade liberalisation that resulted from WTO dispute settlement and compliance.

Undercutting liberalisation with new forms of protection is neither a new trick nor a WTO dispute settlement process-specific phenomenon. Before the WTO was even established, Marvel and Ray (1984) showed that GATT Members used non-tariff barriers to counteract the trade liberalising effects of the Kennedy Round. Kono (2006) provides evidence that democracies obfuscate their trade policies and hide their level of protection by switching tariffs and 'core' non-tariff barriers for less visible 'quality' non-tariff barriers, such as product standards. Hofmann and Schaffer (2009) demonstrate that members of the eurozone have substituted 'natural' barriers to trade – such as currency risk and transaction costs – with the more generous provision of subsidies to ailing industries following the launch of the single currency in 1999. Jagdish Bhagwati has even coined a term for this protectionist switcheroo: 'the law of constant protection' (Bhagwati 1988: 53).

Thus, this chapter also analyses the role of trade policy substitutes in affecting the flow of trade between disputing parties following the settlement of disputes. The empirical analysis tests the second hypothesis that if a respondent utilises trade policy substitutes in the post-dispute period, imports from the complainant in the disputed sector will decline over time. This expectation is not limited to the cases of formal compliance, but applies to all disputes that have reached some form of settlement.

D Research Design

The analysis employs a panel dataset that tracks trade between WTO Members involved in formal disputes with at least a request for consultations, as documented on the WTO website. The unit of analysis is the dispute-dyad-year, formed by pairing the respondent(s) with each of the complainants for a given year of a dispute.[2] We employ data on compliance dates from Hofmann and Kim (2010), utilising individual case histories from the WTO website updated with the latest information from the WTO on the status of the disputes.[3] We also rely on data compiled by Horn and Mavroidis (2008) that identify the Harmonized System (HS) codes of products that are involved in the disputes in order to calculate the value of trade between disputing parties across the stages of WTO disputes. The dataset includes WTO disputes initiated and

[2] Overlapping disputes, i.e. disputes that involve the same respondent, products and WTO obligations but are initiated separately by different complainants, were coded as one dispute.

[3] www.wto.org/english/tratop_e/dispu_e/dispu_status_e.htm. Last accessed 8 August 2013.

concluded during the years 1995–2009. Disputes are initiated when a complainant files a request for consultations vis-à-vis a respondent, and they are concluded when a settlement is notified to the DSB. A dispute may be settled at the consultation stage, at the panel or Appellate Body stage, or in the implementation stage. Settlement can take various forms, including an MAS through private negotiations at any stage of the DSU process, or through formal compliance reported to the DSB following the adoption of a panel or Appellate Body report with recommendations.

The type of dispute settlement that is of central interest in this chapter – formal compliance – involves the issuing of a panel or Appellate Body report with recommendations and the subsequent report by the respondent of their implementation by the end of the reasonable period of time. This respondent report is sometimes contested by the complainant, but we code the case as resulting in formal compliance if no further litigation activity is reported.[4] These cases of formal compliance are distinguished from those cases which are resolved through negotiations, either at (i) the consultation stage or (ii) at the panel stage before the panel concludes its deliberations and thus without the circulation of a panel report. Another two categories of dispute outcomes include cases that never moved beyond the request for circulations and those in which the complainant lost the dispute, that is, a dispute in which the panel report found in favour of the respondent. These last two categories are excluded from the analysis, as there is no record of dispute settlement in the former case; in the latter, the panel found no evidence of WTO-inconsistent measures by the respondent.

I Dependent Variable

The dependent variable is the value of the respondent's imports from the complainant of the product or products identified in the WTO dispute. Imports are observed, where data are available, in the five years preceding the formal request for consultations, the years during which the dispute is ongoing, and five years following the settlement of the dispute by negotiation or by arbitration.[5] These trade values capture

[4] In cases where a MAS is reported during the implementation/compliance stage, we take the date of the MAS agreement as the compliance date.

[5] For disputes ending in the years 2007, 2008, and 2009, the data include, respectively, only four, three, and two years of post-dispute data. These disputes were included to maximise the sample available for analysis.

the economic effectiveness of WTO rulings in promoting trade following the resolution of a trade conflict. We utilise the information compiled by Horn and Mavroidis (2008) on the products, classified according to the HS, which are formally identified in official WTO documents associated with the dispute. Product-level data on annual imports by the respondent from the complainant were obtained from the UN Comtrade database.[6] Import values, converted to constant (2005) US dollars, were aggregated across all products identified in the dispute for each respondent–complainant pair. The analysis employs the log-transformed value of imports.

II Independent Variables of Interest

1 Compliance with recommendations of panel or Appellate Body report

The analysis uses the date on which the respondent reports formal compliance with, i.e. implementation of the recommendations of the panel or Appellate Body as the 'treatment' variable.

Compliance equals 1 from the year in which the respondent reports to the DSB that it has complied with the recommendations of the panel or Appellate Body, the implementation report is uncontested, and this report or, in some cases a MAS, marks the last official communication/documentation on the dispute. The measure updates the data on compliance originally compiled by Hofmann and Kim (2010). In this analysis, we investigate whether the respondent's imports from the complainant of the contested product(s) increase in the post-dispute compliance period. We expect the respondent's imports from the complainant to increase in this period as a result of the former's removal of trade barriers following the recommendations of the panel or Appellate Body report.

Settlement outcomes. In focusing on cases of compliance, the analysis distinguishes between different types of dispute settlement outcomes. In particular, the disputes which result in a compliance process following the adoption of a panel or Appellate Body report are compared with those that were resolved through negotiation and resulted in a MAS between the parties, whether these cases were paneled or not. In addition, a supplementary analysis also differentiates between paneled and non-paneled cases, in order to examine whether the institutional

[6] http://comtrade.un.org/.

mechanisms of 'escalating' a dispute from the request for consultations to the panel-formation stage also yields economic consequences.

Trade policy substitutes. Consistent with the second question addressed in this paper, the analysis examines the impact of trade policy substitutes, or the availability of policy alternatives to which governments may resort to address continued pressures for protectionism from domestic interest groups. We employ several measures to investigate the role of trade policy substitutes in influencing product-level trade flows. First, we employ the average applied tariff rate of the respondent country in a given year.[7] This is an imperfect proxy for the general level of a country's protectionism, but the measure does offer wider temporal coverage than other available indicators that did not provide enough data points.[8] Data on tariff rates were obtained from the World Development Indicators (WDI). In addition, we also employ the number of trade remedy investigations undertaken by the respondent in a given year. They include investigations for the adoption of anti-dumping duties, countervailing duties and safeguards. Data were obtained from the Temporary Trade Barriers Database compiled by Bown (2010).[9] These measures – tariffs and trade remedy investigations – capture the tendency of countries with a record of protectionist policies to appeal to them again, employing alternative measures from this menu of trade policy instruments and even other less visible non-tariff barriers in the post-compliance period to meet domestic pressures.

III Control Variables

The analysis also controls for factors that may affect both trade flows and the independent variables of interest: compliance and the availability of trade policy substitutes. The control variables include trade openness, as a proxy for general economic openness and a liberal foreign economic policy regime more broadly; the gross domestic product (GDP) of the respondent and complainant countries to capture their respective market

[7] We employ the simple (unweighted) mean of tariff rates across all products. This avoids the downward bias of import-weighted averages, in which products with higher tariffs (and less trade) have lower weights (WDI 2013).

[8] A more suitable measure would have been the record of states' usage of 'core' non-tariff barriers complied by Nicita and Olarreaga (2006). However, this database did not contain sufficient data points to make the analysis feasible.

[9] The data include information on initiations, investigations and outcomes of trade remedy investigations. Initiations were employed to maximise data availability.

size; the growth in GDP to reflect the disputing parties' respective positions in the business cycle; and a linear trend variable to capture time effects during the years of the dispute.

Trade openness. The analysis controls for the level of trade openness of the respondent and complainant. Trade openness is measured as the sum of exports and imports as a proportion of GDP. The data were obtained from the WDI (2013). Trade openness is an indicator of a country's economic integration into the global economy and the extent of its diversification in trade partners. Applied to this analysis, high levels of trade openness are indicative of numerous sources of supply for imports. Thus where the respondent's trade openness increases over time and the sources of its imports are increasingly distributed across different countries, this is likely to depress imports from the complainant country (or from any one country in particular, for that matter).[10]

Market size and economic growth. The size of the economy is measured as the dollar value, in constant (2005) US dollars, of the disputing countries' GDP figures. Data were obtained from the WDI (World Bank). The model differentiates between the respondent's GDP and that of the complainant. The GDP of the respondent is an indicator of its capacity to absorb imports from the complainant and thus its capacity to implement the recommendations of the panel or Appellate Body report. The size of the respondent's market is therefore expected to have a positive impact on trade flows. The complainant's GDP is an indicator of its relative power vis-à-vis the respondent. The expectation is that the higher the GDP of the complainant, the more successful the complainant is likely to be in compelling the respondent to comply, as it will involve access to a larger market and the possibility of exclusion in the event of noncompliance. The analysis also controls for economic growth, measured in terms of the annual growth rate of GDP. Data were also obtained from the WDI. Economic growth is also a measure of capacity, but reflects the short-term effects of the respondent's position in the business cycle. High levels of economic growth enhance the capacity of the national economy to absorb imports, whereas lower levels of economic growth are likely to depress trade flows.

Linear trend. We include a measure that indicates the cumulative years since the beginning of the dispute, that is, the year in which the complainant files its request for consultations, as well as the

[10] This expectation rests on the assumption that the product in question (and involved in the dispute) does have a wide range of supplying countries.

cumulative years of the post-dispute compliance period. This control variable has two functions in the analysis. First, the measure captures the long-term effects of WTO disputes. Bechtel and Sattler (2015) have identified an interesting pattern to trade flows following the adoption of panel or Appellate Body reports, in which disputing parties experience an initial two-year increase in trade that tapers off and declines in the subsequent two years. This analysis takes a longer-term view of trade patterns by controlling for time effects throughout the life of the dispute. In addition, the linear trend captures time effects that have a systemic effect on all trade flows, including but also going beyond trade between disputing parties.

IV Methodology

This study employs a fixed-effects panel model to examine changes in imports by respondents from complainants before and after the reported implementation of panel or Appellate Body reports. The 'treatment' of interest is the shift to the post-dispute compliance period resulting from an uncontested report of implementation from the respondent of the panel or Appellate Body report's recommendations. The analysis thus examines whether product-level respondent imports are significantly different between the two time periods – the years in which the dispute is ongoing and the post-dispute compliance years, controlling for the confounding factors described above.

The fixed effects model analyses over-time variation in trade flows between disputing countries. In this way, the method takes account of the unobserved heterogeneity of the units –the dispute dyads, whose unobserved individual-level factors affect both compliance and trade flows. Controlling for unit heterogeneity reduces the likelihood of heterogeneity bias due to the correlation between the unobserved unit-level effects and the error term, including cases where individual-level effects are systematically related to one or more independent variables – that is, the relationship between individual-level factors and the independent variables is non-random (Wooldridge 2009: 402–488). This method is appropriate for analysing the trade effects of WTO disputes in which compliance has been achieved, as non-random factors at the dispute-dyad level may be systematically related to whether a case actually advances to the panel stage and results in a panel or Appellate Body report.

The analysis consists of two parts. The first examines the life of the dispute, comparing the trade effects of compliance cases – cases that have been settled through arbitration and resulted in a panel or Appellate Body report to which a respondent must formally respond with implementation of the recommendations – with cases that have been settled through negotiations. The second part of the analysis examines the post-dispute period only, and again compares the compliance cases with the negotiated cases, and investigates the impact of trade policy substitutes. This reveals the extent to which post-dispute trade flows are influenced by a respondent's protectionist tendencies, in the form of high tariffs and trade remedy investigations.

E Findings

We report two main findings from the empirical analysis. First, trade flows between respondent and complainant are significantly different between compliance cases and negotiated cases. Negotiated cases, that is, cases that are settled with the issuing of a panel report, led to an increase in trade flows, while respondent imports fall for compliance cases. Second, in the post-settlement period, trade flows for compliance cases are depressed in the presence of extensive trade remedy actions by the respondent, but this result does not hold for negotiated cases. We discuss each of these findings in turn below.

I Pre- and Post-settlement Trade Flows: Compliance Versus Negotiated Cases

Table 8.1 shows the results the first analysis comparing respondent imports from the complainant of the product during the years of the dispute – from initiation to settlement – and the years following settlement. The results indicate the extent to which a respondent's imports of products at issue in the dispute change as a result of the settlement of the dispute. They show that dispute and post-dispute trade flows differ between compliance cases and negotiated cases.

Trade flows at the compliance stage experience a downturn in the post-settlement period relative to the years in which the dispute is ongoing. That is, in the post-settlement period, the respondent's imports of the disputed product from the complainant decrease by an average of about 20 per cent relative to the previous period. However, in negotiated cases,

Table 8.1 *Pre- and Post-dispute Trade Flows*

Compliance cases	−0.198**
	(0.096)
Negotiated cases	0.139*
	(0.075)
Trade openness (respondent)	−0.014**
	(0.005)
Trade openness (complainant)	−0.001
	(0.003)
GDP (respondent)	2.526***
	(0.366)
GDP (complainant)	−0.182
	(0.428)
GDP growth (respondent)	0.031***
	(0.008)
GDP growth (complainant)	0.004
	(0.008)
Linear trend	0.013
	(0.020)
Constant	−48.044***
	(15.92)
R-squared	0.202
N	2736
Dispute dyads	257

Source: Created by the authors.
* $p < 0.10$, ** $p < 0.05$, *** $p < 0.001$

an increase in trade flows of about 14 per cent is observed.[11] The results present an interesting puzzle regarding compliance cases, where we would expect a recovery of trade flows once the respondent has lifted trade barriers that have been specifically and explicitly identified in panel or Appellate Body reports. At the same time, the rise in trade for negotiated cases provides some support for Kucik and Pelc's (2016) finding that the immediate parties to the dispute benefit from settlement, although this particular analysis does not make the comparison with third parties or other WTO Members.

[11] This effect is not as strong as for the compliance cases. For these negotiated disputes, the result is statistically significant at the $p < 0.10$ level.

Among the control variables, the linear trend term, though positive, does not have a strong effect on product-level trade flows between disputing parties. Similarly, neither the trade openness of the respondent nor that of the complainant, though in the expected negative direction, are associated with changes in trade flows. The economic growth and the economic size of the respondent, however, have a positive effect on its imports from the complainant. They indicate that the economic capacity to comply with the recommendations of the panel or Appellate Body report help trade to recover after settlement.

II Trade After Implementation in Paneled Disputes

Table 8.2 compares trade flows between compliance and negotiated cases in the post-dispute period, focusing on the role of trade policy substitutes. These results follow up on the previous analysis, which found that trade flows take a negative turn in the post-dispute period. We examine one possible explanation for the decline in trade flows in the post-dispute period: the usage of trade policy alternatives. Table 8.2 reports the results for two main measures: the average applied tariff rate of the respondent in a given year and the number of trade remedy investigations (anti-dumping, countervailing duties, safeguards) initiated by the respondent in a given year of the post-dispute period.

The effects of respondent tariffs on trade flows between the respondent and complainant are weak. Indeed, the direction of the effect is the opposite of what was expected: respondent's imports of the disputed product from the complainant appear to increase for compliance cases but decrease for negotiated cases, although neither of the results is statistically significant. They do suggest, however, that the tariff rate of the respondent – the simple average of tariffs across all product categories – may be a weak proxy for trade policy alternatives as it is an aggregate measure that has little bearing on product-level trade flows.

The number of trade remedy investigations initiated in a given year of the post-dispute period has a negative effect on imports by the respondent in compliance cases. The results show that respondent's imports of disputed products from the complainant decrease by about 1.6 per cent in the post-dispute period for compliance cases. This is not a 'large' effect, especially as it concerns specific products. However, it does indicate how the usage of alternative trade policy instruments may be made to serve domestic interests in achieving non-compliance by other means. These measures – tariffs and trade remedy investigations – certainly do not

Table 8.2 *Post-implementation Trade Flows: Respondent's Tariffs and Trade Remedy Investigations*

TR investigations compliance cases	−0.016**
	(0.006)
TR investigations negotiated cases	0.004
	(0.003)
Tariffs compliance cases	0.017
	(0.056)
Tariffs negotiated cases	−0.017
	(0.024)
Trade openness (respondent)	−0.014**
	(0.006)
Trade openness (complainant)	0.009
	(0.006)
GDP (respondent)	1.875**
	(0.830)
GDP (complainant)	1.860**
	(0.929)
GDP growth (respondent)	−0.006
	(0.013)
GDP growth (complainant)	0.022
	(0.142)
Linear trend	−0.036
	(0.037)
Constant	−86.43**
	(31.73)
R-squared	0.244
N	985
Dispute dyads	232

Source: Created by the authors.
* $p < 0.10$, ** $p < 0.05$

exhaust the range of policy instruments available to governments that are facing continued pressures from domestic interest groups. Nevertheless, they are indicative of the impact of a country's ability to deploy alternative policy instruments to affect trade flows when facing the pressures for compliance in the aftermath of a WTO dispute.

Among the control variables, the respondent's trade openness is associated with a decrease in trade flows between the disputing parties.

The effect of economic size is positive, while the effect of economic growth is negative but weak. The effect of the linear trend term is negative but is suggestive of long-term trends following dispute settlement. Although this effect is also weak, for each year after dispute settlement, the respondent's imports from the complainant of the product at issue in the dispute continue to decline. This is consistent with Bechtel and Sattler (2015), who also find that trade flows, while showing an initial rise following the adoption of a panel or Appellate Body report, start to drop in subsequent years.

F Conclusion

While the WTO's dispute settlement process has a positive record of juridical compliance, the focus of this study has been on 'economic' compliance, whether the legal resolution of a trade dispute and the implementation of the rulings and its judicial success is matched in the economic realm by the resumption of trade between complainants and respondents. This chapter analysed pre- and post-dispute trade flows among disputing dyads, differentiating between cases that involve formal arbitration and compliance with a panel or Appellate Body report and those that were settled through negotiations between parties to the dispute. This study has found that trade flows do not comply, that is, trade flows do not recover following dispute resolution. Dispute settlement has a positive but weak effect in negotiated cases, and trade flows decline further for cases that go through formal arbitration.

This study has also examined why trade flows may not resume following dispute settlement, and, in particular, why they do not do so for cases that involve compliance with explicitly stated recommendations found in panel or Appellate Body reports. We have advanced an explanation that relies on trade policy substitutes, or alternative trade policy instruments that provide avenues for non-compliance by other means. The empirical analysis investigated the effect of two possible instruments – tariffs and trade remedy investigations. The results show that the decline in trade flows between the respondent and complainant at the post-dispute stage are strongly associated with the number of trade remedy investigations.

Our assessment of the economic effectiveness of the WTO's dispute settlement system is less sanguine than the positive pronouncements on the aquis accumulated in the case history of the WTO's DSU. The rate of legal compliance appears high, as noted in the interaction of respondents with complainants, as the former make their reports of implementation to the Dispute Settlement Body of WTO Members. It seems likely that there is indeed successful legal implementation of panel and/or Appellate Body reports. Measures are withdrawn or adjusted to meet the implementation requirements of WTO dispute settlements. However, the economic impact is less than 'compliant', as trade flows continue to remain depressed even after implementation. This chapter suggests that a respondent country's level of protectionism, i.e. the heavy usage of alternative policy instruments that expand the menu for protectionism for respondent countries, may well be the explanation for economic non-compliance and low trade flows. The lack of responsiveness of trade flows to dispute settlement suggests trade disputes are also enduring conflicts, as states continue their trade fights beyond the confines of the DSU, compensating for the withdrawal of one trade measure with the imposition of another in its place. Future work will benefit from a closer look at the range and composition of policy substitutes and how they influence states' economic compliance with WTO disputes when facing continued domestic pressures for protection.

References

Abbott, Kenneth W., Keohane, Robert O., Moravcsik, Andrew, Slaughter, Anne-Marie and Snidal, Duncan. 2000. 'The Concept of Legalization'. *International Organization* 54 (3): 401–419.

Baier, Scott L. and Bergstrand, Jeffrey H. 2007. 'Do Free Trade Agreements Actually Increase Members International Trade?' *Journal of International Economics* 71 (1) 72–95.

Bhagwati, Jagdish. 1988. *Protectionism*. Cambridge, MA: MIT Press.

Bechtel, Michael M. and Sattler, Thomas. 2015. 'What Is Litigation in the World Trade Organization Worth?' *International Organization* 69 (2): 375–403.

Bello, Judith H. and Holmer, Alan F. 1998. 'GATT Dispute Settlement Agreement: Internationalization v. Elimination of Section 301'. *International Lawyer* 26: 795–803.

Bown, Chad P. 2004. 'On the Economic Success of GATT/WTO Dispute Settlement'. *Review of Economics and Statistics* 86: 811–823.

Bown, Chad P. 2010. '*Temporary Trade Barriers Database*'. World Bank. Available online at http://go.worldbank.org/W5AGKE6DH0.

Busch, Marc L. and Reinhardt, Eric. 2001. 'Bargaining in the Shadow of Law: Early Settlements in GATT/WTO Disputes'. *Fordham International Law Journal* 24: 158–172.

Busch, Marc L. and Reinhardt, Eric. 2002. 'Testing International Trade Law: Empirical Studies of GATT/WTO Dispute Settlement'. In *The Political Economy of International Trade Law. Essays in Honor of Robert E. Hudec*, edited by Daniel Kennedy and James Southwick, 457–481. New York, NY: Cambridge University Press.

Busch, Marc L. and Reinhardt, Eric. 2003. 'Developing Countries and GATT/WTO Dispute Settlement'. *Journal of World Trade* 37: 719–735.

Busch, Marc L. and Reinhardt, Eric. 2006. 'Three's a Crowd: Third Parties and WTO Dispute Settlement'. *World Politics* 58: 446–477.

Büthe, Tim and Milner, Helen V. 2008. 'The Politics of Foreign Direct Investment into Developing Countries: Increasing FDI through International Trade Agreements?' *American Journal of Political Science* 52 (4): 741–762.

Cameron, James and Campbell, Karen. 1998. *Dispute Resolution in the World Trade Organization*. London: Cameron May.

Chayes, Abram and Handler Chayes, Antonia. 1993. 'On Compliance'. *International Organization* 47: 175–205.

Chaudoin, Stephen, Kucik, Jeffrey, and Pelc, Krzysztof. 2016. 'Do WTO Disputes Actually Increase Trade?' *International Studies Quarterly*, 60 (2): 294–306.

Dai, Xinyuan. 2007. *International Institutions and National Policies*. New York: Cambridge University Press.

Davis, Christina L. and Blodgett Bermeo, Sarah. 2009. 'Who Files? Developing Country Participation in GATT/WTO Adjudication'. *Journal of Politics* 71: 1033–1049.

Downs, George W., Rocke, David M. and Barsoom, Peter N. 1996. 'Is the Good News About Compliance Good News About Cooperation?' *International Organization* 50: 379–406.

Esserman, Susan and Howse, Robert. 2003. 'The WTO on Trial'. *Foreign Affairs*. https://www.foreignaffairs.com/articles/2003-01-01/wto-trial.

Fisher, Roger. 1981. *Improving Compliance with International Law*. Charlottesville, VA: University of Virginia Press.

Gowa, Joanne and Kim, SooYeon. 2005. 'An Exclusive Country Club: The Effects of the GATT on Trade, 1950–94'. *World Politics* 57: 453–478.

Grinols, Earl L. and Perrelli, Robert. 2002. 'Politics, the WTO, and Trade Disputes: Evidence from US Cases'. *Pacific Economic Review* 7 (2): 335–357.

Grinols, Earl L. and Perrelli, Roberto. 2006. 'The WTO Impact on International Trade Disputes: An Event History Analysis'. *Review of Economics and Statistics* 88: 613–624.

Guzman, Andrew and Simmons, Beth A. 2002. 'To Settle or Empanel? An Empirical Analysis of Litigation and Settlement at the World Trade Organization'. *Journal of Legal Studies* 16: 205–235.

Guzman, Andrew and Simmons, Beth A. 2005. 'Power Plays and Capacity Constraints: The Selection of Defendants in World Trade Organization Disputes'. *Journal of Legal Studies* 34: 557–598.

Hafner-Burton, Emilie M. 2005. 'Trading Human Rights: How Preferential Trade Agreements Influence Government Repression'. *International Organization* 59: 593–629.

Helm, Carsten and Sprinz, Detlef F. 2000. 'Measuring the Effectiveness of International Environmental Regimes'. *Journal of Conflict Resolution* 45: 630–652.

Hofmann, Tobias and Kim, SooYeon. 2010. *The Domestic Politics of Compliance: Explaining Time-to-Compliance in WTO Disputes*. Unpublished manuscript.

Hofmann, Tobias, and Kim, SooYeon. 2011. *Picking Fights: Rising Powers in WTO Disputes*. Unpublished manuscript.

Hofmann, Tobias and Schaffer, Lena M. 2009. *Currency Unions and the Demand for Protection*. Unpublished manuscript.

Hollyer, James R. and Rosendorff, B. Peter. 2011. 'Why Do Authoritarian Regimes Sign the Convention Against Torture? Signaling, Domestic Politics and Non-Compliance'. *Quarterly Journal of Political Science* 6: 275–327.

Horn, Henrik and Mavroidis, Petros C. 2008. *The WTO Dispute Settlement Data Set 1995-2006*. Washington, DC: World Bank.

Horn, Henrik, Mavroidis, Petros C. and Nordström, Hakan. 1999. 'Is the Use of the WTO Dispute Settlement System Biased?' *CEPR Discussion Paper* 2340.

Jackson, John H. 2000. *The Jurisprudence of GATT and the WTO: Insights on Treaty Law and Economic Relations*. New York: Cambridge University Press.

Jackson, John H. 2001. 'The Role and Effectiveness of the WTO Dispute Settlement Mechanism'. In *Brookings Trade Forum: 2000*, edited by Susan M. Dollins and Dani Rodrik, 179–219. Washington, DC: Brookings Institution Press.

Kono, Daniel Y. 2006. 'Optimal Obfuscation: Democracy and Trade Policy Transparency'. *American Political Science Review* 100: 369–384.

Kucik, Jeffrey and Pelc, Krzysztof J. 2016. 'Measuring the Cost of Privacy: A Look at the Distributional Effects of Private Bargaining'. *British Journal of Political Science, available on CJO2015*. doi:10.1017/S0007123414000520.

Marvel, Howard P. and Ray, Edward J. 1984. 'The Pattern of Protection in the Industrial World'. *Review of Economics and Statistics* 66: 452–458.

Mitchell, Ronald. 1994. 'Regime Design Matters: Intentional Oil Pollution and Treaty Compliance'. *International Organization* 48: 425–458.

Neumayer, Eric. 2005. 'Do International Human Rights Treaties Improve Respect for Human Rights?' *Journal of Conflict Resolution* 49: 925–953.

Nicita, Alessandro and Olarreaga, Marcelo. 2006. 'Trade, Production and Protection 1976–2004'. *World Bank Economic Review* 21: 165–171.

Peinhardt, Clint and Allee, Todd. 2012. 'Failure to Deliver: The Investment Effects of US Preferential Economic Agreements'. *World Economy* 35: 757–783.

Ragosta, John, Joneja, Navin and Zeldovich, Mikhail. 2003. 'WTO Dispute Settlement: The System Is Flawed and Must Be Fixed'. In International Lawyer 37 (3): 697–752.

Reinhardt, Eric. 2000. *Aggressive Multilateralism: The Determinants of GATT/ WTO Dispute Initiation, 1948–1998*. Unpublished manuscript.

Rose, Andrew K. 2004. 'Do We Really Know That the WTO Increases Trade?' *American Economic Review* 94: 98–114.

Subramanian, Arvind and Wei, Shang-Jin. 2007. 'The WTO Promotes Trade, Strongly but Unevenly'. *Journal of International Economics* 72: 151–175.

Weiss Brown, Edith and Jacobson, Harold K., (eds.). 1998. *Engaging Countries: Strengthening Compliance with International Environmental Accords*. Cambridge, MA: MIT Press.

Wooldridge, Jeffrey M. 2009. Introductory Econometrics: A Modern Approach. 4th edition. Mason, OH: South-Western Cengage Learning.

Young, Michael K. 1995. 'Dispute Resolution in the Uruguay Round: Lawyers Triumph over Diplomats'. *International Lawyer* 29: 389–409.

Young, Oran R. 1979. *Compliance and Public Authority: A Theory with International Applications*. Baltimore, MD: Johns Hopkins University Press.

PART IV

Zooming in on Specific Debates

9

Twenty Years of Third-Party Participation at the WTO

What Have We Learned?

KRZYSZTOF J. PELC

A Introduction

The issue of participation has always loomed large in the World Trade Organization. The question is, who is allowed into the room? When it comes to dispute settlement, the issue largely falls under a single mechanism. The one means by which countries other than the litigants can enter the room during WTO disputes is by joining as third parties. Third-party status allows Members to become privy to otherwise private consultations, as well as to voice their views to the panel and AB during litigation and have them recorded in the final ruling. Third-party status has only gained in importance through time, as the institution has encouraged participation and gradually expanded third-party rights. Since 1995, Member States have entered the room on nearly a thousand occasions, to observe dispute proceedings or make their views heard. This chapter asks, what have we learned from twenty years of third-party participation?

Broader participation seems innocuous. International organisations such as the WTO have long been called on to open their procedures to greater scrutiny. Doing so within the membership seems like an uncomplicated step. It contributes to internal transparency and is seen as reducing the much lamented 'participation deficit' of international organisations. Yet what I seek to demonstrate in this chapter is that participation actually has complex and far-reaching effects. Although countries join disputes for strategic reasons, their presence and participation leads to a series of unintended consequences for the membership as a whole. Some of these are positive, while others are arguably less so. I also suggest that there is evidence that countries do take these unintended consequences into consideration when choosing whether to participate. I attempt to net these different effects, to assess whether the aggregate impact of third-party participation has been a positive one. I close by mapping the third-party submissions in relation to one another, thus taking a first step in examining the content of third-party submissions.

Third-party status lets countries guard their interests in a number of ways. States may enter to ensure that any private settlement reached between a dispute's litigants does not impinge on their trade interests. They may also join a dispute to weigh in on matters of legal interpretation which they think may impact the future of the institution. One European representative expressed this view by stating that 'the fundamental purpose of increased third party access was to give all Members an opportunity to contribute to the development of WTO law'.[1] This ability to influence jurisprudence without filing a formal challenge as a complainant takes on added importance in view of emerging findings about the barriers to participation imposed by legal capacity.[2] For developing countries and recently acceded Members, especially, third-party participation can also serve as a means of learning. Legal capacity has been found to be driven not only by country wealth, but also by experience.[3] Evidence suggests that third-party participation can fulfil this capacity-bolstering function.

The WTO's third-party mechanism is a lens through which to look at participation in international organisations writ large. By illustrating both the benefits of wider participation and its potential drawbacks, it pits some of the fundamental objectives of the institution against one another: transparency comes at the possible cost of dispute settlement effectiveness, which comes at the possible cost of non-discrimination. Third parties also give true meaning to the trade-off expressed in US diplomat Harlan Cleveland's famous phrase, 'how do you get everyone into the action and still get action?' By carefully examining both the incentives of countries joining and the systemic effects of their presence in the room, we can arrive at a better understanding of both the origins of the widely held 'participation deficit' in global governance and the best solutions to address it.

The remainder of this chapter proceeds as follows. After a brief overview of participation in the WTO, I examine the unintended consequences that the presence of third parties may exert, and how these lead to inevitable

[1] European representative, Special Session of the Dispute Settlement Body, November 2003, WTO document TN/DS/M/14, para. 47.

[2] Busch, Reinhardt and Shaffer (2009).

[3] Davis and Bermeo (2009).

trade-offs between fundamental objectives of the institution – transparency, dispute settlement effectiveness and non-discrimination. These considerations then lead me to the question of who decides to participate, and for what reasons. Finally, I take a brief look at the content of third-party submissions and how these relate to one another.

B Background: The Question of Participation in the WTO

The way in which international organisations aim at equality among sovereigns has had the natural effect of elevating the question of participation: to put it simply, equality does not result unless all countries are privy to the proceedings. The question pervades both multilateral bargaining among states, and dispute settlement.

In the early days of the institution, multilateral trade rounds consisted largely of closed-door meetings between the membership's various caucuses, the results of which were then presented to the remainder of the membership for approval. This practice largely circumvented the aim of the consensus voting rule, leading to what some have described as 'organised hypocrisy'.[4] To this day, the 'green room' where these early meetings among major powers took place, remains a common metaphor used by critics to conjure the exclusionary nature of WTO decision-making, even as multilateral negotiation procedures have since evolved. Despite some changes, developing country Members often complain of insufficient internal transparency. In a representative instance, Bolivia, Cuba, Ecuador and Nicaragua claimed in a recent ministerial that 'the WTO has become an organization that is not led by its Members, in which decision-making ... is not governed by consensus, and negotiation meetings are not open to participation by all Members'.[5] It is thus in great measure because of formal rules aiming at egalitarian decision-making that the prior question of who is in the room has taken on such importance.

The analogous debate over participation has long existed in dispute settlement. In fact, one of the most heated debates in the institution's history has been waged over who can submit their views during a dispute. In the *US – Shrimp* dispute, the AB ruled that it could accept views

[4] See Steinberg (2002). In the earliest days of the GATT, decisions were designed to be voted on. Since at least 1959, almost all legislative decisions have been taken by consensus – except decisions over issues like country accession, which require a supermajority to agree on the working party proposal (Pelc 2011).

[5] WTO document WT/MIN(11)/W/4, December 2011.

submitted by private parties, called amicus briefs (or 'friend of the court' submissions), if these could provide relevant facts to the dispute. It faced unprecedented pushback from the membership.

This controversy erupted in spite of the fact that the AB has never actually considered an amicus brief to be either 'pertinent or useful',[6] and that there was never any question of allowing these private parties inside the room to actually witness the proceedings. Yet the possibility of allowing more voices into the room nonetheless grew into one of the more contentious issues in the interpretation of WTO rules. This wrangling illustrates how high the stakes of participation are. As things stand, the AB retains the discretion to accept briefs when these are relevant, but private parties have no right under WTO rules to be heard in the process. There is only one mechanism addressing participation in disputes beyond the litigants and that is third-party status.

I WTO Rules on Third Parties

Since the start of the General Agreement on Tariffs and Trade (GATT), the institution has had in place some provisions allowing Members other than the litigants to be privy to dispute proceedings. In the WTO's Dispute Settlement Understanding (DSU), the question of third-party participation is nominally covered by Article 10 (Third Parties). Yet third parties come up at an earlier dispute stage, during consultations, and it is arguably there that they exert their biggest impact. As DSU Article 4.11 reads:

> Whenever a Member other than the consulting Members considers that it has a substantial trade interest in consultations being held pursuant to paragraph 1 of Article XXII of GATT 1994, . . . such Member may notify the consulting Members and the DSB . . . of its desire to be joined in the consultations.

Several points in this paragraph are worth noting. First, countries wishing to join a dispute during consultations must demonstrate 'a substantial trade interest' in the matter at hand. This is a higher threshold than the 'substantial interest' requirement that Members face to join a dispute at the panel stage as laid out in Article 10, reflecting a desire to afford greater leeway for parties that prefer to negotiate in private. In this respect, however, the discretion of parties to allow third parties in or block their entry lies in the condition that follows: 'in consultations

[6] WTO Dispute Settlement System Training Module: Section 9.3 Amicus Curiae submissions.

being held pursuant to paragraph 1 of Article XXII of GATT'. This reference to the GATT text is a somewhat arcane one, yet it has considerable implications. It is an often overlooked point that complainants have the means to block third parties from entering consultations.

To this day, any complaining party must choose to file every WTO legal challenge under either Article XXII:1 or XXIII:1 of the GATT. This apparently small difference determines whether other Members can join as third parties during consultations. As a result, it largely determines third-party participation throughout the dispute.[7] This choice is a weighty one. As the WTO itself puts it in a manual to the intent of Member States, 'the choice between Articles XXII:1 and XXIII:1 of GATT 1994 is a strategic one, depending on whether the complainant wants to make it possible for other Members to participate'.[8]

This choice allows us rare insight into countries' preferences about participation. States must choose whether to open up the proceedings to participation or not.[9] Historically, countries have chosen each option in about half of all disputes. Over time, the option of opening up participation under Article XXII has gained favour slightly. But what is most interesting is that the choice of whether to open to third parties is not reducible to the country: that is, it is not that some countries are systematically more likely to choose to promote versus prevent third-party participation (except for China, which has been significantly more likely to prevent third-party participation when it has been a complainant). Rather, the variation appears to be at the case level. Specifically, the source of variation seems to be case quality: consistent with some earlier anecdotal observations, complainants choose the Article XXII route, promoting third-party participation, if they stand to profit from 'kibitzing' by third parties (Davey and Porges 1998). That is, complainants appear more likely to open the door to third-party participation if they have a weak case. Johns and Pelc (2014) have expressed this by saying that third parties act as 'insurance' for complainants: they politicise the proceedings in a way that benefits complainants with weak cases. Third parties submissions can function as a form of plebiscite on a Member's measures that can modulate the effect of the verdict itself.

[7] The average number of third parties in consultations for an Article XXII case is 2.5, while the average number of third parties for an Article XXIII case is 0.8. The difference is highly statistically significant, and remains through all the stages of the average dispute.

[8] WTO Dispute Settlement System Training Module: Chapter 6.2.

[9] Defendants can always block countries from entering, but rarely do so, since defendants would rather allow a third party in the room than have it file a complaint of its own.

Thus, in the Section 301 dispute that challenged the US unilateral legislative tool used to pressure other Members into modifying their policies (Pelc 2010), the United States won on the merits, but it lost on the politics, precisely because a large portion of the membership joined as third parties to condemn the US measures. The panel itself underscored this point, noting that '[i]n addition to the EC, twelve of the sixteen third parties [that filed third-party submissions] expressed highly critical views of this legislation'. It also went out of its way to increase the third parties' voice in the proceedings: 'Given the intense criticism of Sections 301–310 articulated in the submissions of third parties before this Panel, we expressly invited the EC and all third parties to submit to us any evidence of WTO-inconsistent conduct by the US corresponding to the complaints of the EC.'[10] Third parties, in other words, add voices and issues to a dispute. These politicise cases in a way that can benefit a complainant which risks losing on the merits. This belief has verifiable testable implications: promoting participation is associated with significantly decreased odds of winning a case. Specifically, Article XXII:1 cases, which allow participation, are half as likely to result in a fully pro-complainant ruling than those that block third-party participation.[11] To be clear, this is entirely a selection effect, not a causal one: weak cases are the ones that seek third-party support and gain from the kind of ambiguity that the presence of many third parties often injects into the proceedings.

As noted above, the threshold for entering a dispute as a third party drops once litigation begins. Members can then claim a 'substantial interest', which need not involve a specific trade interest: it is sufficient that there be a claim to a broader systemic interest. A country can thus join a dispute over e.g. steel safeguards even if it does not trade in steel, but is concerned about the implications for the membership of the interpretation of rules on safeguards. The relevant text of the DSU reads:

Article 10: Third Parties

1. The interests of the parties to a dispute and those of other Members under a covered agreement at issue in the dispute shall be fully taken into account during the panel process.
2. Any Member having a substantial interest in a matter before a panel and having notified its interest to the DSB (referred to in this

[10] *US – Section 301*, WT/DS152/R, adopted 27 January 2000, para. 7.11.

[11] This result accounts for the effect that the presence of third parties initially has on the odds of litigation, which I will examine in greater detail.

> Understanding as a 'third party') shall have an opportunity to be heard by the panel and to make written submissions to the panel. These submissions shall also be given to the parties to the dispute and shall be reflected in the panel report.

Third-party status thus affords Members the right to be privy to the main substantive meetings between the panel and the litigants, and to submit views to the panel, either in written or in oral form. To this, parties and the AB have begun to grant 'enhanced third-party rights', for which there is no textual support, but which allow countries to be present throughout all sessions between the panel and the litigants, and to make their voices heard earlier, from the first meeting onwards.[12] Usually, enhanced third-party rights are granted by the panel only if a third party has an especially significant trade interest in the dispute at hand. It is telling of the considerable involvement of third parties in dispute proceedings that the WTO texts expressly disallow drawing panelists from the country of either litigant, or any of the third parties.[13] Third parties are seen as active Members in the dispute.

The rights of due process afforded by Article 11 of the DSU mean that the litigants have the right to respond and comment on third-party submissions, and they frequently do. More interesting still is that the panel and AB frequently engage with third-party views – even when the litigants disagree with them. In fact, they frequently seem swayed by third-party views, as in the case of Section 301 cited above. This was not an isolated instance by any means. In one of the most recent panel reports, in *US – Animals*, the panel thus felt obliged to engage with a view submitted by the EU in this third-party submission, although

[12] In a representative instance, Brazil asked for enhanced third-party rights (on account of its systemic interest in the dispute, leading to a discussion of whether those third parties citing systemic interests were in any way distinguished from the other third parties citing a substantial interest, and thus whether they might obtain different rights), which included the right: (1) 'to attend the entirety of all substantive meetings of the Panel with the parties'; (2) 'to present oral statements and oral observations at the substantive meetings of the Panel with the parties'; (3) 'to receive copies of all submissions to the Panel, including answers to the questions posed by the Panel or the parties'; and (4) 'to review and comment on the interim Panel Report, in particular the summary of Brazil's arguments in the draft descriptive part of the Panel report'. In that case, the panel chose not to extend these rights to the third parties.

[13] DSU Article 8:3: 'Citizens of Members whose governments (6) are parties to the dispute or third parties as defined in paragraph 2 of Article 10 shall not serve on a panel concerned with that dispute, unless the parties to the dispute agree otherwise.'

neither the complainant (Argentina) *nor* the respondent (the United States) agreed with the third-party views.[14]

Third parties often serve as a proxy for the concerns of the membership, in a way that litigant submissions hardly can. When a large number of third-party Members weigh in on a measure, as they did in Section 301, panelists and AB Members appear to take note. Busch and Pelc (2010) find, for instance, that panels grow significantly more likely to decline to rule on a given claim, citing judicial economy, when third parties offer 'mixed' submissions, i.e. ones that take sides with neither litigant. Indeed, a majority of third parties take pro-complainant positions (56 per cent), while a minority take pro-respondent positions (32 per cent). The remaining 12 per cent are mixed, insofar as they side with neither party, but rather take the opportunity of their submission to voice their concern about the possible jurisprudential implications of a ruling. Panelists appear to heed the cue in these submissions, and they tread more carefully. The result is that a single mixed submission is associated with 27 per cent greater odds of judicial economy being exercised. Three mixed submissions increase those odds by an average of 67 per cent. In short, panels look to third parties for a reliable indicator of the feelings of the membership about the legal issues in dispute, and they consistently act on the basis of these feelings.

C The Externalities of Third-Party Participation

I have reviewed some of the ways in which the broader participation of third parties affects the proceedings: third parties tend to politicise rulings, and may thus act as insurance for complainants, which leads to an association between legal merit and third-party presence. Panels and the AB also actively seek third parties' views, and act on their submissions, as when they grow more likely to decline to rule on a claim on the basis of mixed third-party submissions. Yet the biggest impact of third parties actually occurs before litigation even begins.

[14] 'The European Union argued in its third-party submission that Article 10.1 is too vague to be the subject of dispute settlement. Neither Argentina nor the United States indicated that they shared this view. That being said, the Panel is nonetheless under an independent obligation pursuant to Article 11 of the DSU to make an objective assessment of the matter' (*US – Animals* Panel Report, para. 7.689).

I *Effects on Settlement Odds*

What may be the most established empirical finding in the study of WTO dispute settlement pertains to participation: third parties make settlement less likely. This belief emerged early[15] and was then empirically confirmed in a number of independent analyses on subsets of disputes and within specific legal issue-areas.[16] In fact, the WTO itself recognises as much, stating that the option of keeping third parties out of consultations (through Article XXIII, as discussed above) 'may be attractive for a complainant who intends to work towards a mutually agreed solution with the respondent without interference from other Members'.[17] The implication is that when third parties are in the room, such mutually agreed solutions become less likely.

There are distinct mechanisms by which the presence of third parties may impede settlement. First, third parties add their own views to consultations, making any potential agreement more complex. More interestingly, third parties may also lead the litigants to posture, misrepresenting their true preferences about reaching agreement, as a means of investing in their reputation as intransigent negotiating parties, with the hope that this may help them secure better bargains in the future when dealing directly with the third-party litigants.[18] The EU may thus have an incentive to act tough if China has joined as a third party (as China often does, regardless of the nature of the dispute, in an apparent bid to accrue legal capacity), with an eye to upcoming consultations with China over a separate case.

The combined effects are substantively important. The presence of third parties decreases the odds of early settlement from 69 per cent (in the absence of third parties) to 31 per cent (if any third parties are present). They drop further still, to 4 per cent, if any of those third parties entered by citing systemic concerns, as this corresponds to disputes over policies with far-ranging effects that are likely to be especially difficult to supplant. If a dispute attracts five or more third parties, the odds of settlement are effectively nil.[19]

This impact on settlement matters. Much of the WTO dispute settlement system is geared towards encouraging settlement. Litigation remains, in international public law as much as in domestic law, an

15 Davey and Porges (1998).
16 Bown (2005); Busch and Reinhardt (2006); Kucik and Pelc (2016).
17 WTO Dispute Settlement System Training Module: Chapter 6.2.
18 Busch and Reinhardt (2006); Stasavage (2004).
19 Busch and Reinhardt (2006).

inefficient outcome (Gilligan, Johns and Rosendorff 2010). Moreover, once litigation begins, some evidence suggests that any concessions on the part of the respondent grow unlikely, as both litigants dig in their heels and have less reason to cooperate.[20] A negotiated private settlement allows both litigants to present the outcome in a positive light domestically; once litigation begins, the facts are made plain, the respondent incurs whatever domestic cost is associated with being branded in violation and the motivation to concede is diminished. In short, the odds of cooperation are greatest if the parties can agree to resolve the matter before a panel report brings out all the facts of the case. Given how the presence of third parties is the single clearest determinant of early settlement, it is no exaggeration to say that broader participation may be the greatest obstacle to the DSU's core aim: settling disputes.

1 Distributional effects

In the context of multilateral trade, observers frequently warn that some Members may be left out of concessions offered to other Members. A quota may be reallocated, or a standard favourably redrawn, such that one Member's interests are served at the expense of another. The core principles of reciprocity and nondiscrimination are targeted at preventing such 'bilateral opportunism', yet as Bagwell and Staiger (2004) make clear in their work on the subject, these ground rules are at best a 'first line of defence' against this issue. Early settlements are one way through which litigants can reach arrangements that come at the expense of the remainder of the membership, even as such discriminatory deals are explicitly proscribed by the rules. Indeed, the most-favoured nation (MFN) principle extends to any agreement that results from dispute settlement.[21] If the defendant offers some concession in response to the complainant's grievances, this concession must be extended to the remainder of the membership. This constraint rule is often flouted. A number of cases where the content of settlements was disclosed, often by accident, bear witness to the danger of bilateral opportunism during private consultations.[22]

[20] Busch and Reinhardt (2001).

[21] See Article 3.2 of the DSU, which reads that 'All solutions to matters formally raised under the consultation and dispute settlement provisions of the covered agreements . . . shall be consistent with those agreements and shall not nullify or impair benefits accruing to any Member under those agreements.'

[22] Kucik and Pelc (2016).

We already know that the presence of third parties renders private settlement less likely. Yet an equally interesting finding is that third parties affect the content of those settlements that are reached. By examining trade flows before and after disputes, it is possible to measure the increase in trade that occurs in the wake of early settlements, and compare this across the membership, to verify any reallocation of trade.

Kucik and Pelc (2016) do just that, and arrive at two related findings. The first is that the concerns of Bagwell and Staiger (2004), and much of the membership, are well founded: bilateral opportunism does appear to take place, and the privacy afforded by early settlement makes it considerably more likely. That is, complainants appear to gain disproportionately more, in terms of the trade-flow increases following early settlement, than the rest of the membership. Tellingly, and in keeping with the view that privacy is what makes bilateral opportunism possible, this disproportionate gain for complainants is only present following early settlements. Complainants do not gain more than everyone else in the wake of disputes that move on to a panel ruling, once the facts of the case are made public, and expectations emerge about what should constitute a satisfactory outcome.

The second finding qualifies the concern over third parties spelled out above. The presence of third parties appears to close the gap between complainants and the remainder of the membership, in terms of trade increases following consultations. That is, when third parties are present, the remainder of the membership – those countries not in the room – captures a greater proportion of the trade increase following early settlements. By contrast, as one might expect, the presence of third parties has no effect on the distribution of concessions for disputes that went on to litigation. Once a panel rules on a case, its facts become public, expectations about the content of a settlement converge and the opportunities for bilateral opportunism decrease. These findings hold when controlling for a number of possible determinants of the level and distribution of the respondent's concessions.

It is important to clarify that countries do not enter a dispute as third parties in order to prevent discriminatory settlements. But by their sheer presence, they act as unwitting enforcers of MFN rules, making discriminatory deals less likely, on average. This empirical finding confirmed earlier similar beliefs. As Bown (2009: 61) puts it, third parties 'minimiz[e] the likelihood that settlements between litigating parties result in discrimination against exporting firms from third countries'. The WTO itself has made claims consistent with this view, opining that countries joining as third parties may have 'an interest in being present at discussions on any mutually agreeable solution because such a solution may affect its interests'.[23]

The effects of third parties when it comes to settlement thus run in two opposite directions. Their presence makes settlement less likely, yet it also increases the 'fairness' of those settlements that do occur. One charitable way of reading these opposing effects is to suggest that third parties may be preventing those settlements that would not have benefitted the remainder of the membership.

D Why Do Countries (Not) Join Disputes as Third Parties?

In view of the above, we can now advance a number of reasons why countries exercise their right to join a dispute as a third party. To recap, being in the room during consultations is a means of preventing bilateral opportunism. Countries join as third parties because they may have a material stake in the matter at hand, and they want to be in the room to ensure that their trade interests are not encroached on through a bilateral deal between the litigants. As shown above, this also leads to positive unintended consequences for the remainder of the membership.

Once litigation begins, third parties may also gain from making their voice heard. In fact, this is often portrayed as the main advantage of third-party participation – after all, it is over this issue that the amicus briefs controversy erupted: who gets to submit their beliefs to the panel, and have these views recorded in the ruling?[24]

There is considerable ambiguity in WTO rules, and especially as multilateral negotiations are presently stalled, litigation has become the main way in which these gaps are clarified.[25] Hence the oft-quoted phrase that international courts 'legislate interstitially'. Third-party participation is a cheap means of influencing judicial interpretation of these rules. In fact, it is in many respects the only means for smaller countries to have an impact on WTO jurisprudence.

Given these incentives, who participates? Figure 9.1 shows rates of participation by Member State, for all countries that acted as third parties on more than five occasions. The figure shows 'formal' third-party

[23] WTO Dispute Settlement System Training Module: Chapter 6.2.
[24] See note 1.
[25] Pelc (2014).

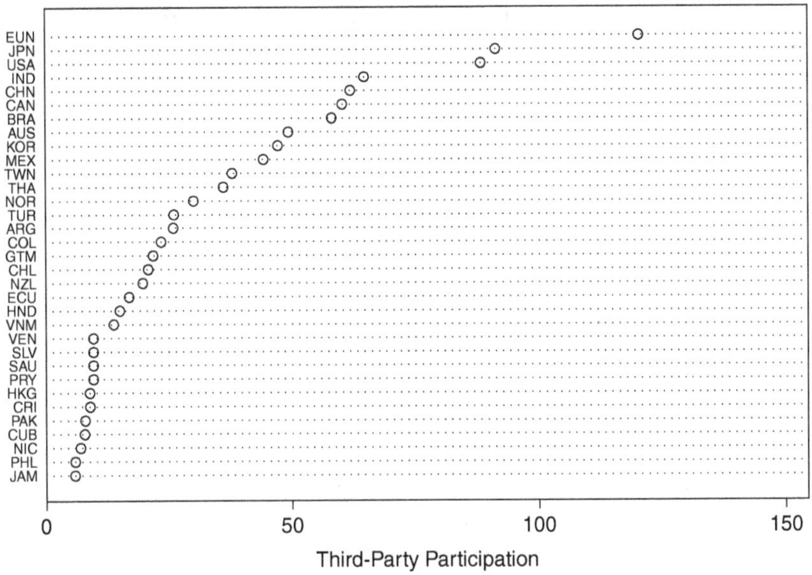

Figure 9.1. Most frequent third-party members, 1995–2014.
Source: Created by the author.

participation under Article 10, that is, during panel proceedings, and thus it underestimates third-party participation during consultations, since most disputes never make it to a panel. Yet the variation across states is instructive. The European Union finds itself at the very top, ahead of Japan and -the United States, the two other top third-party participants. India and China come next, and are, as might be expected, the top developing country participants. Note that this breakdown is also partly a reflection of litigation rates: since a party cannot be a third party if it is a litigant, frequent litigators thus appear to join fewer disputes. The rate of participation of the United States, especially, is thus 'artificially' low, given how often it finds itself as either the complainant or respondent.

Overall, third-party participation thus includes all the usual suspects, but it also counts a number of smaller countries, such as Turkey, Colombia, Guatemala, Venezuela and Vietnam near the top. What Figure 9.1 illustrates is thus the extent to which third-party participation is also a tool of smaller Members. There is no doubt that the option to join in litigation as a third party has successfully enlarged the franchise, as it were, by opening up participation to a set of countries that lacks the capacity to file their own challenges. It also shows that this mechanism has its limitations: the cost of third-participation is low, but not so low that least-developed countries avail themselves of it in any meaningful way.

I *Choosing to Stay Out*

In light of the considerable benefits of third-party participation, the question that remains is why we do not observe *more* of it. Practitioners have also asked themselves this very question.[26] The average dispute, after all, counts less than four third-parties. If we consider the traded products at issue in every dispute, and each country's stake in those products, we should expect this number to be closer to fourteen countries (Johns and Pelc 2016). And this does not include Members that might have a non-trade interest, related to a systemic aspect of the dispute. If third-party participation is a cheap means of guarding one's interests, of increasing poor countries' legal capacity, while offering Members a voice in the proceedings, why are there not more countries seeking to enter the room?

First, it is important not to overstate the low cost of third-party participation. While in actual terms, it may involve sending a single representative into a room, it requires the legal capacity to recognise trade interests worth defending. Just as importantly, third-party participation may come with some political costs. The aforementioned fact that most third parties take a pro-complainant stance in their submissions also means that it is rarely a neutral position. Some evidence suggests that in cases like the *US – Upland Cotton* dispute, the fear of irking the defendant has deterred countries from joining as third parties: Elsig and Stucki (2011) show that African cotton-producing countries were reluctant to join the dispute – even as third parties – from fear that the aid they received from the United States could be jeopardised as a result. While such fears can become an issue when the legal matter being challenged concerns developing countries, and the complainant is a major power, this does not appear to be the main driver of third-party participation across the board.

Recent evidence suggests that while countries may indeed all gain from third-parties status on average – both in terms of access to concessions,

[26] Horlick (1998).

and influence over the proceedings – states may nonetheless have reason to stay out of the room. Why is this? Precisely because of that most established of findings concerning third parties: while participation may be beneficial 'all else equal', the fact is that all else is not equal. By entering the room, third parties make it less likely that the litigants will reach a settlement. Settlements represent the fastest means of resolving a dispute. And while bilateral opportunism remains a risk at the margin, defendants who settle do often lift trade barriers in ways that favour the entire membership. What this means is that there exists a point at which the effect of an additional third party on the odds of settlement outweighs the benefit to that country of being in the room. One way of thinking about this is that by joining as a third party, a given country may obtain a bigger slice of the proverbial pie (if concessions offered by the respondent favour the Members in the room), but it may end up being a bigger slice of a much smaller pie (if no settlement is reached, and litigation drags on for many years, with an uncertain final outcome).

Johns and Pelc (2016) test these beliefs by looking at every country's decision to enter every dispute in the WTO's caseload. The model is identified by looking at every country's trade stake in the products traded in the dispute,[27] and assuming that the greater the trade stake, the more likely a country is to enter, all else equal. The paradoxical finding is that after accounting for a battery of controls, WTO Members become individually significantly less likely to join the more third parties are expected to be in the room. In short, countries appear to shy away from overcrowding.

Countries may thus reason that in a given case, it is 'preferable to let the litigants sort it out themselves'. It may also be that there is tacit delegation at play: countries may look to some focal players to prevent bilateral opportunism between the litigants. But whatever heuristic countries employ to make these choices, in aggregate, decisions over participation are highly consistent with a wish to avoid overcrowding. It is also an explanation for otherwise puzzling behaviour: why would countries themselves spurn participation which seems, on its face, so beneficial?

The sum of these findings goes some way to qualifying the main effect of third parties on settlement. Not only do third parties improve the fairness of those private settlements that do result, but countries actually appear to take into account their effect on the odds of settlement in their

[27] These trade data are collected at the appropriate level of aggregation, ranging from the two-digit to the six-digit Harmonized System (HS) level.

decision to join in the first place, limiting the negative externality of opening up participation.

E The Content of Third-Party Submissions

Given the glimpse they offer into issues of transparency and participation in international institutions, WTO third parties have been studied from many angles. Yet until now, little attention has been paid to the actual content of third-party submissions. As noted above, we know that most third parties take pro-complainant positions. Yet do most third parties agree with one another? Do they take more aggressive stances than the complainant? Are there consistent cleavages across the membership where some country clusters favour liberalisation, while others protect state sovereignty? Third-party submissions provide a rich record of country preferences on a wide array of legal questions.

In a first attempt to get at this variation, I collect the texts of all third-party submissions. I then use a text analysis algorithm similar to those found in plagiarism software to code each third-party submission in terms of its similarity, or textual proximity, to every other submission in the same dispute. The resulting variable is a dyadic measure bound between 0 and 1, where measures closer to 1 indicate more similar submissions. There are 12,086 such pairs, covering all countries that have ever joined a dispute as a third party.

It is possible to represent the resulting relationships between countries, on the basis of their submissions, in a single two-dimensional space. The method of multidimensional scaling (MDS) graphically represents the similarities and dissimilarities between various points. If one entered the distances between all the world's capital cities, the resulting MDS output would be a recognisable world map. In this case, instead of geographical distances, I visually represent the textual dissimilarities between country submissions.

Since for this initial application, it makes little sense to compare third-party submissions across different disputes, I only compare submissions within disputes. I then take the average distance of these pairings across the caseload. The result is a single average distance between the EU and the United States that takes into account the distance between each EU and US submission in every dispute where both countries file third-party submissions.

This approach means that many countries are never directly compared to one another, if they never found themselves as third parties in the same dispute. For those pairs of countries, dissimilarity is calculated on the basis of their relative distance to a third country with whom a direct measure is possible. For these reasons, however, the results of the multidimensional scaling model should be interpreted with caution; it is without a doubt less reliable than all the empirical findings cited above, which are based on more traditional regression techniques.

Nonetheless, the results, presented in Figure 9.2, are the best approximation of the relative distance between third-party submissions across the institution's first twenty years. For greater reliability, I focus on the top third-party participants – a country with e.g. a single third-party submission would lead to large potential errors. Several stylised relationships emerge from this first look. The two superpowers appear like median countries and are quite close to one another. India and China are outliers and on opposite poles. Similarly, traditionally

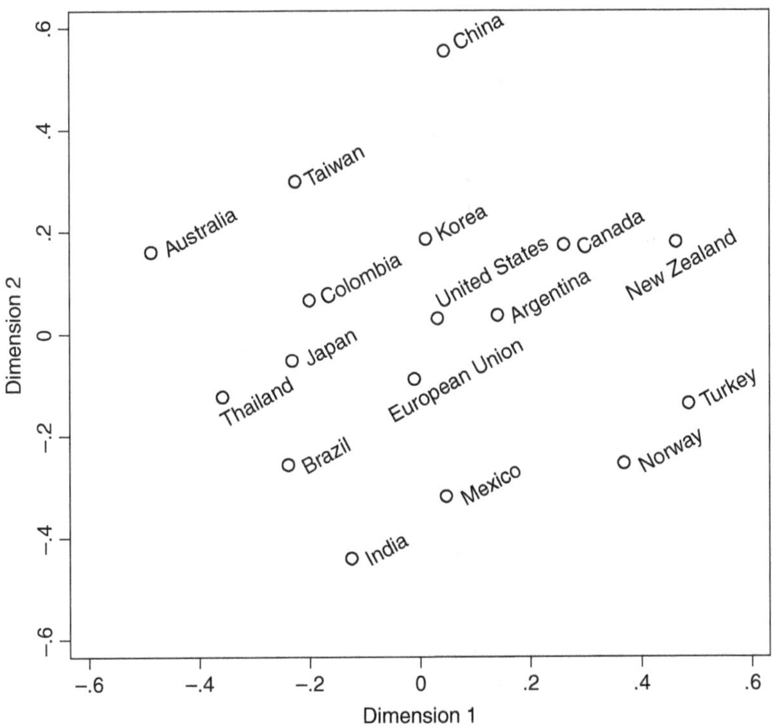

Figure 9.2. Multidimensional scaling of third-party submissions, 1995–2014.
Source: Created by the author.

antagonistic pairs like Australia and New Zealand also appear to submit divergent views, if judged by the textual content of their third-party submissions.

It is also possible to estimate the distance between these submissions using ordinary least squares (OLS), and seeking to explain dissimilarity between pairs through country characteristics, or structural variables. Doing so reveals, for instance, that third parties with similar wealth profiles tend to produce more similar submissions. This relationship is robust to a number of specifications (Daku and Pelc 2016).

F Conclusion

In this chapter, I have sought to summarise and extend the accumulated knowledge about third-party participation over the WTO's first twenty years. Countries join disputes for strategic reasons: they seek to guard their trade interests against discriminatory deals; they want to influence the jurisprudence that results from litigation; and they strive to increase their legal capacity by learning from other countries' proceedings. Yet by their sheer presence in the room, third parties have unintended consequences. Some of these are positive, while others are less so. Third-party status pits some of the fundamental objectives of the institution against one another: transparency comes at the possible cost of dispute settlement effectiveness, which in turn comes at the possible cost of nondiscrimination.

The most established finding in this regard is that third-party participation reduces the odds of settlement, going against a fundamental goal of the institution. Yet third parties also render those settlements that do occur less likely to be discriminatory, which benefits the remainder of the membership. Finally, there is also some indication that countries themselves take their own impact on the odds of settlement into account when deciding whether to join as third parties. The result is that states are more likely to stay out of the room when it is overly crowded, given the marginal effect of their presence on the odds of a swift resolution to the dispute. Countries prefer to have a smaller slice of a larger expected pie.

Third-party status has only grown in importance over the institution's first twenty years. This is a positive development. While early findings struck a note of caution about the net impact of opening up participation to third parties, in light of recent research, it appears that the positive effects of transparency more than outweigh its possible drawbacks.

References

Bagwell, K. and Staiger, R.W. 2004. 'Multilateral Trade Negotiations, Bilateral Opportunism and the Rules of GATT/WTO'. *Journal of International Economics* 63(1): 1–29.

Bown, Chad P. 2005. 'Participation in WTO Dispute Settlement: Complainants Interested Parties, and Free Riders'. *World Bank Economic Review* 19: 287–310.

Bown, Chad P. 2009. *Self-Enforcing Trade: Developing Countries and WTO Dispute Settlement*. Washington, DC: Brookings Institution Press.

Busch, Marc L. and Reinhardt, Eric. 2001. 'Bargaining in the Shadow of the Law: Early Settlement in GATT/WTO Disputes'. *Fordham International Law Journal* 24: 158–172.

Busch, Marc L. and Reinhardt, Eric. 2006. 'Three's a Crowd: Third Parties and WTO Dispute Settlement'. *World Politics* 58: 446–477.

Busch, Marc L., Reinhardt, Eric and Shaffer, Gregory. 2009. 'Does Legal Capacity Matter? Explaining Dispute Initiation and Antidumping Actions in the WTO'. *World Trade Review* 8: 559–577.

Busch, Marc L. and Pelc, Krzysztof J. 2010. 'The Politics of Judicial Economy at the World Trade Organization'. *International Organization* 64: 257–279.

Daku, Mark and Pelc, Krzysztof J. 2016. 'Who Holds Most Influence Over WTO Jurisprudence?' Working Paper, McGill University.

Davey, William J. and Porges, Amelia. 1998. 'Comments on Performance of the System I: Consultations and Deterrence'. *International Lawyer* 32: 695–707.

Davis, Christina L. and Bermeo, Sarah Blodgett. 2009. 'Who Files? Developing Country Participation in GATT/WTO Adjudication'. *Journal of Politics* 71: 1033–1049.

Elsig, Manfred and Stucki, Philipp. 2011. 'Low-Income Developing Countries and WTO Litigation: Why Wake Up the Sleeping Dog?' *Review of International Political Economy* 19: 292–316.

Gilligan, Michael, Johns, Leslie and Rosendorff, B. Peter. 2010. 'Strengthening International Courts and the Early Settlement of Disputes'. *Journal of Conflict Resolution* 54: 5–38.

Horlick, Gary N. 1998. 'The Consultation Phase of WTO Dispute Resolution: A Private Practitioner's View'. *International Lawyer* 32: 685–693.

Johns, Leslie and Pelc, Krzysztof J. 2014. 'Who Gets to Be in the Room? Manipulating Participation in WTO Disputes'. *International Organization* 68: 663–699.

Johns, Leslie and Pelc, Krzysztof J. 2016. 'Fear of Crowds in WTO Disputes: Why Don't More Countries Participate?' *Journal of Politics* 78 (1): 88–104.

Kucik, Jeffrey and Pelc, Krzysztof J. 2016. 'Measuring the Cost of Privacy: A Look at the Distributional Effects of Private Bargaining'. *British Journal of Political Science* 46 (4): 861–889

Pelc, Krzysztof J. 2010. 'Constraining Coercion? Legitimacy and Its Role in US Trade Policy, 1975–2000'. *International Organization* 64(01): 65–96.

Pelc, Krzysztof J. 2011. 'Why Do Some Countries Get Better WTO Accession Terms Than Others?' *International Organization* 65(4): 639–672.

Pelc, Krzysztof J. 2014. 'The Politics of Precedent in International Law: A Social Network Application'. *American Political Science Review* 108(3): 547–564.

Stasavage, David. 2004. 'Open-Door or Closed-Door? Transparency in Domestic and International Bargaining'. *International Organization* 58: 667–703.

Steinberg, Richard H. 2002. 'In the Shadow of Law or Power? Consensus-based Bargaining and Outcomes in the GATT/WTO'. *International Organization* 56: 339–374.

10

Mind the Gap

Navigating Between the WTO Agreement and Its Accession Protocols

JULIA Y. QIN

A Introduction

One new development in the world trading system has been the institutionalisation of country-specific rules via accession agreements to the World Trade Organization (WTO). When the WTO was established twenty years ago, its generally uniform rule structure was considered a major achievement, as compared to the somewhat fragmented rule structure of the General Agreement on Tariffs and Trade (GATT), under which different contracting parties could be subject to different rules, an approach known as 'GATT à la carte'. However, twenty years later, the WTO rule system is once again fragmented, except that this time the countries subject to different rules are a group of acceded Members. To date, more than thirty countries have become WTO Members through accession. Most of them are subject to country-specific rules set out in their accession protocols. These country-specific rules may confirm, elaborate, expand on or deviate from the standard provisions of the WTO Agreement. The scope and contents of such rules vary from Member to Member, depending on the result of specific accession negotiations. Except for a small number of provisions with built-in expiration dates, most of these Member-specific rules are permanent in duration.

In the past decade, the Member-specific rules have given rise to claims in more than twenty WTO disputes, most of them involving China,

I would like to thank Joost Pauwelyn and Ruosi Zhang for their insightful comments and Milan Hejtmanek for his editorial suggestions. Earlier drafts also benefited from comments by the participants at the World Trade Forum 2015, held in Bern, Switzerland in September 2015.

which accepted a large number of special rules when it acceded to the WTO in 2001. A major challenge presented by these disputes is how to define the relationship between the Member-specific rules of the accession protocol and the provisions of WTO multilateral agreements. Although each of the accession protocols has been formally designated as an 'integral part' of the WTO Agreement, the precise status of the accession protocols under the WTO Agreement and their relationship with WTO multilateral agreements are largely undefined by the treaty text. Consequently, WTO adjudicators have had to fill large gaps through treaty interpretation. Judicial interpretations thus far have not succeeded in clarifying these issues. In some cases, they have led to problematic jurisprudence, creating systemic incoherence and inconsistencies in WTO law and policy.

This chapter has two main objectives. First, it seeks to clarify the relationship between the WTO Agreement and its accession protocols. To that end, it re-examines the legal basis for Member-specific rulemaking, assesses relevant WTO jurisprudence and proposes a new approach to navigating the relationship. Second, it seeks to address four specific interpretive issues arising from the relationship between the WTO Agreement and its accession protocols: (i) how to determine the availability of the general exceptions contained in WTO agreements to Member-specific obligations; (ii) how to determine the scope of derogation from WTO provisions of the Member-specific rules; (iii) relevance of accession protocols to the interpretation of WTO multilateral agreements; and (iv) relevance of the accession protocol of one Member to the interpretation of the accession protocol of another Member. These interpretive issues have arisen in one form or another in WTO disputes, but not all of them have been properly resolved and some have not even attracted much attention.

The chapter will proceed as follows. Section A provides an overview of WTO accession law, the disputes involving accession rules and the special interpretive challenges that arise. Section B analyses the fraught relationship between accession protocols and WTO multilateral agreements. In this section, I will question the commonly accepted legal basis for Member-specific rulemaking under WTO law, critique the existing jurisprudence on the said relationship, and advocate a focus on systemic coherence in navigating between accession protocols and WTO multilateral agreements. Section C discusses the four specific interpretive issues identified above. It will demonstrate that there has been a disconnect between the formal status of accession protocols as an integral part of the WTO Agreement and the actual treatment of the accession protocols in treaty interpretation.

Before proceeding, a clarification of the terminology is necessary. In this chapter, the term 'WTO agreements' is used interchangeably with 'WTO multilateral agreements'. They both refer to the set of multilateral agreements adopted in the Uruguay Round of multilateral trade negotiations, which include the Marrakesh Agreement Establishing the World Trade Agreement ('Marrakesh Agreement' or 'WTO Agreement') and the 'Multilateral Trade Agreements' set out in Annexes 1, 2 and 3 thereto. The term 'WTO provisions' is used to refer to the provisions of WTO multilateral agreements.

B Overview

I Unique Accession Law of the WTO: Country-Specific Rules for Acceded Members

Since its inception, the WTO has expanded its membership significantly. Of the current 164 Members, thirty-six are acceded Members, which include major trading powers such as China, Taiwan, Vietnam and Russia.[1] A further 19 countries are in the process of accession negotiations. Despite the importance of accession to the world trade regime, WTO accession law is riddled with unanswered questions. These all stem from a unique feature of the WTO: unlike any other international organisation, the WTO has required its acceded Members to adhere to more stringent rules than those set out in the provisions of the WTO Agreement and has offered no official explanation for the differential treatment between its original Members and acceded Members (Charnovitz 2008; Tyagi 2012; Kennedy 2013; Qin 2015).

1 Unclear legal status of accession protocols

The country-specific rules are made pursuant to Article XII of the Marrakesh Agreement, which provides that any state or fully autonomous customs territory may accede to the WTO on 'terms to be agreed between it and the WTO'. Initially, the terms of accession were understood to comprise the scheduling of market access commitments of the acceding country and its assurance of compliance with the WTO agreements (Parenti 2000). Over time, however, the terms of accession

[1] See Accessions, World Trade Organization, www.wto.org/english/thewto_e/acc_e/acc_e.htm.

have expanded to include country-specific rules that expand on or deviate from the provisions of the WTO agreements. The quantity and content of such rules vary from country to country, depending on the outcome of particular accession negotiations. Typically, the country-specific rules are expressed in non-standard treaty language as specific 'commitments' of the acceding country, which are scattered throughout a lengthy accession working party report and are incorporated into the accession protocol by reference. The only exception is China's accession protocol, which contains seventeen sections of China-specific rules in the main text of the protocol, as well as 143 specific commitments in the accession working party report that are incorporated into the protocol by reference.[2] It is unclear how many country-specific rules have been made thus far, and what their exact contents are, since there is no official catalogue or compilation of all such rules publicly available.

The legal status of accession protocols is not defined in the Marrakesh Agreement. The only indication of such status is the 'integration clause' contained in each of the accession protocols, stating that the protocol 'shall be an integral part of the WTO Agreement'.[3] Formally, an accession protocol is a bilateral treaty between the WTO (an international organisation) and an acceding country. It is unclear how these two parties, neither of which is a party to the WTO Agreement, could effectively incorporate their bilateral treaty into the WTO Agreement, a multilateral treaty among individual Members. Nonetheless, the Members and WTO adjudicators have all accepted the legal effect of the integration clause, and moreover have treated accession protocols as 'covered agreements' enforceable under the Dispute Settlement Understanding (DSU), despite the lack of such a formal designation by the DSU.

The unclear legal status of accession protocols within the WTO legal framework and the lack of clear rationale for country-specific rulemaking have given rise to interpretive issues in disputes involving accession protocols. Absent textual guidance in treaty provisions, WTO adjudicators have had to fill the large gap through treaty interpretation. Specifically, they need to determine how the country-specific rules that expand on or deviate from the WTO provisions interact with the provisions of the WTO agreements.

[2] Protocol on the Accession of the People's Republic of China, WT/L/432 (10 November 2001); Report of the Working Party on the Accession of China, WT/ACC/CHN/49 (1 October 2001) ('China WPR').

[3] See WTO Secretariat, Technical Note on the Accession Process, Addendum, WT/ACC/10/Rev.4/Add.1 (25 May 2010): 4.

2 Five categories of WTO accession terms

The substantive provisions of WTO accession protocols may be divided into five categories, each of which denotes a different type of relationship with the WTO agreements:

(a) Commercial commitments set out in the goods and services schedules of the acceded Member. As for all other Members, the schedules of an acceded Member are incorporated into the General Agreement on Tariffs and Trade (GATT 1994) and the General Agreement on Trade in Service (GATS), thereby becoming part of the multilateral trade agreements.

(b) Affirmation of obligations under the Multilateral Trade Agreements. For example, paragraph 7.2 of China's Accession Protocol provides: 'In implementing the provisions of Articles III and XI of the GATT 1994 and the Agreement on Agriculture, China shall eliminate and shall not introduce, re-introduce or apply non-tariff measures that cannot be justified under the provisions of the WTO Agreement.' This type of provision is technically redundant, since the acceded Member is already obligated to comply with all the requirements of the WTO Agreement.

(c) Elaboration of existing provisions of the Multilateral Trade Agreements. For example, paragraph 8.1 of China's Accession Protocol specifies a number of measures that China shall undertake in implementing the Agreement on Import Licensing Procedures, including a commitment to 'issue import licences for a minimum duration of validity of six months'. The minimum duration of six months appears to elaborate the requirement of Article 3(5)(g) of the Agreement on Import Licensing Procedures that 'the period of licence validity shall be of reasonable duration and not be so short as to preclude imports'.

(d) Expansion of existing obligations under the Multilateral Trade Agreements. The terms of accession that expand WTO obligations are also known as 'WTO-plus', as they prescribe obligations that go beyond the existing requirements of the WTO agreements. Well-known examples in this category include the obligations undertaken by a number of acceded Members to bind and/or eliminate export duties,[4] and China's obligations to practise a market economy, to

[4] They include Mongolia, Latvia, Croatia, China, Saudi Arabia, Vietnam, Ukraine, Montenegro, Russia, Tajikistan, Kazakhstan, Liberia and Afghanistan. For a detailed discussion, see Qin (2012a).

improve domestic governance and to extend enhanced national treatment to foreign investment (Qin 2003).

(e) Derogation from existing obligations under the Multilateral Trade Agreements. The terms of accession that derogate from WTO obligations can be described as 'WTO-minus', as they reduce the burden of existing WTO disciplines for other Members in their trade relations with the acceded Member.[5] Major examples in this category are the special anti-dumping, countervailing and safeguard measures contained in China's Accession Protocol and in Vietnam's Accession Protocol.[6]

Of these five categories, only the last two deviate from or go beyond the scope of the WTO Agreement, thus raising the issue of relationship with the WTO provisions. Except for a small number of provisions with built-in expiration dates, all the country-specific rules are permanent provisions by design.[7]

II Disputes Arising from Accession Protocols

To date, accession commitments have given rise to claims in more than twenty WTO disputes, most of which concern China.[8] The first such claims were brought in 2006 in *China – Auto Parts*,[9] in which the complainants accused China of breaching a specific commitment on auto parts contained in China's Accession Working Party Report. The panel accepted the enforceability of the accession commitment in WTO dispute settlement, even though the accession protocol is not a 'covered agreement' under the DSU.[10] Since then, a whole slew of

5 As a conceptual matter, since WTO-minus rules also increase the burden of acceded Members, they may also be described as WTO-plus. However, distinguishing the two types is useful because WTO-plus and WTO-minus rules have given rise to different legal issues in practice.

6 China's Accession Protocol, sections 15 and 16; China WPR, para. 242; Report of the Working Party on the Accession of Viet Nam, WT/ACC/VNM/48 (27 October 2006), para. 255.

7 Almost all WTO-plus obligations are permanent. Among WTO-minus provisions, the special countervailing rules in the protocols of China and Vietnam are without expiration dates.

8 For a list of WTO disputes involving accession protocols, see Disputes by agreement. www.wto.org/english/tratop_e/dispu_e/dispu_agreements_index_e.htm?id=A30.

9 Appellate Body Reports, *China – Auto Parts*, WT/DS339, DS340, DS342/AB/R (15 December 2008).

10 Panel Reports, *China – Auto Parts*, WT/DS339, 340, 342/R (18 July 2008), para. 7.740.

disputes brought against China have made claims on the basis of China's additional rule commitments. They include: (i) *China – Publications and Audiovisual Products,*[11] a central claim of which was that China violated its accession commitments on trading rights; (ii) *China – Financial Information Services,*[12] which contained a claim regarding China's specific commitment on regulatory independence in the service sectors; (iii) *China – Taxes,*[13] which included claims concerning China's specific commitments on subsidies and internal measures; (iv) *China – Grants, Loans and Other Incentives,*[14] which included a claim on China's commitment not to maintain any export subsidy on agricultural products; (v) *China – Raw Materials*[15] and *China – Rare Earths,*[16] which are two high-profile cases built on claims concerning China's special commitments on export duties; (vi) *China – Wind Power,*[17] *China – Auto Parts Subsidies,*[18] and *China – Tax Measures,*[19] each of which included claims regarding China's special commitments on transparency; and (vii) *China – Textile,*[20] a dispute brought by Mexico

11 Appellate Body Report, *China – Publications and Audiovisual Products*, WT/DS363/AB/R (21 December 2009).

12 *China – Financial Information Services*, DS372, DS373, DS378. The case was settled with China's agreement to withdraw the measures at issue. See www.wto.org/english/tratop_e/dispu_e/cases_e/ds372_e.htm.

13 *China – Taxes*, DS358, DS359. The case was settled. See www.wto.org/english/tratop_e/dispu_e/cases_e/ds358_e.htm.

14 *China – Grants, Loans and Other Incentives*, DS387, DS388, DS390. The case was settled with China withdrawing all the measures in question. See https://ustr.gov/about-us/policy-offices/press-office/press-releases/2009/december/united-states-wins-end-china's-"famous-brand"-sub.

15 Appellate Body Reports, *China – Raw Materials*, WT/DS394, 395, 398/AB/R (30 January 2012).

16 Appellate Body Reports, *China – Rare Earths*, WT/DS431, 432, 433/AB/R (7 August 2014).

17 Request for Consultations by the United States, *China – Measures Concerning Wind Power Equipment*, WT/DS419/1 (6 January 2011) (claiming, *inter alia*, that China failed to make available a translation of the measures at issue into one or more of the official languages of the WTO).

18 Request for Consultations by the United States, *China – Certain Measures Affecting the Automobile and Automobile Parts Industries*, WT/DS450/1 (20 September 2012) (claiming that China breached several special commitments on the publication, notification, and translation of its trade measures).

19 Request for Consultation by the United States, *China – Tax Measures Concerning Certain Domestically Produced Aircraft*, WT/DS501/1 (8 December 2015) (claiming that China breached several special commitments on the publication, notification, comment period and translation of its measures).

20 Request for Consultations by Mexico, *China – Measures Relating to the Production and Exportation of Apparel and Textile Products*, WT/DS451/1 (18 October 2012).

claiming, *inter alia*, that China breached thirty-eight of the accession commitments contained in its Accession Working Party Report.

In addition, China has launched a number of disputes of its own involving WTO-minus rules of its Accession Protocol. They include: (i) four cases against US anti-dumping and countervailing measures,[21] (ii) one case against US special safeguards[22] and (iii) two disputes against EU anti-dumping measures.[23] In all these cases, China claimed that the respondent acted inconsistently with the special trade-remedy rules of its accession protocol.

Besides China, at least two other acceded Members have been involved in disputes over their accession protocols. One is Vietnam, which has brought two separate cases against the United States, claiming that US anti-dumping measures on Vietnamese shrimp were inconsistent with the provisions of its accession protocol.[24] The other is Armenia, whose specific accession commitments on customs duties and internal taxes have become the legal basis for claims in a dispute brought by Ukraine.[25]

III *Interpretive Challenges*

Accession protocols have presented special interpretive challenges to the WTO judiciary. Such challenges stem primarily from the lack of clear textual guidance as to the relation between country-specific rules and provisions of the WTO agreements. Ideally, such systemic issues should be addressed by the 'legislative' body of the WTO – the Ministerial Conference and the General Council – through their exclusive authority

[21] Appellate Body Report, *US – Countervailing Measures (China)*, WT/DS437/AB/R (18 December 2014); Appellate Body Report, *US – Countervailing and Anti-Dumping Measures (China)*, WT/DS449/AB/R (7 July 2014); Appellate Body Report, *US – Anti-Dumping and Countervailing Duties (China)*, WT/DS379/AB/R (11 March 2011); Request for Consultations by China, *US – Preliminary Anti-Dumping and Countervailing Duty Determinations on Coated Free Sheet Paper from China*, WT/DS368/1 (18 September 2007).

[22] Appellate Body Report, *US – Tyres (China)*, WT/DS399/AB/R (5 September 2011).

[23] Panel Report, *EU – Footwear (China)*, WT/DS405/R (28 October 2011); Appellate Body Report, *EC – Fasteners (China)*, WT/DS397/AB/R (15 July 2011).

[24] Panel Report, *US – Shrimp (Viet Nam)*, WT/DS404/R (11 July 2011); Panel Report, *US – Shrimp II (Viet Nam)*, WT/DS429/R (17 November 2014).

[25] Request for the Establishment of a Panel by Ukraine, *Armenia – Measures Affecting the Importation and Internal Sale of Cigarettes and Alcoholic Beverages*, WT/DS411/2/Rev.1 (8 October 2010).

to adopt multilateral interpretations.[26] In practice, however, the WTO judiciary has decided to fill the large gaps in the treaty texts on its own.

'WTO-plus' and 'WTO-minus' provisions have given rise to different interpretive issues. With respect to 'WTO-plus' obligations, a major issue has been the availability of public policy exceptions. The accession protocols contain numerous rule commitments that go beyond the requirements of the WTO agreements, but do not provide general exceptions similar to those in GATT Articles XX and XXI or GATS Articles XIV and XIV *Bis*. The question, therefore, is whether the additional obligations under WTO accession protocols are entitled to such policy exceptions at all, and if so, on what legal basis. This issue has come up in several disputes. In each case, the Appellate Body made its decision based on whether it could identify a 'textual link' in the protocol provision to the WTO Agreement. Thus, it accepted the availability of GATT Article XX to the trading-rights obligations under China's Accession Protocol,[27] but denied such availability to the export-duty obligations under the same.[28] This strict textualist approach has led to systemically inconsistent and inequitable results. For one thing, it is inexplicable why the additional obligations undertaken by an acceded Member to limit the use of export duties should be denied of the public policy exceptions that are available to all obligations under GATT and GATS, including the obligations of most-favoured-nation (MFN) treatment and national treatment, two fundamental principles of the WTO system.[29]

With respect to 'WTO-minus' provisions, the main issues of interpretation have concerned either the legality of such provisions or the scope of their derogation from the generally applicable WTO rules. As noted above, China has launched a number of cases challenging trade-remedy measures taken by other Members under the 'WTO-minus' provisions of its Accession Protocol. Of these cases, the one that best demonstrates the interpretive challenge is *US – Tyres (China)*.[30] At issue were the special tariffs levied on certain Chinese tyres by the United States under Section 16 of China's Accession Protocol. Section 16 allows WTO Members, during the first twelve years after China's accession, to invoke safeguard measures against imports from China without doing the same against like products from other countries. Section 16, therefore, directly

[26] WTO Agreement, Article IX: 2.
[27] Appellate Body Report, *China – Publications*, paras. 229–233.
[28] Appellate Body Reports, *China – Raw Materials*, para. 291.
[29] For a general critique, see Qin (2012b).
[30] Appellate Body Report, *US – Tyres (China)*, above note 22.

derogates from the MFN requirement in GATT Article I:1 and Article 2.2 of the Agreement on Safeguards;[31] yet China's Accession Protocol provides no rationale for the derogation. In its complaint, China made a primary claim that the US safeguard measures were inconsistent with GATT Article I:1,[32] thus effectively challenging the legality of the China-specific safeguards. Remarkably, the panel managed to avoid addressing the issue altogether. It did so by characterising the MFN claim as 'entirely dependent' on China's other claims under Section 16,[33] even though violation of GATT Article I:1 had been clearly listed as the primary claim in both China's consultation request and its panel request.[34] While politically savvy, the panel's approach contrasted sharply with previous jurisprudence in cases such as *EC – Tariff Preferences*, where the Appellate Body went to great lengths to clarify the relationship between GATT Article I:1 and the Enabling Clause,[35] and *US – Wool Shirts and Blouses*, where the Appellate Body carefully distinguished, for the purpose of allocating the burden of proof, between the nature of the transitional safeguard mechanism provided in the Agreement on Textiles and Clothing and that of GATT exceptions.[36]

C The Fraught Relationship Between Accession Protocols and WTO Agreements

The issue of the relationship between accession protocols and WTO multilateral agreements arises because of potential inconsistencies between the country-specific rules of the protocols and provisions of the WTO agreements. To define this relationship, it is necessary first to

31 Article 2.2 specifically provides: 'Safeguard measures shall be applied to a product being imported irrespective of its source.'

32 Request for Panel by China, *US – Tyres (China)*, WT/DS399/2 (11 December 2009).

33 Panel Report, *US – Tyres (China)*, WT/DS399/R (13 December 2010), para. 7.418. The panel explained the reason for this treatment in a footnote: 'The dependent nature of China's GATT 1994 claims is shown by China's argument that there is "also" a GATT 1994 violation . . . (*See* China's First Written Submission, paras. 417 and 421).' See also fn.557 to para. 7.418. Thus, the Panel based its ruling on the MFN claim solely on the word 'also' in a written submission, instead of China's formal consultation and panel requests.

34 Above note 32; Request for Consultations by China, *US – Tyres (China)*, WT/DS399/1 (16 September 2009). Interestingly, China did not appeal the Panel ruling on the issue.

35 Appellate Body Report, *EC – Tariff Preferences*, WT/DS246/AB/R (7 April 2004), paras. 79–125.

36 Appellate Body Report, *US – Wool Shirts and Blouses*, WT/DS33/AB/R (25 April 1997), at p. 16.

examine the legal basis for making country-specific rules in accession protocols.

I The (Questionable) Legal Basis for Country-Specific Rulemaking

1 Does Article XII authorise country-specific rulemaking?

It is commonly assumed that Article XII of the Marrakesh Agreement authorises the making of all country-specific rules in accession agreements. This assumption, however, is questionable.

Article XII Accession provides:

1. Any State . . . may accede to this Agreement, on terms to be agreed between it and the WTO. Such accession shall apply to this Agreement and the Multilateral Trade Agreements annexed thereto.
2. Decisions on accession shall be taken by the Ministerial Conference. The Ministerial Conference shall approve the agreement on the terms of accession by a two-thirds majority of the Members of the WTO.

Article XII:1 makes accession to the WTO Agreement subject to the 'terms to be agreed' between the acceding country and the WTO, but does not specify what types of terms may be agreed between them. According to the Appellate Body:

> The 'terms' of accession referred to in the first sentence of Article XII are not defined. Thus, apart from the stipulation in the second sentence of Article XII . . . this provision does not spell out the content of, or impose limitations on, such 'terms'. Rather, such terms are to be 'agreed' upon by the WTO and the individual acceding Member during a specific accession process.[37]

The Appellate Body, therefore, appears to agree that the absence of an express limit on the 'terms of accession' authorises the making of any country-specific rules via accession protocols.

However, does the lack of definition on the 'terms' of accession in Article XII mean that the WTO Agreement, as a whole, does not place any limit on such terms? Pursuant to the interpretive rules of the Vienna Convention on the Law of Treaties (VCLT), the 'terms' of accession in Article XII must be interpreted in its 'context' and in the light of the object and purpose of the treaty. Such 'context' shall comprise the 'text' of the WTO Agreement, including its preamble and annexes, as well as 'any

[37] Appellate Body Reports, *China – Rare Earths*, above note 16, para. 5.27.

agreement relating to' the WTO Agreement 'which was made between all the parties in connection with the conclusion' of the WTO Agreement.[38]

One of the highly relevant contexts of Article XII should be Article XI:1, which provides the criteria for the original membership of the WTO:

Article XI Original Membership

1. The contracting parties to GATT 1947 as of the date of entry into force of this Agreement, and the European Communities, which accept this Agreement and the Multilateral Trade Agreements and for which Schedules of Concessions and Commitments are annexed to GATT 1994 and for which Schedules of Specific Commitments are annexed to GATS shall become original Members of the WTO.

The provision sets out two conditions for an existing GATT contracting party to become a Member of the WTO: (1) it accepts the Marrakesh Agreement and the multilateral trade agreements, and (2) it has a GATT schedule and a GATS schedule. The first condition is about the acceptance of WTO rules, which apply to all Members generally and uniformly. The second condition concerns the making of specific commercial commitments, the scope and content of which vary from country to country depending on the result of trade negotiations.

Unless there is reason to believe that the Uruguay Round negotiators intended to create two different classes of WTO Members, the substantive conditions for the original membership should also be the substantive conditions for acceded Members. Accordingly, the 'terms of accession' should consist of (1) the acceptance by the acceding country of the WTO rules as provided in the Marrakesh Agreement and the Multilateral Trade Agreements, and (2) specific commercial commitments by the acceding country to be included in its GATT and GATS schedules.

But is there reason to believe that the Uruguay Round negotiators intended to treat acceded Members as a different class from the original Members? There is no treaty language suggesting such an intention. On the contrary, the WTO Agreement provides a 'one-Member one-vote' decision-making mechanism;[39] its preamble confirms one of its objectives as 'the elimination of discriminatory treatment in international trade

[38] Vienna Convention on the Law of Treaties, Vienna, 23 May 1969, in force 27 January 1980, 1155 UNTS 331, Article 31.

[39] WTO Agreement, Article IX:1.

relations'; and the multilateral trade agreements impose various MFN obligations that require equal treatment of all Members in respect of the subject matters thereunder. Moreover, the 'single package undertaking' design of the WTO, which prohibits individual reservations under the WTO Agreement,[40] embodies the intention of the drafters to maintain a uniform set of WTO rules. And the stringent rules for amendment of the WTO Agreement make it extremely difficult to change this design.[41] All these provisions of the WTO Agreement, and the overall design and structure of the WTO legal framework, constitute relevant 'contexts' for understanding the 'terms of accession' under Article XII.

The intention of the Uruguay Round negotiators to treat acceded Members and original Members equally was also explicitly expressed in the Ministerial Decision on the Acceptance of and Accession to the Agreement Establishing the World Trade Organization of 15 April 1994.[42] The Decision was intended to clarify several situations during the transition period from the adoption of the Uruguay Round agreements to the entry into force of the WTO Agreement. Its preamble declares that the Ministers:

> Recogniz[e] that the WTO Agreement does not distinguish in any way between WTO Members which accepted that Agreement in accordance with its Articles XI and XIV [i.e. the original Members] and WTO Members which acceded to it in accordance with its Article XII . . .

The formal recognition that the WTO Agreement 'does not distinguish in any way' between its original Members and acceded Members confirmed a basic principle of WTO membership as originally understood. The Decision was one of the several Ministerial Decisions and Declarations that were adopted, together with the WTO Agreement, as 'an integral part' of the Final Act Embodying the Results of the Uruguay Round of Multilateral Trade Negotiations.[43] Thus, for the purpose of treaty interpretation, the Decision constitutes an 'agreement relating to' the WTO Agreement 'which was made between all the parties in connection with the conclusion of' the WTO Agreement within the meaning of VCLT Article 31(2)(a). And as such, it must also be taken into account as the treaty 'context' for the interpretation of Article XII.

[40] WTO Agreement, Article XVI:5.

[41] WTO Agreement, Article X.

[42] 'Decision on the Acceptance of and Accession to the Agreement Establishing the World Trade Organization'. In World Trade Organization (1999: 409).

[43] Final Act Embodying the Results of the Uruguay Round of Multilateral Trade Negotiations, 15 April 1994, 1867 U.N.T.S. 14, para. 1.

To say that the terms of accession under Article XII should be the same as the conditions for the original membership under Article XI, however, does not preclude the making of any country-specific rules in an accession. If the relevant conditions in the acceding country differ from those in the original Members in such a fundamental way as to render the application of WTO rules meaningless or largely ineffective, it might be desirable or even necessary to prescribe country-specific rules to remedy the situation. In addition, to ensure effective application of the WTO Agreement, it might be desirable to seek the assurance of the acceding country that it will abide by particular WTO rules in specified situations. However, any country-specific rules in derogation of the generally applicable WTO rules should be transitional in nature and should not exceed the scope of the existing provisions of the WTO Agreement.

The above understanding on the 'terms of accession' is also borne out by the history of the world trade system. Article XII of the WTO Agreement is closely modelled after the accession provision of GATT 1947.[44] During the GATT era, the terms of accession were commonly understood as tariff and non-tariff concessions included in the GATT schedules. Although an accession protocol might contain terms pertaining to GATT rules, they were typically reservations in derogation of a specific GATT provision.[45] The only exceptions were Poland, Romania and Hungary. When these countries acceded to the GATT, they each maintained a central-planned economy, in which all imports and exports were controlled by government plans. Since tariffs and traditional non-tariff measures were not used to restrict trade in these countries, the GATT disciplines would be largely ineffective. To address this systemic incompatibility, the GATT contracting parties negotiated certain special provisions of accession, such as annual increases in imports and special safeguard provisions, so as to achieve a perceived level of reciprocity in market access.[46] The limited number of country-

[44] GATT 1947, Article XXXIII.

[45] See GATT Analytical Index, Article XXXIII, p. 1023, at www.wto.org/english/res_e/booksp_e/gatt_ai_e/gatt_ai_e.htm.

[46] See Protocol for the Accession of Poland (30 June 1967), GATT Basic Instruments and Selected Documents [BISD] (15th Supp.) at 46, 52 (1968); Protocol for the Accession of Romania to the General Agreement on Tariffs and Trade (15 October 1971), BISD (18th Supp.) at 5, 10 (1972); Protocol for the Accession of Hungary to the General Agreement on Tariffs and Trade (8 August 1973), BISD (20th Supp.) at 3, 4 (1974). Unlike these three countries, none of the acceded Members to the WTO, including China and Vietnam, maintained a central-planned economy at the time of accession.

specific rules in GATT accession agreements, therefore, did not exceed the scope of the GATT provisions.

To summarise, when Article XII is interpreted in its treaty context, it becomes clear that the 'terms of accession' should be essentially the same as the criteria for the original membership prescribed in Article XI. That is to say, the country-specific terms of accession should, in principle, be limited to the commercial concessions in the GATT and GATS schedules. Country-specific terms deviating from WTO rules should only be made when there is a need to ensure effective integration of the acceding country into the system. This understanding is consistent with prior GATT accession practice. It also explains why the WTO Agreement, a carefully-drafted constitutive treaty for the world trading system, does not contain any provision regarding the status of accession protocols – if the 'terms of accession' would all be incorporated into GATT and GATS schedules and only on rare occasions would country-specific rules be made, there should be no need to separately provide for the status of accession protocols in the constituent instrument.

2 Subsequent practice of the WTO as the legal basis for Member-specific rulemaking

Despite its questionable legal basis under Article XII, country-specific rulemaking has become standard practice in WTO accessions. Such practice has affected the WTO Agreement in a variety of ways:

- It has changed the meaning of 'terms of accession' under Article XII, from that originally intended, to include substantive rules that modify the provisions of WTO agreements as between existing WTO Members and each acceded Member. Consequently, the meaning of 'terms of accession', as interpreted by subsequent practice of the WTO, is no longer consistent with the treaty contexts of Article XII.
- It has turned Article XII into a gateway to modify provisions of the WTO agreements that affect the rights and obligations of all Members, in circumvention of the amendment provisions of the WTO Agreement.
- It has designated all country-specific rules of the accession protocols as integral parts of the WTO Agreement, even though none of the signatories to the accession protocols is a party to the WTO Agreement.
- It has made accession protocols 'covered agreements' under the DSU, despite the absence of such a designation under the DSU.

A treaty may be modified by subsequent practice of its parties. This method of treaty modification was recognised by a draft provision of the VCLT, although the provision was never adopted.[47] The lack of codification notwithstanding, international practice has continued to develop in this regard.[48] As a concept, 'subsequent practice' is broad, as it may encompass not only that of individual states, but also that of international organisations. This understanding has been confirmed by the opinions of the International Court of Justice (ICJ), which has relied on subsequent practice of the United Nations (UN), rather than that of its Member States, to justify de facto modifications of the UN Charter.[49] The ICJ cited the evolving practice of the UN over time and the general acceptance of such practice by the UN members as the basis for its opinions.[50] Judging by the ICJ standards, we may find that using accession protocols to modify the WTO Agreement has been an evolving practice of the WTO and that such practice has been generally accepted by the WTO Members. In fact, the world trade regime has a particularly rich tradition of developing law through subsequent practice.[51] As a result of historical circumstances, nearly the entire institutional apparatus of the GATT, including its Council and dispute settlement mechanism, was created through subsequent practice of the contracting parties. Furthermore, the GATT's subsequent practice has sanctioned serious derogations from the provisions of GATT 1947. A prominent example is the adoption of the 'Enabling Clause by the CONTRACTING PARTIES' in 1979, which created a permanent exception to the MFN clause in Article I:1 without following the

[47] Draft Article 38 of the VCLT provides: 'A treaty may be modified by subsequent practice in the application of the treaty establishing the agreement of the parties to modify its provisions.' See 'Reports of the International Law Commission on the second part of its seventeenth session and on its eighteenth session', *Yearbook of the International Law Commission* (1966), Vol. II, U.N. Doc. A/CN.4/SER.A/1966/Add.1, at 236. The debate on draft Article 38 was summarised in Nolte (2013): 169.

[48] See Nolte (2013: 201–202) (referring to several cases decided by the International Court of Justice and other international tribunals).

[49] See ICJ, Legal Consequences for States of the Continued Presence of South Africa in Namibia (South West Africa) Notwithstanding Security Council Resolution 276 (1970), Advisory Opinion, 1971 I.C.J. 16 (21 June) (concerning the meaning of Article 27(3) of the UN Charter); Legal Consequences of the Construction of a Wall in the Occupied Palestinian Territory, Advisory Opinion, 2004 I.C.J. 136 (9 July) (concerning the meaning of Article 12(1) of the UN Charter). For detailed treatment, see Arato (2013: 289–357). *See* also Nolte (2013: 201–202).

[50] See ICJ, above note 49.

[51] See generally, Berrisch (1991: 497).

procedures for treaty amendment of GATT 1947.[52] It appears that the WTO practice of using accession protocols to modify the WTO Agreement is in keeping with GATT tradition.[53] While the legal basis for country-specific rulemaking may be found in the subsequent practice of the WTO, we must recognise the negative implications of such practice for the WTO legal system. Formally, making country-specific rules for selected WTO Members on a permanent basis has destroyed the uniformity of WTO rules. Substantively, the practice has created a new exception to the non-discrimination principle of the WTO – the acceded Members as a group may be treated less favourably than the original Members under the WTO Agreement – without clear justification. As is more fully explained elsewhere, the unprincipled rulemaking in WTO accessions undermines the legitimacy of the WTO (Qin 2015). In a sense, the practice reflects an institutional failure – the WTO as a major international organisation is unable to safeguard the integrity of its legal regime. And the practice will continue so long as the WTO remains a 'Member-driven' organisation.[54]

II WTO Jurisprudence on the Relationship Between Accession Protocols and WTO Agreements

Although the first WTO dispute involving China's Accession Protocol was brought in 2006, it was not until the case of *China – Rare Earths*[55] in 2014 that the WTO adjudicators engaged in an extensive discussion on the relationship between accession protocols and the WTO Agreement. The issue triggering the assessment was the applicability of the general exceptions of GATT Article XX to China's WTO-plus obligation on the use of export duties under Paragraph 11.3 of its Accession Protocol. The parties in the dispute debated how Paragraph 11.3 of the Protocol

[52] Decision of the Contracting Parties on 28 November 1979, *Differential and More Favourable Treatment Reciprocity and Fuller Participation of Developing Countries*, BISD (26th Supp.) 203 (1980).

[53] It is important to note, however, that because GATT 1947 never entered into force itself and instead was brought into effect through the Protocol of Provisional Application in 1947 and a series of protocols of accession thereafter, there was no formal legal obstacle preventing the contracting parties from modifying the application of GATT provisions through subsequent agreements. For major differences in treaty structure between the GATT and the WTO, see Qin (2015).

[54] See 'Whose WTO Is It Anyway?' at. www.wto.org/english/thewto_e/whatis_e/tif_e/org1_e.htm.

[55] Above note 16.

should be integrated into the WTO Agreement. According to China, because the use of export duties is concerned with a GATT issue, Paragraph 11.3 should be deemed to be an integral part of GATT 1994; consequently, GATT Article XX should be available to justify a breach of Paragraph 11.3. The complainants disagreed, arguing that the Protocol should be integrated into the Marrakesh Agreement itself, or be deemed akin to a new annex to the Marrakesh Agreement, parallel to the Multilateral Trade Agreements; either way, a breach of Paragraph 11.3 of the Protocol would not be entitled to the GATT exceptions.[56]

1 Panel's ruling and dissenting opinion

The panel was split on the issue. The majority of the panel disagreed with China, finding that China's Accession Protocol is, in its entirety, an integral part of the Marrakesh Agreement and not that the individual provisions thereof are also 'integral parts' of the Multilateral Trade Agreements annexed to the Marrakesh Agreement.[57] One panelist dissented.[58] In his view, the location of a specific term of accession within the WTO Agreement should be determined 'in light of the subject matter and the underlying rationale' of that commitment.[59] Because Paragraph 11.3 'adds to the basic obligations of the GATT 1994 relating to border tariffs', the panelist reasoned, its provision must be read 'cumulatively and simultaneously' with related GATT provisions on export tariffs and 'as an integral part of the GATT system of rights and obligations'.[60]

2 Appellate Body's assessment

On appeal, the Appellate Body declined to determine the precise location of China's Accession Protocol within the WTO legal framework. It considered the question 'not dispositive' of the issue regarding the relationship between a specific provision of the Protocol on one hand, and provisions of the Marrakesh Agreement and the Multilateral Trade Agreements on the other.[61] Nonetheless, the Appellate Body found no error in the majority panel's conclusion that individual provisions of

[56] See Panel Reports, *China – Rare Earths*, WT/DS394, 395, 398/R (26 March 2014), para. 7.126.

[57] Panel Reports, *China – Rare Earths*, para. 7.93.

[58] Panel Reports, *China – Rare Earths*, paras. 7.118–7.138 (separate opinion by one panelist).

[59] Panel Reports, *China – Rare Earths*, paras. 7.131–7.132.

[60] Panel Reports, *China – Rare Earths*, para. 7.138.

[61] Appellate Body Reports, above note 16, para. 5.73.

China's Accession Protocol are *not* integral parts of the Multilateral Trade Agreements.[62] As for the separate opinion of the dissenting panelist, the Appellate Body summarily dismissed it in a footnote without discussion.[63]

The key conclusions of the Appellate Body's assessment on the relationship between the Accession Protocol and the WTO agreements are as follows:

(a) The integration clause in Paragraph 1.2 of China's Accession Protocol 'serves to build a bridge' between the package of Protocol provisions and the package of existing rights and obligations under the Marrakesh Agreement and the multilateral trade agreements.[64] Just like the multilateral trade agreements, China's Accession Protocol is 'an integral part' of the Marrakesh Agreement and thereby forms 'an integral part' of the 'single package of WTO rights and obligations'.[65]
(b) Within this single package, 'neither obligations nor rights may be automatically transposed from one part of the legal framework into another'. Just 'like the approach to ascertaining the relationship among provisions of the Multilateral Trade Agreements, the specific relationship between the provisions of China's Accession Protocol, on the one hand, and the provisions of the Marrakesh Agreement and the Multilateral Trade Agreements, on the other hand, must also be determined on a case-by-case basis'.[66]
(c) The questions of whether a particular Protocol provision at issue 'has an objective link' to existing obligations under the Marrakesh

62 Appellate Body Reports, above note 16, para. 5.73.

63 Appellate Body Reports, above note 16, fn. 504. The footnote, which is to paragraph 5.68 that dismisses China's argument on the 'intrinsic relationship' between specific provisions of its Accession Protocol and WTO provisions, reads in its entirety as follows: 'For these reasons, we also see no basis for the opinion of the dissenting panelist in these disputes that "the defences provided in the GATT 1994 are automatically available to justify any GATT-related obligations, including border tariff-related obligations – unless a contrary intention is expressed by the acceding Member and WTO Members". Indeed, the Appellate Body rejected arguments by China to this effect in *China – Raw Materials*.'

64 Appellate Body Reports, above note 16, paras. 5.73; 5.50. The Appellate Body also stated that the integration clause, together with Article XII:1 of the Marrakesh Agreement, 'serves the function of integrating China's Accession Protocol into the single package of WTO rights and obligations, just as Article II:2 of the Marrakesh Agreement serves the same function with regard to the Multilateral Trade Agreements'. Appellate Body Reports, above note 16, para. 5.49.

65 Appellate Body Reports, above note 16, para. 5.57.

66 Appellate Body Reports, above note 16, para. 5.57.

> Agreement and the Multilateral Trade Agreements, and whether the exceptions under those agreements may be invoked to justify a breach of such Protocol provision 'must be answered through a thorough analysis of the relevant provisions on the basis of the customary rules of treaty interpretation and the circumstances of the dispute'.[67]

Thus, it appears that the Appellate Body, while declining to identify the precise location of accession protocols within the WTO legal framework, has effectively viewed accession protocols as parallel to the Multilateral Trade Agreements, akin to new annexes to the Marrakesh Agreement. Indeed, in reaching the above conclusions, the Appellate Body referred to its jurisprudence on the relationship between GATT Article XIX and the Agreement on Safeguards[68] and the relationship between GATT Article XX and the Agreement on Technical Barriers to Trade (TBT Agreement).[69] It also referred to the express terms in the Agreement on Trade-Related Investment Measures (TRIMs) regarding the relationship between TRIMs obligations and GATT exceptions.[70] It was upon making these references that the Appellate Body concluded that, just like the relationship between the multilateral trade agreements, neither obligations nor rights may be 'automatically transposed' between accession protocols and other parts of the WTO legal framework.

3 A critical appraisal

The Appellate Body's affirmation that an accession protocol forms 'an integral part' of the 'single package of WTO rights and obligations' lays the basic foundation for understanding the relationship between protocol provisions and WTO multilateral agreements. Once that foundation is laid, the task is to determine how a specific provision of the protocol interacts with other components of this single package. In this regard, it is sensible for the Appellate Body to view the accession protocols as akin to the Multilateral Trade Agreements in terms of their relationship to the Marrakesh Agreement. If, as the majority of the panel had found, the accession protocols should be deemed as integral parts of the Marrakesh Agreement, then, in accordance with Article XVI:3 of the Marrakesh

67 Appellate Body Reports, above note 16, para. 5.74.
68 Appellate Body Reports, above note 16, paras. 5.53; 5.54.
69 Appellate Body Reports, above note 16, para. 5.56.
70 Appellate Body Reports, above note 16, para. 5.56.

Agreement,[71] the Member-specific rules would prevail over all provisions of the Multilateral Trade Agreements, which could lead to absurd results.[72] However, it is one thing to regard the accession protocols as akin to the Multilateral Trade Agreements in respect of their relationship to the Marrakesh Agreement, but it is quite another to view the relationship between an accession protocol and the Multilateral Trade Agreements as essentially the same as the relationship between the Multilateral Trade Agreements. That is because there are important differences between these two types of relationships. First of all, the accession protocols differ from the Multilateral Trade Agreements in their purpose, design and structure. While each of the Multilateral Trade Agreements is designed to provide a multilateral discipline on a distinct aspect of trade, the accession protocol is a legal instrument designed to bring a particular country into the WTO system. Over time, this instrument has evolved into an agreement of ad hoc rules that are targeted at specific situations in the acceding country. These rules typically cover subject matters along the entire spectrum of the WTO legal framework. As such, they are meant to supplement and modify the Multilateral Trade Agreements as applied between the acceded Member and other Members, rather than to provide a new generally applicable discipline separate from the Multilateral Trade Agreements. It is owing to this special design that the accession protocol, as pointed out by China, 'does not include most of the important features that many of the Multilateral Trade Agreements possess, such as proper general exceptions, security exceptions or a modification clause'.[73] It is also owing to this special design that the interpretation of a specific provision of an accession protocol may well require *treating* such provision as 'integrated' with provisions of one or more of the Multilateral Trade Agreements. In other words, provisions of one or more of the Multilateral Trade Agreements may constitute an *indispensable* textual

[71] Article XVI:3 provides: 'In the event of a conflict between a provision of the Marrakesh Agreement and a provision of any of the Multilateral Trade Agreements, the provision of the Marrakesh Agreement shall prevail.'

[72] For example, it might raise a question as to whether China's export duty obligations under Paragraph 11.3 are subject to the MFN obligation. Since Paragraph 11.3 does not mention MFN, the omission could be interpreted as prevailing over GATT Article I:1 which requires an MFN application of export duties.

[73] Appellate Body Reports, above note 16, para. 5.69. China characterised its Accession Protocol as not a 'self-contained agreement'. The Appellate Body dismissed the term as not being 'an apt descriptor' of any of the agreements contained in the integrated WTO framework. Appellate Body Reports, above note 16, para. 5.70.

context for a specific provision of the accession protocol. If we perceive there is a 'wall' between different agreements within the WTO legal framework, the 'wall' separating an accession protocol from the Multilateral Trade Agreements is necessarily very thin and porous. Moreover, the circumstances of the negotiation and conclusion of accession protocols are markedly different from those of the Multilateral Trade Agreements. Instead of being subject to multilateral checks and balances, an accession protocol is negotiated between the applicant country on the one hand, and existing Members of the WTO on the other. As a result, the content of country-specific rules in a given protocol and the quality of their drafting depend heavily on the negotiating ability, including the level of legal capacity, of a particular acceding country. (The very existence of the large gaps in China's Accession Protocol, which the Appellate Body was compelled to fill, is an indication of the inferior quality of its drafting as compared to that of the Multilateral Trade Agreements.) Also, unlike the Multilateral Trade Agreements, the negotiation records of accession protocols are generally unavailable, making it harder to ascertain the original intent of the parties behind those loosely drafted texts. In sum, the relationship between an accession protocol and the Multilateral Trade Agreements is not the same, and should not be treated in the same way, as the relationship among the Multilateral Trade Agreements. While neither obligations nor rights may be 'automatically' transposed from one part of the WTO legal framework to another, the integration of accession protocols into the WTO Agreement may require the treaty interpreter to *deem* a specific right or obligation of the protocol as an organic part of one or more WTO agreements.[74] In theory, the relationship between a specific provision of the accession protocol and the Multilateral Trade Agreements can always be ascertained by applying the general approach set out by the Appellate Body, which approximates the interpretive principles of VCLT:

> The analysis must start with the text of the relevant provision in China's Accession Protocol and take into account its context, including that provided by the Protocol itself and by relevant provisions of the Accession Working Party Report, and by the agreements in the WTO legal framework. The analysis must also take into account the overall architecture of the WTO system as a single package of rights and obligations and any other relevant interpretive elements, and must be applied to

[74] See Kennedy (2013: 66–69) (explaining the need to read accession provisions together with relevant WTO provisions in every case).

> the circumstance of each dispute, including the measure at issue and the nature of the alleged violation.[75]

The difficult task in practice, however, is to determine which parts of the agreements and which other elements in the vast universe of the WTO legal framework should be taken into account in the interpretation of a particular relationship. In this regard, the Appellate Body has suggested the need to find 'an objective link' between a specific protocol provision and a WTO agreement.[76] But what is 'an objective link'? And how should such a link be identified? The notion seems to raise more questions than providing answers.[77]

III *Finding the Lodestar for Navigation: Systemic Coherence*

Instead of 'an objective link', it is suggested here that navigation between accession protocols and WTO agreements needs to fix on 'systemic coherence' as its lodestar. 'Coherence is valued positively owing to the connection it has with predictability and legal security. Moreover, only a coherent legal system treats legal subjects equally.'[78] In WTO jurisprudence, it has been well established that provisions of the WTO agreements should be interpreted in 'a coherent and consistent manner, giving meaning to all applicable provisions harmoniously'.[79] While it may not always be feasible to make a 'harmonious' reading of the Member-specific rules with the WTO agreements, a 'coherent' interpretation of the two sets of provisions should be achievable. When guided by the notion of 'systemic coherence', WTO adjudicators would be encouraged to discover the inner logic and underlying rationale shared by the Member-specific rules and the WTO multilateral agreements, so that such rules can be interpreted, to the largest extent possible, as integral parts of coherent WTO disciplines.

[75] See above Appellate Body Reports, para. 5.74.

[76] See above Appellate Body Reports, paras. 5.61; 5.74.

[77] See text at above note 68. This criterion has its origin in *China – Publications and Audiovisual Products*, in which the Appellate Body interpreted the Protocol language that China's trading rights obligation is 'without prejudice to China's right to regulate trade' and found that China's measures at issue had 'a clearly discernible, objective link' to its regulation of trade. Appellate Body Report, above note 11, para. 230.

[78] International Law Commission (ILC), Report of the Study Group, *Fragmentation of International Law: Difficulties Arising the Diversification and Expansion of International Law*, UN Doc. A/CN.4/L.682 (13 April 2006), para. 491.

[79] Appellate Body Reports, *EC – Seal Products*, WT/DS400, DS401/AB/R (22 May 2014), para. 5.123.

1 Achieving systemic coherence through conflict rules

Technically, to achieve systemic coherence it is necessary to employ the tool of conflict rules. The issue of relationship between accession protocols and WTO agreements arises because the protocols contain provisions that are inconsistent with the WTO multilateral agreements. Hence, without identifying and resolving such inconsistencies, it will not be possible to construe the relationship between the protocols and the WTO agreements in a truly coherent and consistent manner.

The WTO Agreement contains various conflict clauses, but none of them addresses the priority between an accession protocol and any of the WTO agreements.[80] Absent an express conflict provision, the generally accepted legal doctrines, such as *lex specialis* and *lex posterior*, will apply by default. The maxim *lex specialis* suggests that 'whenever two or more norms deal with the same subject matter, priority should be given to the norm that is more specific'.[81] An accession protocol is *lex specialis* in the sense that it specifies how WTO agreements shall be applied to a particular Member.[82] The doctrine of *lex posterior* has been codified in VCLT Article 30, which provides that in the case of successive treaties relating to 'the same subject matter', priority should be given to the later treaty. An accession protocol is *lex posterior* in the sense that it is concluded after the WTO Agreement.[83] Under either doctrine, a protocol provision will prevail over a WTO provision in the event of conflict. But this precedence is limited to the extent of the conflict. While the country-specific rules may depart from the WTO provisions, the WTO provisions, as the general law, will 'continue to give direction for the interpretation and application' of the country-specific rules and will 'become fully applicable in situations not provided for by the latter'.[84] The critical question, then, is how to determine whether a conflict exists

80 E.g. General Interpretive Note to Annex 1A of the WTO Agreement provides that in the event of conflict between a provision of GATT 1994 and a provision of another agreement on trade in goods contained in Annex 1A to the WTO Agreement, 'the provision of the other agreement shall prevail to the extent of the conflict'. For an overview of WTO conflict clauses, see Pauwelyn (2003: 356–357).

81 ILC, *Conclusions of the Work of the Study Group on the Fragmentation of International Law: Difficulties Arising from the Diversification and Expansion of International Law* (2006), para. 5, UN Doc. A/61/10, para. 251.

82 The application of *lex specialis* is highly complex. See ILC, above note 78, paras. 56–122; Pauwelyn, (2003: 385–418).

83 Pursuant to VCLT Article 30(4)(b), the principle of *lex posterior* may apply where the parties to the successive treaties are not identical.

84 ILC, above note 81, para. 9.

between a protocol provision and a WTO provision. A straightforward way to identify the existence of conflict is to see whether the two provisions can be applied to the same measure simultaneously without leading to contradictory results. For example, Paragraph 11.3 of China's Accession Protocol (which prohibits the use of export duties on most products) and GATT Article XI:1 (which explicitly permits the use of export duties on any products) cannot be applied to China's levy of export duties simultaneously without leading to contradictory results; hence, there is a conflict between the two provisions.[85] When in conflict, the two provisions necessarily relate to the same subject matter,[86] which is the basis for applying conflict rules. Identifying whether the two provisions relate to the same subject matter is particularly useful for interpreting WTO-plus provisions. Thus, in the example above, we can conclude that, given their conflict, Paragraph 11.3 and GATT Article XI:1 must relate to the same subject matter.[87] Consequently, while the special obligation of Paragraph 11.3 should prevail over the permission under Article XI:1 – which is the extent of conflict – the rest of the GATT provisions, including the GATT MFN clause and general exceptions, should remain applicable and 'continue to give direction for the interpretation and application' of Paragraph 11.3. Note that a conflict so-defined is broad in extent. Under this definition, conflict exists not only when the two provisions prescribe inconsistent obligations, but also where one provision prescribes an obligation that is inconsistent with a right recognised under the other provision.[88] Notably, this type of conflict was recognised by the Appellate Body when it held that 'the explicit export subsidy disciplines' contained in the various provisions of the Agreement on Agriculture (AoA) 'must clearly take precedence over the *exemption* of primary products from export subsidy disciplines in Article XVI:4 of the GATT 1994'.[89] Indeed, the inconsistency recognised

[85] The purpose of defining a conflict broadly in this context is to achieve a systemically coherent reading of WTO-plus provisions and the WTO multilateral agreements. See below Section C.I for further explanation.

[86] See ILC, above note 78, para. 22.

[87] Hence, the majority of the panel in *China – Rare Earths* was mistaken in concluding that '[t]he obligation in Paragraph 11.3 of China's Accession Protocol does not relate to the same subject-matter as Articles II or XI of the GATT 1994'. Panel Reports, above note 57, para. 7.95.

[88] In contrast, a narrower definition only recognises conflict between two contradicting obligations. See Pauwelyn (2003: 179–188) (analysing four situations of conflict).

[89] Appellate Body Report, *US – FSC*, WT/DS108/AB/R (24 February 2000), para. 117 (emphasis original).

by the Appellate Body between the AoA provisions (the specific and new obligation not to use export subsidies on agricultural products) and GATT Article XVI:4 (the explicit permission to use such export subsidies) is exactly analogous to the inconsistency between Paragraph 11.3 of China's Accession Protocol (the specific and new obligation not to use export duties) and GATT Article XI:1 (the explicit permission to use export duties).[90] With respect to the accession protocols, such a broad definition of conflict is essential in that it can help the treaty interpreter to identify inherent connections between ad hoc accession rules and WTO multilateral disciplines so as to achieve maximum systemic coherence between them.

2 Systemic coherence based on the principle of non-discrimination

In addition to the technical tool of conflict rules, systemic coherence needs to be achieved normatively by adhering to the principle of non-discrimination. In addressing the relationship between accession protocols and WTO agreements, a treaty interpreter should be mindful of the discriminatory effect of WTO-plus and WTO-minus rules. These country-specific rules result in less favourable treatment of acceded Members than that of the original Members under WTO law. Without clear justification, they are inconsistent with the fundamental principle of non-discrimination, thereby undermining the integrity of the WTO system. Thus, to achieve systemic coherence, a treaty interpreter should strive to construe the relationship between the country-specific rules and WTO agreements in a way that will reduce the discriminatory effect to the greatest extent possible. Would such an interpretive approach amount to 'judicial activism', in the sense that it might 'add to or diminish the rights and obligations' provided in the WTO treaties?[91] Insofar as the interpretive issues arise from the gaps or ambiguities in treaty texts, the answer should be no. In the absence of 'legislative' guidance, it is up to the WTO judiciary to provide legal reasoning that can link an unclear provision to the objectives and rationale of the WTO system as a whole. Hence, unless the express wording of treaty texts

[90] Notably, the permission in GATT Article XVI:4 (Members shall cease to grant any form of subsidy on the export of any product 'other than' a primary product . . .) is formulated similarly to that in GATT Article XI:1 (No prohibition or restriction 'other than' duties shall be instituted or maintained . . .).

[91] DSU, Article 3.2.

otherwise requires, an interpretive approach that aims to preserve the fundamental principle of non-discrimination cannot be considered to add to or diminish the rights and obligations provided in the WTO treaties. In this context, we must discredit the 'entry fee' theory offered by the panel in *China – Raw Materials* to justify all Member-specific rules of accession. According to this panel:[92]

> Most accession processes take several years to complete and lead to detailed negotiated provisions … The negotiated agreement between the WTO membership and the acceding Member results in a delicate balance of rights and obligations, which are reflected in the specific wording of each commitment set out in [the accession] documents. *Ultimately, the acceding Member and the WTO membership recognize that the intensively negotiated content of an accession package is the 'entry fee' to the WTO system.* (emphasis added)

This 'entry fee' theory is highly problematic. Legally, this theory ignores the basic distinction drawn by the WTO treaty structure between the commercial commitments set out in GATT and GATS schedules on the one hand, and the rule obligations contained in the provisions of WTO agreements on the other. Unlike the commercial commitments in GATT and GATS schedules, which are country-specific and negotiated on a reciprocal basis between individual Members, the provisions of WTO agreements are uniform and generally applicable to all Members. Also, unlike the commercial commitments in GATT and GATS schedules, which may be modified or withdrawn unilaterally at any time pursuant to certain procedures,[93] the provisions of the WTO agreements are permanent and their amendment requires ratification of either all or of a qualified majority of WTO Members.[94] Furthermore, in the event of a conflict, a scheduled commitment must yield to the provisions of WTO agreements.[95] According to this systemic design, an acceding country is expected to negotiate its commercial commitments, but not to bargain against the provisions of WTO agreements. By characterising all country-specific rules that modify or derogate from WTO provisions as the 'entry fee' to WTO membership, the panel obliterated the qualitative

[92] Panel Reports, *China – Raw Materials*, WT/DS394, 395, 398/R (5 July 2011), para. 7.112.

[93] GATT Article XXVIII, GATS, Article XXI.

[94] WTO Agreement, Article X. To date, the WTO has adopted two amendments, but neither has become effective owing to the insufficient number of ratifications.

[95] Panel Reports, *China – Rare Earths*, above note 57, para. 7.124 (Separate Opinion, citing Appellate Body Report of *EC – Export Subsidies on Sugar*, paras. 220–223, and Appellate Body Report of *EC – Bananas III*, paras. 155–158). See also, Pauwelyn (2003: 357).

differences between the two types of treaty obligations under WTO law. Normatively, the entry-fee theory is harmful because it is purported to justify unprincipled Member-specific rulemaking that undermines the WTO rule of law. The theory takes for granted that WTO rules can be bargained for in the same way as market access for goods and services, without regard for the basic principles of the WTO system. While rule-bargaining may have become a political reality in WTO accession practice, the adjudicators, as the judicial branch of the WTO, should at least be mindful of the detrimental impact of such a practice on the WTO rule of law. When tasked to interpret the Member-specific rules, they should be obliged to provide legal reasoning that would lessen such impact, rather than offering a legal cover for the practice.

D Specific Interpretive Issues

This section analyses four situations that require an assessment of the relationship between an accession protocol and the WTO agreements. In each situation, the analysis is made in the light of the principle of systemic coherence as explained above.

I WTO-Plus Obligations: Availability of WTO General Exceptions

By definition, WTO-plus provisions prescribe new obligations that go beyond the requirements of the WTO Agreement. There has been no question that a WTO-plus obligation shall prevail over the existing rights under the WTO agreements. The major interpretive issue, instead, has been the applicability of the general exceptions contained in the WTO agreements to China's Accession Protocol, which does not contain general exceptions of its own and is otherwise silent as to such applicability. To date, the issue has arisen in three cases. The first is *China – Publications and Audiovisual Products*, in which China invoked the public morals exception of GATT Article XX(a) to defend a breach of its trading-rights obligation under Paragraph 5.1 of its Accession Protocol. The trading-rights obligation is WTO-plus because it requires China to abolish most of its state-trading monopolies, whereas such monopolies are explicitly permitted under GATT 1994.[96] The Appellate Body held that China may invoke GATT Article XX(a) in this case, on the grounds that Paragraph 5.1 contains a textual link to the WTO

[96] See GATT Articles. II:4, XVII and XX(d).

Agreement (the introductory phrase of Paragraph 5.1 states that the trading rights commitments are '[w]ithout prejudice to China's right to regulate trade in a manner consistent with the WTO Agreement').[97] The second and third cases are *China – Raw Materials* and *China – Rare Earths*. In both these cases, China invoked the health and environment exceptions under GATT Article XX to defend the breach of its export duty obligations under Paragraph 11.3 of its Accession Protocol. In *Raw Materials*, the Appellate Body held that China may not invoke the Article XX exceptions in this case in light of 'the lack of any textual reference to Article XX of the GATT 1994' in Paragraph 11.3.[98] This ruling has attracted strong criticism (e.g. Bronckers and Maskus 2014: 393–408; Kennedy 2013; Baroncini 2013: 1–34; Gu 2012: 1007; Qin, 2012b: 237–246). When the same issue arose again in *Rare Earths*, several third parties sided with China and one panelist wrote a separate opinion disagreeing with the Appellate Body's prior ruling.[99] In response, the Appellate Body seemed to have backed down somewhat from its previous position, stating that 'express textual references, or the lack thereof, to a covered agreement (such as the GATT 1994) or a provision thereof (such as . . . Article XX of the GATT 1994), or "the WTO Agreement" in general, are *not* dispositive in and of themselves'.[100] Having made that statement, however, the Appellate Body went on to reaffirm its ruling in *Raw Materials*.[101] Thus, as WTO jurisprudence stands now, it remains uncertain as to whether, absent express textual references, the general exceptions under the WTO Agreement will be available to WTO-plus obligations of an accession protocol. This legal uncertainty, however, is unnecessary. Conceptually, there is no inherent conflict between an obligation and an express exception to the obligation, because the two occupy different spheres of application.[102] Within the WTO system, the general exceptions are those applicable to all the obligations in a given WTO agreement, which are typically based on public policy, such as public morals, health and environmental protection, and national security.[103] The presence of these generally applicable exceptions in all

[97] Appellate Body Report, above note 11, paras. 229–233. For critiques of the Appellate Body's ruling, see Roessler (2011: 119); Pauwelyn (2010).

[98] Appellate Body Reports, above note 15, para. 306.

[99] Above note 59.

[100] Appellate Body Reports, above note 16, para. 5.61 (emphasis original).

[101] Appellate Body Reports, above note 16, para., 5.63 (declaring that its ruling in *Raw Materials* was made 'on the basis of a holistic analysis of all elements').

[102] See Pauwelyn (2003: 162–163).

[103] E.g. GATT Articles XX and XXI; GATS Articles XIV and XIV *bis*; TBT Article 2.2; Agreement on Trade-Related Aspects of Intellectual Property Rights (TRIPS), Article 8.1.

major WTO agreements reflects a clear policy choice of the system: the WTO's trade obligations are without prejudice to certain non-trade interests that are vital to the societies of its Members. We have no reason to believe that the WTO has abandoned this basic design of the system with respect to its accession agreements. After all, the purpose of accession is to integrate more countries into the multilateral trade system. While an accession protocol may expand WTO obligations for the acceded Member, it does not create a new system. Hence, just as there is no conflict between existing WTO obligations and the generally applicable exceptions under the WTO Agreement, there is no inherent conflict between a WTO-plus obligation and such general exceptions, unless a WTO-plus obligation directly contradicts a particular exception. To illustrate, as noted above, the obligation of China not to use export duties under Paragraph 11.3 of its Accession Protocol conflicts with the explicit permission to use export duties under GATT Article XI:1; thus, with respect to China, Article XI:1 has been effectively modified to the following effect:

> *Subject to Paragraph 11.3 of China's Accession Protocol,* [n]o prohibitions or restrictions other than duties, taxes or other charges, . . . shall be instituted or maintained by any Member on the importation of any product of the territory of any other Member or on the exportation or sale for export of any product destined for the territory of any other Member. (modification in italics)

This modification, however, merely expands China's obligations under Article XI:1. While Paragraph 11.3 supersedes Article XI:1 with respect to China's export duties, it does not affect the application of GATT Article XX or XXI. Paragraph 11.3 (the additional obligation of China) and Articles XX and XXI (the general policy exceptions) can apply to China's export-duty measures simultaneously, as they have different scopes of application. To further illustrate, in the case of Paragraph 5.1 of China's Accession Protocol, China's trading rights obligation is inconsistent with the explicit permission for maintaining state trading monopolies under GATT Article XX(d). Thus, insofar as China is concerned, GATT Article XX(d) has been effectively modified to the following effect:

> [N]othing in this Agreement shall be construed to prevent the adoption or enforcement by any Member of measures:
>
> . . .
>
> (d) necessary to secure compliance with laws or regulations . . . relating to . . . the enforcement of monopolies operated under paragraph 4 of

> Article II and Article XVII, *except as otherwise provided in Paragraph 5.1 of China's Accession Protocol*, . . . (modification in italics)

Notably, this modification is made to one of the GATT general exceptions, which provides 'a conditional right'[104] to maintain state trading monopolies. Hence, this is a case where a WTO-plus provision contradicts and supersedes a specific provision of the general exceptions. Other than this particular conflict, however, Paragraph 5.1 does not affect the application of any other exception under Article XX (such as public morals). That is, Paragraph 5.1 and the other general exceptions can apply to China's trading-rights measures at the same time, as they have different scopes of application.[105] To summarise, a WTO-plus provision shall prevail over provisions of the WTO Agreement *only* to the extent of its inconsistency with the latter. While a WTO-plus obligation is inconsistent with, and hence shall prevail over, an existing permission under the WTO Agreement, there is no inherent conflict between a WTO-plus obligation and a generally applicable exception under the WTO Agreement. Thus, as a matter of principle, absent express language to the contrary, the general exceptions under a given WTO agreement should be made available to all WTO-plus obligations of an acceded Member relating to the subject matters of that agreement. In other words, when the text is silent as to the availability of a general exception to a WTO-plus obligation, the silence should be interpreted in favour of finding such availability. Accepting this interpretive principle will eliminate the uncertainty associated with this issue and ensure the internal coherence of the WTO rule system with respect to all WTO-plus obligations.

II WTO-Minus Provisions: Determining the Scope of Derogation

By definition, WTO-minus provisions derogate from existing obligations of Members towards an acceded Member under the WTO Agreement. A key issue in interpreting a WTO-minus provision is to determine the extent of such derogation. To achieve a maximum extent of systemic coherence, the derogation should be construed restrictively and in light of the underlying rationale of such derogation. To date, this issue has

[104] Pauwelyn (2003: 163) (explaining that an exception can be considered 'as a conditional right, delinked from the general rule' to which the exception applies).

[105] Note that this is a completely different legal basis from that provided by the Appellate Body.

arisen in five cases. One of these is *US – Tyres* discussed above. As noted, China challenged the US safeguard measure taken under Section 16 of its Accession Protocol and lost the case completely. The outcome was not surprising. Instead of derogating from specific WTO safeguard provisions, Section 16 established an entirely separate safeguard mechanism that was to be applied parallel to the WTO safeguard discipline. The openly discriminatory mechanism was the result of political compromise and had no apparent justification under WTO law. Although the adjudicators sought guidance from WTO safeguard jurisprudence where identical words are used in both Section 16 and the Agreement on Safeguards, the distinct design of Section 16 led them to reject all of China's claims.[106] In the end, this case provided no particular insight into how to delineate the scope of derogation from specific provisions of the WTO Agreement. The other four cases addressed the issue of the relationship between specific provisions of the Anti-dumping Agreement (AD Agreement) and the non-market economy (NME) provisions in the accession protocols of China and Vietnam. The NME provisions permit an importing Member, when 'determining price comparability under Article VI of the GATT 1994 and the Antidumping Agreement', to 'use a methodology that is not based on a strict comparison with domestic prices or costs' in China or Vietnam 'if the producers under investigation cannot clearly show that market economy conditions prevail' in the relevant industry.[107] In practice, the NME provisions allow an importing Member to substitute third-country prices as the 'normal value' of products from China and Vietnam, which typically leads to positive dumping determinations and high dumping margins. The NME provisions have a built-in expiration date of 11 December 2016 for China, and 31 December 2018 for Vietnam. The NME provisions depart from the provisions of GATT Article VI and Article 2 of the AD Agreement, which require the use of domestic prices or costs in the exporting country to determine the normal value of the product under investigation. Note that a similar departure from this requirement is authorised by the second *Ad* Note to GATT Article VI:1, but only in the case of imports from 'a country which has a complete or substantially complete monopoly of its trade and where all domestic prices are fixed by the State'.[108] Since neither China nor Vietnam fitted

106 See Charnovitz and Hoekman (2013: 273–296).

107 China's Accession Protocol, Section 15; Vietnam's Accession Protocol, para. 255.

108 GATT Ad Article VI:1, Note 2. This provision is reaffirmed by Article 2.7 of the AD Agreement.

the profile of such a country at the time of accession,[109] the NME provisions of the two protocols derogate directly from GATT Article VI and Article 2 of the AD Agreement. The precise extent of such derogation was at issue in the four cases. In *EC – Fasteners*,[110] China challenged the EU regulation that assigned countrywide anti-dumping duties to producers from NME countries instead of individual duties as required by Articles 6.10 and 9.2 of the AD Agreement. The EU argued that the NME provisions under Section 15 of China's Accession Protocol permit a flexible application of the rules under the AD Agreement. The Appellate Body disagreed, stating that 'while Section 15 of the Accession Protocol establishes special rules regarding the domestic price aspect of price comparability, it does not contain an open-ended exception that allows WTO Members to treat China differently for other purposes under the Anti-dumping Agreement and the GATT 1994, such as the determination of export prices or individual versus countrywide margins and duties'.[111] The Appellate Body also rejected the EU's claim that it is entitled to presume that in NMEs the State and exporters constitute a single entity and hence a single duty can be assigned to them. The Appellate Body again emphasised that Section 15 'only permits derogations in respect of the use of domestic prices and costs – that is, normal value' and that it cannot be interpreted as 'authorizing WTO Members to treat China as an NME for matters other than the determination of normal value'.[112] The other three cases are *EC – Footwear*,[113] in which China challenged the same EU measure as in *EC – Fasteners;* and *US – Shrimp* (Vietnam)[114] and *US – Shrimp II* (Vietnam).[115] In the two shrimp cases, Vietnam challenged the US measures that treated all shrimp exporters in Vietnam as a single entity controlled by the government of Vietnam, relying on the NME

[109] As the Appellate Body observed: 'The second *Ad* Note to Article VI:1 would thus not on its face be applicable to lesser forms of NMEs that do not fulfil both conditions, that is, the complete or substantially complete monopoly of trade and the fixing of all prices by the State.' Appellate Body Report, *EC – Fasteners*, para. 285, fn. 460.

[110] Appellate Body Report, *EC – Fasteners*, para. 285.

[111] Appellate Body Report, *EC – Fasteners*, para. 290.

[112] Appellate Body Report, *EC – Fasteners*, paras. 365–366. In the subsequent compliance proceedings, China challenged the EU regulation implementing the WTO rulings as inconsistent with various other provisions of the AD Agreement and GATT Article VI:1. The Appellate Body found for China in all the challenges. Appellate Body Report, *EC – Fasteners (21.5).*, WT/DS397/AB/RW (18 January 2016).

[113] Panel Report, WT/DS405/R, above note 23.

[114] Panel Report, WT/DS404/R, above note 24.

[115] Panel Report, WT/DS429/R, above note 24.

provisions in paragraph 255 of Vietnam's accession protocol. The panels in these three cases all decided that the scope of derogation by the NME provisions is limited to the determination of normal value only, consistent with the Appellate Body's position in *EC – Fasteners*. Thus, it appears that when the WTO-minus provisions specify the context of the WTO agreements in which they shall apply, as in the case of the NME provisions, WTO adjudicators have construed the scope of derogation narrowly, based strictly on the text of the protocols. In contrast with the interpretation of WTO-plus provisions, the strict textualist approach adopted in the interpretation of the NME provisions has thus far worked to achieve a maximum extent of systemic coherence between the protocol provisions and WTO agreements. Yet, a major dispute on the horizon may bring new challenges to the interpretation of the NME provisions. Contrary to the common understanding that China's NME status would expire on 11 December 2016 (fifteen years after the date of accession), new arguments have been raised in the United States and the EU maintaining that an importing country may continue to use NME anti-dumping methodologies against China after that date (O'Connor 2015; Price, Brightbill and Nance 2015; Oliver, Donnan and Mitchell 2015). According to this line of argument, the expiration date set out in Paragraph 15(d) of China's Accession Protocol applies only to the provision of Paragraph 15(a)(ii), which contains the condition for the use of an NME methodology, and not to the main clause in Paragraph 15(a), which authorises the use of an NME methodology generally.[116] While it is

[116] Paragraphs (a) and (d) of Section 15 provide:

'(a) In determining price comparability under Article VI of the GATT 1994 and the Anti-Dumping Agreement, the importing WTO Member shall use either Chinese prices or costs for the industry under investigation *or a methodology that is not based on a strict comparison with domestic prices or costs in China based on the following rules*:

(i) If the producers under investigation can clearly show that market economy conditions prevail in the industry producing the like product with regard to the manufacture, production and sale of that product, the importing WTO Member shall use Chinese prices or costs for the industry under investigation in determining price comparability;

(ii) The importing WTO Member may use a methodology that is not based on a strict comparison with domestic prices or costs in China if the producers under investigation cannot clearly show that market economy conditions prevail in the industry producing the like product with regard to manufacture, production and sale of that product.'

'(d) Once China has established, under the national law of the importing WTO Member, that it is a market economy, the provisions of subparagraph (a) shall be terminated provided that the importing Member's national law contains market economy

a mystery why the expiration clause should refer only to Paragraph 15(a)(ii) – no negotiation record is publicly available to shed light on this issue[117] – a contextual reading of the provisions of Section 15 should lead to the conclusion that the expiration of subparagraph (a)(ii) will render the use of any NME methodology under Section 15 baseless. Indeed, this seemed to be the understanding of the Appellate Body suggested in an earlier case.[118] However, when all the arguments are presented in this case, it is uncertain whether the adjudicators will adopt a narrow textualist approach, which could lead to a very different conclusion. Guided by the principle of systemic coherence, it is submitted here that any ambiguity in the text of Section 15 should be resolved in favour of minimising the derogation from anti-dumping disciplines of GATT Article VI and the AD Agreement. Most critically, the terms 'non-market economy' and 'market economy' are not defined anywhere in the WTO treaties; and the Protocol does not articulate any rationale for the derogation from WTO anti-dumping disciplines. Hence, there is no systemically coherent reason to construe any 'gap' in the text of Section 15 as permission for the derogation to last indefinitely. (The same is true for the interpretation of the NME provisions in Vietnam's accession protocol.) It remains to be seen how the WTO judiciary will meet the interpretive challenge presented by this WTO-minus provision.

III *Relevance of Accession Protocols to the Interpretation of WTO Agreements*

In theory, since an accession protocol is 'an integral part' of the WTO Agreement, it also constitutes part of the treaty 'context', against which the terms of the WTO Agreement should be interpreted.[119] As the

criteria as of the date of accession. *In any event, the provisions of subparagraph (a)(ii) shall expire 15 years after the date of accession.* In addition, should China establish, pursuant to the national law of the importing WTO Member, that market economy conditions prevail in a particular industry or sector, the non-market economy provisions of subparagraph (a) shall no longer apply to that industry or sector.' (emphasis added)

[117] Negotiation records for WTO accessions are rarely made publicly available, unlike the negotiation records for the Uruguay Round trade agreements, most of which have been published.

[118] Appellate Body Report, *EC – Fasteners (China)*, para. 289 (stating 'Paragraph 15(d) of China's Accession Protocol establishes that the provisions of paragraph 15(a) expire 15 years after China's date of accession (that is, 11 December 2016).').

[119] VCLT Article 31.

Appellate Body observed: 'The realm of "context" as defined in [VCLT] Article 31(2) is broad. "Context" includes all of the text of the treaty – in this case, the WTO Agreement.'[120] Of course, not all parts of the treaty context are relevant to the interpretation of a particular WTO provision. According to the Appellate Body, 'context is *relevant* for a treaty interpreter to the extent that it may shed light on the interpretative issue to be resolved, such as the meaning of the term or phrase at issue'.[121] Thus, the criterion articulated by the Appellate Body is both simple and broad: context is relevant so long as it may shed light on the interpretive issue at hand. Given that an accession protocol concerns the application of WTO agreements to a specific acceded Member, it is very likely that the protocol provisions 'may shed light' on the meaning of WTO provisions when applied to the acceded Member. Furthermore, for those protocol provisions that fall into the category of elaborating existing provisions of WTO agreements, they may also shed light on the meaning of the existing WTO provisions when applied to other Members generally. In practice, however, highly relevant provisions of the accession protocol have been ignored in the interpretation of WTO provisions. The case of *US – AD/CVD (China)*[122] illustrates this curious situation, as discussed below.

1 Accepting China's accession protocol as context for the SCM Agreement

One of the issues involved in *US – AD/CVD (China)* was whether the United States acted inconsistently with the Agreement on Subsidies and Countervailing Measures (SCM Agreement) by imposing, concurrently, anti-dumping duties calculated on the basis of an NME methodology and countervailing duties on the same products, without assessing the effect of 'double remedies'. SCM Article 19.3 provides that a countervailing duty shall be levied 'in the appropriate amounts in each case'. The interpretive question was whether the phrase 'in the appropriate amounts in each case' prohibits the levy of countervailing duties that result in double remedies. The panel concluded that the drafters of the SCM Agreement did not intend to address the question of double remedies in Article 19.3. In arriving at this conclusion, the panel considered different 'elements of context', including China's Accession

[120] Appellate Body Reports, *China – Auto Parts*, above note 9, para. 151.
[121] Appellate Body Reports, *China – Auto Parts*, above note 9, para. 151.
[122] Appellate Body Report, *US – Anti-Dumping and Countervailing Duties (China)*, above note 21.

Protocol, which it found 'contains no provision explicitly addressing the issue of double remedies even though it appears to allow the use of countervailing duties while China remains an NME'.[123] On appeal, the Appellate Body reversed the panel's ruling. Concerning the relevance of the Protocol, the Appellate Body stated:[124]

> We do not agree with the Panel that the fact that China's Accession Protocol does not explicitly address the issue of double remedies suggests that Articles 19.3 and 19.4 of the *SCM Agreement* do not address double remedies. In our view, the fact that China's Accession Protocol does not exclude the application of countervailing duties to China while it remained an NME may equally be read as suggesting a shared understanding that China would be protected against the imposition of double remedies by the provisions of the *SCM Agreement*. On balance, however, we are not persuaded that the absence of a provision addressing double remedies in China's Accession Protocol suggests anything regarding the interpretation of Articles 19.3 and 19.4 of the *SCM Agreement*.

Although the Appellate Body disagreed with the panel on the significance of the absence of a provision addressing double remedies in China's Accession Protocol, by discussing the relevance of the Protocol to the interpretation of SCM provisions, the Appellate Body seems to have accepted the Protocol as part of the context for the SCM Agreement.

2 Curious omission: Protocol provisions and interpretation of 'public body'

Despite their general acceptance that China's Accession Protocol can be relevant to the interpretation of SCM provisions, the parties and the adjudicators paid scant attention to the Protocol provisions in the resolution of a major interpretive issue in the case: whether China's state-owned enterprises (SOEs) are 'public bodies', i.e. subsidy providers, for the purposes of the SCM Agreement. Under SCM Article 1.1(a)(i), 'any public body' within the territory of a Member is defined as part of the 'government', but the term 'public body' is not separately defined.[125] In its countervailing duty investigations, the United States had determined that China's SOE input suppliers and state-owned commercial

[123] Panel Report, *US – Anti-Dumping and Countervailing Duties (China)*, WT/DS379/R (22 October 2010), para. 14.121.

[124] Appellate Body Report, *US – Anti-Dumping and Countervailing Duties (China)*, fn. 559.

[125] It seems the term 'public body' first appeared in footnote 22 of the Tokyo Subsidies Code of 1979, with no definition provided. The Code was superseded by the SCM Agreement. See Pre-WTO Legal Texts, available at www.wto.org/english/docs_e/legal_e/prewto_legal_e.htm.

banks (SOCBs) were 'public bodies', based principally on government ownership in the SOEs and SOCBs. China challenged this ownership-based definition of 'public body'. The panel agreed with the United States, interpreting the term 'public body' to mean 'any entity controlled by a government' and finding 'government ownership to be highly relevant and potentially dispositive evidence of government control'.[126] The Appellate Body reversed the panel's interpretation, finding that a public body within the meaning of SCM Article 1.1 'must be an entity that possesses, exercises or is vested with governmental authority'.[127] According to the Appellate Body, while government control may serve 'as evidence that the relevant entity possesses governmental authority and exercises such authority in the performance of governmental functions', such control 'in itself, is not sufficient to establish that an entity is a public body'.[128] Ultimately, the Appellate Body found that the United States had acted inconsistently with Article 1.1 by treating the SOE input suppliers as public bodies, but that China had not established that the United States was wrong in characterising the SOCBs as public bodies. Note that the issue of whether SOEs can be categorically deemed 'public bodies' has a special significance for China. Normally, whether a government or a public body has made a financial contribution (as defined in SCM Article 1.1) is viewed as 'a completely neutral event', since the financial contribution must result in 'a benefit' to the recipient to become a subsidy covered by the SCM Agreement (Cartland, Depayre and Woznowski 2012: 1006). This event, however, is hardly neutral in the case of China. That is because under current WTO law China is particularly vulnerable to the finding of a 'benefit' conferred by a government financial contribution. A 'benefit' is found by reference to relevant market benchmarks. Under existing SCM jurisprudence or pursuant to Section 15(b) of China's Accession Protocol,[129] domestic prices in China may be considered distorted due to a predominant role of

[126] Panel Report, above note 123, paras. 8.94, 8.134.

[127] Appellate Body Report, *US – Anti-Dumping and Countervailing Duties (China)*, para. 317.

[128] Appellate Body Report, *US – Anti-Dumping and Countervailing Duties (China)*, paras. 318, 320.

[129] Section 15(b) permits an importing Member to use an alternative methodology in identifying and measuring subsidy benefits under Article 14 of the SCM Agreement against Chinese products, which is equivalent to NME methodologies in anti-dumping actions. Section 15(b) has no built-in expiration date. Interestingly, neither China nor the United States invoked Section 15(b). See Panel Report, above note 123, paras. 10.9–10.12.

the government in the market, hence unsuitable to serve as market benchmarks; instead, external (foreign) prices can be used as appropriate benchmarks in determining the existence of a benefit.[130] Similar to the use of an NME methodology in anti-dumping investigations, the use of external market benchmarks in a benefit determination can easily lead to a positive finding of the existence of a subsidy. Given the prevalence of Chinese SOEs in the infrastructure, resource sectors and upstream industries, the ownership-based definition of 'public body', combined with the use of external benchmarks, could potentially subject most Chinese products to charges of government subsidisation. In its analysis, the Appellate Body cautioned that, 'just as no two governments are exactly alike, the precise contours and characteristics of a public body are bound to differ from entity to entity, State to State, and case to case'.[131] Accordingly, to determine whether SOEs in China should categorically constitute public bodies, one would need to investigate the legal status and functions of Chinese SOEs and their actual relationship with the Chinese Government. Because China had a large number of SOEs at the time of its accession, China's Accession Protocol contains a number of provisions pertaining to SOEs, including provisions directly related to the SCM Agreement. These provisions should be of special interest to the parties and judges in determining the meaning of public body in the particular context of China. Yet, these provisions were left out of the analysis, as if they had no relevance at all to the issue. The only exception was the discussion in the Panel Report on paragraph 172 of China's Accession Working Party Report (WPR), which reads as follows:

> Some members of the Working Party, in view of the special characteristics of China's economy, sought to clarify that when state-owned enterprises (including banks) provided financial contributions, they were doing so as government actors within the scope of Article 1.1(a) of the SCM Agreement. The representative of China noted, however, that such financial contributions would not necessarily give rise to a benefit within the meaning of Article 1.1(b) of the SCM Agreement. He pointed out that China's objective was that state-owned enterprises, including banks,

[130] See Appellate Body Report, *US – Softwood Lumber IV*, WT/DS257/AB/R (19 January 2004), para. 103 (finding that 'an investigating authority may use an external benchmark other than private prices of the goods in question in the country of provision, when it has been established that those private prices are distorted, because of the predominant role of the government in the market as a provider of the same or similar goods.').

[131] Appellate Body Report, *US – Softwood Lumber IV*, WT/DS257/AB/R (19 January 2004), para. 317.

> should be run on a commercial basis and be responsible for their own profits and losses. The Working Party took note of this commitment.

According to the Panel Report, the United States pointed to the discussion in Paragraph 172 as 'relevant context' showing that 'China accepted that its state-owned enterprises (including banks) are government actors, or at least public bodies, within the meaning of the SCM Agreement'.[132] Three third parties in the panel proceeding also expressed their views in this regard. Australia considered that 'paragraph 172 of China's Working Party Report provides historical evidence of the nature of Chinese SOEs (including banks), rather than evidence of their current nature, but that such historical evidence could be relevant for assessing whether an entity is a "public body" within the meaning of the SCM Agreement'.[133] The European Communities stated in general that 'the Panel should examine China's Working Party Report in assessing whether the SOEs at issue are "public bodies"'.[134] Saudi Arabia disagreed, stating that 'China's Working Party Report should not be used as the basis for interpreting the term "public bodies", i.e. the Working Party Report contains commitments specific to China, while the WTO Agreement, including Article 1 of the SCM Agreement, applies to all WTO Members'.[135] In the end, the panel considered it unnecessary to analyse the language of the Working Party Report in light of its conclusions based on the text of the SCM provision, noting also that the United States did not rely directly on this language and did not argue that it constitutes 'a commitment by China as to any particular interpretation' of SCM Article 1.1(a)(1).[136] Indeed, the first two sentences of Paragraph 172 contain merely a discussion (which can be understood to indicate China's acceptance that its SOEs might provide financial contributions under SCM Article 1.1), and not a commitment by China, hence were not incorporated into China's Accession Protocol.[137] Consequently, they are not part of the WTO Agreement and do not constitute treaty 'context' within the meaning of VCLT Article 31(2).

[132] Panel Report, above note 123, para. 8.93.
[133] Panel Report, above note 123, para. 8.43.
[134] Panel Report, above note 123, para. 8.46.
[135] Panel Report, above note 123, para. 8.51.
[136] Panel Report, above note 123, para. 8.93.
[137] Only 'commitments' set out in the WPR are incorporated into the Accession Protocol. See China's Accession Protocol, Article 1.2; and WPR, para. 342. The nonbinding contents of the WPR provide a historical context of China's accession, and as such, may be used as supplementary means of interpretation in accordance with VCLT Article 32.

In contrast, the last sentence of Paragraph 172 does set out a commitment of China on its objective to run SOEs on a commercial basis, which was incorporated into China's Accession Protocol. In addition to this commitment, China's Accession Protocol contains several other provisions regarding SOEs:

(i) Paragraph 10.2 of the Protocol designates SOEs as a specific group of subsidy recipients. It provides: 'For purposes of applying Articles 1.2 and 2 of the SCM Agreement, subsidies provided to state-owned enterprises will be viewed as specific if, inter alia, state-owned enterprises are the predominant recipients of such subsidies or state-owned enterprises receive disproportionately large amounts of such subsidies.'

(ii) Annex 5A of the Protocol contains China's subsidy notification pursuant to Article 25 of the SCM Agreement, which includes lists of subsidies provided by the central and local governments to certain loss-making SOEs; Annex 5B of the Protocol contains a list of subsidies to be phased out, which also includes subsidies provided to certain loss-making SOEs.

(iii) Paragraph 46 of China's Accession Wording Party Report (WPR) sets out two commitments of China that are incorporated into the Protocol: (1) 'China would ensure that all state-owned and state-invested enterprises would make purchases and sales based solely on commercial considerations, e.g., price, quality, marketability and availability'; and (2) 'the Government of China would not influence, directly or indirectly, commercial decisions on the part of state-owned or state-invested enterprises, including on the quantity, value or country of origin of any goods purchased or sold, except in a manner consistent with the WTO Agreement'.

(iv) Paragraph 47 of the WPR provides that 'without prejudice to China's rights in future negotiations in the Government Procurement Agreement, all laws, regulations and measures relating to the procurement by state-owned and state-invested enterprises of goods and services for commercial sale, production of goods or supply of services for commercial sale, or for non-governmental purposes would not be considered to be laws, regulations and measures relating to government procurement. Thus, such purchases or sales would be subject to the provisions of Articles II, XVI and XVII of the GATS and Article III of the GATT 1994.' This commitment is incorporated into the Protocol.

Unlike the first two sentences in Paragraph 172 of the WPR, these Protocol provisions are legally 'integral parts' of the WTO Agreement, thereby falling within the formal boundaries of 'context' as defined in VCLT Article 31(2). Accordingly, WTO judges are obligated to consider these provisions if they 'may shed light' on the issue of whether Chinese SOEs are 'public bodies' within the meaning of SCM Article 1.1.

There should be no question that these Protocol provisions can shed such light, as they all pertain to the nature and function of Chinese SOEs. Paragraph 10.2 and Annexes 5A and 5B expressly indicate that Chinese SOEs, as a group, are recipients of government subsidies under the SCM Agreement. Paragraphs 46 and 47 of the WPR confirm that Chinese SOEs will operate solely on commercial considerations and will not be exempted from GATT and GATS disciplines. Taken together, these provisions embody a common intention of China and WTO Members that SOEs should in principle behave like private enterprises, rather than acting as government agencies, in all matters subject to WTO disciplines.

The China-specific SOE provisions reflect a historical reality: China's economy was evolving from one in which most economic actors were SOEs to one in which SOEs would coexist and compete with private entities. While the private sector in China was rapidly expanding, the government did not engage in a large-scale privatisation of its state sector. Instead, its objective was to turn SOEs, many of which were loss-making at the time, into competitive and profit-making entities in the marketplace. Given China's SOE policies, the main concern of WTO Members in the accession negotiations was the continuing governmental influence over the decisions and activities of SOEs. This background was set out in various provisions of the accession documents, in particular, in the subsection titled 'State-Owned and Stated-Invested Enterprises' in the WPR.[138]

It is important to note that the SOE provisions of the Protocol do not exclude the possibility that individual SOEs might act as subsidy providers within the meaning of SCM Article 1.1. Just as a private firm may be entrusted or directed by the government to provide subsidies, an SOE may do so under the instruction of its government shareholder.[139] Indeed, the government may find it particularly convenient to use SOEs as a conduit for providing subsidies. However, whether that is the

[138] See China's WPR, paras. 6, 43–45, 110 and 173.

[139] For the many similarities between SOEs and private enterprises in China's institutional environment, see Milhaupt and Zheng (2015: 665–722).

case is a factual matter that needs to be proved and not assumed. When China's Accession Protocol explicitly requires that SOEs operate on a commercial basis like a private entity, and when it specifically designates SOEs as a group of subsidy *recipients* for the purposes of SCM Articles 1.2 and 2, the same SOEs cannot simultaneously and categorically be deemed as a group of subsidy *providers* under SCM Article 1.1. In other words, the SOE provisions of China's Accession Protocol can be understood to have established a rebuttable presumption that its SOEs are *not* 'public bodies' within the meaning of SCM Article 1.1. To assume otherwise would create a major inconsistency between SCM Article 1.1 on one hand, and SCM Articles 1.2 and 2 on the other, at least in their application to China. Given that the China-specific SOE provisions are legally 'integral' parts of the WTO Agreement, it is rather surprising that they were completely ignored by the parties as well as the WTO adjudicators when determining the nature of Chinese SOEs under the SCM Agreement.[140] In contrast, in their 'public body' analyses, a great deal of attention was devoted to the ILC Draft Articles on Responsibility of States for Internationally Wrongful Acts, a document extrinsic to the WTO Agreement.[141] Although the Appellate Body's ultimate conclusions appear to be consistent with the tenets of the Protocol provisions, the failure to consider the highly relevant contexts of Protocol provisions is not without legal consequences. Critically, under the Appellate Body's interpretation, there is no rebuttable presumption that Chinese SOEs do not constitute public bodies within the meaning of SCM Article 1.1. Instead, the burden is on China to prove that the countervailing Member acted inconsistently with SCM Article 1.1 in characterising SOEs as public bodies.

3 Accession protocol as subsequent agreement interpreting the WTO Agreement

An accession protocol is an agreement concluded subsequent to the WTO Agreement, and as such, some of its terms may reflect an updated common understanding among WTO Members regarding the meaning of a particular WTO provision, albeit in the context of its application to a specific Member. In this sense, accession provisions may constitute 'subsequent agreement between the parties regarding the interpretation

[140] While it is understandable that the United States should point to the nonbinding discussion in paragraph 172 of the WPR to buttress its argument, it is puzzling why China did not refer to any of the SOE provisions of the Protocol to support its position.

[141] See Panel Report, paras. 8.85–8.91; Appellate Body Report, paras. 305–316.

of the treaty or the application of its provisions' within the meaning of VCLT Article 31(3)(a).[142] In WTO jurisprudence, the Appellate Body has more than once recognised WTO legal instruments as subsequent agreement within the meaning of Article 31(3)(a). To the Appellate Body, it is the substance, rather than the form, of an agreement that matters for the purpose of Article 31(3)(a). Thus, it has found that paragraph 5.2 of the Doha Ministerial Decision can be characterised as a subsequent agreement interpreting the term 'reasonable interval' in Article 2.12 of the TBT Agreement, since paragraph 5.2 'clearly expresses a common understanding, and an acceptance of that understanding among the Members' on the meaning of that term.[143] It has also found that a particular decision of the TBT Committee can qualify as a subsequent agreement interpreting the TBT Agreement, noting that 'the membership of the TBT Committee comprises all WTO Members and that the Decision was adopted by consensus'.[144] Regarding the substantive requirement, the Appellate Body is of the view that a subsequent agreement referred to in Article 31(3)(a) must bear 'specifically upon the interpretation of a treaty' or specify 'how existing rules or obligations in force are to be "applied"'.[145] In light of the Appellate Body jurisprudence, an accession protocol, which is adopted by the Ministerial Conference by consensus, may certainly qualify as a subsequent agreement within the meaning of Article 31(3)(a), provided that its terms specifically bear upon the interpretation or application of existing provisions of the WTO Agreement. Of the five types of accession terms discussed in Section A above, those that elaborate existing WTO

[142] It may seem illogical that an accession protocol should constitute 'context' under VCLT Article 31(2) and at the same time some of its provisions may also constitute 'subsequent agreement' under VCLT Article 31(3)(a) with respect to the existing Members. For all practical purposes, however, the distinction between the two categories does not matter, since a treaty interpreter is obligated to take into account both 'context' as defined in Article 31(2) and 'subsequent agreement' as defined in Article 31(3) and there is no hierarchical relationship between the two. See Gardiner (2007: 204) (quoting the ILC Commentary that while the elements in Article 31(3) are 'extrinsic' to the text, they 'are all of obligatory character and by their very nature could not be considered to be norms of interpretation in any way inferior to those which precede them'. [1966] Yearbook of the ILC, v. 2: 220, para. 9).

[143] Appellate Body Report, *US – Clove Cigarettes*, WT/DS406/AB/R (4 April 2012), para. 267.

[144] Appellate Body Report, *US – Tuna II (Mexico)*, WT/DS381/AB/R (16 May 2012), paras. 371–372.

[145] Appellate Body Report, *EC – Bananas (21.5) II*, WT/DS27/AB/RW2/ECU, WT/DS27/AB/RW/USA (26 November 2008), paras. 390–391.

provisions appear to meet this criterion. For example, Paragraph 8.1 of China's Accession Protocol, as previously noted, specifies how the Agreement on Import Licensing Procedures should be applied in China. Its requirement that all import licences must have a minimum duration of six months may reflect a consensus among Members on the meaning of 'reasonable duration' of the licence period under Article 3(5)(g) of that Agreement. Another example is Paragraph 10.2 of China's Accession Protocol discussed above, which stipulates how SCM Articles 1.2 and 2 (Specificity) should be 'applied' when SOEs are among the recipients of a government subsidy. Notably, the wording of Paragraph 10.2 is general and does not mention China in particular. Thus, it may be reasonable to assume that the provision reflects a common understanding of WTO Members regarding the application of Articles 1.2 and 2 wherever SOEs are involved as subsidy recipients. Furthermore, as already discussed, in light of the provision of Paragraph 10.2, SOEs in China cannot be categorically defined as public bodies within the meaning of SCM Article 1.1, since the same SOEs cannot be deemed as a group of subsidy providers under Article 1.1 when they have been specifically designated by Paragraph 10.2 as a group of subsidy recipients for the purposes of SCM Article 2. To the extent the SOE-based specificity criterion reflects the common understanding of the Members on the application of SCM Article 2, the same logic should apply generally to similar situations elsewhere. In addition, by introducing state ownership into the application of SCM Article 2, Paragraph 10.2 of China's Accession Protocol may have opened the door for defining the specificity of a subsidy on the basis of other types of ownership of recipients. For instance, the United States has found that tax incentives and other benefits provided to all foreign-invested enterprises (FIEs) in China are specific subsidies, thus treating FIEs as 'a group of enterprises' within the meaning of SCM Article 2.[146] This is in spite of the fact that FIEs in China are numerous and are engaged in many different industries. Unlike state ownership, foreign ownership of subsidy recipients is not mentioned in China's Accession Protocol. Presumably, the United States may apply the same logic to any other Member that provides financial incentives to foreign investors. If the legality of the US practice is ever contested in the WTO, Paragraph 10.2

[146] See e.g. US International Trade Administration, *Crystalline Silicon Photovoltaic Cells, Whether or Not Assembled Into Modules, From the People's Republic of China: Preliminary Affirmative Countervailing Duty Determination*, 77 Fed. Reg. 17439 (26 March 2012).

of China's Accession Protocol can be used to justify such an ownership-based criterion of specificity.

Lastly, it should be noted that, to the extent this ownership-based criterion is new,[147] Paragraph 10.2 may also be considered as a subsequent agreement modifying instead of merely interpreting SCM Article 2.[148] The line between treaty interpretation and treaty modification, therefore, can be rather blurred.

IV Relevance of One Accession Protocol to the Interpretation of Another Accession Protocol

At first glance, it may seem unlikely that one accession protocol should be relevant to the interpretation of another, since each of them contains rules that are specific to the particular acceding country. Yet, when all accession protocols are made 'integral parts' of the WTO Agreement, they also constitute 'context' for each other within the meaning of VCLT Article 31(2). The question is whether they can be 'relevant context' for each other, i.e. whether the accession terms of one Member can 'shed light' on the interpretive issues arising from the accession terms of another Member. In practice, although the terms of WTO accession protocols are country-specific, they are formulated following a certain general pattern of subject matters.[149] Thus, while the country-specific obligations may differ from Member to Member on a given topic, such obligations may concern the same subject matter under WTO law. For example, a number of acceded Members have undertaken obligations on export duties, even though the specifics of such obligations vary from one to the other.[150] It is therefore quite possible that the provisions of one accession protocol may 'shed light' on the interpretive issue arising from the provisions of another accession protocol addressing the same subject matter. To date, the WTO adjudicators have not paid attention to the potential relevance of one accession protocol to the interpretation of

[147] The provision of Paragraph 10.2 appears to depart from the ownership-neutral philosophy of the world trade regime See Qin (2004: 899–902).

[148] The Appellate Body has distinguished an agreement that specifies the application of existing rules, which falls within VCLT Article 31(3)(a), from an agreement that modifies them. Thus, in *EC – Bananas (21.5) II*, it found that the Doha Article I Waiver, which extended the EC's waiver on the tariff quota concession, is not an agreement within the meaning of Article 31(3)(a) because the waiver 'modified or changed' the content of existing obligations of the European Communities. Above note 145, paras. 391–393.

[149] See WTO Secretariat, 'Technical Note on the Accession Process', above note 3.

[150] See above note 5.

another accession protocol. The first case involving such a potential is *China – Publications and Audiovisual Products*. A major interpretive issue in that case was whether China was entitled to invoke the public morals exception of GATT Article XX(a) to defend a breach of its Protocol obligations to liberalise trading rights with respect to the imports of cultural products. As previously noted, the Appellate Body found that China may do so on the grounds that the Protocol introduces the trading rights commitments by the phrase 'without prejudice to China's right to regulate trade in a manner consistent with the WTO Agreement'.[151] Rather than relying on this extremely broad language, the Appellate Body could have placed its decision on a more solid footing by considering the highly relevant contexts of GATT Articles II:4, XVII and XX(d), which explicitly concern state trading monopolies (Qin 2011: 297–299), and additionally, the trading rights provisions of Vietnam's accession protocol. Like China, Vietnam also undertook to liberalise trading rights upon accession; but unlike China, it excluded from its trading-rights commitments the importation of certain cultural products, citing 'society morals' as the rationale for the exclusion.[152] Presumably, 'society morals' is not a different concept from that of 'public morals' in GATT Article XX(a).[153] (Since Vietnam did not take on the obligation regarding cultural imports, it would not have been appropriate to refer to the exception of GATT Article XX(a) in the context.) The provision of this rationale is significant – it indicates that, as a matter of WTO law, the Members have accepted that state monopolies in the imports of cultural products can be justified by the reason of public (society) morals. Unfortunately, this highly relevant context was completely overlooked in this case. Similarly, on the issue of whether China's export-duty obligations are entitled to the GATT general exceptions, the relevance of other accession protocols was ignored in the interpretive process. As noted above, a number of acceded Members undertook WTO-plus obligations on the use of export duties. The scope of such obligations ranges from a complete elimination of export duties on all products, to that on a single product only, to the

[151] Above note 97.

[152] Vietnam's Accession Working Party Report, para. 146 and Table 8(c), which were incorporated into Vietnam's Accession Protocol, WT/ACC/VNM/48 (27 October 2006).

[153] Panel Report, *China – Publications and Audiovisual Products*, WT/DS363/R (12 August 2009), para. 7.759 (adopting the panel interpretation in *US – Gambling* that 'the term "public morals" denotes standards of right and wrong conduct maintained by or on behalf of a community or nation').

binding of export duties at specific levels on various products.[154] The majority of these accession protocols are silent as to whether the GATT general exceptions apply to the export duty commitments, but some do make a textual reference to GATT 1994 in connection with their export duty commitments. In this respect, Ukraine's accession protocol in 2008 stands out; it explicitly provides that 'Ukraine would not increase export duties, nor apply other measures having an equivalent effect, unless justified under the exceptions of the GATT 1994'.[155] In *China – Raw Materials*, the Panel mentioned in a footnote that several other acceded Members had made commitments on export duties,[156] but made no use of this fact. On appeal, the Appellate Body noted the submission of the United States and Mexico that the language in Paragraph 11.3 of China's Accession Protocol, which contains China's export duty commitments, 'is in "contrast" to the language in the accession documents of other WTO Members with respect to their obligations on export duties', referring specifically to Ukraine's accession document.[157] Having noted this submission, however, the Appellate Body did not make a comment. What, then, is the relevance of the fact that a number of other acceded Members also made commitments on export duties, but only a few of them linked such commitments explicitly to GATT 1994? At the minimum, it should have indicated to the treaty interpreter that the question of whether the GATT general exceptions should be made available to export duty commitments is a systemic one, the resolution of which would affect the rights of a group of WTO Members. If the WTO judges had examined other Members' accession documents on the same issue, they might have looked into the reasons behind the different language on the export duty commitments. In so doing, they might have found that the lack of reference to the GATT general exceptions in the context of export duties was understandable, since there is no obligation under the GATT to eliminate or bind export duties. They might also have found that Ukraine negotiated and finalised the language of its export commitments well after the issue on the applicability of GATT exceptions to China's export duties was raised within the WTO.[158] More importantly, they might have appreciated how

[154] For details, see Qin (2003) above note 4.

[155] Report of the Working Party on the Accession of Ukraine to the World Trade Organization, WT/ACC/UKR/152 (25 January 2008), para. 240.

[156] Panel Reports, above note 92, fn. 186.

[157] Appellate Body Reports, above note 15, para. 301, fn. 588.

[158] The issue concerning legal justification for China's export duties on raw materials was raised within the WTO well before Ukraine finalised its accession package in early 2008.

the circumstances of accession negotiations differ from the multilateral rulemaking process at the WTO, and have been willing to take such circumstances into consideration as instructed by VCLT Article 32. In short, the relevant contexts provided by other Members' accession documents could have shed much light on how the silence in China's Accession Protocol regarding the availability of GATT exceptions to the export duty obligations should be interpreted. In sum, when interpreting the country-specific rules of one accession protocol, WTO adjudicators, as well as the parties involved in dispute, should not ignore the country-specific rules in other accession protocols addressing the same subject matter. Instead, they should consider the systemic connection between them, and resolve the interpretive issue in favour of finding consistency and coherence among them.

E Conclusions

This chapter makes several contributions to the understanding of the relationship between the WTO Agreement and its accession protocols. First, it demonstrates that, contrary to the conventional understanding, Article XII of the Marrakesh Agreement does not give carte blanche to enact country-specific rules for acceded Members. The conventional understanding that Article XII does not place any limit on 'the terms of accession' is based on a reading of Article XII out of its treaty context. When read in its relevant treaty context, as is required by the interpretive principles of VCLT, it should become clear that 'the terms of accession' should be essentially the same as the criteria of the original Membership. That is, each acceded Member must accept the Marrakesh Agreement and the Multilateral Trade Agreements, and must have its own GATT and GATS schedules. Member-specific rules differing from the WTO agreements can only be made when such rules are necessary for the application of existing WTO agreements to the acceded Member. Thus, the current practice of Member-specific rulemaking in a routine and unlimited fashion is without proper legal basis under the Marrakesh Agreement. Rather, such practice can only be explained as 'subsequent practice' of the WTO effectively modifying the Marrakesh Agreement

See WTO Transitional Review Mechanism Pursuant to Paragraph 18 of the Protocol on the Accession of the People's Republic of China, *Questions from the European Communities to China*, G/C/W/538 (8 November 2005); *Questions from the United States to China*, G/C/W/560 (6 November 2006); *Questions from Japan to China*, G/C/W/586 (2 November 2007).

and its annexes. Secondly, it explains that, contrary to what the Appellate Body seemed to suggest, the relationship between an accession protocol and the Multilateral Trade Agreements is not the same as the relationship among the Multilateral Trade Agreements. Although they all form 'integral parts' of the WTO Agreement, the accession protocol has a very different purpose, design and structure from that of the Multilateral Trade Agreements. And the circumstances of their conclusions are also markedly different from each other. If we perceive there is a 'wall' separating different agreements within the WTO treaty framework, the 'wall' between an accession protocol and the Multilateral Trade Agreements is necessarily thin and porous. While neither obligations nor rights may be 'automatically' transposed from one part of the WTO legal framework to another, the integration of an accession protocol into the WTO Agreement may require us to read a specific right or obligation of the protocol as an organic part of a WTO agreement that addresses the same subject matter. Third, the chapter proposes that navigation between accession protocols and WTO multilateral agreements needs to find its lodestar in the notion of 'systemic coherence'. To maintain systemic coherence between ad hoc rules of accession and the provisions of WTO multilateral agreements, it is suggested that the treaty interpreter needs to identify and resolve the potential conflicts between them by utilising the tools of conflict rules. Furthermore, any gaps and ambiguities in the text of accession provisions should be construed in a way that will preserve the WTO's fundamental principle of non-discrimination. Applying this approach, the chapter demonstrates how major issues in the relationship between accession terms and the provisions of WTO agreements can be resolved in the manner that achieves a maximum degree of systemic coherence. Specifically, it explains why, as a matter of principle, the general exceptions of a WTO agreement should be made generally available to all WTO-plus obligations relating to the subject matters covered by that agreement, whereas derogations from WTO provisions by WTO-minus rules should be strictly construed. Finally, the chapter contributes to the study of the relationship between the WTO Agreement and its accession protocols by examining two major issues that have hitherto not attracted much attention. One is the relevance of an accession protocol to the interpretation of WTO multilateral agreements; the other the relevance of the accession protocol of one Member to the interpretation of the accession protocol of another Member. It has found that, despite the formal designation that each accession protocol is an integral part of the WTO Agreement and thereby constitutes the treaty context for all WTO provisions, and despite the fact that protocol provisions can be highly relevant to, or even dispositive of, the interpretive issue at hand, participants in disputes and WTO adjudicators have generally ignored accession protocols in the interpretation of other WTO provisions. The disconnect between the formal status of accession protocols and the actual treatment of accession protocols in WTO jurisprudence is astonishing, and it needs to be remedied in the future. Looking forward, finding a way to navigate between the WTO Agreement and its accession protocols so as to bridge the gap between them in a systemically coherent way will continue to pose serious challenges to the WTO treaty interpreters. Whether the challenges can be successfully met will depend on the collective wisdom of the WTO legal community.

References

Arato, Julian. 2013. 'Treaty Interpretation and Constitutional Transformation: Informal Change in International Organizations'. *Yale J. Int'l L.* 38: 289–357.

Baroncini, Elisa. 2013. 'The Applicability of GATT Article XX to China's WTO Accession Protocol in the Appellate Body Report of the *China – Raw Materials* Case: Suggestions for a Different Interpretive Approach'. *China-EU L.J.* 1 (3): 1–34.

Berrisch, George M. 1991. 'The Establishment of New Law Through Subsequent Practice in GATT'. *N.C.J. Int'l L. & Com. Reg.* 16: 497.

Bronckers, Marco and Maskus, Keith E. 2014. '*China – Raw Materials*: A Controversial Step Towards Evenhanded Exploitation of Natural Resources'. *World Trade Review* 13 (2): 393–408.

Cartland, Michel, Depayre, Gérard, and Woznowski, Jan. 2012. 'Is Something Going Wrong in the WTO Dispute Settlement?' *J. World Trade* 46 (5): 979–1015, at 1006.

Charnovitz, Steve. 2008. 'Mapping the Law of WTO Accession'. In *The WTO: Governance, Dispute Settlement & Developing Countries*, edited by Merit E. Janow, Victoria Donaldson and Alan Yanovich, 855–920. Cambridge: Cambridge University Press.

Charnovitz, Steve and Hoekman, Bernard. 2013. '*US – Tyres*, Upholding a WTO Accession Contract – Imposing Pain for Little Gain'. *World Trade Review* 12 (2): 273–296.

Gardiner, Richard K. 2007. *Treaty Interpretation*. Oxford: Oxford University Press, 204.

Gu, Bin. 2012. 'Applicability of GATT Article XX in *China – Raw Materials*: A Clash within the WTO Agreement'. *J. Int'l Econ. L.* 15 (4) 1007.

Kennedy, Matthew. 2013. 'The Integration of Accession Protocols into the WTO Agreement'. *J. World Trade* 47 (1): 45–75.

Milhaupt, Curtis J. and Zheng, Wentong. 2015. 'Beyond Ownership: State Capitalism and the Chinese Firm'. *Georgetown Law J.* 103 (3): 665–722.

Nolte, Georg. 2013. 'Reports for the ILC Study Group on Treaties Over Time'. In *Treaties and Subsequent Practice*, edited by Georg Nolte. Oxford: Oxford University Press, 169.

O'Connor, Bernard. 2015. 'The EU Does Not Have to Make China a Market Economy in 2016'. www.lexology.com/library/detail.aspx?g=c13fe452-8e29-40d5-87d9-bc792daf15a7

Oliver, Christian, Donnan, Shawn and Mitchell, Tom. 2015. 'US Warns Europe over Granting Market Economy Status to China'. *Financial Times* 28 December 2015.

Parenti, Antonio. 2000. 'Accession to the World Trade Organisation: A Legal Analysis'. *Legal Issues of Economic Integration* 27 (2): 141–57.

Pauwelyn, Joost. 2003. *Conflict of Norms in Public International Law: How WTO Law Relates to Other Rules of International Law*, 356–357. Cambridge: Cambridge University Press.

Pauwelyn, Joost. 2010. 'Case Note, Squaring Free Trade in Culture with Chinese Censorship: The WTO Appellate Body Report on China – Audiovisuals'. *Melbourne Journal of International Law* 11 (1): 1–22.

Price, Alan H., Brightbill, Timothy C. and Nance, D. Scott. 2015. 'China Can Still Be Treated as a Nonmarket Economy After 2016'. www.wileyrein/publication/159_China-Can-Still-Be-Treated-As-A-Nonmarket-Economy-After-2016.pdf

Qin, Julia Y. 2003. '"WTO-Plus" Obligations and Their Implications for the WTO Legal System: An Appraisal of the China Accession Protocol'. *J. World Trade* 37 (3): 483–522.

Qin, Julia Y. 2004. 'WTO Regulation of Subsidies to State-Owned Enterprises (SOEs) – A Critical Appraisal of the China Accession Protocol'. *J. Int'l Econ. L.* 7 (4): 863–919, at 899–902.

Qin, Julia Y. 2011. 'Pushing the Limits of Global Governance: Trading Rights, Censorship and WTO Jurisprudence – A Commentary on the *China – Publications* Case'. *Chinese J. Int'l L.* 10 (2): 271–322.

Qin, Julia Y. 2012a. 'Reforming WTO Discipline on Export Duties: Sovereignty over Natural Resources, Economic Development and Environmental Protection'. *J. World Trade* 46 (5): 1147–1190

Qin, Julia. Y. 2012b. 'Editorial Comments, The Predicament of China's "WTO-Plus" Obligation to Eliminate Export Duties: A Commentary on the *China – Raw Materials* Case'. *Chinese J. Int'l L.* 11 (2): 237–246.

Qin, Julia Y. 2015. 'The Conundrum of WTO Accession Protocols: In Search of Legality and Legitimacy'. *Virginia J. Int'l L.* 55 (2) 369–450.

Roessler, Frieder. 2011. 'Comment, Appellate Body Ruling in China – Publications and Audiovisual Products'. 10 *World Trade Review* 119.

Tyagi, Mitali. 2012. 'Flesh on a Legal Fiction: Early Practice in the WTO on Accession Protocols'. *J. Int'l Econ. L.* 15: 391–441.

World Trade Organization. 1999. *The Legal Texts: The Results of the Uruguay Round of Multilateral Trade Negotiations.* Cambridge: Cambridge University Press.

11

The Age of Innocence

The Evolution of the Case Law of the WTO Dispute Settlement: Subsidies as a Case Study

LUCA RUBINI[1]

A The Goal of the Chapter

The case law on subsidies and countervailing duties is topical and salient. The Agreement on Subsidies and Countervailing Measures (SCM Agreement) is the third-most litigated legal instrument in the World Trade Organization (WTO), after the General Agreement on Tariffs and Trade 1994 (GATT 1994) and the Understanding on Rules and Procedures Governing the Settlement of Disputes (DSU).[2] This significant and recurring litigation happens for essentially three main reasons. First, subsidies are a very important and common policy tool of governments, involving often high political stakes. Secondly, several measures can produce subsidy-like effects (i.e. creating economic and competitive advantages, tipping the 'playing field', creating possible obstacles to trade) with the result that the contours of what we mean by 'subsidies' are blurred. Thirdly, as a key instrument of government economic policy, subsidies are often motivated by legitimate public policy goals, which, in a global context, need to be traded off against the possible negative spillovers onto others. Hence, not only do we often not know what a subsidy is but also what constitutes a good or bad subsidy.

[1] I am grateful for the useful comments and suggestions received by Lorand Bartels, Tomer Broude, Ben Cznapnik, Claus-Dieter Ehlermann, Gary Horlick, Simon Lester, Petros Mavroidis, Joost Pauwelyn, Mona Pinchis and Julia Qin on previous versions of this chapter. Special thanks go to Isabelle Van Damme. Any mistake remains mine.

[2] Focusing on appeals only, in the 1996–2014 period, after the DSU (100) and the GATT (85), there were 35 appeals implicating the SCM Agreement. See Appellate Body, *Annual Report for 2014*, WT/AB/24, 3 July 2015, p. 15.

This multifactorial complexity explains why, during the Uruguay Round negotiations (and indeed the Tokyo Round), very different views on the regulation of subsidies clashed. The conclusion of an agreement was thus both a challenge and a success.[3] But a hefty price had to be paid. Subsidy rules lack clarity – paradigmatically.[4] This vagueness is a true test for those called to interpret the rules and make them operative. Consequently, subsidy jurisprudence represents a useful case-study of the WTO adjudicating bodies' attitude to legal interpretation. It is only when dealing with hard cases and difficult interpretative questions that a court's action is seriously verified.

WTO jurisprudence, and especially the decisions of the Appellate Body, are increasingly subject to criticism. Of particular interest is perhaps the disapproval expressed by people that have participated in negotiating the rules or held key positions in the GATT/WTO.[5] Given the prominent part subsidy laws play, it comes as no surprise that decisions on subsidies and countervailing duties are often in the dock. Crucially, the criticism is not necessarily that the WTO dispute settlement organs sometimes take disputable or even wrong decisions, although this may happen and for various reasons. The gist of these criticisms is that certain decisions are wrong because they overlook the nature of WTO law, the 'negotiated balance' underlying it, and the corresponding role of WTO dispute settlement. This is particularly so for Appellate Body (also 'AB') reports (and less so for Panel ones). This chapter explores this line of criticism further, using the jurisprudence of subsidy laws as a testing ground. In so doing, the very interesting statements by current or former Members of the Appellate Body, writing or speaking extrajudicially, are also considered, since they often assist in understanding the hermeneutic approach of the world trade court.[6]

The chapter is structured as follows. After briefly outlining in Section B the jurisdiction and the rules of interpretation of panels and the Appellate Body, and introducing the concept of 'negotiated balance' in Section C, in Section D I sketch a few hypotheses with respect to the interpretative methods of panels and Appellate Body in subsidy cases. Sections E and F

[3] A recent account can be found in Rubini (2016).

[4] The first example that is usually given to justify this statement is the lack of preamble to the SCM Agreement which reflects the huge divergences in positions of the negotiators.

[5] See e.g. Roessler (2015); Greenwald (2013: 261–272); Cartland, Depayre and Woznowski (2012: 979–1016). See also Stewart, McDonough, Smith and Jorgensen (2013: 390–412).

[6] See, e.g, Ehlermann (2002: 606); Abi-Saab (2006); Bacchus (2005: 499–523); Hillman (2010–2011: 269–284); Graham (2013). See also Pauwelyn (2013).

set out to analyse two samples of cases where the dispute settlement bodies have arguably taken good and bad decisions respectively. Section G makes an initial assessment. Then Section H specifically examines the examples of good and bad decisions and investigates whether the search for the said 'negotiated balance' (could have) played any role in the interpretative process.

B The Nature of WTO Law and Its Dispute Settlement

Space constraints permit only a few remarks about the nature of WTO law and of its dispute settlement system.[7] In a nutshell, and at the risk of oversimplifying, my view is that, at least at its current stage of development, WTO law is more comparable to a contract (between parties) than to a constitution (of a community). Through this perhaps stark distinction, I define the fundamental premise of my argument, which is directly connected to the different attitudes the interpreter should have towards contractual vis-à-vis constitutional norms.[8] The interpretation of provisions of contractual nature normally involves placing special emphasis on the objective meaning coming out of their terms, these being the direct expression of the negotiations of the contracting parties and hence of their historical intent.[9] By contrast, (*pace* originalism's claims) constitutional provisions, especially those pertaining to general principles or fundamental rights, reflect a living document that relies less on historical intent and more on the present and future expectations of the community – while adhering perhaps to basic principles that are embedded in the document and depend on the special circumstances of its genesis. For these reasons, constitutions more easily lend themselves to creative and evolutive interpretation or require the continuous balancing of different interests and values.[10]

[7] It is a topic that has generated an abundance of, and often very differing, opinions. See, for example, Jackson (2006); Hudec (1999); Weiler (2000); Pauwelyn (2003).

[8] I will immediately explain what I mean by these two terms. The 'contract' versus 'constitution' distinction should not be confused with that between 'rules' and 'standards'. See Kaplow (1992–1993: 557).

[9] This intent does not necessarily refer to agreeing a norm of clear and precise content, be it a principle or a right/obligation. The parties may simply agree on an ambiguous language, which is the expression of an 'agreement to disagree'. As I note in Section C of this chapter, the interpreter will thus have to do her or his best to identify this and proceed accordingly, for example by identifying any general common ground or, at the very least, what was certainly not contemplated by the parties.

[10] As noted, I am aware of the severity of the dichotomy I have introduced and of the possible freezing effect on the development of WTO law that this may imply. But the main issue, in my view, is that, in the WTO, the Members – and not the dispute

This premise involves that, at their current stage of evolution, WTO dispute settlement organs, and above all the Appellate Body, cannot be compared to domestic constitutional courts, or to international courts, like the Court of Justice of the European Union, that de facto have, or indeed have acquired, a constitutional status.[11] WTO panels and the Appellate Body cannot fill *significant* gaps or perform balancing acts of constitutional relevance.[12] They are akin to agents that have to respect the precise mandate given to them by their principals. If it is true that interpretation is always an act of construction of meaning,[13] in the WTO context it is also particularly true that there are rather defined limits to what the interpreter can and should do, especially when the rules are the result of a careful balancing between different positions. Against a world made up of compromises and creative ambiguity, and, crucially, in the absence of a clear mandate to 'complete the contract',[14] I am of the view that deference and restraint become imperative. Therefore, in my view, adjudicating bodies in the WTO are not – and cannot be – 'engines of change',[15] as, for example, the European Court of Justice has often been, at times when the political arm of the EU was stalled.[16] Finally, the fact is

settlement – should be the main actors in the development of the law. Limited judicial adjustment to new circumstances may be acceptable but the dispute settlement cannot become the route for the fundamental upgrading of the normative framework of the system, on penance of creating serious unbalances. As we are about to see, Appellate Body Members, speaking or writing extrajudicially, have consistently shared this view.

[11] See e.g. the seminal account by Mancini (1989: 595–614).

[12] In other words, there is no way around the gap-filling that occurs with vague legal texts. There will always be gaps. But there are certainly different degrees of gap-filling, which can be more or less constrained.

[13] Bengoextea, MacCormick and Moral Soriano (2001: 43–44).

[14] See Mavroidis (2016: para. 5.3), noting that the Appellate Body was not heavily negotiated and was 'more of an afterthought': 'The fact that only one article of the DSU is dedicated to the highest organ of dispute adjudication is proof enough that this has indeed been the case . . . The framers of the DSU paid little time in designing the entities that would adjudicate, but precious time in putting in place a system of compulsory third party adjudication' (ibid.). See also Van den Bossche (2006: 289–325); Marceau (2015).

[15] This *is* the main pressure on interpretation. What if there is need for change but, as I argue here, change cannot be accommodated by the law as it currently stands? Former AB Member Jennifer Hillman has commented as follows: '[i]n the absence of a legislative function waiting in the wings [the WTO is notorious for lack of legislative activity], judges often become very conservative, fearing to branch out very far since there is such a limited chance for timely course correction. Yet, this very real and understandable conservatism will come under ever increasing strain if cases come in areas in which there is little WTO law to apply, such as climate change or financial regulation, and little ability for the WTO to write new law in those areas if the negotiating process is not working efficiently' (Hillman, n. 6 above, p. 283).

[16] See Mancini, n. 11 above.

that, in the WTO, it is the Members, acting as the Dispute Settlement Body (DSB), that adopt the rulings and recommendations of the panels and the Appellate Body (while, conversely, the latter simply 'assist' the DSB)[17] that is symbolically and legally important.[18]

If this is correct, two corollaries should be put forward. First, the attitude and focus of the interpreter or adjudicator should be more on 'discovering' rather than on 'inventing' meaning (which is the key point of this chapter). This is the essence of being simply agents with a limited mandate, and not principals crafting negotiating scenarios and possibilities. The Panel in *US – Softwood Lumber IV* masterfully expressed this:

> We consider that, if the Members feel the rules as laid down in the WTO Agreements do not address certain situations in what they consider to be a satisfactory manner, they should raise this issue during negotiations. Our task consists of interpreting the Agreement to explain what it means, not what in our view it should mean, nor are we allowed to read words in to the text of the Agreement which are not there, even if we were to consider that the text inadequately addresses certain specific situations.[19]

Former Appellate Body Members have also insisted on this role of the WTO dispute settlement system. Writing in 2002, with considerations that are very much valid today, Claus-Dieter Ehlermann lucidly noted:

> The WTO is characterised by an imbalance between the strong (quasi-) judicial structure set up by the DSU and the weak political decision-making process which is all too often blocked, between major trade rounds, by the traditional consensus rule. The work of Panels and the AB would be facilitated if the political filters of the WTO, i.e., the committees established by different covered agreements, functioned better, and if the Ministerial Conference or the General Counsel were able to adopt interpretations and amendments, pursuant to Articles IX and X of the Marrakesh Agreement. Instead of advocating mechanisms weakening the dispute settlement process, all efforts should be concentrated on strengthening the political arm of the WTO.[20]

This led him to conclude:

> In view of the weakness of the political decision-making process, the responsibility of the AB is enormous. It must proceed with extraordinary

[17] See Article 11 of the DSU.

[18] Thus, though we live in a world of reverse consensus, strictly speaking, 'judicial power' still formally resides with Members (rather than with the panels or the Appellate Body).

[19] Panel Report, *US – Softwood Lumber IV*, para. 7.60.

[20] Ehlermann, n. 6. For a discussion on the imbalance between judicial and legislative function in the WTO, see also Hudec (2002: 211–222).

circumspection and care. It is therefore advisable to pursue the cautious, case-specific approach that the AB has adopted in motivating its findings and conclusions.[21]

Secondly, adjudicators should not pay attention to pressures, expectations or vague legitimacy claims.[22] What they should care about, something for which they will never be censured, is the legality and correctness of their decisions.

The remarks above find confirmation in the rules on jurisdiction and interpretation that apply to the panels and the Appellate Body. These can be found in Article 3.2 of the Dispute Settlement Understanding that reads:

> The dispute settlement system of the WTO is a central element in providing security and predictability to the multilateral trading system. The Members recognise that it serves to preserve the rights and obligations of Members under the covered agreements, and to clarify the existing provisions of those agreements in accordance with customary rules of interpretation of public international law. Recommendations and rulings of the DSB cannot add to or diminish the rights and obligations provided in the covered agreements.

The drafters of the Dispute Settlement Understanding have repeatedly referred to the 'rights and obligations' embodied in the covered agreements.[23] More specifically, they have expressly indicated that the dispute settlement system 'serves to preserve' these rights and obligations and that the latter also represent the limit of adjudication (it should be noted that even the Dispute Settlement Body – and not only the panels and the Appellate Body assisting it – 'cannot add to or diminish' rights or obligations).[24] The fact that the drafters expressly – and repeatedly – introduced this language is significant.

Article 3.2 requires the dispute settlement system to 'clarify' WTO law by having recourse to the 'customary rules of interpretation of public international law'. While to reference to the 'clarification' of the law simply reiterates the point just made, the reference to the use of the 'customary rules of interpretation of public international law' is arguably superfluous.[25] It is known that this expression has been intended to refer to the relevant provisions of the Vienna Convention on the Law of

21 Ibid.

22 See Rubini (2014: 895–936).

23 See also Article 19.2 DSU on 'Panel and Appellate Body recommendations'.

24 The only route to changes of this type is treaty amendment (see Article IX of the Agreement Establishing the World Trade Organization).

25 See Van Damme (2010: 605, 608).

Treaties (VCLT; see Articles 31 to 33).[26] I will delve on these provisions in the next section. Suffice here to say that the principles of interpretation in these provisions put the treaty text at the centre stage of the hermeneutic activity of the interpreter. This is natural. It is the text that was negotiated and agreed. It is through the text that the parties expressed themselves and defined the contours of their rights and obligations. The text is both the starting point and the limit of interpretation.

It now looks clear how – through this approach to the interpretation and application of WTO law – the negotiators envisaged that the WTO dispute settlement system would provide 'security and predictability' to the multilateral trade system.

C The Crucial Search for the 'Negotiated Balance' and Its Evidence

This section introduces two core concepts that will be used to enrich our analysis of subsidies case law.

I The Concept of 'Negotiated Balance'

The main thesis put forward in this chapter is that, in interpreting WTO law, panels and the Appellate Body should search for the 'negotiated balance' of the rules they interpret. What the interpreter has to look for – always – is the equilibrium of the negotiated deal, what was agreed to (or was not agreed to) in its essence and, if possible, in its details. It is the identification of this balance that guides the act of giving meaning to a certain language or requirement in the treaties. This is a reflection of the contractual nature of WTO law underlined above. It is also, in my view, what former Appellate Body Member James Bacchus expressed when saying that, in WTO law, the 'deal' is the

> careful balance of rights and obligations of all WTO Members that was agreed in negotiating and concluding the treaty, and that is expressed in the words of the treaty and *only* in the words of the treaty.[27]

To perform this action of discovery of the negotiated balance, the customary rules of interpretation in international law are the necessary tools.

[26] Appellate Body Report, *US – Gasoline*, at 16–17; Appellate Body Report, *Japan – Alcohol*, at 104; Appellate Body Report, *US – Softwood Lumber IV*, para. 59.

[27] Bacchus, n. 36: 512–513.

The first paragraph of Article 31 of the VCLT, which lays down the 'general rule of interpretation', requires that

> A treaty shall be interpreted in good faith in accordance with the ordinary meaning to be given to the terms of the treaty in their context and in the light of its object and purpose.

The text and the language of the treaty is thus at the centre of the hermeneutic process. As noted above, this is obvious. It is through the text that the negotiating parties defined their rights and obligations. The meaning of the text should be arrived at also by considering the relevant context and the object and purpose of the treaty. It is known that, far from outlining a mechanic process or an exhaustive catalogue of rules of interpretation, Article 31 simply provides for some of the main principles of interpretation which should be considered together – holistically – to give meaning to a given language. In sum, the main evidence of the negotiated deal and the intention of the parties remains the text of the treaty, duly contextualised.[28]

Article 32 of the VCLT deals with the 'supplementary means of interpretation', reading:

> Recourse may be had to supplementary means of interpretation, including the preparatory work of the treaty and the circumstances of its conclusion, in order or confirm the meaning resulting from the application of article 31, or to determine the meaning when the interpretation according to article 31:
> (a) Leaves the meaning ambiguous or obscure; or
> (b) Leads to a result which is manifestly absurd or unreasonable.

Thus, after outlining the 'general rule of interpretation' in Article 31, the VCLT provides the interpreter with further tools to help her or him to give meaning to the treaty text. Although these rules, which give specific relevance to the negotiations and their context, have traditionally been given less weight than those of Article 31, they are important inasmuch as they help to complete or enhance the hermeneutic activity already conducted. It should also be noted that, like in practice, a rigid separation between the various steps of Article 31 is not possible, the same could be said with respect to the relationship between Article 31 and 32.[29] The act of interpretation is a holistic process.[30]

[28] See Van Damme (2009a: 298, 326 et seq.).

[29] Finally, Article 33 deals with the interpretation of treaties authenticated in more languages.

[30] See Abi-Saab, n. 6 above.

Now, if there is admittedly nothing controversial about saying that panels and the Appellate Body should exercise their jurisdiction in the manner intended by the drafters, and that a proper reading of the VCLT seems to confirm that their hermeneutic efforts should always result in an interpretation that represent the deal that was negotiated,[31] it is a fact that it may not always be easy to find the negotiated meaning with precision.

Undoubtedly, in some cases, the lack of clarity or ambiguity of the law is simply justified by the fact that there was no agreement or, indeed, there *was* an agreement but to disagree. This results in what is called deliberate or creative ambiguity.[32] If this is the case, and in order to avoid undue gap filling or law making, the panel or the Appellate Body should arguably take – as highlighted by Claus-Dieter Ehlermann – the most circumspect and cautious approach permissible in the circumstances. This duty is not simply expressed by saying that the interpreter should respect the text of the covered agreements. It is much more than that. It more radically concerns the attitude of the interpreter that should make every effort in discovering meaning from the text, rather than imposing or inventing it. This is after all the deep meaning of the

[31] This, in my view, comes out from the following passage by former AB Member, Abi-Saab, n. 6 above: 'In practice ... much of the reasoning in interpretation is informed by the object and purpose, either consciously or subconsciously, where they can be identified, even though they many not figure explicitly as such in the analysis. Indeed, they are frequently disguised in the search for "*effet utile*", or even the initial common intention of the Contracting Parties.'

[32] As Richard Posner noted, '[d]eliberate ambiguity may be a necessary condition of making the contract; the parties may be unable to agree on certain points yet be content to take their chances on being able to resolve them, with or without judicial intervention, should the need arise. It is a form of compromise like "agreeing to disagree"'. See Posner (2004–2005: 1581, 1583). It is interesting to quote at this stage one passage from a recent article, written by three key actors in the negotiations of the Uruguay Round, and within it more specifically subsidy rules: 'These [WTO] Agreements had been negotiated with the GATT dispute settlement in mind; a system much less legalistic than the new one. Therefore, negotiators, sometimes deliberately, were creating some ambiguities in the negotiated texts or were defining certain issues in rather general terms, in the belief that no interpretation which had not been agreed by them could be imposed on them.' The final twist is telling: 'There is no doubt that had the negotiators known that their agreements would be submitted to as a legalistic system such as the present WTO dispute settlement, the Uruguay Round would have not been concluded or would have been concluded much later, after a long process of clarification of the new rules, their ambiguities and consequences.' Cartland, Depayre, and Woznowski (2012: 986). Pondering these statements, one could note that, already at the time of the Uruguay Round negotiations, GATT panels were rather legalistic and rule-oriented in their approach. Equally, one wonders how different negotiating tables could be operating in 'clinical isolation' between each other.

oft-repeated mantra (which is in fact a legal requirement)[33] that dispute settlement cannot add or diminish rights or obligations, and that the adjudicating bodies' mandate is simply one of 'clarification' of the law.[34] If the precise meaning of a certain provision or requirement may be elusive, what is sometimes less elusive is the (at least) general balance point the negotiators wanted to convey through the agreed text. This may refer to few basic elements where there was common ground. This balance, however general, can and should represent the main guiding principle for the adjudicator who shall then take position accordingly. Furthermore, if what the negotiators wanted, and indeed agreed to, may not be clear, it is sometimes easier to determine what they did *not* want to – the *outer boundaries* of the law.[35]

The gist of this approach is that the interpreter of WTO law should always seek what the negotiators meant, or, alternatively, could and would have meant, by including a certain legal requirement, using a certain language, resorting to a certain legal architecture. If this is not possible, the concern should be to pinpoint what they could *not* and would *not* have meant. The interpreter cannot perform fundamental acts of reconstruction of the law. She or he does not have a completely clean sheet.[36] To say that the interpreter should look for the negotiated balance is also expressing an attitude towards the treaty text and its possible meaning. Once again: every effort should be made to discover (as opposed to impose) meaning out of the text under examination.

[33] See Article 3.2 and 19.2 of the DSU.

[34] John Jackson once noted: 'arguably, [this language] resonates in the direction of a caution to the Panels and appeal divisions to use "judicial restraint", and not to be too activist'. (Jackson 1998: 91). One may even advance the idea that it is part of the duty of the adjudicator to simply acknowledge that there are possible gaps in the law, and that it is not for her or him, but for the legislator, to deal with them.

[35] I concur with Lorand Bartels when he suggests that, should the law be so indeterminate that no meaning can be identified, the panels and the Appellate Body would be discharging their duty to 'address' the relevant provisions and legal issues and 'assist' the Dispute Settlement Body, by simply making a statement to this effect (Bartels 2004: 877). This would serve to highlight any lacuna in the law and shift the responsibility to those that are responsible for filling it – the Members.

[36] I believe that the same ethos comes out from the writing of several AB Members when they are at pains to highlight their 'circumspection and care' in interpreting WTO law. They invariably refer to the importance of a textual approach (see Ehlermann, n. 20 above, pp. 615–616), of the 'trust in the written words' because 'words matter. So words must have meaning . . . The Members of the Appellate Body trust in words also, and, not least, because the Members of the WTO have clearly told them to do so . . . are of the view that the Members of the WTO meant what they said when putting words into the WTO treaty' (Bacchus 2005: 509–511).

II *Searching for Evidence: The Importance of the Negotiating History and Its Context*

But what was the intention of the parties? The key issue then becomes how to establish what the negotiators and the drafters wanted. To what materials should panels and the Appellate Body resort to find this intention? As noted, the main evidence of that intention remains the text of the treaty, but what if this is (as often happens) not conclusive?

As the VCLT warrants, the negotiating history and its context should play a role.[37] It is only through a careful analysis of the history of the negotiations and drafting of the legal text, that the interpreter can identify the balance of the legal disciplines.[38] The initial point of reference are therefore the negotiating documents that first and foremost can elucidate on the various positions and degree of agreement (or disagreement) reached between the parties and offer the necessary third dimension to the legal text. But the problem is that most negotiating documents often are unclear or, in any event, do not say anything about the intention of 'all of the drafters' as a collective unit. If anything, that should come out from the final treaty text. Most documents reflect the position of one or more parties and can hardly be used as a basis for proof of the intention of all the drafters.[39] What they may be useful at, however, is in helping (at least) to identify the, even conflicting, terms of the discussions, their outer boundaries. Most importantly, whatever the informative value of the negotiating documents may be, it may be necessary to consider the 'surrounding circumstances' of the negotiations.

This way of proceeding is reflected in Article 32 of the VCLT which, as noted, is not simply about the use of the *traveaux préparatoires*. This

[37] The views expressed extrajudicially by AB Members are mixed in this respect. The 'low value' attributed to the *traveaux préparatoires* is generally justified by the 'lack of reliable sources, and the ambiguities resulting from the presence of contradictory statements of the negotiating parties' (see Ehlermann, n. 20 above, p. 616; see also Bacchus, n. 36 above, p. 506). But the fact that this is not an objection in principle but a practical consideration is confirmed by the suggestion that WTO Members should write a 'common and official negotiating history' of the pending Doha Development Round (Bacchus, n. 36 above, p. 521). The significance of preparatory works, that are 'sometimes overlooked', and of what negotiators meant to convey has also been very recently reaffirmed by current AB Member Thomas Graham, n. 6, above.

[38] This is leading the Court of Justice of the European Union to increasingly rely in certain areas on *traveaux préparatoires* of legislation, especially those that are publicly available. See the interesting analysis by Koen Lenaerts, the current President of the Court of Justice of the European Union, in Lenaerts and Guitiérrez-Fons (2013: 19–24).

[39] For a detailed analysis of the role of negotiating history in interpretation see Van Damme (2009b: Chapter 8).

provision rather refers to the 'supplementary means of interpretation', which include (*but certainly are not limited to*) the 'preparatory work of the treaty and the circumstances of its conclusion'.[40]

Thomas Graham, one of the current Appellate Body Members, thus recently noted:

> A helpful record of the preparatory work often may not be available. So what help are 'the circumstances of its conclusion' for checking or confirming an interpretation that we've given to a WTO agreement? What were those circumstances, and which are relevant?[41]

What could these circumstances be? One has to look for the broader diplomatic, political and economic context within which the negotiations took place and the negotiators operated.[42] The examination of the main issues that were relevant in the build-up of the negotiations and during them is the starting point. The second step is the reconstruction of the main, prevailing positions vis-à-vis those issues, as reflected, for example, in the domestic laws, litigation, official speeches, policy and academic literature. All these investigations have always to be set against what actually happened in the negotiations and is, despite its deficiencies, reported in the *traveaux préparatoires* – and, eventually, what could be reflected (or not) in the treaty text.

Certainly, legal interpretation does not require adjudicators to become historians. But, much as historians can make reference to various sources (such as diaries or memoires) and make use of them to give meaning and interpret historical events, I do not see any legal obstacle,[43] or any reason why even adjudicators should not decide to enrich their toolbox and, for example, use the most authoritative historical works or commentaries that can provide additional depth to the context of the negotiations. As Van Damme perceptively notes, it is often more an issue of evidence than of interpretation.[44] Thus the question is certainly not *what* may be used but *how* it can be used.[45]

40 Also the 'subsequent practice' of the parties that, within the framework of the Vienna Convention is considered 'together with the context', can play a role in giving meaning to the negotiated balance.

41 Graham, see n. 6 above.

42 The Appellate Body has treated this as context rather than as a supplementary means of interpretation. *EC – Chicken Cuts.*

43 As just noted, the VCLT is certainly not an obstacle to the suggested practice.

44 Van Damme, n. 39 above, p. 353: 'these principles [of interpretation] are as much about evidence and burden of proof as they are about treaty interpretation'.

45 If reference is made to scholarship, the main question then becomes to aptly separate (when this is possible) the reconstruction of a factual record of what happened in the negotiations (which we could tag 'objective narrative'), which may be relevant, from the

Incidentally, the time is ripe to highlight a paradox here. It is still not clear to me why, despite the obvious importance of identifying the negotiators' intention and the context of the negotiations, with very limited exceptions, WTO dispute settlement bodies are reluctant to cite literature (while it is common knowledge they use it, or heavily rely on it in their work). Would it really be completely inappropriate to rely on classic accounts such as the works of John Jackson, Bob Hudec or Kenneth Dam? Or, in the specific area of subsidies, the still highly relevant and fresh analyses of those actors and commentators who were writing during, or in the immediate aftermath of, the negotiations?[46] Are we sure that, discounted any known biases, the knowledge and awareness, the sense and sensibility of these people are of no use at all when it comes to making legal sense of GATT and WTO laws and, going back to the claim of this chapter, detecting the 'balance point' of the disciplines?[47] It is known how in these papers negotiators elucidated and summarised their positions and scholars reacted to them. These pieces constitute an important body of literature that constitutes evidence of the context and circumstances of the negotiations. If literature coeval to the negotiations may be particularly relevant, more contemporary analysis may be valuable too. Serious historical studies on the GATT and the WTO, carried out with strong methodology and with access to several sources, are increasingly common.[48] Shall we simply ignore them once we enter the doors of the temple of WTO dispute settlement? Or, rather should we welcome and promote this type of scholarship and underline its practical relevance? Again – I have not heard or read any plausible explanation of why the WTO wants to be (or to appear?) virtually and completely immune to serious scholarly work.

more subjective assessment of that factual record (the 'subjective narrative'), which may be less relevant.

[46] The list is very long. I include only a few names here: Gary Horlick, Peggy Clarke, Judy Bello, Mike Levine, Alan Holmer, Dan Hunter, Susan Haggerty, John Greenwald, Gerard Depayre, Mauro Petriccione, Gary Hufbauer, Joanna Shelton-Erb, Richard Diamond, Terry Collins-Williams, Geny Salembier.

[47] Suffice it to read Article 38(1)(d) of the Statute of the International Court of Justice which reads that the ICJ is also to apply 'judicial decisions and the teachings of the most highly qualified publicists of the various nations, as subsidiary means for the determination of rules of law'. It is also known that, in the EU law practice, academic scholarship is widely used. One good example is given by the Opinions of the Advocates General to the Court of Justice of the European Union, which are replete with academic citations.

[48] See, for example, Irwin, Mavroidis, Sykes (2010).

Finally, at the risk of stating the obvious, it is clear that the 'negotiated balance' in the relevant laws will not come out – as such – from the negotiating documents (or the most authoritative commentary). In other words, it is always the interpreter–adjudicator who is in the driving seat and has to make full sense of all the evidence available, put it into its context and make use of her or his logical ability to carry out the act of interpretation, and to carry out the act of interpretation – which, as Lord McNair once said – is more an art than a science.[49]

D The Interpretative Attitude of the Panels and Appellate Body in Subsidy Cases

This section outlines the key questions of the chapter and provides the reader with a brief conceptual roadmap.

Against the paradigmatically unclear regulatory framework of the SCM Agreement, what was the attitude of the panels and the Appellate Body towards treaty interpretation in these first twenty years? In particular, is there a difference between the approach of panels and that of the Appellate Body? Can we identify different phases, in particular more self-restrained periods or more activist approaches to the law? Has one clearly given way to another? Or are trends difficult to detect?

As regards the first question, this chapter assumes that more consistency, or indeed an evolution, can more easily be found in the case law of the Appellate Body than for the panels. The Appellate Body is a permanent body and, although it sits in three-Member divisions, there is known to be a considerable degree of collegiality in the deliberation of each case, with meetings extended to non-division Members and opinions sought from them,[50] all to the benefit of consistency of jurisprudence (and partly compensating for changes in composition). Moreover, it benefits from the support of a dedicated and separate secretariat. By contrast, panels are established on an ad hoc basis. Panelists differ in terms of their expertise and knowledge of trade law.[51] The WTO Secretariat certainly plays a supporting and possibly a unifying role in the panels' work but its impact on the actual decisions is not clear. In any case, even assuming there is a strong influence of the secretariat on the adjudicating process, it is difficult to identify its specific impact on

[49] Sinclair (1984: 118). See also Brown and Jacobs (2000: 323).
[50] See Rule 4(3), and also Rule 4(1), of the Working Procedures of the Appellate Body.
[51] Which has led many to advocate the creation of a permanent panel system.

particular cases or issues. And it is equally difficult to speculate on whether, within the specific context and design of WTO dispute settlement (with the above-mentioned two-tier adjudicating system), it is reasonable to expect that the panels' attitude tends to be restrained rather than activist.

For these structural reasons, it is more difficult to identify a 'panels' jurisprudence' and assess whether it evolves or changes. By contrast, the Appellate Body's work is more naturally suited to constitute 'jurisprudence' and can be scrutinised. The reader should bear this caveat in mind.

During the past twenty years, the WTO dispute settlement system has produced eighty-one decisions on subsidies on industrial goods only (not agriculture), issuing 96 reports. In this chapter, we review twenty-four of those reports (some directly, and others, dealing with the same issues in other cases or in the same cases in the first instance, indirectly). These cases have been selected because they focus almost exclusively on substantive issues, mostly related to the definition of 'subsidy', have (almost all) attracted significant attention and, in some cases, generated controversy. Chronologically these reports are evenly spread during the period of 1999 to late 2014 (see Table 11.1).[52] Although this review is not complete, and there are notable omissions,[53] this selection is sufficiently representative and comprehensive to identify directions and trends in subsidy jurisprudence.

I analyse these reports by dividing them into two groups: the 'jurisprudence of discovery' and the 'jurisprudence of invention'. These refer to those decisions where the panels and the Appellate Body respectively have, or have not, searched and found the 'negotiated balance' underlying the provisions at issue. After analysing each group, I will provide a more general assessment.

[52] Seventeen out of those twenty-four reports were adopted during first ten years of dispute settlement activity. This predominance is, however, fully in line with the fact that 66 per cent of the WTO disputes took place during that period. See Mavroidis (2016: para. 5.3).

[53] Most importantly, *EC – Sugar* (265, 266, 283) and *US – Cotton* (267), adopted in 2004 and 2008, which, despite their huge importance, did not raise any significant definitional issue. The absence of the reports in *EC – Aircraft* (316) and *US – Aircraft* (353), which were initiated in 2004 and are still pending, is important but any significant analysis of the issues raised in those cases would have demanded much more space. Finally, disputes raising important procedural or remedial issues, such as *Australia – Leather (21.5)*, are also excluded.

Table 11.1 *Disputes and Reports Reviewed*

Year	1996	1997	1998	1999	2000	2001	2002	2003	2004	2005	2006	2007	2008	2009	2010	2011	2012	2013	2014	Total
Panel				3		2	1	1		3					1		2		1	14
Appellate Body				1	2		2		1	1						1		1	1	10

Source: Created by the author.

E The 'Jurisprudence of Discovery': The WTO Dispute Settlement Gets It Right

In this section, I single out a few decisions, spanning from 1999 to 2012, which, in my view, represent true turning points in the creation of the *acquis* on subsidy laws. They all focus on definitional issues, which, for its intricate interplay of technical and policy issues, is the real testing ground of any effort at adjudication of subsidy rules.[54] All these cases can be grouped under the term 'jurisprudence of discovery' because they involved panels and the Appellate Body discovering the essence of the balance of the subsidies disciplines which were negotiated and agreed upon during the Uruguay Round.

Three key concepts emerge. The first is the *market-orientation* of the definition of subsidy that, conversely, also means that non-market (read: policy) considerations are not taken into account. The second notion relates to the inevitable *formalism* and, to some extent, *simplicity* of the type of assessment required for defining what is a subsidy. The third concept is the importance of the fact that subsidy laws, in particular the rules determining their material scope, are often the result of a delicate balancing of the different positions prevailing during the negotiations. As will be seen, there is indeed a *balance* point between conflicting forces and even goals that the definition has to satisfy.

I *Canada: Measures Affecting the Export of Civilian Aircraft (Canada – Aircraft) (DS 70)*

Both the Panel and the Appellate Body in *Canada – Aircraft* were called upon to interpret the term 'benefit', which is one of the two prongs of the definition of subsidy. Under Article 1 of the SCM Agreement, for a subsidy to exist there must be one of the specific forms of financial contribution outlined therein or, alternatively, any form of income or price support, and either of this should confer

[54] As a result of this, by far the large majority of subsidy cases have raised important questions about Article 1 of the SCM Agreement, to an extent that is probably not comparable to what has happened with respect to definitions under other covered agreements. The main reason is that key concepts of the definition of subsidy, such as the requirement that a 'benefit is conferred', can more easily open up to policy considerations. See Rubini, note n. 22 above, p. 923.

a benefit.[55] Both the Panel and the Appellate Body found that whether the governmental action at issue confers a benefit (or not) depends on the 'marketplace'. This is 'an appropriate basis for comparison' (Appellate Body)[56] or, with even firmer language, 'the only logical basis' (Panel).[57]

Those findings reflect the choice for a progressive construction of WTO subsidy laws on the basis of the main concern subsidies may cause for the trading systems, i.e. the potential to cause distortions and spillovers. To put it another way, subsidies cause apprehension and are an issue for the trading system because they may distort the market (although, crucially, they may often correct it – but this is a separate issue and does not represent the key rationale for regulating subsidies in a multilateral trading system).[58] Viewed from this perspective (i.e. the potential to distort trade and competition), it is then clear why the Panel and the Appellate Body applied the same approach, not only in terms of outcome, but also virtually using the same language.[59] The point I am making is fully clear if we consider the oft-repeated passage from the Appellate Body report:

[55] Article 1.1 reads: For the purpose of this Agreement, a subsidy shall be deemed to exist if:

(a)(1) there is a financial contribution by a government or any public body within the territory of a Member (referred to in this Agreement as 'government'), i.e. where:
- (i) a government practice involves a direct transfer of funds (e.g. grants, loans, and equity infusion), potential direct transfers of funds or liabilities (e.g. loan guarantees);
- (ii) government revenue that is otherwise due is foregone or not collected (e.g. fiscal incentives such as tax credits);
- (iii) a government provides goods or services other than general infrastructure, or purchases goods;
- (iv) a government makes payments to a funding mechanism, or entrusts or directs a private body to carry out one or more of the type of functions illustrated in (i) to (iii) above which would normally be vested in the government and the practice, in no real sense, differs from practices normally followed by governments;

or

(a)(2) there is any form of income or price support in the sense of Article XVI of GATT 1994;

and

(b) a benefit is thereby conferred.

[56] Appellate Body, *Canada – Aircraft*, para. 157.

[57] Panel, *Canada – Aircraft*, para. 9.112.

[58] See Rubini (2009: Chapter 2).

[59] Compare, Appellate Body, para. 157, and Panel, para. 9.112. It is also important to note that this anchorage to the marketplace is found in many other Panel and Appellate Body reports passed subsequently, which are not included in this brief review.

> The marketplace provides an appropriate basis for comparison in determining whether 'benefit' has been 'conferred', because the trade-distorting potential of a 'financial contribution' can be identified by determining whether the recipient has received a 'financial contribution' on terms more favourable than those available to the recipient in the market.[60]

This reference to the market is not always fully appreciated. It is true that there are difficulties in identifying and quantifying a precise benchmark against which the governmental action has to be tested.[61] Markets are complex, actors do not always act as expected (i.e. rationally) and governmental intervention in the economy can seriously distort the working of market forces.[62] Some thus suggest that the assessment would only constitute 'market mimicry'[63] or could only work if resort is made to 'fictions'.[64] While not negating these obvious difficulties,[65] it is clear that the market is the place where trade and competition occur, and which is impacted by public action in the form of subsidies. It is therefore inevitable to look for benefit benchmarks there. In this sense, the market is much more than a paradigm in the benefit benchmarking and more generally is a key test to assess trade distortions in subsidy laws. It is a common sense and logical necessity.[66]

II United States: Tax Treatment for 'Foreign Sales Corporations' (US – FSC) (DS 108)

Through four reports between 1999 and 2002, *US – FSC* provided the opportunity to gain a better understanding of the test to establish when the government is not acting in the economy as a market operator (for example by investing or lending) but as a sovereign, through taxation. The predominant legal criterion to establish whether a tax measure is

60 Appellate Body Report, para. 157.

61 Moreover, another line of criticism attacks the reference to the market because it would not take into account the crucial determinant of public intervention in the market, i.e. the public interest. For a full discussion, see Rubini, n. 58 above, pp. 252–259.

62 See the perceptive analysis of Sykes (2010: 473–523).

63 Tarullo (1986/1987: 546, 570–579).

64 Lang (2014).

65 For a full analysis of these issues see Rubini (2009: Chapter 8).

66 It should be clear that I am not advocating here the use of a paradigmatic and pure market benchmark. I am simply referring to the market and its conditions at the time when the government actually intervenes with the measure that is under examination. Furthermore, one key inevitable corollary of the market orientation of the benefit analysis is that the policy motivations of government action have not been traditionally considered at this level. See Rubini, n. 58 above, Chapter 8.

a subsidy is whether the government foregoes, or does not collect, revenue 'otherwise due'.[67]

At issue, first in the original and then in the implementation proceedings were two US statutes (the Foreign Sales Corporation Act and Extra-Territorial Income Act) that essentially exempted a portion of the income earned outside the United States by certain qualifying companies from taxation. Crucially, both statutes derogated from the principle of 'worldwide taxation' which prevails in US tax law and which taxes worldwide income earned by residents. Other countries, and in particular European countries, adopted the principle of territoriality, whereby only the income earned in the territory (by both residents and non-residents) is taxed. The US move was justified by the need to redress the competitive disadvantage that US multinationals were allegedly suffering vis-à-vis their European competitors. Indeed, from an *economic* perspective, the broader scope of application of worldwide systems, with the associated disincentive to exploit the opportunities of low-tax jurisdictions, seems to put US groups at a disadvantage in international activities compared to European groups. Through ingenious transfer-pricing, the latter could move even very sizeable portions of their income to off-shore jurisdictions and eventually pay no tax at all, anywhere. The economic goal and effect of the US statutes under review were to rebalance the playing field.

Two Panels and the Appellate Body twice provided arguably four different tests and gave some meaning to the expression 'otherwise due'.[68] Through these tests, they all essentially rebuke the US practice of maintaining a broader general rule and then introducing selective exceptions for certain firms. What the United States was doing through the Foreign Sales Corporation Act first and the Extra-Territorial Income Act afterwards was foregoing revenue that would have been otherwise due – i.e. in the absence of those two legislative measures and in the light of the prevailing principles of US tax law.

The reports highlight the difference in approach between legal and economic analysis.[69] In my view, these rulings are formally and even substantially correct – certainly in legal terms, although maybe not in terms of economic logic. This formalism, this rigidity (and lack of

[67] See Article 1.1(a)(1)(ii) of the SCM Agreement.

[68] See Panel Report, paras. 7.43–7.46; Appellate Body Report, paras. 90–91; Panel Report (Article 21.5 DSU), paras. 8.14–8.30; Appellate Body Report (Article 21.5 DSU), para. 91. These four tests are discussed in Luca Rubini, n. 58 above, Chapter 9.

[69] Mavroidis (2012: footnote 27 to p. 534), underlines that the 'rationale' behind the US law is 'immaterial'. See also Hudec (2003: 175).

sensitivity towards any compensatory logic: remember: the US tax measures had been introduced to level – and not to tip – the playing field) is correct.[70] It is much more in line with the idea that the WTO agreement is a contract and that the dispute settlement system is simply ensuring that it is respected, than a different approach that would have done justice to the ultimate policy objectives of the United States and the simply compensating effect of its tax exemption.[71] In other words, the issue was simply whether the US measures did or did not constitute a subsidy, and not whether this policy of support was desirable or legitimate (which is, both conceptually and practically, a separate question).

III United States: Measures Treating Export Restraints as Subsidies (US – Export Restraints) (DS 194)

The third dispute is *US – Export Restraints* which was decided in 2001 by a Panel decision only. This is probably the most important report relating to subsidy laws.[72] This is a landmark decision because it casts light on both the function and interpretation of the requirement of the existence

[70] Formalism is not necessarily negative. It is in the nature of the law to often rely on ex ante and pre-made assessments that take the shape of 'per se' rules like presumptions. In other words, the value that the law brings in these cases is that the rules of the game are settled for a certain period of time and that renegotiation (with its costs and uncertainty) is not possible. The only issue is whether this normative approach is appropriate to achieve the goal of the provision and that any relevant under- or over-inclusion is tolerable. If not, the system should design the rule as a 'standard', continuously attuned to the factual circumstances in the context of an individual assessment. See Rubini (2014: 895–938; footnote 103 to p. 104): 'Note that there is nothing ontologically wrong with formalism, or conversely inherently right with "substantialism". The important points to have in mind are both the practical nature of law – law has to be applied to certain conducts and events – and the objectives of the specific discipline at hand. This double analysis will tell whether, in the specific circumstances, it is better to have a rule requiring a formal or a substantial analysis.'

[71] Ironically despite the initially neutrality of WTO law with respect to tax decisions, the dispute settlement rulings ultimately force countries to choose certain tax systems. The negative integration nature of the WTO agreement – WTO law cannot impose a choice of tax system – gives way to the responsibility of countries to abide fully by the contract they have signed.

[72] A full analysis can be found in Rubini (2009: Chapter 4). A couple of significant biographical circumstances explain the special position of the Panel. The first relates to the composition of the Panel, which was chaired by Michael Cartland, the diplomat largely responsible for negotiations of the SCM Agreement. The Rules Division of the Secretariat, which supported the Panel, was chaired by Jan Woznowski who, during the Uruguay Round negotiations, assisted Cartland in the subsidies negotiations and, in particular, in drafting various iterations of the Chairman's texts. All this gave a comprehensive insight into the delicate negotiations of the notion of subsidy and of

of a financial contribution, and represents the prototype of the correct approach to WTO law. The main issue was whether an 'export restraint' could constitute a financial contribution in the form of a government-entrusted or government-directed provision of goods in the sense of Article 1.1(a)(1)(iii) and (iv) of the SCM Agreement.[73]

In response to the effects-based (and hence informal) approach advocated by the United States, the Panel underlined that the determination of whether a financial contribution exists must concentrate on the examination of the nature of the action by the government (read: form) and not on its effects (and, I would add, its objectives).[74] A different interpretation whereby, irrespective of its nature, any governmental action producing a certain 'subsidy-like' result would effectively amount to a financial contribution, would eventually mean reading the requirement of a financial contribution out of the definition of a 'subsidy' and leaving dangerously open the notion of subsidy and the application of the rules. According to the Panel, the focus of the financial contribution assessment must therefore be on the government's action rather than its possible effects on, or the reactions of, those specifically affected, even if those effects or reactions can be expected.

The financial contribution requirement plays a crucial *limiting* role within the context of subsidy rules. In this light, the Panel went on to clarify the function of the fourth subparagraph of the Article 1.1(a)(1) of the SCM Agreement, which applies where the governments act indirectly through a private body that has been entrusted or directed to carry-out one of the three exhaustive forms of financial contribution. According to the Panel, the objective of this fourth subparagraph is certainly not to extend the coverage of the definition of subsidy (by adding new forms of public action to those already listed), but rather to act as a crucial anti-circumvention device and avoids the risk that a government could jeopardise the effectiveness of the discipline by acting through a private body.

Once again, we notice a discrepancy between this legal (and formal) approach and an economic approach based on the effects. What matters is whether a certain measure belongs to one of those that the drafters wanted to be covered by the definition of subsidy and this irrespective of whether *other* measures producing similar or identical effects are left out. The findings of the Panel are crucial, and should be positively welcomed.

the spirit of the delicate balance reached in the final agreement, and probably also goes some way in explaining why there was no appeal.

73 See Panel Report, paras. 8.15–8.76.

74 See n. 66 above.

They focus on the inner logic between the various parts of the definition of a 'subsidy', and, in doing so, also recognise the role of the definition, which is to distinguish what should and should not be regulated by the disciplines of the SCM Agreement. We may disagree on how well or how appropriately the boundaries of the definition of subsidy are set (what they do is to go some way towards leaving 'regulatory acts' out of the concept of subsidy) – and maybe, with the benefit of hindsight, even the same drafters may have misgivings – but, to opine otherwise and enlarge the definition too much, would fundamentally disregard the function of the financial contribution requirement and ultimately of the notion of subsidy. It would disregard its balance.

IV China: Countervailing and Anti-dumping Duties on Grain Oriented Flat-rolled Electrical Steel from the United States (China – GOES) (DS 414)

The Panel in *China – GOES* adopts the same ethos and the same findings as the Panel in *US – Export Restraints*, with respect to the phrase 'any form of income or price support' of Article 1.1(a)(2) of the SCM Agreement.

The Panel found that the concept of 'price support' involves the direct 'setting and maintaining' of a price. However, it does not cover a random change in price that is merely a 'side effect' of a government measure. The concepts of 'income' and 'price support' must thus be interpreted as being influenced by the same spirit of the financial contribution requirement, i.e. not every government measure that produces certain subsidy-like effects is covered. It follows that the focus is more on the nature (read: the form) of the government action than simply on its effects or objectives. This means that, despite its potentially broad scope, Article 1.1(a)(2) covers those types of governmental conduct that raise 'price' or 'income' in a direct and immediate way.

Our (positive) assessment of this case is the same as that of *US – Export Restraints*.

F The 'Jurisprudence of Invention': When the WTO Dispute Settlement Gets It Wrong

Other reports, which also relate mostly to definitional issues, do not contribute to the proper understanding of WTO subsidy laws. Testing them against the benchmark of whether they capture and reflect the negotiated balance of the relevant provisions, I divide them in three categories: those that raise serious doubts about their correctness, those that are wrong and those that are arguably seriously wrong.

I United States: Imposition of Countervailing Duties on Certain Hot-Rolled Lead and Bismuth Carbon Steel Products Originating in the United Kingdom (US – Lead Bars II) (DS 138) and United States – Countervailing Measures Concerning Certain Products from the European Communities (US – CVDs on EC Products) (DS 212)

In these disputes, which took place from 1999–2000 and 2002–2003, first the Panels and then the Appellate Body were confronted with the issue of the effects of privatisation on prior subsidisation. In particular, should an arm's length sale for a fair market value and in compliance with normal market conditions extinguish the benefit of the subsidy received by the seller?

The United States had imposed countervailing duties on imports produced by companies that, before being privatised, had received subsidies. The United States crucially argued that the circumstances of the privatisation, and in particular whether the company or its assets had been transferred under commercial terms, were irrelevant and that what mattered for subsidy laws was the continuance of the productive operations. In both cases, however, the focus of the Panels and the Appellate Body differed from the United States. They key focus was on the change in ownership and its conditions, and in particular on their compliance with a market benchmark. They thus both concluded that the payment of a 'fair market value' was capable of excluding any benefit to the buyer from the transaction (and hence there was no subsidy).[75]

These decisions have been strongly criticised on the grounds that the adjudicating bodies completely neglected that the requirement at issue was whether a benefit continues to exist.[76] The price paid for the firm and

[75] In *US – CVDs on EC products*, there was some variance between the Panel, which established an absolute presumption of extinction of the benefit, and the Appellate Body, which was more cautious and, after underlining the ability of governments to direct privatisations so as to 'influence the circumstances and conditions of the sale', underlined that no automatic presumption is acceptable and the need for a case-by-case analysis.

[76] Grossman and Mavroidis (2003: 170); Grossman and Mavroidis (2005: 78); Diamond (2008: 649).

the financial wealth of its owners is irrelevant in this respect. What counts is whether the competitive position of the firm *continues* to be advantaged even after the transaction.[77] By being economically ill informed, these rulings are therefore not correct.

II United States: Final Countervailing Duty Determination with respect to certain Softwood Lumber from Canada (US – Lumber IV) (DS 257)

In this dispute from 2004, one of the key questions was how to define the appropriate market benchmark when there has been a significant commercial presence of the government in the market. In these circumstances, is the market distorted? If so, is it possible to refer to reliable commercial benchmarks?

The US Department of Commerce (DOC) had found that, by granting the right to harvest timber on Crown Land, Canada was providing a financial contribution in the form of provision of goods (under Article 1.1(a)(1)(iii) of the SCM Agreement) to lumber producers. The issue was whether these goods were also provided at less than adequate remuneration thereby conferring a benefit pursuant to Article 14 (d) of the SCM Agreement. More specifically, subparagraph (d) of this provision reads:

> the provision of goods or services or purchase of goods by a government shall not be considered as conferring a benefit unless the provision is made for less than adequate remuneration, or the purchase is made for more than adequate remuneration. The adequacy of remuneration shall be determined *in relation to prevailing market conditions* for the good or service in question *in the country of provision or purchase* (including price, quality, availability, marketability, transportation and other conditions of purchase or sale).[78]

In its determination, the US DOC had found that the prices of private timber sales in Canada did not represent a commercial market baseline because they were distorted by government intervention. In particular, the supply of 'public' timber was so dominant in the market that the prices of the few private suppliers were not determined independently

[77] While accepting the validity of this criticism, what remains to be seen is *where* in the SCM Agreement this 'competition' analysis should be more properly done – in the context of the benefit/definition or rather when adverse effects/injury are assessed. See Diamond, id, and Rubini, n. 58 above, footnote 44 to page 349, for a full analysis on this point.

[78] Emphasis added.

but were necessarily depressed and aligned to the lower level of governmental prices. Since these prices were not reliable, the US DOC used the prices of stumpage in certain bordering states in the north of the United States as a benchmark, making adjustments to account for differences in conditions between those states and Canadian provinces.

But – importantly – was it legitimate to look outside the 'country of provision', as the letter of the law clearly stated, in the search for appropriate benchmarks?

The Panel found that 'prevailing market conditions' refer to the market conditions 'as they exist' or 'which are predominant' in the country of provision.[79] Thus, the US argument that the term 'market' means 'fair market value' or market 'undistorted by government intervention' was rejected.[80] In particular, the Panel underlined that, 'as long as there are prices determined by independent operators following the principle of supply and demand, even if supply or demand are affected by the government's presence in the market, there is a "market" in the sense of Article 14(d) [of the] SCM Agreement.'[81]

Crucially, the Panel, while appreciating the 'economic logic' of the US argument, considered it to be impossible – against the express and clear text of Article 14(d) – to 'substitute its economic judgment for that of the drafters' of the SCM Agreement.[82] In these circumstances, the only usable benchmarks should have been found *within* – and not outside – the country of provision.

The Appellate Body, however, took a different view. The Panel's interpretation was 'overly restrictive' and, in some cases, the prices of the 'country of provision' many not be informative. This required consideration of alternative benchmarks rather than the private prices in the country of provision, if the purposes of Article 14(d) of the SCM Agreement 'are not [to be] frustrated'.[83]

The reasoning of the Appellate Body has been criticised for being too liberal and too far from the text of the provision at issue.[84] This is a clear instance of interpretation plainly *contra legem*.

[79] Panel Report, para. 7.50. A similar finding was made by the previous Panel in *US – Lumber III*, para. 50.

[80] Panel, *US – Lumber IV*, paras. 7.50–7.51.

[81] Ibid., para. 7.60.

[82] Ibid., para. 7.59.

[83] Appellate Body, *US – Lumber IV*, para. 101.

[84] See e.g. Horn and Mavroidis (2006: 130–145).

III *United States: Countervailing Duty Investigation on Dynamic Random Access Memory Semiconductors (DRAMS) from Korea (US – DRAMS) (DS 296)*

In 2005 the Appellate Body was called upon to interpret, once again, the meaning of the terms 'entrust' and 'direct' of subparagraph (iv) of the financial contribution requirement. Since the Panel Report in *US – Export Restraint*, there had been a few cases in which panels had adopted a progressively more flexible interpretation of those terms. Thus, whereas the Panel in *US – Export Restraint* had concluded that the ordinary meaning of the concepts of 'entrust' and 'direct' necessarily conveyed an idea of 'explicit and affirmative action [of] delegation or command', the Panels in *US – DRAMs (DS 296), Korea – Commercial Vessels (DS 273)* and *EC – DRAMs (DS 299)* relaxed those standards a bit. They agreed that the terms 'entrust' and 'direct' must respectively contain 'an element of delegation or command', and that they should invariably take the form of an 'affirmative' act. However, they disagreed as to whether these actions necessarily needed to be explicit insofar as they could be 'explicit or implicit, informal or formal'.[85]

In *US – DRAMs*, the Appellate Body took a significant step further along this trajectory of relaxing the legal standard [of what]. It rejected the view that the concepts of entrustment and direction be limited to the notions of delegation or command. For example, in addressing the concept of 'direction', the Appellate Body found that this is connected with the exercise of governmental authority over a private body. 'A "command" ... is certainly one way in which a government can exercise authority over a private body ... but governments are likely to have other means at their disposal to exercise authority over a private body', some of which *are more subtle* or '*may not involve the same degree of compulsion*'.[86] Moreover, as regards the complexity of the act of entrustment or direction, the Appellate Body (unlike all previous panels) did not require that the action of the government be 'affirmative'.

There is a concern that the Appellate Body's interpretation of 'entrust' or 'direct' is too wide and vague and thus introduces a serious element of imbalance within the financial contribution requirement and the definition of a 'subsidy' as a whole.[87] The Panel Report in *US –Export Restraints*

[85] Panel, *US – DRAMS*, para. 7.33; Panel, *Korea – Commercial Vessels*, para. 7.370; Panel, *EC – DRAMS*, para. 7.57.

[86] Appellate Body, *US – DRAMS*, para. 111 (Emphasis added).

[87] See Luca Rubini, n. 58 above, pp. 113–115.

had made it clear that subparagraph (iv) of the financial contribution requirement performs two different – indeed opposing – functions. On the one hand, it does not widen the types of financial contribution covered. On the other hand, it operates as an anti-circumvention device. The main focus of the Panel in *US – Export Restraint* was to show that the financial contribution requirement *covers only* certain forms of public intervention. Hence, in this context, one can understand why the standards of imputability of the notions of 'entrust' and 'direct' were particularly rigorous. This changes with the subsequent cases. The role of delimitation of the financial contribution was no longer an issue. Consequently, the second purpose of subparagraph (iv) – i.e. the anti-abuse device – gains centre stage. It thus becomes important for the financial contribution requirement to catch practices that otherwise would escape the scope of the definition of subsidy. Consequently, the standards of imputability of 'entrust' and 'direct' are interpreted more generously.

The bottom line is that you always a need to strike the right balance between the two functions of subparagraph (iv) and that an unduly generous construction of its key legal requirement may risk enlarging unduly the scope of the financial contribution and thus of the definition of a 'subsidy'. Arguably, this is what happened with the very flexible interpretation of the Appellate Body's decision in *US – DRAMS*.

IV United States: Definitive Anti-dumping and Countervailing Duties on Certain Products from China (US – AD/CVD) (DS 379)

In 2011 *US – AD/CVD*, the Appellate Body similarly neglected the need for balance within the definition of a 'subsidy'. Unlike the Panel,[88] the Appellate Body imposed a strict test for determining whether an entity is a 'public body'. Under the prevailing case law, public control over an organisation was necessary and sufficient to classify it as a 'public body'.

The Appellate Body changed the game in *US – AD/CVD* and found that the notion of 'public body' does not simply refer to any entity controlled by a government. It refers, more specifically, to those entities that perform governmental functions, or are vested with and exercise the authority to perform such functions.[89]

[88] And indeed in previous panels' decisions not considered in this review.

[89] See Appellate Body, *US – AD/CVD*, para. 290.

Does this finding make it more difficult to qualify measures as subsidies? (A problem that, according to some, would be particularly acute with China because of the pervasiveness of state-owned enterprises in its economy.) An initial answer might be that, if such undertakings cannot be considered as public bodies, they would necessarily qualify as 'private bodies', for the purposes of Article 1.1(a)(1)(iv) of the SCM Agreement. It would thus be necessary to prove in each case that the conduct at issue had been 'directed or entrusted' to such a body, but, as we have just seen, after the *US – AD/CVD* case, the attribution of conduct to a government can more easily be established.[90]

The definition of 'entrust' or 'direct' is not, however, the last step of the analysis. Subparagraph (iv) includes two final provisos that essentially require that the transaction at issue is 'normal governmental conduct' (it is in particular necessary to show that the function of, say, transferring funds or purchasing goods is one 'which would normally be vested in the government and the practice, in no real sense, differs from practices normally followed by governments'). But the language of these two provisos – which are themselves guarding against the abuse of subparagraph (iv) – is extremely unclear. As noted elsewhere, to give meaning to this idea of 'normal governmental conduct' is far from easy.[91] To sum this up, '[t]he notion of *normality* is … an uncertain criterion that may be interpreted in various ways'.[92]

To sum up, the use of a particularly demanding notion of 'public body' may lead to under-inclusion, i.e. a scenario where certain measures that

[90] Hence – paradoxically – one lack of balance could remedy another possible lack of balance in the definition. This requires further explanation.

[91] Rubini (2012: 525, 541–544).

[92] Rubini, n. 91 above, at p. 543. 'In a brief paragraph, the Appellate Body has recently shed some light on its reading of the two final sentences of subparagraph (iv) by referring to "*what would ordinarily be considered part of governmental practice in the legal order of the relevant Member*" and "*within WTO Members generally*" [Appellate Body, *US – AD/CVD*, WT/DS379), para. 297]. This apparently disposes of more abstract or philosophical approaches about what government is or should be in favour of a more factual one. Crucial issues remain open though. How does one defined "ordinarily"? What is the relevant baseline? Is there a minimum recurrence or a certain pattern that makes something "ordinary"? Furthermore, moving to the interpretation of "practices normally followed by governments", how do we define what "WTO Members generally" do? Does this mean "what most governments do"? If so, is there a minimum number of governments that is required to satisfy the evidential burden? In our view, the open-ended nature of these questions shows the inherent flexibility of the concept of "normality" that cannot rest on a simple examination of legal systems or on empirical surveys. A qualitative judgment is eventually called for, one that is (more) prone to conclusions based (also) on policy preferences.'

should be covered by subsidy rules may in fact be left outside the scope of the disciplines. One truly wonders whether this result is in line with that the drafters intended.

V Canada: Certain Measures Affecting the Renewable Energy Generation Sector and Canada – Measures Relating to the Feed-in Tariff Program (Canada – Renewable Energy/FIT) (DS 412, 426)

In the recent *Canada – Renewable Energy/FIT*, both the Panel and the Appellate Body interpreted the requirement of a 'benefit'. They called into question the established 'market-orientation' of the benefit test and, at the same time, injected the analysis of public policy objectives into the analysis of the benefit. The majority of the Panel controversially found that the various benchmarks put forward by the complainants could not be accepted.[93] This decision was justified by the fact that:

> competitive wholesale electricity markets, although a theoretical possibility, will only rarely operate in a way that remunerates the mix of generators needed to secure a *reliable* electricity system with enough revenue to cover their all-in costs, let alone a system that pursues *human health and environmental* objectives through the inclusion of facilities using solar PV and wind technologies into the supply mix.[94]

After defining the relevant product market as including renewable (i.e. wind and solar) energy only,[95] the Appellate Body introduced a distinction between government interventions that 'create' markets that would not otherwise exist and government interventions in support of certain players in already existing markets. While the former would not in and of itself be subject to subsidy law scrutiny, in particular *if* certain conditions of proportionality are satisfied, the latter would, by contrast, be fully subject to subsidy laws and market benchmarking.

Although the implications of these potentially far-reaching findings are not yet clear, there is broad agreement that they may offer a carve-out for many policies in support of renewable energy and even beyond this

93 One Panelist dissented and concluded that the Canadian measure did confer a benefit and constitute a subsidy.

94 Panel Report, para. 7.309 (emphasis in the original). The dissenting Panelist opined that an appropriate benchmark could be found, even in a hypothetical competitive market, in the wholesale market that 'could' exist in Ontario. He was also quite adamant that public policy objectives should not interfere with the market analysis of the benefit test.

95 This conclusion was based on a wrong application of market definition analysis, unwarrantedly borrowed from the antitrust toolbox.

sector. The eventual outcome is that certain 'subsidy' measures are not covered by the 'subsidy' definition with possible serious systemic implications. It therefore comes as no surprise that these decisions have been strongly criticised in the literature.[96]

VI Canada: Certain Measures Affecting the Renewable Energy Generation Sector and Canada – Measures Relating to the Feed-in Tariff Program (Canada – Renewable Energy/FIT) (DS 412, 426)

In *US – Carbon Steel*, the Appellate Body interpreted the expression 'a government practice involves a direct transfer of funds', which is the first type of financial contribution under Article 1.1(a)(1) of the SCM Agreement.

The Appellate Body contrasted the adjective 'direct', which would indicate 'something occurring immediately, without intermediaries or interference',[97] with the word 'involves' which would suggest that the government action does not necessarily need to consist of a transfer of funds but 'may be a broader set of conduct in which such a transfer is implicated or included'.[98] Even more explicitly the Appellate Body went on to say that '[t]he term also appears to introduce an element suggesting a lack of immediacy to the extent that it does not prescribe that a government must necessarily make the direct transfer of funds, but only that there be a "government practice" that "involves" the direct transfer of funds'.[99] This inevitably led to the conclusion that this form of financial contribution might include a transfer effectuated through an intermediary.[100]

The Appellate Body then perceptively noted:

> We also do not consider that the foregoing interpretation of the scope of Article 1.1(a)(1)(i) renders Article 1.1(a)(1)(iv) [which primarily regulated 'indirect' financial contributions] inutile. Depending on the nature of the involvement of an intermediary in the transfer of an alleged subsidy, the outcome may differ under subparagraph (i) and subparagraph (iv). For instance, there may be circumstances where the intermediary acts as 'entrusted' or 'directed' by the government. In yet other circumstances, the intermediary may not have been accorded sufficient entrustment or direction in order to effect the type of financial contribution contemplated under Article 1.1(a)(1)(iv), but may yet still qualify under Article 1.1(a)(1)(i).[101]

96 See e.g. Cosbey and Mavroidis (2014: 1–37); Charnovitz and Fischer (2015: 177–210); Rubini, n. 70 above. For a comprehensive literature review, see Rubini (2015: 211–237).
97 Appellate Body Report, para. 4.89.
98 Ibid., para. 4.90.
99 Ibid., para 4.90.
100 Ibid., para. 4.94.
101 Ibid., para. 4.95.

This passage is crucial to the interpretation of the definition of subsidy. One wonders whether the Appellate Body is ingeniously uncovering a difference that, to the best of our knowledge, nobody has ever noted before, and, in so doing, it is splitting hairs, or, in other words, is indulging in a unduly pedantic exercise of textual hermeneutics with exaggerated semantics that ends up betraying the object and purpose of the provision. Moreover, how can two arguably opposing forces embodied in the financial contribution – on the one hand, the requirements for 'directness', on the other that of 'lack of immediacy' – be operationally reconciled? How can scenarios under subparagraph (i) really be distinguished from those under subparagraph (iv)?

Indeed, the adopted interpretation carries two risks. The first concerns the 'internal' balance within the definition of subsidy, and the real danger of emptying the fourth subparagraph of Article 1.1(a)(1) of the SCM Agreement of its clear function (which is convincingly elucidated, also with reference to the negotiating history, in the *US – Export Restraints* Panel Report commented above). The second affects the 'external' balance of the definition (i.e. that pertaining the scope of the notion of subsidy) and is similar to that of the arguably too broad prevailing construction of the terms 'entrust' and 'direct' after *US – DRAMs* as analysed above. In simple terms, the Appellate Body may have created new inroads into the scope of the disciplines in a manner that was not intended by those who negotiated and drafted them.

One final gloss which shows how one error may lead to another. At issue were two different bodies, i.e. the Steel Development Fund (SDF) and the Joint Plant Committee (JPC). The US DOC had imposed CVDs after concluding that the SDF, and in particular its Managing Committee, was a public body and that it had made all the decisions related to the loans at issue, whose disbursements were however administered by the JPC. Because the SDF Managing Committee made all the decisions regarding the issuance of the loans, the Panel concurred with the US DOC and accepted that the former was directly involved in their provision. It may well be that, had the notion of 'public body' still relied on governmental control (despite the Appellate Body's dictum in *US – AD/CVD*), *all* relevant bodies in this case (i.e. both the SDF and the JPC) might easily have been considered to be public bodies, making the issue analysed in this section redundant and avoiding the need for the Appellate Body to step into dangerous territory.

G Taking Stock: Initial Observations

At this stage, it may be useful to group together the various decisions analysed so far. As noted above, there are four types of decisions, according to the assessment given: correct decisions, those raising serious doubts, wrong decisions and finally seriously wrong decisions. The standard of assessment focuses on whether, and if so to what extent, the relevant adjudicating body has followed the negotiated balance of the provisions at issue (a more detailed analysis of this assessment follows in Section H). Table 11.2 offers a visual aid and also shows the decisions attributed to Panels (P) or the Appellate Body (AB).

Very basic data analysis shows that, of 24 decisions, 14 have been assessed as correct, 7 wrong to a varying degree and 3 as highly dubious. Of the 14 correct ones, the large majority (11) comes from panels. This

Table 11.2 *Summary of Assessments of Reviewed Decisions*

Correct Decisions	Decisions Raising Serious Doubts	Wrong Decisions	Seriously Wrong Decisions
Canada – Aircraft (P, AB)	*US – DRAMs* (AB)	*US – Lead Bars II* (P, AB)	*US – Lumber IV* (AB)
US – Export Restraints (P)	*US – AD/ CVDs* (AB)	*US – CVDs on EC Products* (P, AB)	*Canada – Renewable Energy/FIT* (P, AB)
US – FSC (P, AB)	*US – Carbon Steel* (AB)		
US – FSC (21.5) (P, AB)			
China – GOES (P)			
US – Lumber IV (P)			
US – DRAMS (P)			
Korea – Commercial Vessels (P)			
EC – DRAMS (P)			
US – AD/ CVDs (P)			
US – Carbon Steel (P)			

Source: Created by the author.

contrasts to the set of questionable decisions, of which 7 (out of 10) were adopted by the Appellate Body.

Assuming the sampling is meaningful and the assessment is correct, this seems to immediately indicate that panel decisions in the subsidy field are on the whole more likely to follow the negotiated balance of the law than those of the Appellate Body. This result is particularly significant because of the greater number of panel (14) vis-à-vis Appellate Body (10) decisions reviewed. That being said, we need a little more analysis before reaching a more definite conclusion.

H Have the Panels and Appellate Body Searched for the 'Negotiated Balance'?

It is now time to specifically apply the concepts of 'negotiated balance' and 'point of balance' to the samples of good and bad cases analysed above. Have the relevant panels and the Appellate Body made use of these concepts and, if so, to what extent? In other words, have they referred to what the drafters meant (by looking at what they said in the negotiating documents) or must have meant, or not have meant (by logical implication)? If not, to what extent did their reasoning differ from the negotiated balance?

In the cases exemplifying what I call 'jurisprudence of discovery' there is good evidence that the relevant panels and Appellate Body paid considerable attention to detecting the 'negotiated balance' or the 'balance point' of the relevant provisions and disciplines. For example, in *Canada – Aircraft* they did so by considering the objective of the agreement, which, however vague, was identified in the need to control trade-distorting subsidies, and then directly making a connection between that objective and the use of the marketplace as the inevitable benchmark. It is only by reviewing what happens – or would happen – in the market as it exists when the government intervenes that one can identify the trade-distorting potential of the action of the government,[102] which is what ultimately matters in WTO subsidy disciplines. In *US – FSC* they struggled to identify a clear logical expression for the test required by the 'otherwise due' language. However, they rightly found this to be a formal test, largely based on whether the US measures at issue were derogating (or otherwise) from the conduct previously established by the same United States. In so doing, they implicitly rejected the

[102] Appellate Body Report, para. 157.

possibility of *defining* subsidies by taking into account their broader political and economic objectives or effects, such as the need to equalise or compensate for the impact of other competing tax systems. This is – in our view – part and parcel of the inherent logic of the SCM Agreement. Finally, in *US – Export Restraints* and, by reference, in *China – GOES*, the two Panels expressly sought illumination from the negotiating history. In so doing, they avoided that the parties re-opened hard-fought agreements and respected the delicate balance that the compromised definition of Article SCM 1 enshrines.

By contrast, in the cases belonging to the 'jurisprudence of invention' the Appellate Body and panels go against the balance and logic of the SCM Agreement, of the relevant provision or even of the legal requirement at issue. In some cases, this happens because, by not being economically informed in highlighting what matters in the benefit analysis (i.e. do we still have a distortion in the market?), they go against the general objective of the SCM Agreement (see *US – Lead Bars II* and *EC – CVDs on EC Products*). The same outcome is evident in the *Canada – Renewable Energy/FIT* dispute, where both the Panel and the Appellate Body intentionally inject public policy considerations into the benefit determination, and thus clearly depart from the conception of benefit and subsidy that the negotiators had in mind. In *US – Lumber IV* this is taken in an even more dramatic direction. The Appellate Body goes against the clear letter of the law and substitutes itself for the drafters. Finally, in other decisions, the Appellate Body (not the panels) takes adventurous paths and produces novel interpretations that, by expanding or reducing the meaning of certain legal requirements, seriously risk unsettling the balance of the definition and hence of the disciplines themselves (see *US – DRAMS; US – AD/CVD; US – Carbon Steel (India)*).

The analysis seems to confirm that, at least in the context of subsidy jurisprudence, panels have on the whole been more self-restrained (and correct).[103] Equally, it looks like the Appellate Body has become increasingly 'innovative' in its subsidy jurisprudence. If we leave aside the odd *US – Softwood Lumber IV* decision of 2004, and the difficult privatisation cases, it can probably be argued that it is only very recently that the Appellate Body has adopted subsidy decisions that can be tagged as

[103] One good explanation may be that the panels adhere more closely to the text and the intention of the drafters because, at least until 2008, they had – through the Secretariat – access to Jan Woznowski. By having closely assistant the Chair during the Uruguay Round negotiations, he was familiar with the nuances in the text, the negotiation history, the positions of the different Members and any 'gentlemen's agreements'.

'seriously wrong' (*Canada – Renewable Energy/FIT*) or that raise serious doubts, at least with respect to some important issues of law (*US – AD/CVD; US – Carbon Steel (India)*). Compared to the initial years of subsidy jurisprudence, it is becoming increasingly difficult to find correct decisions issued by the Appellate Body in the field. If one draws an imaginary vertical line just after 2005 and thus splits the jurisprudence in the two decades, this trend shift is very clear. In the 1995–2005 period, the AB's case law is mixed: three correct decisions, three wrong decisions and one, raising serious doubts, in the middle. By contrast, in the 2010–2015 period, the three decisions considered (one seriously wrong and two raising serious doubts), makes a considerable contribution to shifting the assessment (Figure 11.1).

More radically, if we focus on the attitude towards treaty interpretation, it looks like this change in the Appellate Body's jurisprudence over time can be explained by a progressive disjunction from the interpretative method (which, for the sake of simplicity, we can tag 'textual')[104] that the world trade court had itself originally established in its early years and that contributed so much to fostering its acceptance and legitimacy.[105] Following the narrative of this chapter, this means that the 'early' Appellate Body, through its ingenious 'textual' approach, was arguably better in adopting interpretations reflecting the negotiated balance.

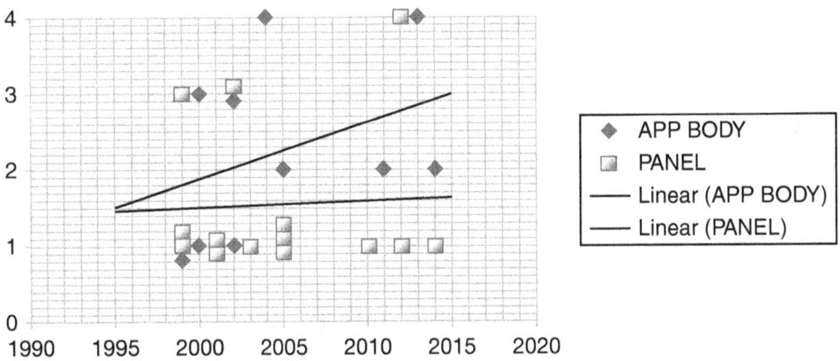

Figure 11.1. Different attitudes! Different phases?
Source: Created by the author.

[104] For an accurate exposition, see the accounts by Ehlermann Bacchus and Abi-Saab, n. 6 above.

[105] See the very recent and cogent account by Howse (2016: 9–77); see also Van Damme, n. 25.

I The Age of Innocence

Recently, on the occasion of a luncheon address at a conference marking the twentieth anniversary of the WTO Appellate Body,[106] Professor Joseph Weiler emphatically argued that the 'first' WTO jurisprudence was characterised by some sort of infancy or immaturity and showed lack of self-confidence by continuing to refer to the negotiating history of the relevant WTO provisions. Then – so the argument went – came the age of maturity and the adjudicators were finally liberated from this burden and able to walk on their own two feet.[107] For the reasons expressed in this brief chapter, I do not agree with this interpretation.

The reference and reliance on the justification of the law, which in the contractual context of the WTO goes back to its roots and origins in the negotiations, is not a symptom of lack of experience or self-confidence, nor of subscribing to any (neo-liberal) agenda, but rather a sign of maturity of the court. This, of course, cannot be stated in general terms for any legal system and any court. But, we believe, it is certainly valid in the context of a political and legal system such as the WTO and with respect to its uniquely successful dispute settlement system.

On the occasion of its twentieth anniversary, recent scholarship has concentrated on general assessments of WTO dispute settlement.[108] This is often looked at through the lens of the notion of legitimacy. This is not limited to offering learned narratives about the Appellate Body's contribution to the building of WTO law through its case law,[109] but extends to its assessment through empirical evidence. In particular, interviews with key WTO practitioners would thus show how the WTO adjudicating bodies, and in particular the Appellate Body, can be said to have succeeded in using various jurisprudential, procedural and rhetorical devices to specifically respond to the demands of their different audiences.[110]

[106] The 'WTO Appellate Body @ 20: Taking Stock and Looking Forward', 15 May 2015, European University Institute, Florence.

[107] Rob Howse has recently provided a new interpretation of the Appellate Body's disengagement from the negotiating history, which would put the WTO era in stark contrast to the GATT period. The effective downgrading of negotiating history (and even the express reliance on Article 32 of the VCLT, which frames the latter within the 'supplementary means of interpretation') would represent an intentional device to gain independence from the WTO 'institution' and its political-diplomatic trade circle. See Howse, n. 105 above, p. 32.

[108] See e.g. Mavroidis (2016).

[109] The best example in point is Howse, n. 105 above, pp. 9–77.

[110] See Shlomo-Agon (2015: 539–590).

Be that as it may, in this chapter I have presented a different narrative of the case law, and suggested a different approach to the interpretation of the WTO covered agreements, using subsidy jurisprudence as case study. To put it another way, this chapter has an important normative – not sociological – point to make. There are various meanings of legitimacy[111] but, ultimately, I believe that adjudicators, and in particular those acting in the specific political and legal context of the WTO, *should* pay attention to the legitimacy that inevitably flows from the legality of their decisions and reasoning. And the legality of judicial decisions must be measured against their formal correctness. Key to this, as this chapter has argued, is the WTO judges' effort to rely on what the negotiators have agreed to – no more no less.

At twenty, the age of innocence is definitely over. At the time of writing, very dark clouds are gathering over the Appellate Body – and the WTO at large.[112] It would be extremely unfortunate if these events, determined by political forces, would undermine the success story of the WTO dispute settlement system. If external, and largely illogical, events cannot be controlled, the WTO dispute settlement system can, however, certainly reflect on its story, weigh up its success, carefully consider its crucial and delicate role in the WTO system, and, in the most crucial step, it must measure up to it.

References

Abi-Saab, Georges. 2006. 'The Appellate Body and Treaty Interpretation'. In *The WTO at Ten: The Contribution of the Dispute Settlement System*, edited by Giorgio Sacerdoti, Alan Yanovich and Jan Bohanes Cambridge: Cambridge University Press, 453–464.

Bacchus, James. 2005. 'Appellators: The Quest for the Meaning of and/or'. *World Trade Review* 4 (3): 499–523.

Bartels, Lorand. 2004. 'The Separation of Powers in the WTO: How to Avoid Judicial Activism'. *International and Comparative Law Quarterly* 53 (4): 877.

Bengoextea, Joxerammon, MacCormick, Neil, and Moral Soriano, Leonor. 2001. 'Integration and Integrity and Legal Reasoning of the European Court of

111 Weiler juxtaposes a 'sociological' approach to legitimacy and a 'normative' one. See Weiler (2013: 235).

112 The USA has announced that it will block the reappointment of one Member of the Appellate Body (Seung Wha Chang) essentially because he participated in decisions against the USA. See Shaffer (2016).

Justice'. In *The European Court of Justice*, edited by Grainne De Burca and Joseph Weiler, Oxford: Oxford University Press, 43, at 44.

Brown, Neville and Jacobs, Francis. 2000. *The Court of Justice of the European Communities*, 5th edition. London: Sweet and Maxwell.

Cartland, Michael, Depayre, Gérard, and Woznowski, Jan. 2012. 'Is Something Going Wrong in the WTO Dispute Settlement?' *Journal of World Trade* 46 (5): 979–1016.

Charnovitz, Steve and Fischer, Carolyn. 2015. 'Canada – Renewable Energy. Implications for WTO Law on Green and Not-So Green Subsidies'. *World Trade Review* 14 (2): 177–210.

Cosbey, Aaron and Mavroidis, Petros C. 2014. 'A Turquoise Mess: Green Subsidies, Blue Industrial Policy and Renewable Energy: the Case for Redrafting the Subsidies Agreement of the WTO'. *Journal of International Economic Law* 7 (1): 1–37.

Diamond, Richard. 2008. 'Privatization and the Definition of Subsidy: A Critical Study of Appellate Body Texturalism'. *Journal of International Economic Law* 11 (3): 649.

Ehlermann, Claus-Dieter. 2002. 'Six Years on the Bench of the "World Trade Court" – Some Personal Experiences as Member of the Appellate Body of the World Trade Organization'. *Journal of World Trade* 36 (4): 606.

European University Institute. 2015. 'WTO Appellate Body @ 20: Taking Stock and Looking Forward'. 15 May 2015. Florence: EUI.

Graham, Thomas. 2013. 'Present at the Creation'. Speech at Hofstra University Law School, 6 February 2013.

Greenwald, John D. 2013. 'A Comparison of WTO and CIT/CAFC Jurisprudence in Review of US Commerce Department Decisions in Antidumping and Countervailing Duty Proceedings'. *Tulane Journal of International and Comparative Law* 21 (2): 261–272.

Grossman, Gene and Mavroidis, Petros C. 2003. 'Here Today? Gone Tomorrow?' In *The WTO Case Law of 2001*, edited by Henrik Horn and Petros C. Mavroidis. Cambridge: Cambridge University Press, 170.

Grossman, Gene and Mavroidis, Petros C. 2005. 'Recurring Misunderstandings of Non-Recurring Subsidies'. In *The WTO Case Law of 2002*, edited by Henrik Horn and Petros C. Mavroidis. Cambridge: Cambridge University Press, 78.

Hillman, Jennifer. 2010–11. 'An Emerging International Rule of Law? – The WTO Dispute Settlement System's Role in its Evolution'. *Ottawa Law Review* 42 (2): 269–284.

Horn, Henrik and Mavroidis, Petros. 2006. 'United States – Final Determination with Respect to Certain Softwood Lumber from Canada (AB-2003–6, WT/DS257/AB/R)'. *World Trade Review* 5 (S1): 130–145.

Howse, Robert. 2016. 'The World Trade Organization 20 Years On: Global Governance by Judiciary'. *European Journal of International Law* 27 (1) 9–77.

Hudec, Robert. 1999. *Essays on the Nature of International Trade Law.* London: Cameron May.

Hudec, Robert. 2002. 'Free Trade, Sovereignty, Democracy: The Future of the World Trade Organization'. *World Trade Review* 1 (2): 211–222.

Hudec, Robert. 2003. 'Industrial Subsidies: Tax Treatment of "Foreign Sales Corporations"'. In *Transatlantic Economic Disputes – The EU, the US, and the WTO,* edited by Ernest-Ullrich Petersmann and Mark A Pollack. Oxford: Oxford University Press, 175.

Irwin, Douglas, Mavroidis, Petros, and Sykes, Alan O. 2010. *The Genesis of the GATT.* Cambridge: Cambridge University Press.

Jackson, John H. 1998. *The World Trade Organization – Constitution and Jurisprudence.* London: Royal Institute of International Affairs.

Jackson, John H. 2006. *Sovereignty, the WTO, and the Changing Fundamentals of International Law.* Cambridge: Cambridge University Press.

Kaplow, Louis. 1992–93. 'Rules Versus Standards: An Economic Analysis'. *Duke Law Journal* 42: 557.

Lang, Andrew. 2014. *Governing 'As If': Global Subsidies Regulation and the Benchmark Problem.* LSE Legal Studies Working Paper No. 12/2014 (http://ssrn.com/abstract=2432642 or http://dx.doi.org/10.2139/ssrn.2432642).

Lenaerts, Koen and Guitiérrez-Fons, José. 2013. *To Say What the Law of the EU Is: Methods of Interpretation and the European Court of Justice.* AEL 2013/9 Academy of European Law Distinguished Lectures of the Academy.

Mancini, Federico. 1989. 'The Making of a Constitution for Europe'. *Common Market Law Review* 26 (4): 595–614.

Marceau, Gabrielle (ed.). 2015. *A History of Law and Lawyers in the GATT/WTO – The Development of the Rule of Law in the Multilateral Trading System.* Cambridge: Cambridge University Press.

Mavroidis, Petros. 2012. *Trade in Goods.* Oxford: Oxford University Press.

Mavroidis, Petros. 2016. *Dispute Settlement in the WTO: Mind over Matter.* Research Paper No. RSCAS 2016/04. Italy: Robert Schuman Centre for Advanced Studies.

Pauwelyn, Joost. 2003. *Conflict of Norms in Public International Law. How WTO Law Relates to Other Rules of International Law.* Cambridge: Cambridge University Press.

Pauwelyn, Joost. 2013. 'The Balancing Act of Keeping Up "Respect" for AB Rulings (according to an AB Member)'. *International Economic Law and Policy Blog* 15 February 2013.

Posner, Richard. 2004–05. 'Law and Economics of Contract Interpretation'. *Texas Law Review* 83: 1581, 1583.

Roessler, Frieder. 2015. 'Changes in the Jurisprudence of the WTO Appellate Body during the Past Twenty Years'. Working Paper 2015/72. Italy: Robert Schuman Centre for Advanced Studies, Global Governance Programme.

Rubini, Luca. 2009. *The Definition of Subsidy and State Aid: WTO Law and EC Law in Comparative Perspective*. Oxford: Oxford University Press.

Rubini, Luca. 2012. 'Ain't Wastin' Time No More. Subsidies for Renewable Energy, the SCM Agreement, Policy Space, and Law Reform'. *Journal of International Economic Law* 15 (2): 525, 541–544.

Rubini, Luca. 2014. 'The Good, the Bad, and the Ugly. Lessons on Methodology in Legal Analysis from the Recent WTO Litigation on Renewable Energy Subsidies'. *Journal of World Trade* 48 (5): 895–936.

Rubini, Luca. 2015. 'The Wide and the Narrow Gate. Benchmarking in the SCM Agreement after the Canada – Renewable Energy/FIT Ruling'. *World Trade Review* 14 (2): 211–237.

Rubini, Luca. 2016. *What Shapes the Law? Reflections on the History, Law, Politics and Economics of International and European Subsidy Disciplines*. Italy: European University Institute, Global Governance Programme.

Shaffer, Greg. 2016. *Will the US Undermine the World Trade Organization? The World Post*.

Shlomo-Agon, Sivan. 2015. 'Clearing the Smoke: The Legitimation of Judicial Power at the WTO'. *Journal of World Trade* 49 (4): 539–590.

Sinclair, Ian. 1984. *The Vienna Convention on the Law of Treaties*. Manchester: Manchester University Press.

Stewart, Terence P., McDonough, Patrick J., Smith, Jennifer M., and Jorgensen, Sandra K. 2013. 'The Increasing Recognition of Problems with WTO Appellate Body Decision-Making: Will the Message Be Heard?' *Global Trade and Customs Journal* 8 (11/12): 390–412.

Sykes, Alan O. 2010. 'The Questionable Case of Subsidy Regulation: A Comparative Analysis'. *Journal of Legal Analysis* 2 (2): 473–523.

Tarullo, Dan K. 1986–87. 'Beyond Normalcy in the Regulation of International Trade'. *Harvard Law Review* 100: 546, 570–579.

Van Damme, Isabelle. 2009a. 'Jurisdiction, Applicable Law, and Interpretation'. In *The Oxford Handbook of International Trade Law*, edited by David Bethlemen, Donald McRae, Rodney Neufeuld and Isabelle Van Damme, Oxford: Oxford University Press, 298, 326.

Van Damme, Isabelle. 2009b. *Treaty Interpretation by the WTO Appellate Body*. Oxford: Oxford University Press.

Van Damme, Isabelle. 2010. 'Treaty Interpretation by the WTO Appellate Body'. *European Journal of International Law* 21 (3): 605, 608.

Van den Bossche, Peter. 2006. 'From Afterthought to Centrepiece: the WTO Appellate Body and Its Rise to Prominence in the World Trading System'.

In *The WTO at Ten*, edited by Giorgio Sacerdoti, Alan Yanovic, and Jan Bohanes. Cambridge: Cambridge University Press, 289–325.

Weiler, Joseph. 2000. *The EU, the WTO, and the NAFTA – Towards a Common Law of International Trade*. Oxford: Oxford University Press.

Weiler, Joseph. 2013. 'Epilogue: Judging the Judges – Apology and Critique'. In *Judging Europe's Judges – The Legitimacy of the Case Law of the European Court of Justice*, edited by Maurice Adams, Henri de Waele, Johan Meeusen and Gert Straetmans. Oxford and Portland, Oregon: Hart Publishing, 235.

PART V

Interactions Within and Across Regimes

12

The Presence of the World Trade Organization Within Preferential Trade Agreements

TODD ALLEE AND MANFRED ELSIG

A Introduction

The increase in venues for regulating economic exchange in the global trading system has spurred debates on the fragmentation of international economic law and the challenges brought about by regime overlap (e.g. Busch 2007; Alter and Meunier 2009). Most notably, the rise of preferential trade agreements (PTAs) has been accompanied by a vigorous discussion of how their ascendancy affects the multilateral trading system that has the World Trade Organization (WTO) at its core. The early debate was WTO-centric, as the question actively debated was whether PTAs represent a stepping stone or a stumbling block for the Geneva-based organisation (e.g. Srinivasan 1998; Bhagwati and Panagariya 1996). Studies on the economic effects of PTAs mollified the critics somewhat, as they showed a substantial positive impact of PTAs on trade flows (e.g. Baier and Bergstrand 2007; Dür et al. 2014).

Yet concerns are still being raised. As most major developments in trade cooperation continue to occur at the bilateral and regional levels, scholars have begun to search for ways to reconcile this trend with the multilateral system. In order to address possible frictions, new ideas have been put forward as to how to 'multilateralise regionalism' (Baldwin 2006). Recent legal work has hinted further at a dialectical relationship between PTAs and the WTO system (Cottier et al. 2015). On the one hand, specific regulatory approaches developed over time within the multilateral system can be introduced into PTAs. On the other hand, regulatory innovation may be debated first in the framework of a PTA (e.g. North American Free Trade Agreement (NAFTA)) and then partially or fully adopted in the

We wish to thank the participants at the World Trade Forum 2015 for their insightful comments. We further thank Andrew Lugg for excellent research assistance and acknowledge generous financial support from the Swiss National Science Foundation (www.nccr-trade.org).

multilateral negotiations. Anecdotal evidence suggests a multidirectional relationship. However, what is lacking in this debate is more systematic evidence – at the level of treaty contents – to show exactly how much WTO law is already embedded in PTA law.

This chapter answers this question, but from a different angle and with unique empirical insights. From the vantage point of PTAs, we assess the overlap with WTO law and show how and to what extent PTAs incorporate WTO treaty obligations. By doing so, we aim to shed light on the long-standing debate about the actual presence of the WTO in today's negotiations on the contents of PTAs. This allows us to get a better handle on measuring the fragmentation or coherence of WTO and PTA obligations.

We analyse the texts of hundreds of PTAs in two novel ways, building on the ongoing work of two different projects. The first is based on a comprehensive, manual approach to coding PTAs (Dür et al. 2014). The second is the calculation of text similarities using textual-analysis software (Allee and Elsig 2015a). The former looks at explicit references to the WTO found in PTAs and their sub-areas, and the latter provides percentage scores for WTO–PTA text overlap within a given issue area.

Our analyses, particularly using the first approach, reveal that the WTO has a significant 'presence' in PTAs. For seven of the ten trade issues we examine, about half or more of the PTAs refer to the prevailing WTO agreement in some way. Additionally, some PTAs consistently make reference to the WTO across all their provisions. We find that PTAs actually do copy and paste language verbatim from WTO agreements, but this finding is less consistent. Nevertheless, we uncover dozens of PTAs that take 60 per cent or 70 per cent (or more) of their text from a parallel WTO agreement. It also seems that the two methods – references and copy-pasting – tend to be positively associated and thus reinforce one another. Overall, then, we uncover a strong presence of the WTO within PTAs, which suggests that the two venues are perhaps more compatible than is often suggested. This could also be interpreted as good news for WTO performance.

B The Presence of the WTO in Other Trade Agreements

Why would we expect the WTO to be 'present' in PTAs? If PTAs give preferences to PTA partners, why should we assume that these agreements take into account WTO rights and obligations?

WTO law might be important for various reasons. First, WTO treaties are well established. Some WTO law is based on a very long history, with some agreements dating back to 1947. They have been negotiated and implemented over many years and have become prominent instruments of international economic law. Second, active use of available dispute settlement mechanisms throughout the history of the General Agreement on Tariffs and Trade (GATT)/WTO regime has helped to clarify rules and therefore to complete to a significant degree the existing incomplete contracts. This increasingly clearer meaning of legal terms and obligations means that drawing directly upon WTO texts and agreements should entail less uncertainty than crafting new phrasings, the meaning of which could be more ambiguous. Third, the WTO today enjoys nearly universal applicability. It has 161 official Members, and twenty-two observers are in accession talks. It is no longer perceived as a club of Organisation of Economic Co-operation and Development (OECD) States, and its laws are binding on the nearly-complete universe of participating members. Fourth, trade negotiators for PTAs are also well-versed in WTO law. They are trained in, and exposed to, the WTO rulebook in their respective areas of expertise; they tend to follow developments in Geneva quite closely and are part of a wider trade law community. Overall, these factors lead to the development of shared expectations and acceptance of WTO trade rules, providing the foundational elements for the global trading system. This suggests that we should observe a significant presence of the WTO within PTAs.

Perhaps unsurprisingly, research on the relationship between the WTO and PTAs has proceeded largely according to the assumption of WTO centrism noted above. Some have looked more selectively at PTA provisions that go beyond existing WTO obligations (WTO-plus) or that cover areas that the WTO is not engaged in (WTO-extra). For instance, Horn et al. (2009) compare these elements within fourteen European Community (EC) and fourteen US agreements. For the WTO-plus category they find that 'the EC and US sets of agreements have a large number of legally enforceable obligations with significant undertakings in areas covered by the current WTO mandate, such as tariff cuts in goods, Customs Administration, Anti-dumping, Countervailing Measures, Agriculture, and Trade-Related Intellectual Property Rights (TRIPS)' (Horn et al. 2009: 23). Although they provide useful examples of additional trade commitments that are legally binding, their analysis does not explicitly capture the degree to which these go beyond the status quo, nor does it allow for generalisation beyond the United States and EC.

In addition, some contributions focus on selected areas, such as services commitments that surpass commitments under the General Agreement on Trade in Services (GATS) and existing service offers tabled in the Doha Round (Roy 2011). This research, however, does not provide direct evidence of WTO presence in the first place, but focuses on additional commitments.

In terms of measuring actual treaty overlap, some research already has established that PTAs are far from unique and that copy-pasting from other PTAs is widespread (Allee and Elsig 2015a). In fact, for the majority of PTAs, more than 60 per cent of the text is lifted from another PTA – with this figure often reaching 90 per cent or more. An important predictor for the most heavily borrowed texts is whether a common country is present across agreements, thus providing an obvious past 'source' for language used in a future treaty. For PTA partners, then, their earlier PTAs constitute a direct channel from which they can borrow.[1] Yet we also believe there may be indirect channels for borrowing. Most notably, GATT and WTO treaty texts may serve as important sources for copy-pasting. Our goal, therefore, is to systematically explore the various ways in which the WTO obligations could be incorporated into PTAs, including but not limited to this type of copy-pasting.

C Instruments of WTO Presence

How can we measure the presence of the WTO in PTAs? We pursue two different approaches. The first approach considers that PTAs may refer explicitly to other international economic law, namely WTO law. This is an often-used approach in international treaty-making and may be evident in the preamble and/or in the body text of PTAs. By making a reference to the WTO body of law, negotiators: (a) show that they are aware of important linkages to other international agreements, and (b) attempt to describe to the degree possible the relationship to these agreements.

As an illustration of the different possible forms, consider the WTO's TRIPS Agreement, one of the pillars of the multilateral system. The most comprehensive approach may be to defer fully to the TRIPS agreement and incorporate it completely, including its future evolution. For

[1] Interesting in this context is the question of which of the PTA partners' earlier PTAs serves as the template from which to borrow and which text is utilised in cases of disagreement. Also, some PTAs might borrow from landmark PTAs to which their members are not a party (e.g. from the North American Free Trade Agreement (NAFTA)).

instance, Article 9.1 of the Canada–Israel trade agreement states that 'the rights and obligations of the Parties relating to intellectual property rights shall be governed by the Agreement on Trade-Related Aspects of Intellectual Property Rights, Annex 1 C of the WTO Agreement, and any subsequent amendments to that Agreement'.[2]

Other agreements go in a similar direction, although not quite so far. Some state that the PTA obligations will not contradict WTO law. The US–Chile agreement, for example, states in Article 17.1 that 'nothing in this Chapter concerning intellectual property rights shall derogate from the obligations and rights of one Party with respect to the other by virtue of the TRIPS Agreement'. Other agreements might focus on specific TRIPS obligations.[3]

Beyond these references, all of which suggest full respect for WTO law, other references are more prospective. One example is the suggestion that PTA partners in the Cotonou Agreement between the EC and the African, Caribbean and Pacific (ACP) Group of States adhere to the WTO TRIPS Agreement.[4] Although this reference is phrased in a non-binding way, its impact could turn out to be very significant because it invites non-WTO members to accept WTO and other international obligations to which they have not been subject in the past.[5]

As the example of the TRIPS references suggests, the identification of WTO 'presence' could involve the counting of references to the WTO and the categorisation of different types of references for different sub-sections of PTAs. For instance, Valdes and McCann (2014) find that reaffirmations of WTO TRIPS obligations occur in 61 per cent of PTAs involving intellectual property rights provisions. Their findings, gener-

[2] In this respect Valdes and McCann write that 'reaffirmation ... may be seen as an acceptance of TRIPS Agreement provisions, including substantive standards and public policy safeguards and flexibilities, and thus recognition that it may serve as a kind of benchmark for a balanced and comprehensive IP system' (2014: 14).

[3] For instance in the Canada–Chile agreement (in the section on Geographical Indications) the treaty states that 'as set out in Annex C-11 and taking into account the TRIPS Agreement, the Parties shall protect the geographical indications for the products specified in that Annex'.

[4] Article 46 of this agreement on the protection of intellectual property rights states that both parties 'underline the importance, in this context, of adherence to the Agreement on Trade-Related Aspects of Intellectual Property Rights (TRIPS)' and 'they also agree on the need to accede to all relevant international conventions on intellectual, industrial and commercial property as referred to in Part I of the TRIPS Agreement, in line with their level of development'.

[5] This leads to other potential problems, as Valdes and McCann (2014) point out.

ated using an approach similar to ours, suggest that specifically mentioning the WTO in PTA provisions could be an often-applied negotiation instrument. We probe more widely for such mentions, across ten different PTA provisions.

A second way to identify 'presence' is by assessing for each provision of a PTA the amount of treaty overlap with the GATT or WTO agreement that provides the multilateral rules for each area. By incorporating existing GATT/WTO texts, PTA negotiators signal that the contracting parties base their bilateral treaty obligations on the multilateral system. Borrowing text from the GATT/WTO can occur for the full range of relevant trade issues, from market access commitments and behind the border rules, to the use of escape-clause measures and procedures for dispute settlement. Substantively, these texts can borrow core obligations of the WTO system, such as most-favoured nation (MFN) or national treatment commitments, as well as certain procedural rules.

As an illustration of a core WTO value that is copied, we focus briefly on Article 3 of the WTO Government Procurement Agreement (GPA), which refers to national treatment and non-discrimination. It states that:

1. With respect to all laws, regulations, procedures and practices regarding government procurement covered by this Agreement, each Party shall provide immediately and unconditionally to the products, services and suppliers of other Parties offering products or services of the Parties, treatment no less favourable than:
   (a) that accorded to domestic products, services and suppliers; . . .
2. With respect to all laws, regulations, procedures and practices regarding government procurement covered by this Agreement, each Party shall ensure:
   (a) that its entities shall not treat a locally-established supplier less favourably than another locally-established supplier on the basis of degree of foreign affiliation or ownership; and
   (b) that its entities shall not discriminate against locally-established suppliers on the basis of the country of production of the good or service being supplied, provided that the country of production is a Party to the Agreement in accordance with the provisions of Article IV.

If we compare this wording with the government procurement provisions in the Japan–Mexico PTA of 2004, we find nearly identical wording for the section on national treatment. For example, Article 120 on National Treatment reads (<u>underlined</u> words are exactly the same):

1. With respect to any measures regarding government procurement covered by this Chapter, each Party shall provide immediately and unconditionally to the goods, services and suppliers of the other Party offering goods or services of the other Party, treatment no less favorable than that accorded to domestic goods, services and suppliers.
2. With respect to any measures regarding government procurement covered by this Chapter, each Party shall ensure:
   (a) that its entities shall not treat a locally-established supplier less favorably than another locally-established supplier on the basis of the degree of affiliation to, or ownership by, a person of the other Party; and
   (b) that its entities shall not discriminate against locally-established suppliers on the basis of the country of production of the good or service being supplied, provided that the country of production is the other Party in accordance with the provisions of Article 121.

We can expand to all WTO sub-areas to find additional sources for copy-pasting. Because the WTO has also attracted attention in the area of dispute settlement, some elements of the Agreement on Dispute Settlement (DSU: Understanding on Rules and Procedures Governing the Settlement of Disputes) could also be taken up in PTAs. For instance, we observe that the WTO approach (retaliatory measures) to inducing compliance in case of non-implementation as described in Article 22 of the DSU is often replicated in some way in PTAs.[6] To illustrate the overlap in wording, consider first the WTO Article which states that:

(a) the general principle is that the complaining party should first seek to suspend concessions or other obligations with respect to the same sector(s) as that in which the panel or Appellate Body has found a violation or other nullification or impairment;
(c) if that party considers that it is not practicable or effective to suspend concessions or other obligations with respect to other sectors under the same agreement, and that the circumstances are serious enough, it may seek to suspend concessions or other obligations under another covered agreement.

If we compare this article with Article 21.12 of the Australia–Chile agreement of 2008 we find the following text (underlined words are exactly the same):

[6] This article is titled 'Compensation and the suspension of concessions' and it gives the right to the complainant party to suspend concessions in the same sector where non-compliance has occurred, potentially followed by similar steps in another area or sector (cross-sector).

(a) the complaining Party should first seek to suspend concessions or other obligations with respect to the same sector(s) as that in which the report of the arbitral panel referred to in Article 21.10 has found a failure to comply with the obligations under this Agreement, or nullification or impairment of benefits in the sense of Article 21.1 (c); and

(b) if the complaining Party considers that it is not practicable or effective to suspend concessions or other obligations with respect to the same sector(s), it may suspend concessions or other obligations with respect to other sectors.

This example, and perhaps many others, illustrates that there could be significant copy-pasting occurring from WTO agreements to PTAs. Next we examine whether such copy-pasting is rampant and whether it occurs alongside potentially widespread references in the text to WTO agreements and their associated obligations.

D Methodology

We utilise two very different methodologies to produce two distinct indicators for possible WTO presence. The two approaches, however, do share a few common features. Both organise PTAs by trade issue, which mirrors the article-based structure of the agreements and also maps directly onto the way in which WTO agreements are negotiated by sector or measure. Accordingly, for both methods of analysis we study only those PTAs signed during or after 1994, when the final WTO (Uruguay Round) agreements were concluded and became publicly known – and therefore could have been referenced or served as a type of template.[7]

The first method involves coding the PTAs manually for references to the relevant WTO agreement (and then tabulating the number of such references and percentage of PTAs that include them). To do this, we utilise the Design of Trade Agreements (DESTA) dataset (Dür et al. 2014), which codes numerous design-feature variables for post-war PTAs, including variables on whether each trade issue addressed in the PTA includes some type of reference to the prevailing WTO agreement.[8]

[7] In a few instances we also explore patterns for post-GATT (1947) or post–Tokyo Round (1979) agreements, although we do not emphasise these findings here.

[8] For details on coding showing how the WTO typically is referenced in each area, see Dür et al. (2014) and the associated codebook.

Using this approach, we identify ten trade issues within PTAs that frequently have their own provision or article, each of which maps to a parallel WTO agreement. This approach captures the fact that a necessary condition for the PTA being able to evoke the WTO (on a given trade issue) is that the PTA actually addresses the issue (i.e. contains the provision) for which the WTO has an existing agreement. The ten issues we examine for such references include: anti-dumping, general services, subsidies, technical barriers to trade (TBTs), sanitary and phytosanitary measures (SPS), public procurement, intellectual property, safeguards, dispute settlement and investment.

The second method, used to examine text similarity between WTO agreements and PTAs, is more novel and requires a bit more elaboration. Once again, we subdivide the PTAs according to issues – this time identifying eleven important and distinct trade issues on which the WTO has a specific agreement.[9] This delineation captures the fact that each WTO agreement could serve as a template from which text can be copied and pasted into the corresponding sections of PTAs.[10] Accordingly, for each PTA, we extract the PTA text that addresses each of these eleven areas for comparison to each parallel WTO agreement.[11] Table 12.1 lists the eleven issues for which we compare WTO agreements to PTA text on the same issue.

Now that the appropriate WTO agreements and PTA texts have been identified, we proceed to systematically compare how much of the WTO language has been appropriated directly into each PTA. First we standardise the texts of all agreements to prepare them for analysis. Since nearly all PTA texts (and WTO agreements) are in pdf format, we first convert those texts to Microsoft Word before ultimately converting them to plain text format.[12] To analyse the amount of text in each PTA subsection that matches language in the corresponding WTO agreement, we utilise DupeFreePro, a text-comparison software package whose 'Bulk Compare' feature allows one to compare hundreds of texts to all other texts (or in our case, hundreds of PTA subsets to the corresponding WTO agreement) and calculates the

[9] Nine of these are the same issues on which the DESTA data codes for WTO references.

[10] Note that a PTA might not include language on all eleven issues.

[11] For most trade issues, and for the overwhelming majority of PTAs, the relevant information is clearly delineated and contained in one (or more) articles in the PTA. Nevertheless, for situations in which the relevant information on a trade topic is spread across articles or found in multiple places in the PTA, we develop a set of detailed coding rules for compiling all of the relevant PTA text on that issue. These coding guidelines are available from the authors upon request.

[12] In a handful of situations a treaty text was damaged and we could not repair it or identify an undamaged alternative.

Table 12.1 *Trade Issues for Text Comparison and Corresponding WTO Agreement*

Trade Issue	Corresponding WTO Agreement
Financial services	Understanding and Annexes on Financial Services (1995)
General services	General Agreement on Trade in Services (GATS) (1994)
Telecom	Telecommunications Reference Paper and Annex (1996)
Safeguards	Agreement on Safeguards (1994)
Anti-dumping	Article VI and Agreement on Implementation of Article VI of the General Agreement on Tariffs and Trade (1994)
Intellectual property	Agreement on Trade-Related Aspects of Intellectual Property Rights (TRIPS) (1994)
Procurement	Agreement on Government Procurement (1994)
TBT	Agreement on Technical Barriers to Trade (1994)
SPS	Agreement on the Application of Sanitary and Phytosanitary Measures (1994)
Dispute settlement	Understanding on Rules and Procedures Governing the Settlement of Disputes (Dispute Settlement Understanding) (1994)
Investment	Agreement on Trade-Related Investment Measures (TRIMs) (1994)

Source: Created by the authors.

percentage of content that is shared among (or is unique to) all pairings of treaties. It also allows for the visual, side-by-side comparison of any two texts and highlights areas of text overlap. Also helpful is that DupeFreePro allows one to specify different parameters for matching and comparison. Most notably, we specify seven words to constitute a match (consistent with industry standards)[13] and take a number of steps to enhance the validity of our comparisons, which on the whole are probably somewhat conservative.[14]

[13] Several studies that compare the text of opinions written by US Supreme Court justices to various written briefs submitted by the parties involved or interested in the case match on six words, which is the default setting for the software used in those studies (e.g. Collins et al. 2013; Corley et al. 2011; Feldman 2015).

[14] We include common words in our matches, because theoretically we expect large passages of texts to be copied, and all words should be part of the copy-pasting process.

E Findings on the Presence of the WTO in PTAs

The findings for both sets of results, together with several follow-up analyses, are presented in Tables 12.2–12.6b. Overall the findings indicate a sizeable presence for the WTO in PTAs, particularly in terms of PTAs, including references to the WTO within their key provisions. Some PTAs, in fact, reference the WTO across all nine or ten major provisions they contain. We also uncover some, albeit less widespread, support for the conjecture that PTAs might copy language directly from WTO agreements. Such dynamics are most visible in less developed trade areas, and we observe dozens of cases in which a majority of the text in a PTA subsection is taken verbatim from a WTO agreement. The evidence also suggests that references to the WTO and copy-

Table 12.2 *References to the WTO in PTAs*

Trade Issue	PTAs (with relevant provision) That Reference the WTO (%)	PTAs with Relevant Provision
Anti-dumping	82.1	392
Subsidies	70.4	371
Services	68.7	280
TBT	64.4	292
SPS	58.1	320
Procurement	52.7	226
Intellectual property	47.7	260
Safeguards	38.1	458
Dispute settlement	23.2	483
Investment	2.3	304

Source: Created by the authors.

Excluding common words would break strings of copied text and generate false mismatches. In order to further calibrate matching, we identify a series of words that might be spelled differently across treaties (with or without hyphens, US versus UK spellings) so that these minor differences do not disrupt matches. We ignore numbers and Roman numerals (and accompanying punctuation) that are used in headings and lists, since these vary from treaty to treaty in idiosyncratic ways. Notwithstanding the aforementioned rules, some remaining text simply will not be matched properly owing to minor differences associated with proper nouns, punctuation, spelling and spacing that we cannot address systematically. In general, we believe these parameters constitute a relatively conservative approach to identifying 'matching' text between WTO agreements and PTAs.

pasting of WTO text tend to serve as complements rather than substitutes. Finally, some initial exploration of which PTAs tend to incorporate a strong WTO presence indicate that a diverse set of actors evoke the WTO, including some of the most notable state actors (United States, China, Japan, Australia) and regional actors (Association of Southeast Asian Nations (ASEAN), European Free Trade Association (EFTA)) actors in the global trading system.

Table 12.2 presents the findings for the first method of comparison – the one that probes for some form of reference to the WTO with a given PTA provision. Overall we find that PTAs systematically do include references to the WTO across important provisions, with particularly high rates of inclusion on notable trade topics. For six of the ten trade issues, more than half of PTAs reference the WTO in some way. In fact, more than four-fifths of PTAs make such references with regard to anti-dumping, and approximately 70 per cent do so with regard to subsidies and services. In general, we view the findings reported in Table 12.2 as broad and fairly sweeping evidence for a strong, general presence for the WTO within PTAs.

Nevertheless, we observe wide variation in terms of the issues in PTAs that make reference to the WTO. As noted above, anti-dumping (AD) is an area in which we see widespread acknowledgement of WTO obligations and standards. This is perhaps not surprising, since AD is an issue that is highly developed within the WTO regime. Multiple AD agreements have been negotiated over the GATT/WTO regime's lifetime, and AD is an issue that has been addressed vigorously within the WTO dispute settlement process. Moreover, national AD procedures governing the use of AD tend to flow from the well-specified multilateral rules.

By contrast, references to the WTO are quite rare on issues such as investment and dispute settlement. For investment, the infrequent references likely reflect the fact that the TRIMS agreement plays a less central role in global investment than bilateral investment treaties (BITs) and the investor–state arbitration proceedings that often emerge from BITs. The story for dispute settlement is somewhat different. Nearly all PTAs specify some procedures for dispute settlement, but they are quite heterogeneous in terms of their length and the modes of settlement they allow (Allee and Elsig 2015b). States that create preferential trade arrangements tend to want to establish their own dispute settlement institutions instead of simply importing multilateral ones, perhaps because of the high costs associated with the highly institutionalised WTO dispute settlement system. Moreover, only PTAs with high aspirations beyond economic integration (e.g. Mercosur) are likely to model their dispute settlement mechanisms on the WTO's DSU (Arnold and Rittberger 2013).

The findings thus far are based on a coding standard that looks for any type of reference to the WTO across trade issues, without distinguishing the nature of that reference. Next we take some preliminary steps to uncover the different types of references to the WTO. We explore PTA provisions on intellectual property – an area in which WTO references occur in just under half of PTAs – as an illustrative example that could guide future coding. Our survey of 125 intellectual property provisions in PTAs reveals seven ways that the WTO TRIPS agreement is evoked:

i. affirmation of WTO rights and obligations,
ii. national treatment exceptions in line with TRIPS,
iii. no derogation from TRIPS,
iv. geographical indications protection under TRIPS,
v. statements on the importance of adherence to TRIPS,
vi. cooperation based on TRIPS, and
vii. miscellaneous citations of the TRIPS agreement.

The first is the most prevalent: we identify eighty-eight PTAs (out of the 125) in which the parties affirm their rights and obligations under TRIPS. This language typically occurs at the very beginning of the PTA's intellectual property provision. Next we find twelve instances in which the PTA states that any national treatment exceptions must be in accordance with Articles 3 and/or 5 of the TRIPS agreement. Several of the other types of references occur in between five and ten PTAs. On the whole, then, the references to the WTO in PTA intellectual property rights provisions take both general and specific forms, and tend to tie the PTA signatories more closely to WTO law.

Next we turn to our second methodology, which probes whether language from WTO agreements is incorporated by states directly into their PTAs. We find some support for this type of WTO presence, but the results are less systematic and more nuanced. The second column in Table 12.3 displays the average overlap across issue areas in terms of how much text is copy-pasted from the relevant WTO agreement into the corresponding provision of a PTA.

At first glance the numbers in the second column might seem low – particularly compared to the percentages returned by the other method of comparison. Yet a few important caveats are in order, which we discuss in more detail below. First, *ex ante* we would expect these 'percentage' numbers to be relatively modest. One reason is the nature of this type of

Table 12.3 *Amount of Text from WTO Agreements Copy-Pasted into PTAs*

Trade Issue	Text Copied Directly from Relevant WTO Agreement (average % across all PTAs with relevant provision)	PTAs That Copy 25% or More of Their Text from Relevant WTO Agreement	PTAs That Copy 50% or More of Their Text from Relevant WTO Agreement	PTAs with the Relevant Provision
Financial services	19.0	9	3	39
General services	14.4	31	13	131
Telecom	11.4	9	0	30
Safeguards	5.1	6	1	219
Anti-dumping	4.8	6	2	181
Intellectual property	4.8	3	0	170
Procurement	4.0	8	1	149
TBT	3.8	6	0	174
SPS	2.8	2	1	167
Dispute settlement	2.5	4	0	243
Investment	0.4	0	0	121

Source: Created by the authors.

WTO presence; according to conventional wisdom on international negotiations and bargaining, one should expect trade negotiators to carefully negotiate important PTA provisions instead of copying a substantial amount of language verbatim from a separate, multilateral agreement. Second, the overlap percentages in general are likely to be conservative, for all of the reasons noted earlier. Third, the numbers in the second column of Table 12.3 are averages across all PTAs. Some PTAs actually take more than half of their text directly from the respective WTO agreement, whereas others copy nothing from related WTO documents.

In fact, if we turn our attention to columns 3 and 4 of Table 12.3 the picture shifts towards one where there appears to be a much stronger presence of the WTO, and of WTO language, in particular, in certain PTAs. Column 3 indicates the number of provisions across PTAs in which at least one-quarter of the language is copied directly from a WTO agreement. Some eighty-four PTA-provisions borrow at least 25 per cent or more of their text word-for-word from the WTO. Perhaps more notably, twenty-one PTAs copy and paste 50 per cent or more of their provision directly from the corresponding WTO agreement (see Table 12.3, column 4). Thus, there are clearly some situations in which trade negotiators borrow heavily from WTO law when putting together a PTA. Furthermore, general services provisions comprise approximately three-eighths and five-eighths of these totals, suggesting some further potential differences in the WTO's presence across issues areas.

Returning to the second column of Table 12.3, we do indeed observe notable variation in WTO-based copy-pasting across issue areas. Within some provisions, such as those on financial services, general services and telecoms, the average PTA will copy between 10 and 20 per cent of its text from the corresponding WTO agreement. By contrast, in other areas a PTA will copy on average less than 5 per cent of its text from parallel WTO agreements, with investment provisions copying virtually nothing from TRIMS.[15] Our primary conjecture to explain this pattern is the difference between new and old trade areas. Today's regulatory challenges demand modern solutions. In these newer areas, where there is perhaps less guidance on what to specify in trade agreements and where rules are not well-established, the WTO agreement may serve as a focal point from

[15] We suspect the low results for investment can be explained by the same reasons as discussed previously for references to the WTO.

which negotiators may draw language. In more established areas where WTO law might be more outdated, by contrast, trade negotiators should be less inclined to lean so heavily on WTO language and more likely borrow from innovations that occur in the newer generation of PTAs.

This also raises the issue of whether our two indicators of WTO presence – the first of which captures WTO references and the second of which assesses the amount of WTO-derived copy and pasting – serve as complements or substitutes. That is, does evidence for one type of WTO presence in a PTA make the other type of WTO presence more or less likely to emerge? Or put differently, does including a reference to the WTO serve as a shortcut (replacement) for incorporating WTO language directly? Overall, although the evidence is not definitive, we certainly interpret it as suggesting that the two indicators are complementary.

Table 12.4 presents two types of evidence for the potential complementarity of the two WTO presence indicators. The first type, shown in the second column of the table, depicts the correlations across all PTA provisions between the WTO reference variable and the variable

Table 12.4 *Complementarity of WTO-Reference and Copied-WTO-Text Variables*

Trade Issue	Correlation Between WTO Reference Variable and Text Overlap Variable	Ranking in Terms of Frequency of References to WTO	Ranking in Terms of Percentage of Text Taken from Relevant WTO Agreement
Anti-dumping	−0.264	1	5
Services	0.153	2	2
TBT	−0.043	3	8
SPS	−0.050	4	9
Procurement	−0.068	5	7
Intellectual property	0.349	6	6
Safeguards	0.461	7	4
Dispute settlement	0.433	8	10
Investment	0.324	9	11

Source: Created by the authors.
Note: Lower ranking numbers indicate greater presence of the WTO.

indicating the amount of text taken from the corresponding WTO agreement. The majority of the correlations are positive, indicating that the two variables tend to work in the same direction. Although four of the cross-variable correlations are negative, the comparative magnitude of the positive versus negative correlations nudges us closer to a conclusion of complementarity. Three of the four negative correlations depicted in column 2 are very low, below −0.10. By contrast, all but one of the positive correlations across variables are sizeable, ranging between +0.3 and +0.5. The second type of evidence is shown in columns 3 and 4 of Table 12.4, which depict and compare the relative ranking of how much WTO presence is found in each issue area according to each variable. Notably, both dispute settlement and investment rank at the very bottom (lowest WTO presence) for both the WTO-reference variable and the text-copying variable. Intellectual property is similarly consistent, falling in the middle (ranked sixth) for both indicators. Although there are more 'gaps' between the two rankings on other issues, the patterns there are somewhat ambiguous. Lastly, we identify general services as an issue in which the rankings across the two indicators of presence are consistently high (ranked second for both). Indeed, we had previously identified general services as a topic that reflected a strong WTO presence, according to both methods of analysis. Overall, then, the evidence suggests that the two indicators of WTO presence work more in tandem than they do as alternatives.

Finally, we reveal some patterns in terms of which PTAs and which actors are more likely to evoke the WTO in their agreements. Although a comprehensive treatment of this issue is beyond the scope of this chapter, some preliminary patterns are suggestive. Sticking with the second method, which compares text overlap, Table 12.5 shows the PTAs, and the provisions within them, that copy-paste the greatest percentage of their text from a WTO agreement. Initially one is struck by the diversity in Table 12.5 across actors, geographical regions and time. Upon closer examination, however, a few patterns are evident. Most obviously, some of the overlap percentages are very high. Several PTAs copy between 60 per cent and 80 per cent of their language directly from a WTO agreement – which means they are relying almost completely upon what is specified under WTO law. Our side-by-side comparison of these PTA provisions to their WTO parallel indicates a typical pattern, which is that the PTA provisions tend to be reasonably long in these cases. They tend to copy a few entire paragraphs (articles) from the WTO agreement, and then also to copy selected sentences from other articles. Another pattern revealed is that certain issues continue to be amenable to a strong WTO presence. General services, for instance, is often the locus of the greatest amount of copy-pasting from WTO agreements, followed by government procurement.

Turning now to the actors and their resulting agreements, within Table 12.5 we see many bilateral PTAs, but also broader regional groupings (such as the Baltic Free Trade Area and the Southern African Development Community) as well as regional–state combinations. Asia appears to be well-represented among the countries that borrow most heavily from WTO language. Japan and Singapore, for instance, appear multiple times on the list in Table 12.5. More broadly, major actors in the region such as India and China also copy relatively heavily from the WTO in at least some agreements, as do smaller states such as Brunei. Other WTO-language-borrowers include global players such as the EU as well as the EFTA countries, as a group and individually (Switzerland), and Mexico.

Turning lastly to the original method of identifying references to the WTO in PTAs, Tables 12.6a and 12.6b indicate the countries that include the greatest number of WTO references across their PTA provisions (Table 12.6a) and the highest percentage of provisions that reference the WTO (Table 12.6b). Once again, a certain amount of heterogeneity is evident, but familiar patterns also emerge in terms of who most frequently includes such references. In this pair of tables we see notable multi-actor PTAs (like CAFTA–DR) along with several agreements between regional actors and individual states (Mercosur and ASEAN with various partners). Geographically, Asia and the Pacific Rim are well represented. The two tables include countries that span from India to Malaysia to Korea, and down to New Zealand across to Peru. Also striking is the inclusion on the list of major trade actors. The United States and the EU make the list multiple times, as do India and South Korea, continuing a pattern seen in Table 12.5.

F Conclusion

In this chapter we pursued a two-pronged approach towards systematically testing for the 'presence' of the WTO within PTAs, looking to see whether and how various Uruguay Round agreements have made their way into modern PTAs. Based on our first and more conventional analyses, it is clear that the WTO is indeed present within many provisions in many PTAs. We find widespread references to the WTO across

Table 12.5 *PTAs That Copy the Most Text Language from a WTO Agreement*

PTA	Year	Amount of Text Copied from Relevant WTO Agreement (%)	Trade Issue
Israel–Mexico	2000	77	Procurement
Baltic Free Trade Area	1997	74	SPS
Brunei–Japan	2007	71	Financial services
Japan–Singapore	2002	67	General services
Colombia–EFTA	2008	65	General services
GCC–Singapore	2008	64	General services
Australia–Singapore	2003	62	Procurement
EFTA–Singapore	2002	62	General services
China–Singapore	2008	61	General services
Japan–Switzerland	2009	57	General services
Southern African Development Community (SADC)	1996	57	Safeguards
Australia–Singapore	2003	55	General services
Iran–Syria	2006	54	Anti-dumping
EU–Serbia	2008	53	Procurement
India–South Korea	2009	52	General services
Japan–Philippines	2006	52	General services
China–New Zealand	2008	52	General services
Japan–Vietnam	2005	52	General services
Iran–Pakistan	2004	51	Anti-dumping
India–Singapore	2005	51	General services
Brunei–Japan	2007	50	General services

Source: Created by the authors.

PTAs, on some of the most important trade issues. Moreover, further investigation reveals that these references often explicitly and strongly tie PTA signatories to WTO law. Our second, more novel, analyses reveal another type of WTO presence: certain PTAs copy a sizeable amount of text directly from WTO agreements. This is particularly true in newer trade areas, such as services. Moreover, these two forms of WTO presence often exist simultaneously, and the major trade actors appear to be the most likely to include WTO rights, obligations, and language in their PTAs.

Table 12.6a *PTAs with the Greatest Number of Issue Areas Referencing the WTO*

PTA	Year	Issue Areas That Reference the WTO
South Korea–Singapore	2005	10
CARIFORUM–EU	2008	9
Dominican Republic–Central America Free Trade Agreement (CAFTA–DR)	2004	9
Chile–South Korea	2003	9
EFTA–South Korea	2005	9
EFTA–Singapore	2002	9
South Korea–United States	2007	9
Malaysia–New Zealand	2009	9
Malaysia–Pakistan	2007	9
Morocco–United States	2004	9
Peru–Singapore	2008	9

Source: Created by the authors.

Two avenues are ripe for future research. One is to probe more deeply into the types of references to the WTO that are made and what they entail. A 'pilot' investigation of intellectual property revealed that many different types of references are made, and some are surprisingly strong in binding PTA signatories to their WTO-based obligations. Likewise, across the range of issues covered in our study we hope to showcase the spectrum of WTO references that are made and how strongly they harmonise WTO and PTA obligations. A second pathway is to test more systematically which PTAs, and which actors, are more likely to link their PTAs to WTO law through either of the pathways we identify. Some PTAs clearly evoke the WTO more strongly than others. It certainly appears that prominent state and regional actors, as well as those in Asia, are more likely to do so, which if true would portend well for the future of the WTO. Yet another class of explanations might expect less-developed or less experienced actors to lean more explicitly on WTO agreements. In any event, we believe it is important for various policy debates to show the conditions under which PTAs will be more closely linked to WTO agreements. Moreover, other variations that we uncovered, such as that across issue areas, also warrants further investigation.

Table 12.6b *PTAs with the Highest Percentage of Issue Areas Referencing the WTO*

PTA	Year	Percentage of Issue Areas Referencing the WTO[a]
Afghanistan–India	2003	100
ASEAN–India	2009	100
ASEAN–South Korea	2006	100
Chile–India	2006	100
South Korea–Singapore	2005	100
Malaysia–New Zealand	2009	100
Malaysia–Pakistan	2007	100
MERCOSUR– Southern African Customs Union (SACU)	2004	100
Peru–Singapore	2008	100
Peru–Thailand	2005	100
CARIFORUM–EU	2008	90
CAFTA–DR	2004	90
Chile–South Korea	2003	90
EFTA–South Korea	2005	90
EFTA–Singapore	2002	90
South Korea–United States	2007	90
Morocco–United States	2004	90

Source: Created by the authors.

[a] At least two issue areas required.

Our goal has been to present novel and much-needed empirical insights into an often-debated topic. Some questions have been answered, while new ones have arisen. The relationship between PTAs of various types and the WTO is an important one, and we hope that we have shed light on some interesting aspects of this relationship. It seems safe to assume that the WTO–PTA debate is likely to continue, if not intensify, in the face of mega-regionals and ongoing bilateral agreement-making, coupled with lingering uncertainty about the next steps for the WTO. There are important debates to be had, yet we believe they require more careful and unique empirical investigations, such as the one we have undertaken. Twenty years on we can say that the WTO has contributed much to the global trading system. The conclusion we reach is that the Uruguay Round agreements are much more 'present' in the constellation of PTAs than has generally been realised and therefore an assessment of WTO performance needs to take into account how its 'rights and obligations' travel.

References

Allee, Todd and Elsig, Manfred. 2015a. 'Are the Contents of International Treaties Copied-and-Pasted? Unique Evidence from Preferential Trade Agreements'. Paper presented at the Annual Meeting of the American Political Science Association, San Francisco, CA.

Allee, Todd and Elsig, Manfred. 2015b. 'Dispute Settlement Provisions in PTAs: New Data and New Concepts'. In *Trade Cooperation: The Purpose, Design and Effects of Preferential Trade Agreements*, edited by Andreas Dür and Manfred Elsig. Cambridge: Cambridge University Press, 319–352.

Alter, Karen and Meunier, Sophie. 2009. 'The Politics of International Regime Complexity'. *Perspectives on Politics* 7(1): 13–24.

Arnold, Christian and Rittberger, Berthold. 2013. 'The Legalization of Dispute Resolution in Mercosur'. *Journal of Politics in Latin America* 5(3): 97–132.

Baier, Scott and Bergstrand, Jeffrey. 2007. 'Do Free Trade Agreements Actually Increase Members' International Trade?' *Journal of International Economics* 71(1): 72–95.

Baldwin, Richard. 2006. 'Multilateralising Regionalism: Spaghetti Bowls as Building Blocs on the Path to Global Free Trade'. *The World Economy* 29 (11): 1451–1518.

Bhagwati, Jagdish and Panagariya, Arvind. (eds.). 1996. *The Economics of Preferential Trade Agreements*. Washington, DC: American Enterprise Institute Press.

Busch, Marc. 2007. 'Overlapping Institutions, Forum Shopping, and Dispute Settlement in International Trade'. *International Organization* 61(4): 735–61.

Collins, Paul, Corley, Pamela C. and Hanmer, Jesse. 2013. 'The Influence of Amicus Curiae Briefs on U.S. Supreme Court Opinion Content'. Paper presented at the Annual Meeting of the American Political Science Association, Chicago, IL.

Corley, Paul, Collins, Pamela and Calvin, Bryan. 2011. 'Lower Court Influence on U.S. Supreme Court Opinion Content'. *Journal of Politics* 73(1): 31–44.

Cottier, Thomas, Sieber-Gasser, Charlotte and Wermelinger, Gabriela. 2015. 'The Dialectical Relationship of Preferential and Multilateral Trade Agreements'. In *Trade Cooperation: The Purpose, Design and Effects of Preferential Trade Agreements*, edited by Andreas Dür and Manfred Elsig. Cambridge: Cambridge University Press, 465–496.

Dür, Andreas, Baccini, Leonardo and Elsig, Manfred. 2014. 'The Design of International Trade Agreements: Introducing a New Database'. *Review of International Organization* 9(3): 353–375.

Feldman, Adam. 2015. 'A Brief Assessment of Supreme Court Opinion Language'. Available at SSRN: http://ssrn.com/abstract=2574451.

Horn, Henrik, Mavroidis, Petros and Sapir, André. 2009. *Beyond the WTO? An Anatomy of EU and US Preferential Trade Agreements*. Brussels: Bruegel.

Roy, Martin. 2011. 'Services Commitments in Preferential Trade Agreements: An Expanded Dataset'. WTO Staff Working Paper ERSD-2011–18.

Srinivasan, T.N. 1998. 'Regionalism and the WTO: Is Nondiscrimination Passé?' In *The WTO as an International Organization*, edited by Anne Krueger. Chicago, IL: University of Chicago Press, 329–352.

Valdés, Raymundo and McCann, Maegan. 2014. 'Intellectual Property Provisions in Regional Trade Agreements: Revision and Update'. WTO Staff Working Paper ERSD-2014–14.

13

The WTO and Regional Trading Agreements

Is It All Over for Multilateralism?

L. ALAN WINTERS

A Introduction

The number of operative regional trading agreements (RTAs) in the world has been increasing, and at an increasing rate, over the life of the General Agreement on Tariffs and Trade (GATT) – World Trade Organization (WTO) system – WTO (2011) – and this has been a source of unease for many economists, including myself. However, the trading system has not obviously collapsed during its course and, except possibly for the last few years, the growth of world trade does not seem to have been materially affected.[1] Such observations often seem to lead commentators to conclude that RTAs are neutral or, indeed, benign, fostering international trade and boosting incomes at only the tiniest cost in terms of discrimination. I would argue, on the other hand, that the process has been systemically harmful and that, although the problems have been building up only gradually, they are now of sufficient magnitude to be seriously alarming: although regionalism has always been with us, something fundamentally and qualitatively different has happened in the world of RTAs since 2008.

Three related factors have come together to create my alarm. First, the treatment of RTAs in the WTO has always been highly political and has

I am grateful to colleagues at the following seminars for their constructive comments on an earlier draft: The World Trade Forum 2015 held on 25 and 26 September 2015, at the World Trade Institute, Bern, including my discussants Dirk De Bièvre and Krzysztof Pelc; The FIW/CER Workshop on the 'Political Economy of Trade Policy', Vienna, 22 September 2015, and the University of Sussex WTO Study Group. Naturally, none is responsible for the paper's remaining shortcomings.

[1] See Hoekman (2015) for various analyses and hypotheses about the recent trade slowdown.

actually owed very little to the principles of trade policy or even trade law. Second, the GATT/WTO's success in addressing tariff barriers and the increased propensity of governments to regulate transactions in labour and product markets have switched the focus of trade policy firmly onto non-tariff measures (NTMs) and also extended attention towards areas such as investment and intellectual property. The WTO has found it difficult to respond to these trends. Third, since 2008 we have witnessed the rise of the so-called mega-regionals – RTAs of huge economic size, with geographical spreads far exceeding any plausible notion of political integration – and of global policy ambition. The mega-regionals aim not just to manage trade relations between their members, as have previous RTAs, but quite explicitly to control or circumvent the multilateral discussion of trade policy by creating coalitions of countries that can, more or less, dictate terms to other players.

This chapter sets out the history of regionalism starting from the discussion about it preceding the Havana Charter. Quite understandably (and reasonably), this history was driven by geopolitics rather than simple commercial policy considerations, and, from the start, those politics have been more about separating countries than bringing them together. In the face of such overwhelming forces, economists' analytical attachment to non-discrimination and the GATT/WTO's institutional attachment to it have been able to do little about the march of RTAs. Moreover, I shall argue that because NTMs and the non-trade issues are more 'all-or-nothing' than are tariffs, they make the creation of coalitions of countries to pursue specific rather than global objectives easier. If the WTO's Members insist on negotiating NTMs and related non-trade issues in the mega-regionals, important aspects of multilateralism will be lost and I fear that the rest will be undermined. Realistically, it would take a huge change of attitude to promote the interests of the multilateral system above those of the members of the various mega-regionals, and while I advocate such a change I cannot honestly say that I expect it.

A premise of this chapter is that multilateralism is worth preserving. It has an inherent ethical basis; it has served us well in the past in terms of preserving peace (if not harmony!), and it has clear economic benefits in terms of fostering efficiency. Multilateralism, as opposed to wholly power-based international relations, did not emerge spontaneously but as a conscious goal and with associated birth pangs as part of the post–World War II settlement. It was substantially an American conception and one for which we should be grateful, but over time we have seen the commitment to multilateralism of the United States and of those who model their policy on US ideals erode. Nowhere has this been more obvious than in the spread of RTAs. It is true that by accommodating the rise of preferentialism in the past, the central institution of multilateralism, the GATT/WTO, may have preserved itself and its other functions, and may thus have made the best of a bad hand in maintaining multilateralism. But the analysis of this chapter suggests that in the case of RTAs, at least, it was never able to promote multilateralism above the national demands of its major members and that therefore, absent a major and conscious change in the value placed by such countries on multilateralism, we are unlikely to bequeath an effective multilateral system to the next generation.

B Non-discrimination and Multilateralism

The principle of non-discrimination is the cornerstone of the GATT. We tend to equate it with multilateralism, but this is not really correct. There are arguably at least three dimensions to multilateralism that need to be considered:

- first, procedural – multilateralism as an organising principle by which all parties have appropriate (although not necessarily equal) scope to contribute to debate and decision-making;
- second, whether the result is spread more or less widely across the world economy, which is arguably what we mean by non-discrimination; and
- third, whether there is a multilateral enforcement mechanism for trade agreements which represents the general interest and is tolerably even-handed.

The most frequently cited champion of the principle of non-discrimination is Cordell Hull, US Secretary of State 1933–1944, who wrote in his memoirs (Hull 1948):

> … to me, unhampered trade dovetailed with peace; high tariffs, trade barriers, and unfair economic competition, with war … if we could get a freer flow of trade – freer in the sense of fewer discriminations and obstructions – so that one country would not be deadly jealous of another and the living standards of all countries might rise, thereby eliminating the economic dissatisfaction that breeds war, we might have a reasonable chance for lasting peace. (p. 81)
>
> … you could not separate the idea of commerce from the idea of war and peace … wars were often largely caused by economic rivalry conducted unfairly. (p. 84)

Hull was convinced that the protectionism of the interwar period was an evil both globally and for the US economy itself; he firmly believed that liberalisation was a desirable policy. Following the failure of the London World Economic Conference of 1933, which had hoped to achieve a multilateral de-escalation of trade barriers, Hull largely wrested control of US trade policy from Congress for the Executive with the passing of the Reciprocal Trade Agreements Act (RTAA) of 1934, an act whose authorship may be wholly ascribed to Hull, according to Schwob (2009). The RTAA permitted the president (effectively the State Department) to reduce US tariffs line-by-line by up to 50 per cent in bilateral negotiations with individual trading partners who offered similar concessions; these concessions were then extended to other countries which had signed such agreements via an unconditional most-favoured nation (MFN) clause. For the United States in the 1930s this was not a large set but it was arguably an improvement on the restrictive regime of the period. However, the RTAA process reduced the average US tariff only from 46.7 per cent to 40.7 per cent (Irwin 2012) and was criticised at the time for doing little to address the need to increase US imports as well US exports (Bidwell 1944: 344) or to foster effective trade liberalisation elsewhere in the world (Bidwell 1943: 297).

Bilateralism was not entirely absent from the GATT because negotiations were conducted bilaterally before extension to others, but the key difference from the RTAA process was that all the negotiations occurred together and were adopted and extended to others simultaneously. Schwob (2009: 9) notes Hull's attachment to the principal supplier rule, but argues that the origins of the multilateral approach to negotiations lay elsewhere, with Percy Bidwell and James Meade. He credits the latter pair, rather than Cordell Hull, with being the father(s) of the multilateral trading system, as I will discuss below.

Both the RTAA process and the early GATT embedded a somewhat limited notion of non-discrimination – non-discrimination *within* a club. Clearly the extent of the non-discrimination that club approaches can achieve depends on the size of the club – the set of countries included among those deemed to have signed 'similar agreements'. In both cases the club was small – by 1940 twenty-one partners had signed RTAA-agreements with the United States, and the first GATT negotiation had twenty-three signatories, albeit of greater economic weight than the RTAA-club. But as the GATT and then the WTO was enlarged, the network of multilaterally linked partners was extended and became more nearly global and hence more nearly non-discriminatory.

Schwob (2009) argues that Hull's attachment to bilateral negotiations was not pragmatic so much as born out of a conviction that only bilateralism would allow the United States to exercise its economic muscle in terms of extracting concessions. In fact, Schwob argues (pp. 11–12) that Hull took no steps to encourage multilateral trade negotiations and actually opposed them. Overall, one can see in the way in which Hull approached liberalisation the seeds of the rhetoric currently surrounding the mega-regionals: 'If the global system will not generate the liberalisation we require, we will work individually with like-minded countries to achieve it and extend it in a non-discriminatory way within that set.'

Cordell Hull was an early advocate of multilateral enforcement. As early as 1916 he argued that maintaining non-discrimination required – or at least was greatly aided by – an international body: if he was president, Congressman Hull said, he would

> ... propose ... an international trade conference ... For the purpose of establishing a permanent international trade congress [to consider] all international trade methods, practices, and policies which in their effects are calculated to create destructive commercial controversies or bitter economic wars, and to formulate agreements with respect thereto, designed to eliminate and avoid the injurious results and dangerous possibilities of economic warfare, and to promote fair and friendly trade relations among all the nations of the world. (Hull 1948: 82)

Although according to Toye (2012) Hull used the term 'International Trade Organization' in 1925, he apparently cooled on the idea of an international body quite soon afterwards. Probably for merely practical reasons, during the war the State Department subcontracted thought about the post-war trading system largely to the Council for Foreign Relations, where the leading exponent was Percy Bidwell.[2] Bidwell had thought about an international body in 1938 and made a concrete proposal for an International Trade Agency in 1942; he published his ideas in Bidwell (1943 and 1944). The 1942 proposal was matched on the British side by James Meade's proposal for an International Commercial Union (Meade 1988) and together these formed the basis for the ongoing discussion of the trading system that led eventually to the Havana Charter and, via that, to the GATT. Schwob argues that the origins of the WTO can be much more clearly traced back to Bidwell and Meade than to Hull.

[2] This account is taken substantially from Schwob (2009).

Bidwell was an unashamed multilateralist and liberaliser.[3] He had advocated a multilateral negotiation in 1933 and argued for post-war trade liberalisation not only on the grounds of economic efficiency within the United States but as the only effective way of generating sufficient trade liberalisation, and hence trade, to alleviate the United Kingdom's balance of payments pressures. He felt that negotiations had to be multilateral in order to help governments to overcome the opposition of domestic pressure groups and hence make extensive concessions, to manage the logistics of such a broad negotiation, especially if it was to be viewed as a single item, and to manage trade relations with state-traders such as the Soviet Union. He also argued that multilateral arbitration of trade disputes and oversight of trade agreements would be necessary to keep the partners honest (not his words!). None of this was messianic, however; Bidwell's writing is suffused with the pragmatism and practicality necessary to achieve such a dramatic change in practice from the interwar period.

Meade held similar, but possibly more measured, views to Bidwell's. His proposals would have forbidden import or export quotas and restrictions on current account payments, restricted subsidies to 10 per cent and protection of home producers by any means to 25 per cent. While he did not debate between bilateral and multilateral negotiations, his International Commercial Union would provide for an 'International Commerce Commission of a semi-arbitral semi-judicial nature'. This would interpret the Charter of the Commercial Union and express an opinion on any dispute between members.

C The Early Treatment of Regional Trading Agreements

This section considers the views of Bidwell, Hull and Meade on regional trading agreements. Throughout the wartime and early post-war discussions of the future trading system, British Imperial Preferences figured large. To Cordell Hull these were an abomination, not only as examples of the discrimination he abhorred but as a restriction on US ability to export effectively (Schwob 2009: 12). Meade, as a British government official, could hardly disown Imperial Preferences, but he seems a bit embarrassed by them; he wrote about the International Commercial Union permitting 'moderate preferences' to a 'recognised political or

[3] He also had a very clear view of the United States' existential leadership role in the creation of the post-war era.

geographical group of nations' as the way of grandfathering them. Bidwell was also diplomatic on the specifically British issue.

Hull had little to say practically on preferences more generally, but Bidwell and Meade were very explicit. Both plans recognised a role for preferential trading arrangements but subject to well-defined limits. Discussing his proposed International Trade Authority, Bidwell (1943: 306) writes:

> The definition of 'discrimination' raises the problem of preferential tariffs and customs unions. Present usage does not consider that the most-favored-nation clause is violated when a country accords tariff favors to another country with which it maintains especially close political relations, as for example in the Ottawa Agreements and in our reciprocal preferential arrangement with Cuba. But there is grave danger that the clause may become so weakened by these and other exceptions and interpretations that it will lose all real significance. The wise course, however, would seem to be not to attempt to prevent all discriminations of this type. If customs unions are properly organized they can be useful in promoting a diversification of industries in certain areas. But they and preferential tariff arrangements should be subjected to scrutiny by the Trade Authority, which should have power to recommend to the states belonging to the general organization whether or not they should waive their rights under most-favoured-nation pledges.

Just prior to this Bidwell argues that

> [bilateral trade agreements] should be given close scrutiny by the International Trade Authority, which should attempt to devise substitute policies more in line with the general aims of sound reconstruction policy on the basis of equal treatment. Hence the writer urges the advisability of an agreement that not later than five or ten years after the close of hostilities the nations will undertake to abolish all discrimination in their commercial policies and in the administration of exchange controls.[4]

Meade proposed a limit on the degree of preference that customs unions or other blocs could maintain (p. 32):

> (iii) As exceptions to [the MFN obligation] members could give price preferences up to a maximum of, say, 10 percent to the produce of another state with which it formed a special recognised geographical or political union.

He also clearly included such unions within the ambit of the International Commerce Commission which would oversee the implementation of the Commercial Union's Charter.

[4] 'Exceptions should, of course, be made for frontier trade [small scale trade between immediate neighbours]'. This footnote is from the original.

This brief discussion shows that 'the founding fathers' envisaged a role for customs unions and possibly other preferential trade agreements within the post-war trading system, but subject to conditions:

- maximal degrees of preference or maximal durations,
- restriction to recognised groups or specific circumstances, and
- multilateral oversight to represent the interests of non-partners as well partners in the agreement, with, at least implicitly, the right to veto agreements.

It also seems reasonable to infer that these officials had a greater degree of comfort with customs unions than with other forms of preference, despite their diplomatic efforts to accommodate Imperial Preference.

D The Birth Pangs of Article XXIV[5]

The 'founding fathers' logic followed through to the negotiations around the early drafts of the Charter for what had come to be called the International Trade Organization (ITO), with the United States generally pushing hard against preferences and the British far more ambiguous in view of their wish to keep Imperial Preference. Irwin, Mavroidis and Sykes (2008) lay out the somewhat tortured timetable of trade discussions (and then negotiations) on the post-war trade architecture, from which one can extract the following milestones on Imperial Preferences, which was more or less the only form in which non-customs union preferences were discussed.[6]

The Atlantic Charter of 14 August 1941 called for 'access, on equal terms, to' trade, but subject to 'due respect to … existing obligations', which the British believed grandfathered Imperial Preferences (as did Cordell Hull, to his considerable frustration). *The Mutual Aid Agreement* of 23 February 1942, Article VII, referred back to the Charter but also spoke of 'the elimination of all forms of discriminatory treatment … ', which deepened the ambiguity. *The Washington Seminar* of September–October 1943, an informal meeting between various government economists, agreed to many features of the post-war regimes but not on Imperial Preferences.

[5] The first part of this section draws heavily on the excellent research in Chase (2006) and Irwin, Mavroidis and Sykes (2008).

[6] While this account stresses the international negotiations on the trading system, behind them lay pressing and immediate domestic political pressures and also the desire to construct an international system that helped governments to manage such pressures.

Following the Washington seminar, the discussion stalled as the British became less and less interested in a liberal world trading order. However, preferences resurfaced as a contention in *The British Loan Negotiations*, September–October 1945, which after much acrimony concluded that Imperial Preferences would be negotiated, along with reductions in American tariffs, previous commitments notwithstanding. It was also agreed that the US side would draft Proposals on 'expanding world trade and employment' for discussion among a dozen or so key countries in March 1946. The Proposals were issued in December 1945 but no meeting occurred on them and they were then transformed into the United States' 'Suggested Charter for an International Trade Organization' in September 1946. This fed into *The First Preparatory Meeting*, London, October–November 1946, Article 38 of which permitted customs unions provided that they did not raise the average of the tariffs charged by members prior to the customs union. This position remained unchanged through the *New York Meeting* of January–February 1947, which produced the first draft of the GATT out of the Commercial Policy Chapter of the ITO Charter and the *Second Preparatory Meeting*, Geneva, April–October 1947, which produced the putative definitive draft of the GATT.

The Geneva Draft included, inter alia, a provision grandfathering Imperial Preferences and some other existing arrangements via a qualification to Article I on MFN, and the inspired relegation of the treatment of customs unions to a mere technical question of the definition of a customs territory in a quite separate Article XXIV. In the meantime, however, the Havana Conference of November 1948 to March 1949 was working on the Charter for the ITO and during this meeting the disciplines on preferential trading agreements were suddenly relaxed – and the relaxation then retrofitted into the GATT. Suddenly free trade areas were to be permitted as well as customs unions, arrangements had to cover only 'substantially all trade', interim arrangements were allowed during which even this was not required, and the requirement not to raise the average tariff was replaced by the less operationalisable notion of not increasing 'the general incidence of duties'.

It is sometimes suggested that Article XXIV's general lack of clarity, consistency and practicality arose from the sensitivity over Imperial Preference or in order to make space for economic integration within Europe or between developing countries, aimed at encouraging industrialisation. However, as Chase (2006) so thoroughly documents, a very substantial part of the reason was that the United States was planning – indeed, was already negotiating – a free-trade area with Canada. Thus from a somewhat unforgiving position of 'customs unions only', the United States sought to relax the exceptions to be permitted in the Havana Charter to include free-trade areas and to subject the latter to fewer disciplines than the former. This is the origin of the language that preferential agreements must cover 'substantially all trade' as opposed to 'all trade' which had been the presumption before the United States' change of heart. It also lies behind the wording in Article XXIV Clause 6, which requires that if partners to an agreement raise tariffs subsequent to its creation they are liable to provide compensation to third parties: this applies only to customs unions and not to free-trade areas.[7]

This dramatic change of position by the United States might look like mere opportunism – the pursuit of immediate commercial benefits outweighing long-term principles and the fruit of dispassionate analysis. However, even this requires explanation and Chase argues that change from 1946's restrictive stance to 1947's pragmatic flexibility lay in the security situation (p. 21):

> By early fall 1947, the Truman administration had concluded that a Soviet invasion of Europe was unlikely in the foreseeable future; instead, the Soviet regime would use political and economic means of subversion. . . ..
>
> At Geneva and Havana, its primary objective was to demonstrate cohesion among market-oriented, democratic nations in the face of the Soviet threat. The Canadian trade initiative caused US officials to recognize that preferential arrangements could be employed to serve this larger Cold War strategy. This realization led policymakers to revise their beliefs about multilateralism. Previously, they had preferred a rigid MFN clause so the benefits of trade would be non-excludable: exclusion was repugnant, and it aroused hostility. But after the Canadian proposal, they concluded that international trade institutions, whether multilateral or regional, cemented political bonds among noncommunist countries, deepened commitments to the capitalist model, and mobilized a united front against the Soviet Union.

Chase examines other possible drivers of the relaxation and extension of Article XXIV and largely dismisses them. To facilitate European integration: this may have explained the provisions for interim stages for customs unions but not those for free trade agreements (FTAs) because the United States had decided that Europe needed a customs union not

[7] Given that FTA members each control their own tariffs, however, it is presumably the case that each is liable individually to the normal rules for compensation, so that this asymmetry is of no consequence.

an FTA; to please developing countries: but the United States resisted any amendments that went beyond its precise requirements for Canada; to preserve Imperial Preference: but that was treated elsewhere and, indeed, the British objected to the form of Article XXIV on the grounds that it permitted others to form FTAs but not the Commonwealth, because the latter could never agree to 'substantially all'.

One other question arises – why write universal rules to accommodate the putative US–Canada free-trade area rather than merely insist on an exception, which in the aftermath of the war, the United States could surely have done? Would these rules not eventually lead to a plethora of agreements that discriminated against the United States? Partial answers are that no one expected much use to be made of Article XXIV and that it is just more comfortable diplomatically to be within rather than outside a system you are leading.[8] More satisfying is Chase's argument that by the autumn of 1947, the US Administration had concluded that the Soviet Union was unlikely to pursue its goals in Europe militarily and that US foreign policy should now focus on drawing major Western countries into its market-based economic system.

It seems clear from this account that FTAs were an afterthought which received little analytical scrutiny and which lay awkwardly within the system even though, by dint of clever drafting (treating the matter as one of defining a customs territory), the latter admitted exceptions to non-discrimination in the form of customs unions. The contemporary (pre-Vinerian) view was that by facilitating the internal allocation of resources, customs unions would be welfare-enhancing, but that preferential trade areas were just discriminatory. Claire Wilcox (1949), the United States' Chief Negotiator and Director of the US Department of International Trade Policy, wrote,

> A customs union creates a wider trading area, removes obstacles to competition, makes possible a more economic allocation of resources, and thus operates to increase production and raise planes of living. A preferential system, on the other hand, retains internal barriers, obstructs economy in production, and restrains the growth of income and demand. It is set up for the purpose of conferring a privilege on

[8] Goldstein and Gowa (2002) argue convincingly that the United States saw benefits in tying its hands – in establishing a set of rules and enforcement mechanisms that applied equally to it as hegemon as to other, smaller, players in the trading system. This was to give the others confidence that the trading system would not exploit them and so encourage them to invest in it and in trading activities. From this perspective, it was important to make the FTA consistent with the rule-book rather than to present it as an exception.

> producers within the system and imposing a handicap on external competitors.
>
> . . . a customs union is conducive to the expansion of trade on a basis of multilateralism and nondiscrimination; a preferential system is not.

While we no longer see the distinction in quite these terms, it is not without validity. A customs union demonstrates a serious intention to integrate member economies, and as, for example, Sapir (1995) has argued, almost inevitably leads to deeper integration in areas beyond trade. An FTA is about managing competition between countries. It is only slightly hyperbolic to say that customs unions are domestic policy, FTAs are foreign policy. In the legitimisation of FTAs, the driving force was entirely geopolitics, not economic efficiency.

E The Early Application of Article XXIV

The history of the creation of regional trading agreements since the advent of the GATT has been well documented elsewhere, and so I will not dwell on it (e.g. Mathis 2002; WTO 2011). As negotiators had foreseen, not much use was made of regional trading arrangements in the first decade, but Article XXIV was nonetheless tested severely – indeed, in one sense, to destruction.

The three principal substantive conditions that Article XXIV lays down are that a regional trading agreement (RTA) should:

- cover substantially all trade,
- abolish duties and other regulations on internal trade between members,
- not raise the general incidence of duties against third countries,[9]

and the procedural requirement was that each RTA should be notified to the GATT, which was then permitted 'to make such reports and recommendations to contracting parties as they may deem appropriate'. This is a little vague, but for interim agreements the GATT had the power to prohibit an agreement from coming into or remaining in force if the GATT's recommendations were not followed. To start with each RTA was examined by a Working Group in order to guide the contracting parties about whether it should be acceptable to them.

[9] The Enabling Clause of 1979 allows developing countries to conclude RTAs between themselves without these restrictions.

In principle this structure could have imposed a good deal of discipline on preferentialism within the GATT, but in fact it failed to do so in any explicit fashion.[10] The terms in the Article turned out to be so vague as to defy legal interpretation but this was basically merely a cover for the political difficulties involved in acting against an RTA after it had been established. The first cases examined concerned small countries: South Africa–Rhodesia for a customs union (1949) and Nicaragua–El Salvador for an FTA (1951).[11] In each there was at least room for doubt as to whether the conditions had been satisfied but in each case any determination was put off until full plans or more data had been supplied, by which time the ability to act if ever there had been one would have evaporated. The South Africa–Rhodesia case dissolved as Rhodesia federated with two other states in 1955, while the FTA continued to report on trade relations between the partners, but no action by other contracting parties apparently resulted.

Two key early cases that came to define the GATT's practice on regionalism both concerned the European Economic Community (EEC) – its creation in 1957 and its relationships with its overseas territories (which became a GATT issue in 1958). The EEC's precursor – The European Coal and Steel Community, which liberalised trade in coal and steel between six European countries and more controversially created a steel cartel – had been granted a waiver. When it came to the Treaty of Rome establishing the EEC itself and then the relationship between the EEC and its members' overseas territories, however, politics became central. The European countries concerned were quite clear that European integration was their principal interest in terms of economic institutions. And in this, they were backed by the United States which saw economic integration as the route to economic success and hence a bulwark against both internal and external threats to the democratic/market system.[12] Thus while the EEC arguably violated the injunction against increasing average tariff levels and the agreements with overseas territories those about 'substantially all trade', in neither case could the contracting parties bring themselves to declare the arrangements inconsistent with the GATT.

[10] This is not to say, of course, that the Article had no effect – the scrutiny and the definition of norms it entailed may well have influenced what members proposed. However, once something was proposed the contracting parties were not able or willing to change it materially.

[11] This account is based on Curzon (1965).

[12] Lowenfeld (1996) gives an inside view of the United States' position.

By backing off on European integration, the GATT survived what might have been an existential threat, essentially by bowing to a superior political imperative. And it may well have been right to do so, for the GATT offered more advantages than just controlling RTAs – both economic and in terms of promoting cooperative solutions to global problems. But within the GATT the casualty of the compromise was Article XXIV, which was emasculated (if it ever had any masculinity to lose). Even this might not have been a bad deal – at least, so it seemed until recently. Even a regulation that is almost universally violated may still have a positive effect in the sense that it heads off even worse behaviour. Speeding laws, which are very commonly violated to a degree, are still regarded by most people as worthwhile and as having some influence on traffic speeds. Likewise, the existence and monitoring entailed by Article XXIV may still constrain the degree to which RTAs disadvantage third countries.

F The Middle Years

From the 1960s the number of RTAs has increased dramatically with a burst of activity in the 1970s and another, continuing, one starting in 1992 (WTO 2011). Until 1995 the procedure remained as described above and not a single working group concluded that an RTA was consistent with the GATT – although four concluded that an agreement was broadly consistent with it (Schott 1989) – and none concluded that an agreement was inconsistent with the GATT. That is, the working groups, and hence the contracting parties, sat firmly on the fence – RTAs were just too hot to handle. And neither were any disputes lodged directly against an RTA or even any in which the GATT-consistency of an RTA figured in a significant way. However, given that pre-1994 dispute settlement required the acceptance of a conclusion by both parties to a dispute before it had any effect, one can see why contracting parties might not have bothered. There were claims for compensation for the effects of tariff changes resulting from the enlargement of the EEC under GATT Article XXVIII – see, for example, GATT (1986) which arose from Spain and Portugal increasing certain tariffs to the level of the EEC's common external tariff on their accession – but it is difficult to see these isolated incidents as reflecting any attempt to enforce Article XXIV.

The problems of Article XXIV were well recognised within the GATT community and were the subject of a pretty thorough negotiation in the Uruguay Round. The changes to the Dispute Settlement Procedure will have affected disputes in the area of Article XXIV as much as any other, but the agreement concerning Article XXIV specifically – the Understanding on the Interpretation of Article XXIV of the General Agreement on Tariffs and Trade 1994 – did not advance matters very far. The Understanding clarifies a few terms but avoids any really contentious issues because agreement could not be reached. At least in part this was because the major players, again, found it politically impossible to address the issues: by 1994 the United States had just signed the North American Free Trade Agreement (NAFTA) and the European Union (EU) (as it had now become) had created many RTAs as it sought to integrate the newly liberated Central and Eastern European states into European and world markets. Both were clearly very important foreign policy imperatives and allowing a mere commercial treaty to unpick them was unthinkable.

The Understanding states that notifications of RTAs will be 'examined by a working party'; whether this refers to one working party or one per RTA is unclear to me, but the question was immediately resolved by placing the investigations in the hands of a Committee on Regional Trading Arrangements (CRTA). This, it was hoped, would give the process more expertise and clout and a greater ability and willingness to make comparisons between agreements. It is true that the CRTA managed one definitive conclusion – that the customs union between the Czech and Slovak Republics following the division of Czechoslovakia was GATT-consistent. But otherwise, the CRTA continued the studied agnosticism of the GATT working parties.

In December 2006 the WTO created the Transparency Mechanism for Regional Trading Agreements as a complement to the CRTA's work. As explained by Mavroidis (2011), however, transparency actually provided the context for the CRTA to cease the pretence of assessing RTAs itself – it became a de facto substitute for, not a complement to, the CRTA's role as a judge of new RTAs. The CRTA now circulates a factual document on an RTA to members; the members submit questions which the parties to the RTA must answer in advance and then everyone meets. The formal record contains the document, the Q&As and minutes of the meeting, but does not attempt to come to any decision about the WTO-consistency of the RTA in question. Presumably transparency limits the degree to which new RTAs deviate from Article XXIV, but the membership no longer has any mechanism by which it can express an institutional view, still less seek amendment. It may also provide evidence on which disputes could be launched, but so far that has not happened, and by and large it seems unlikely that responding parties would offer the membership sticks with which to beat them.

While the GATT failed to defend Article XXIV it nonetheless made considerable progress on reducing tariffs, supplemented in the cases of developing countries by the tender mercies of the Bretton Woods institutions' conditionality, which often featured trade liberalisations. Thus after the Uruguay Round had been implemented, it was often stated that tariffs were no longer a major issue for the world trading system. Even though this was not precisely true – plenty of developing countries have significant average tariffs and developed countries have a number of peaks – it clearly illustrated a trend. By simple arithmetic, then, regulatory issues – NTMs and issues surrounding the coverage of agreements – became relatively more important; they also actually increased in importance in a number of spheres – for example, food standards rose, environmental standards were introduced and labour standards extended. Moreover, with leaps in communications technology, production chains fragmented, increasing the integration of economies and, arguably, raising the opportunity costs of the assorted barriers to trade. Global value chains also brought issues such as foreign direct investment (FDI) and intellectual property (IP) more to the fore as large sophisticated global firms sought protection for their activities in developing countries.

Thus, as many scholars have noted, by the twenty-first century, regulation had become the focus of trade discussions, and the WTO proved ill-equipped to deal with it. Developing countries, smarting from what they felt were the asymmetries of the Uruguay Round, were suspicious of attempts to deal with four such issues in the Doha Round – investment, competition policy, government procurement and trade facilitation – and so, after generating a considerable amount of ill will, the first three of these were excised from the agenda in 2004. At the same time, the regulatory issues were the only ones for which large-scale business could work up any enthusiasm. Caught between a rock and a hard place, trade negotiators came up with the idea of treating them outside the WTO in smaller 'coalitions of the willing'. And by packaging them up with preferential access to their markets, the major players realised that they could persuade sets of developing countries to overlook the scruples that developing countries had expressed as a group.

Two features make negotiating tariffs more straightforward than negotiating regulation: tariffs are continuous variables and so may be tweaked to reach acceptable agreements and are 'owned' by trade ministries so that the internal bureaucratic process is much simpler. The regulatory issues, on the other hand, are frequently 'owned' by other ministries or by pseudo-independent agencies and often have a rather all-or-nothing character –

you either have an acceptable regime or you do not, you either meet the standard and can access a market or you do not. This not only makes them harder to negotiate, I would argue, but it also gives a strong first mover advantage to a bloc that can arrive at the global negotiating table with a ready-made proposal. It also makes them much more firmly exclusionary than tariffs: a tariff might be circumvented by reducing prices (preferably after reducing costs), but a regulation leaves no alternative than to accept it or reject it completely. Thus regulatory negotiations seem likely to be more 'take it or leave it' than those on tariffs.

To conclude, the 'middle' years saw two forces coming together – the shifting of attention from tariffs to NTMs and regulations and the confirmation that in matters of RTAs, the trading system bowed to the political demands of the major players. RTAs had become the perfect instrument for dividing up the trading system: they would not be opposed and yet they could very effectively exclude certain countries. Thus the scene was set for the advent of the mega-regional trading arrangements.

G The Mega-regionals

The term mega-regional is not defined, but in common with most commentators I will take it to encompass just three blocs, none of which is yet ratified and implemented. These are:

- **The Trans-Pacific Partnership (TPP)**, which has been signed between twelve countries, namely Australia, Brunei Darussalam, Canada, Chile, Japan, Malaysia, Mexico, New Zealand, Peru, Singapore, the United States, and Vietnam. They have a combined gross domestic product (GDP) of US$27.8 trillion, (37 per cent of global total), total trade of US$11.6 trillion (26 per cent) and have a combined population of about 802 million (11 per cent).[13]
- **The Trans-Atlantic Trade and Investment Partnership (TTIP)** which is being negotiated between the United States and the EU. These two economies have a combined GDP of US$34.6 trillion (46 per cent), total trade of US$19.6 trillion (44 per cent) and have a total population of more than 823 million (12 per cent).
- **The Regional Comprehensive Economic Partnership (RCEP)** which is being negotiated between the ten members of the Association of

[13] All statistics come from World Development Indicators (WDI) online and refer to 2013. Details are in Table 13.1.

Southeast Asian Nations (ASEAN) (Brunei, Cambodia, Indonesia, Laos, Malaysia, Myanmar, the Philippines, Singapore, Thailand and Vietnam) and six larger, economies – Australia, China, India, Japan, New Zealand and South Korea. They have a combined GDP of US$21.8 trillion (31 per cent), total trade of US$12 trillion (27 per cent) and a total population of 3.43 billion (48 per cent).

These huge trading arrangements are unprecedented in terms of the numbers of countries involved (*ab initio*), their total GDP, the variance in their levels of development, the volume of world trade that they account for and the spread and depth of the issues that they seek to address. Moreover, they also include the major hubs in most, if not all, global production networks, account for nearly all the world's patents and generate the bulk of the world's outflows of FDI. They differ from their predecessors not only in scale, however, but also in nature. The largest blocs of yesteryear – the EEC and NAFTA – were smaller and regionally concentrated, with the EEC aiming to become a customs union rather than an FTA. They were not aimed at influencing the architecture of world trade and the world trading system, but at essentially local integration. The mega-regionals, on the other hand, are explicitly global in conception and scope. They aim to define global standards and to create blocs of sufficient size that being outside them would be materially costly. I will argue that the mega-regionals threaten the multilateral trading system both by discriminating and by displacing multilateral functions and activities with regional ones.

I *The Trans-Pacific Partnership (TPP)*

The history of the multilaterals is linear. In 2002 the leaders of three small countries – Chile, New Zealand and Singapore – started talks on a Pacific Three Closer Economic Partnership (P3-CEP). Brunei joined the talks in April 2005, and the Pacific-4 (P4) came into being in 2006. It sought quite deep integration, with, for example, chapters on sanitary and phytosanitary measures (SPS), technical barriers to trade (TBT), trade-related aspects of intellectual property rights, competition policy and government procurement and services. The P4 committed to negotiating financial services and investment within two years of coming into force. It accounted (according to the 2013 data in Table 13.1) for 1 per cent of world GDP, and no one batted an eyelid.

Table 13.1 *Statistics on Mega-regionals, 2013*

	TPP	TTIP	RCEP	Population (millions)	GDP	Imports	Exports
					US$ billions		
Australia	1		1	23.1	1560.4	329.4	310.2
Brunei	1		1	0.4	16.1	5.2	12.3
Cambodia			1	15.1	15.2	11.2	10.0
Canada	1			35.2	1839.0	584.6	555.3
Chile	1			17.6	276.7	91.5	89.7
China			1	1357.4	9490.6	1953.5	2213.3
European Union		1		506.6	17950.1	7055.5	7495.3
India			1	1252.1	1861.8	523.6	468.5
Indonesia			1	249.9	910.5	225.5	218.3
Japan	1		1	127.3	4919.6	934.3	794.6
Republic of Korea			1	50.2	1305.6	638.4	703.4
Lao People's Democratic Republic			1	6.8	11.2	5.2	4.2
Malaysia	1		1	29.7	313.2	226.7	255.8
Mexico	1			122.3	1262.2	411.9	400.6
Myanmar			1	53.3	58.7	..	..
New Zealand	1		1	4.4	188.4	51.9	55.1

Peru	1			30.4	202.4	49.8	48.3
Philippines			1	98.4	272.1	87.0	75.9
Singapore	1		1	5.4	302.2	508.8	579.0
Thailand			1	67.0	387.3	272.2	284.9
United States	1	1		316.5	16768.1	2770.4	2262.2
Vietnam	1		1	89.7	171.2	139.5	143.2

	Population (millions)	GDP	Imports	Exports
TPP	802.1	27819.4	6104.0	5506.2
TTIP	823.0	34718.2	9825.9	9757.5
RCEP	3430.3	21783.9	5912.4	6128.6
	As a Percentage of World Total			
TPP	11	37	27	24
TTIP	12	46	44	43
TPP+TTIP	18	60	58	57
RCEP	48	29	26	27

Source: World Development Indicators Online (11 September 2015).

The P4 also had an open access clause whereby excluded countries could negotiate accession, and in February 2008 the United States (22 per cent of world GDP) announced that it would join the negotiations on finance and investment and explore full accession.[14] United States Trade Representative Susan Schwab said, 'This initiative also will provide another opportunity for the United States to participate in the regional trade architecture that is emerging in the vitally important Asia-Pacific region.' And the press release explained by way of background that 'Asia-Pacific countries are actively pursuing preferential trade agreements, both with one another as well as with partners outside the region. This trend has important commercial and strategic implications for the United States' (USTR 2008).

Thus the overt motivation seems to have been a fear of being on the outside of a nascent Asian-Pacific economic structure. But other forces were perhaps pressing in the same direction.[15] By 2008 the Doha Round was failing, and, according to many, the Uruguay Round had been closed only when the United States pursued NAFTA; why not try to enliven the Doha Round using the same stratagem?[16] Second, US foreign policy was already 'pivoting' towards Asia, and TPP could form part of this. Such a pivot seemed desirable partly on economic grounds – compared to nearly all of Asia, European growth was very disappointing – and partly on geopolitical grounds – Europe exercised declining amounts of leadership or influence in the world and China was becoming more powerful and assertive. By the late 2000s, US policy-makers were becoming much more cautious about China as a trading rival and also as an alternative focal point politically. By binding other Asian countries into an economic bloc, the United States hoped to head off any development of a Chinese-led Asian bloc in the WTO. This would be especially effective while the TPP was being negotiated because at that stage any defection could be punished.

More parochially, there was a general concern that business seemed to have little or no interest in the world trade talks and a deeper but narrower deal with dynamic Asia seemed as if it might address this. A fresh start would enable business to be more influential in the agenda

[14] The United States made clear that it viewed this process as negotiating a new agreement, not accession to an old one.

[15] Fergusson et al. (2013) discuss several of these.

[16] This effect of NAFTA on the Uruguay Round is far from certain, but there is convincing evidence that the creation of the EEC stimulated the United States to negotiate the Kennedy Round – Dür (2010). But the latter was quite a different business from creating a regional bloc as a negotiating ploy.

and also, very probably, dilute the amount of opposition that the United States' business agenda faced. Finally, some commentators argued that President Bush was aiming to wrong-foot the Democrats in the forthcoming election. Becoming ever more sceptical about liberal trade, the Democrats would struggle to define a position over a TPP presented in terms of jobs and opportunities.

Soon, if not immediately, the TPP became the central pillar of US trade policy and unashamedly strategic. For example,

> Our goal is for high standards for the Trans-Pacific Partnership to enter the bloodstream of the global system and improve the rules and norms.

So said Vice President Joseph P. Biden, 5 April 2013 (see Fergusson et al. (2013)), who continued:

> the TPP aims to establish disciplines on new trade issues, such as state-owned enterprises or supply chain facilitation, that could serve as a model for future negotiations bilaterally, regionally, or in the WTO.

And his boss, President Obama, was even more direct in the State of the Union address, 2015,

> China wants to write the rules for the world's fastest-growing region. That would put our workers and our businesses at a disadvantage. Why would we let that happen? We should write those rules . . .
>
> In the Asia Pacific, we are modernizing alliances while making sure that other nations play by the rules – in how they trade . . .

Once the United States had sought membership, as Baldwin and Robert-Nicoud's (2007) juggernaut theory predicts, other countries rushed to join the TPP – so much so, in fact, that negotiators announced in 2013 that no new potential members would be admitted to the negotiations – they would have to wait until the TPP was completed.

The most notable feature of the TPP's coverage, however, is that it excludes China, the largest economic force in Asia. It is true that until the window was shut, China could have applied for membership, but it did not require much imagination to see that many of the rules reportedly being developed in the TPP negotiations would imply huge changes in economic regulation in China. Moreover, China could hardly have expected to be able to influence those rules or to get waivers from them for at least two reasons. First, it is frequently argued in the West that China had benefitted asymmetrically from its WTO accession, getting huge market access benefits while still pursuing non-cooperative mercantilist policies such as state ownership and currency manipulation at the expense of her trading partners. So China receives little sympathy. Second, China is so large that almost every country in the world fears that if it grants market access to China it could be swamped by imports which undermine both domestic production and imports from other 'friendlier' countries. Thus while the TPP will obviously have to stretch to accommodate Vietnam's state ownership and export promotion for some time, China could not expect any such political favours.[17]

In the case of a purely commercial operation one might regret that it excludes important partners, but for an organisation intended to define standards for the global economy one should surely be more severe about the exclusion of the second-largest member in the world trading system.

Even setting China aside, norms agreed between countries accounting for 37 per cent of world output are going to be pretty hard for excluded countries to review or reform even if those countries are brought into a negotiation at a later stage. And this is particularly true if those norms have already been implemented as is likely to be the case if the TPP forms and a WTO Round is then opened. Mavroidis (2015) has coined the phrase 'forum diversion' to describe the phenomenon whereby the creation of an RTA leads specific activities to migrate from one forum to another controlled or created by the FTA. We observe precisely this phenomenon in the TPP and it is quite explicit and deliberate.

It might be argued that if the varied membership of the TPP can collectively agree a set of norms, then surely those norms ought to be suitable for other countries in the world – i.e. that somehow the TPP members are a representative group. Aside from the arrogance of this view, we should also note that TPP members would have accepted the norms as part of a particular package which will not be offered to others even under a supposedly MFN deal. Specifically, the TPP offers preferential access to the US market in return for agreeing the norms, whereas when the norms are offered to all other WTO Members, the preferential component will, by definition, be absent.

II The Trans-Atlantic Trade and Investment Partnership (TTIP)

For smaller Asian-Pacific countries the natural reaction to TPP was to try to join, but this was precluded de facto for China and de jure for Europe,

[17] The United States is blocking China from joining the Trade in Services Agreement (TiSA) talks in the WTO, despite both China and the United States professing to want China to join.

the two other mega-trading powers. As several analytical models (e.g. Andriamananjara 2002), as well as the political economy discussion have suggested, if you are excluded in a regionalising world, the next best thing is to start your own group. Europe and China could indeed have started to negotiate a parallel agreement – and did in fact start on a Bilateral Investment Treaty in 2013 – but Europe too harbours deep fears of China's huge productive potential. Hence Europe was more inclined to pursue a trans-Atlantic trade agreement – which eventually found form in the Trans-Atlantic Trade and Investment Partnership – TTIP.

Trans-Atlantic free trade had been talked about on-and-off since the 1960s and an Economic Council had been established in 2007 to consider a number of regulatory issues. But by 2012 it had become a priority for the EU. Not only did Europe fear economic and political exclusion from the US 'pivot' to Asia but recovery from the financial crisis was painfully slow. Under similar circumstances in the 1980s the European Commission had proposed the Single Market Programme, an imaginative way of stimulating economic activity, which is widely accepted to have helped economic growth. Perhaps deeper integration with the United States would offer the same benefits now. Given the greater homogeneity and sophistication of its membership, the TTIP could go even further than the TPP in the regulatory race, and Europe could leapfrog into a position of leadership in global economic regulation. Moreover, trade agreements are almost the only policy area over which the European Commission holds undisputed sway and so there was a ready-made champion in Europe for any such agreement.

While the EU was the demandeur, an agreement had two attractions for the United States: it offered a chance, perhaps, to open some sensitive markets such as for genetically modified foods or hormone-treated beef and, more importantly, it would reinforce the TPP. European objections to the latter would be muted and any issues on which the TPP and TTIP agreed would have the support of countries producing 60 per cent of world output and nearly 60 per cent of world trade. In addition, for so long as the Europeans were engaged with the United States in negotiating TTIP the latter could be pretty confident that they would not make overtures towards or entertain overtures from the Chinese. Thus, I would argue, TTIP is not merely another mega-regional agreement which seeks to determine important issues for the world trading system within a small group, but it is, wittingly or unwittingly, a further brick in the wall that excludes China from the design of the twenty-first-century trading system.

We examined the United States' ambitions to design global rules, but Europe's were no less vaunting: TTIP aims 'to enshrine Europe and America's role as the world's standard-setters' (European President Van Rampouy – Van Rompuy 2013). This sounds like an agreement to cooperate to make sure that outcomes in the trading system are as the United States and EU want them. With 45 per cent of world GDP between them and a further 15 per cent in the rest of TPP, it suggests that the choice facing other countries will be capitulation versus exclusion. Even if the EU/US rules are the best available, which is contended at least in part, imposing them in this way is likely to spur opposition and is hardly compatible with multilateralism.

III The Regional Comprehensive Economic Partnership (RCEP)

As noted above, in the world of regionalism the advice is 'if you can't join 'em, beat 'em'. China is party to a third mega-regional under negotiation – RCEP. Broached by the ASEAN Summit in November 2011, negotiations between the ASEAN members and the six other members started in August 2012. RCEP was significant in that it represented a truce between Japan and China in their struggles to lead Asian trade discussions. Japan arguably wanted it to reinforce its hand with the United States in the TPP negotiations (the United States was not unambiguously in favour of letting Japan in at the time), but was anxious to avoid China's proposed ASEAN+3 (China, Japan and South Korea) configuration because it wanted to dilute China's influence by bringing in some other significant traders. China, on the other hand, excluded from the TPP, was anxious to have a forum, any forum, in which the United States was not represented.[18]

The RCEP is much less deep in ambition than the TPP, and much less prescriptive in that it recognises the need for different countries to move at different speeds or even to have effectively permanent differences in their regulatory practices. On the other hand, its major members have higher protection than most TPP members and so the bloc has more than the TPP to gain from old-fashioned shallow integration. And with two massive and rapidly growing members – China and India – RCEP appears to offer considerable trading potential. RCEP seems to have made some progress towards fostering freer trade in its region and so in purely commercial, rather than regulatory terms, it cannot be

[18] See Hamanaka (2014) for more on these motivations.

discounted. While not as large as TPP, it still accounts for 29 per cent of world GDP and 27 per cent of world trade – and a massive 48 per cent of world population.

The principal relationship between the TPP and the RCEP is one of competition for influence, but their overlapping membership (Japan and six other states) makes the game more complex than that. There are at least three possibilities. Some commentators talk of combining the two into a Free-Trade Area of Asia and the Pacific (FTAAP) but the two arrangements have different philosophies and so creating a new institution seems unlikely. Second, absorption: attracted by its greater economic mass, the currently excluded countries opt for the TPP, either abandoning the RCEP or letting it wither. Ultimately, as Schott (2014) observes, 'If China decides to participate in the TPP in the coming years, it will cement the TPP as the template for both a FTAAP and an upgrading of the world trade rules.' It is difficult to see Europe, India or Africa providing much of a counterweight to such a bloc, certainly if Europe is co-opted into the arrangement via TTIP.

The third possible outcome is fragmentation. The overlapping members gravitate towards the TPP and the rump of the RCEP creates a looser and shallower arrangement, but one that steadfastly declines further integration with the TPP. Given the size of China and India, this rump could not be considered, and will not behave, as just a minor anomaly; rather it would represent the demise of effective multilateralism.

H Multilateralism

Where does all this leave multilateralism? The WTO, of course, has played no role in the negotiation of the mega-regionals, but one might want to argue that if the mega-regionals are basically about defining unassailable positions from which to impose regulatory standards on the rest of the world, eventually the issues must come back to the WTO. Indeed, it seems likely that if TPP–TTIP or a substantially enlarged TPP/RCEP do come to fruition they will seek a broad WTO Round to consolidate their dominance. But consolidation may well not appeal to the excluded countries and thus such an initiative may be stillborn. This outcome would reflect the excluded countries' sovereignty and thus in a sense be multilateral in process, but it would leave the world trading system fractured and discriminatory.

The prospect of a small number of competing trading blocs is one which preoccupied the international trade profession in the 1990s. Paul

Krugman (1991; 1993) provided a simple model which traded off the benefits of intra-bloc free trade with trade diversion visited on the rest of the world, either with or without an incentive for members to exploit excluded countries by raising their external tariffs; both versions predicted that under many circumstances the pessimum number of blocs was three. Andriamananjara (2002) and Loke and Winters (2012) have shown that once we are down to such small numbers there is no guarantee that the groups would combine into the so-called global coalition of universal free trade because admitting new members to a group dilutes the benefits of discrimination.

The alternative outcome of a mega-regional-dominated WTO Round would be that the non-Member countries felt that they had no option but to accept the mega-regional's offer and terms. This would eliminate the discrimination but would violate multilateralism in the sense of collective decision-making rather than the unfettered exercise of power. Thus the forum diversion inherent in the mega-regionals will violate multilateralism either procedurally or substantively. And even if it is 'merely' the former, the final equilibrium on regulation will probably be different from that which would have emerged from a single multilateral negotiation and for that reason will be less desirable from the point of view of the initially excluded countries. By breaking the negotiation up into stages – first with TPP or TTIP members and then with the remaining countries – the United States is exercising the power in a way that it arguably sought to avoid by creating even-handed rules in the immediate post-war period. And if this is the likely outcome, other countries may decline to play and the post-war multilateral system will collapse. If we were talking about bidding for oil plots, say, rather than designing a trading regime, the United States' own competition laws would outlaw such collusion prior to the final negotiation.

In countering the fears of fragmentation, many commentators argue that harmonising standards between Europe and the United States (or between Japan and the United States) will benefit not only intra-bloc trade but also exports from third countries because they will no longer have to meet two disparate standards. There is clearly some truth to this, but it should be qualified. Chen and Mattoo (2008) show that, when countries harmonise their standards, exports from third countries tend to fall, especially when, as is likely with the two largest and richest economies in the world, those standards are high and rising. Moreover, the view that harmonisation around *any* standard is desirable is not strengthened when one observes the sensitivity of the process of selecting which, or more precisely whose, standard is to be adopted. That is, simply observing the politics of harmonisation would suggest that the benefits of having one's own standard often outweigh those of having a common standard. If TTIP does actually start to define norms, they will not be those of excluded countries and the latter may therefore expect to lose from the process, at least in the short and medium terms.

Although much of what the TPP entails is actually sound policy, and although the final provisions are in several ways more accommodating of developing country members than had been anticipated, TPP members will still often have to approach US regulatory norms faster than is desirable for low- and middle-income countries, and possibly faster than they can effectively administer.[19] For example, the TPP extends copyright to seventy years beyond the author's death rather than the fifty years in the TRIPS agreement. On state-owned enterprises (SOEs) TPP commitments go beyond WTO principles 'in important ways, including by applying subsidies rules to services exports of SOEs and to the operations of SOE manufacturers outside their home territory' (USTR 2015). Third, the TPP's Investor–State Dispute Settlement Chapter does little to address the concerns that have been expressed such as that investor–state dispute settlement gives foreign-owned firms more protections from government action than local firms have and compromises the policy sovereignty of member states. Thus it is not clear that the TPP standards will actually be in the interests of all countries even setting aside concerns about multilateralism.[20]

The final defence offered for the mega-regionals is that even if there is a chance that things go wrong, and the multilateral system is undermined, the benefits of the mega-regionals are so great that the risk is worth it. The simple static gains do not commend such a bet. Plausible estimates suggest that a 'realistic' agreement in TTIP might add about 0.25 per cent to EU GDP and that an 'ambitious' agreement might add 0.5 per cent. The returns to the United States are around the same level (Francois et al. 2013, Table 16).[21] Similarly with the TPP, the United

[19] And likewise for other countries if they feel obliged to follow TPP–TTIP norms.

[20] It has been argued that the TPP actually implies very little change in members' policies; but this would imply that the extensive effort has been just to establish an exclusionary club.

[21] Felbermayr et al. (2014) offer much greater estimates, by 'assuming that the TTIP will reduce transatlantic trade costs by as much as existing bilateral agreements have reduced trade costs between their trade partners'. This is entirely unrealistic and so their estimates must be discounted.

States might gain 0.4 per cent of GDP and the smaller members a bit more (Petri and Plummer 2012, Table 1). Global gains depend what is assumed about the rest of the world: Francois et al. assume that they gain from the integration of standards inside TTIP whereas Petri and Plummer see trade diversion as harming excluded countries. Either way they do not contribute much to the overall total. It is likely that these static benefits are underestimated, but even if they were doubled, the major partners would gain less than one year's normal economic growth in return for isolating China and undermining what has been one of the triumphs of the post-war settlement. To some, it hardly seems worth the risk – e.g. Krugman (2015).

I Conclusion

Multilateralism is under severe threat at present both procedurally and, perhaps following inevitably from that, substantively. The seeds of this threat were sown in the closing stages of the negotiation of the ITO, when for political, not commercial, reasons the exception from MFN was extended from customs unions to free-trade areas. The latter are much less intrusive on domestic policy than the former, with the result that they have become essentially instruments of foreign policy, rewarding current favourites with possibly valuable market access and permitting the explicit exclusion of non-favourites.

When the ITO rules about regionalism passed into the GATT there was still a chance to impose a good deal of discipline on their use, but, again for essentially political reasons (the desire to not to let the GATT prevent European integration), the membership turned a blind eye to their violation. Having done this once, it became almost impossible to reverse, and so not a single notified agreement was rejected or modified after explicit comment by the Contracting Parties.[22] As we moved from the GATT to the WTO, Members were perfectly aware of the problems, but despite considerable negotiating effort they were unable to agree to a tightening of the arrangement. There were procedural adjustments that might have underpinned a change of heart – the CRTA could have evolved into a stronger enforcer of Article XXIV – but without the Members exhibiting the political will to undertake that change of heart

[22] This is not to say that Article XXIV had no effect – it probably did constrain what members of integration schemes proposed – but that it was not enforced sufficiently to prevent the world from slipping away from multilateralism.

it was essentially powerless. With the transparency agreement in 2006, the WTO threw in the towel.

Multilateralism is a delicate flower; while the generation that had experienced the war and the interwar period was willing to pool sovereignty and recognise constraints in order to maintain the multilateral order, such public-spiritedness has become less and less visible as time has gone by. Hegemons have declined and hence been resentful of the cost of maintaining the system and the countries that have gained power during this process, and which were arguably previously marginalised, have been unable or unwilling to pick up the challenge. Thus while everyone knows the script, no country seems willing or able to exert itself to actively reassert the multilateral ideal in fact. It is a classic public- good failure.

Bibliography

Andriamananjara, Soamiely. 2002. 'On the Size and Number of Preferential Trading Arrangements'. *Journal of International Trade & Economic Development* 11(3): 279–295.

Baldwin, Richard. 2012. 'Sequencing Asian Regionalism: Theory and Lessons from Europe'. *Journal of Economic Integration* 27 (1): 1–32.

Baldwin, Richard and Robert-Nicoud, F. 2007. 'A Simple Model of the Juggernaut Effect of Trade Liberalisation'. CEPR Discussion Papers 6607.

Bidwell, Percy W. 1943. 'Controlling Trade after the War'. *Foreign Affairs* 21 (2): 296–311.

Bidwell, Percy W. 1944. A Postwar Commercial Policy for the United States'. *American Economic Review* 34 (1): 340–353.

Chase, Kerry. 2006. 'Multilateralism Compromised: The Mysterious Origins of GATT Article XXIV'. *World Trade Review* 5 (1): 1–30.

Chen, Maggie X. and Mattoo, Aaditya. 2008. 'Regionalism in Standards: Good or Bad for Trade?' *Canadian Journal of Economics/Revue canadienne d'économique* 41 (3): 838–863.

Curzon, Gerard. 1965. *Multilateral Commercial Diplomacy; the General Agreement on Tariffs and Trade and its Impact on National Commercial Policies and Techniques*. London: Michael Joseph.

Dür, Andreas. 2010. *Protection for Exporters: Power and Discrimination in Transatlantic Relations, 1930–2010*. Cambridge: Cambridge University Press.

Felbermayr, Gabriel, Heid, Benedikt, Larch, Mario and Yalcin, Erdal. 2014. 'Macroeconomic potentials of transatlantic free trade: A high resolution perspective for Europe and the world'. *CESifo Working Paper Series* No. 5019.

Fergusson Ian F., McMinimy, Mark A. and Williams, Brock R. 2013. *The Trans-Pacific Partnership (TPP) Negotiations and Issues for Congress.* Washington DC: Congressional Research Service, Report R42694.

Francois, Joseph, Manchin, Miriam, Norberg, Hanna, Pindyuk, Olga and Tomberger, Patrick. 2013. *Reducing Transatlantic Barriers to Trade and Investment – An Economic Assessment.* London: Centre for Economic Policy Research.

GATT 1986. 'Article XXVIII;3 Notification in Response to Actions by the European Economic Community Under Article XXIV Schedule XX T United States'. GATT Document L/5997, 26 May 1986.

Goldstein, Judith and Gowa, Joanne. 2002. 'US National Power and the Post-War Trading Regime'. *World Trade Review* 1 (2): 153–170.

Hamanaka, Shintaro. 2014. 'Trans-Pacific Partnership versus Regional Comprehensive Economic Partnership: Control of Membership and Agenda Setting'. *Working Paper on Regional Economic Integration,* No. 146, Manila: Asian Development Bank.

Hoekman, Bernard. (ed.). 2015. *The Global Trade Slowdown: A New Normal? A VoxEU.org eBook.* London: Centre for Economic Policy Research (CEPR Press).

Hull, Cordell. 1948. *The Memoirs of Cordell Hull.* 2 vols. Macmillan: New York.

Irwin, Douglas. 2012. *Trade Policy Disaster: Lessons from the 1930s.* Cambridge, MA: MIT Press.

Irwin, Douglas, Mavroidis, Petros C. and Sykes, Alan O. 2008. *The Genesis of the GATT.* Cambridge: Cambridge University Press.

Krugman, Paul. 1991. 'Is Bilateralism Bad?' In *International Trade and Trade Policy,* edited by Elhanan Helpman and Assaf Razin. Cambridge, MA: MIT Press.

Krugman, Paul. 1993. 'Bilateralism versus Multilateralism: Analytical Notes.' In *New Dimensions in Regional Integration,* edited by Arvind Panagariya and Jaime de Melo. Cambridge: Cambridge University Press.

Krugman, Paul. 2015. 'TPP at the NABE.' http://krugman.blogs.nytimes.com/2015/03/11/tpp-at-the-nabe/, accessed 26 November 2015.

Loke, Wai-Heng and Winters, L. Alan. 2012. 'Why Is Open Regionalism Not Always Good?' *Journal of Economic Integration* 27: 437–465.

Lowenfeld, Andreas F. 1996. 'USA, the EEC, and the GATT: The Road Not Taken'. *University of Pennsylvania Journal of International Economic Law* 17: 533.

Mathis, James H. 2002. *Regional Trade Agreements in the GATT/WTO: Article XXIV and the Internal Trade Requirement.* The Hague: T.M.C. Asser Press.

Mavroidis, Petros C. 2011. 'Always Look at the Bright Side of Non-delivery: WTO and Preferential Trade Agreements, Yesterday and Today'. *World Trade Review* 10 (3): 375–387.

Mavroidis, Petros C. 2015. 'Dealing with PTAs in the WTO: Falling Through the Cracks between "Judicialization" and "Legalization"'. *World Trade Review* 14 (S1): S107–S121.

Meade, James. 1988. 'A Proposal for an International Commercial Union'. In *The Collected Papers of James Meade*, Volume 3: *International Economics*, edited by Susan Howson, 27–35. London: Unwin–Hyman.

Petri, Peter A. and Plummer, Michael G. 2012. 'The Trans-Pacific Partnership and Asia-Pacific Integration: Policy Implications'. Peterson Institute for International Economics: Policy Brief No. PB12-16.

Sapir, André. 1995. 'Trade Liberalization and the Harmonization of Social Policies: Lessons from European Integration'. *CEPR Discussion Papers* No. 1114.

Schott, Jeffrey J. (ed.). 1989. *Free Trade Areas and US Trade Policy*. Washington, DC: Institute for International Economics.

Schott, Jeffrey J. 2014. 'Asia-Pacific Economic Integration: Projecting the Path Forward'. www.iie.com/publications/papers/schott201404APEC-FTAPP.pdf

Schwob, Claude. 2009. *The Intellectual Origins of WTO: Hull's and Bidwell's views on Organizing the International Trade*. Strasbourg: Bureau d'Economie Théorique et Appliquée, UDS (No. 2009–32).

Toye, Richard. 2012. 'The International Trade Organization'. In *The Oxford Handbook on The World Trade Organization*, edited by Amrita Narlikar, Martin Daunton and Robert M. Stern, Oxford: Oxford University Press, 85–101.

USTR. 2008. 'United States to Join Sectoral Negotiations with Four Asia-Pacific Countries'. *USTR News* 4 February 2008.

USTR. 2015. 'State-Owned Enterprises: Chapter Summary'. *TPP Full Text*. Washington, DC: USTR.

Van Rompuy, Herman. 2013. 'Remarks by President of the European Council Herman Van Rompuy on the Occasion of the Launch of the EU-US Transatlantic Trade and Investment Partnership'. European Commission Press Release EUCO 143/13.

Wilcox, Clair. 1949. *A Charter for World Trade*. New York: MacMillan.

Winters, L. Alan. 1999. 'Regionalism versus multilateralism'. In *Market Integration, Regionalism and the Global Economy*, edited by Richard Baldwin, Daniel Cohen, André Sapir and Anthony Venables. Cambridge: Cambridge University Press, 7–49.

WTO. 2011. *World Trade Report 2011 – The WTO and Preferential Trade Agreements: From Co-existence to Coherence*. Geneva: World Trade Organization.

14

Performance and International Organisations' Borders

The Case of the World Trade Organization

CÉDRIC DUPONT AND MANFRED ELSIG

A Introduction

A widely held perception among practitioners and analysts of international cooperation is that the World Trade Organization (WTO) has been successful in promoting a rules-based multilateral trading system. This perception of a performing organisation, with both active involvement and compliance of major states, has long raised the issue of cooperation with other international organisations (IOs), particularly with those in the United Nations (UN) system paralysed by power politics and lack of compliance. The perceived contrast in terms of compliance performance between the WTO and other UN organisations has pushed powerful Member States to somehow redraw the regulatory borders between existing institutions, prompting a debate generally known in the trade community as the 'trade-and' debate covering diverse fields including finance, climate change, development, health and human rights. Those efforts have had different impacts, however, and the existing literature has so far offered few, if any, systematic accounts of such variation. This chapter aims at addressing this aspect of performance that has been largely overlooked and proposes a new conceptual framework to help us think about the cooperative or conflictual nature of border politics and its impact on the evolution of regulatory borders. Although it focuses on the specific case of the borders of the WTO, our framework can serve as a conceptual tool to understand the politics of IO borders more generally.

For comments on an earlier draft, special thanks go to Todd Allee, Tim Büthe, Dirk De Bièvre, Dan Drezner, Mark Pollack, Gregory Shaffer and Duncan Snidal.

Within the fields of international relations, little attention has been paid to the boundary questions. Regime theorists have shown some interest in linkages across international regimes. Ernst Haas (1980) developed a holistic framework within which the interests of actors and knowledge of experts drive such processes. This work did offer some guidance on understanding the actors' motives and strategies for linking regimes and therefore changing the balance of preferences, yet, given the limited overlap at that time, it did not address the tensions that changing borders may generate. Considering the growth of international rules and institutions in recent years, the relatively little scholarly work on boundaries and intersection issues is more surprising. In particular, leading liberal research programmes on legalisation in international politics and rational design of international institutions (Goldstein et al. 2000; Koremenos et al. 2001) have been largely silent on this question. In addition, other contributions that unpack the politics of IOs (Barnett and Finnemore 2004; Hawkins et al. 2006) do not look at the interplay with other organisations. Some work focuses mainly on interactions within governmental networks (Slaughter 2000) and forms of 'informal international lawmaking' (Pauwelyn et al. 2012), but these contributions do not directly address border questions. Raustiala and Victor observe a 'lack of systematic attention to boundaries' which 'leaves a large hole in the existing body of theory' (2004: 278).[1]

This chapter aims at redirecting attention to the border question and spearheading new analytical avenues. It is organised as follows. The next section presents a categorisation of border dynamics. In Section C, we theorise, using a principal–agent (PA) framework, about the behaviour of dominant actors, present our key explanatory factors that affect interest aggregation and list a series of bivariate relationships between our explanatory factors and border outcomes. In the final section, we illustrate the analytical relevance of our framework with four cases on the WTO and its border relations with other IOs.

B Conceptualising Border Dynamics

In this section, we present our conceptualisation of border dynamics between organisations, our dependent variable. We differentiate 'border dynamics' along two main dimensions, the nature of border delimitation on the one hand and the border movement on the other. Regarding the former, we distinguish between a cooperative

[1] For an exception, see Kim (2012).

type of dynamics and a conflictual one. Regarding the latter, we distinguish whether, for a given episode, borders between IOs shift or remain unchanged, yielding the four groups of generic outcomes illustrated in Table 14.1.

Table 14.1 *Four Types of Border Dynamics*

		Border Delimitation	
		Cooperative	Conflictual
Border movement	*No shift*	Cooperative status quo	Conflictual status quo
	Shift	Agreed shift	Forced shift

Source: Created by the authors.

When characterising border dynamics, we first determine whether border delimitation is a cooperative process or a highly contentious one. Cooperative border management is witnessed through a convergence of expectations among key actors in IOs (and their shareholders) that they can jointly delineate the borders. It is the absence of politicisation that characterises cooperative behaviour. Moreover, we may find formal and informal platforms where IOs exchange information, engage in constructive debates and foster coordination of activities. We speak of conflictual borders when border delimitation is characterised by strong dissent and significant politicisation. One important sign of conflict is public knowledge about intensive border management problems diffused by media reports or through scholarly work. If institutional fora for coordination exist, they are either bypassed or if debates occur, they are characterised by a substantial degree of distrust among actors and by defensive posturing.

We then turn to the question whether borders have been shifting. We talk of shifts when decisions in a given IO are substantially affected by the politics and law of another IO.[2] Measuring the degree of shifts is not a trivial exercise, mainly because borders are generally difficult to

[2] On IO characteristics, we refer in particular to principles and norms as discussed in the regime literature, see Krasner (1983).

define. We do not provide a silver bullet for operationalising the concept of shifts; however, we suggest that border movement is a relative concept describing change in the outside-in influence of another IO. Such a change in influence can be observed in different ways. For instance agenda-setting can take place in other IOs (e.g. the G7 mandating international financial institutions to focus on money laundering or the G20 mandating the Financial Stability Board to work on too-big-to-fail banks); or we could observe that during negotiations leading up to new rules and obligations, reference (e.g. deference) is made to other IO principles and norms in formal treaty texts or informal agreements at a secondary level); or we may observe that tasks are partially transferred to another IO (e.g. the dispute settlement bodies of one IO refer to another IO when adjudicating disputes). Within the category of 'shift', outcomes can vary from small shifts (e.g. some design features are exported) to large shifts (e.g. agenda-setting occurs in another IO and important functions are suddenly carried out by another organisation). The category 'no shift' suggests that the influence exerted through activities in other IOs remain stable over the period of analysis.

As a result of the dichotomous choice in each of our two dimensions, our framework posits four possible categories of border dynamics. We briefly describe them and provide illustrations of the WTO in border relations with other IOs. The first two categories are cooperative; categories three and four are conflictual ones.

1. *Cooperative status quo* refers to a situation where border management is cooperative and does not lead to any border shift. Explicit and cooperative management of border overlap takes place through the collective design of border mechanisms. Overlapping IO mandates are tackled by a consensual approach to regulating these issues and devising conflict management tools.[3] An illustration of a cooperative status quo comes from recent trade and development linkages. Various efforts have been made to create inter-institutional settings to design rules and agree on implementation. Examples of mutual management could come from the area of trade facilitation, where various IOs are called upon to act jointly.[4] An explicit WTO

[3] This is similar to what Raustiala and Victor (2004) refer to as dealing with legal inconsistency by disentangling and demarcation efforts.

[4] Trade facilitation is about reducing impediments to exports, in particular focusing on speeding up transport times (customs procedures) and investing in infrastructure (warehouses, ports and roads).

Ministerial mandate agreed in July 2004 to cooperate with other institutions on this issue (WTO 2004).[5] This mandate has been actively pursued since, culminating in the adoption of the Trade Facilitation Agreement during the 2013 Ministerial Conference in Bali, followed by the Trade Facilitation Agreement Facility in 2014. Trade facilitation stands out as one of the few areas where progress is visible, politicisation is low and inter-institutional cooperation still runs smoothly.

2. *Agreed shift* represents a cooperative situation in which border shift is mutually accepted. To reach this outcome, neighbouring IOs engage in various forms of accommodation to the other side's demands or agenda. In the context of the WTO, we can distinguish between situations in which the WTO extends its scope to others' regulatory turf (shift outward) and those in which the WTO cedes some of its responsibilities to others (shift inward). An illustrative example of the second subtype of controlled shift (in implementation) is the so-called Doha Declaration on the Agreement on Trade-related Aspects of Intellectual Property Rights (TRIPS Agreement) and Public Health. In this instance, a large coalition (excluding the United States) led to a weakening of the TRIPS Agreement by stretching the scope of exceptions for certain policy objectives (WTO 2001). Exponents from both the World Health Organization (WHO) and the World Intellectual Property Organization (WIPO) have collaborated in recent years with the WTO to implement the Doha Declaration. WIPO and WHO expanded their mandate in the field of trade rules, intellectual property rights and public health in particular by developing guidelines and providing technical assistance. Notwithstanding attempts by the United States to restrict its effects (Drezner 2007), a shift has occurred.
3. The case of *conflictual status quo* suggests that IO actors do not cooperate with each other beyond their mandates and that there is substantial distrust and divergence of views. If one side attempts to push the border, the actors in the neighbouring IO fight to 'defend the border' and engage in counter-pressure attempts. Reactions range from containment to open resistance. Each side controls the border

[5] See Annex D: 'In order to make technical assistance and capacity building more effective and operational and to ensure better coherence, Members shall invite relevant international organizations, including the IMF, OECD, UNCTAD, WCO and the World Bank to undertake a collaborative effort in this regard' (Decision Adopted by the General Council on 1 August 2004; WT/L/579, 2 August 2004).

to make sure the forces for shifting remain controlled. An illustration of conflictual status quo is the border between the WTO and the UN Framework on Biodiversity. Members of the latter reacted to an emergent dominance of trade rules through the design of a new agreement: the Cartagena Protocol on Biosafety to the Convention on Biological Diversity. This was an attempt to counter WTO pressures by buffering against dominance of trade rules in trade in genetically modified products. This outcome of pushing the borders back to the status quo was witnessed in the treaty text, where various formulations suggested that WTO law would not apply in this area (see Winham 2003).

4. Lastly *forced shift* depicts a conflictual situation where there is an absence of cooperation in the delimitation of borders. Border shifts occur in an uncoordinated manner and may be difficult to contain. This situation is characterised by one side not reacting to border pressures either owing to lack of capacity, benign neglect or IO officials seeing some benefits of a shift. Forced shifts are usually temporary and subsequently overlap with moves towards a more stable situation over time. An example of a 'forced' shift occurred in the second half of the 1990s between the WTO system and the intergovernmental food standard setting agency Codex Alimentarius. We will discuss this example in greater detail in Section III.

C A Pathway to a More Systematic Understanding of Borders

How can we account for the emergence of the different types of border dynamics that we have just outlined? Ultimately one could say that this will depend on the cost–benefit ratio of various outcomes for members of the various organisations and the power distribution. Yet, given the multiplicity of actors and the complex setting in which they are embedded, a purely interest-based or power-based approach would not sufficiently help us understand border politics and outcomes. We therefore now turn to a discussion of more general factors – conditions – that could exert a significant influence on border dynamics. Before doing so, however, we first briefly focus on the actors. When accounting for their preferences, we adopt general working assumptions that enable us to simplify our task of gauging the effect of our explanatory factors on aggregation of multiple actors' preferences. We suggest that institutional and structural conditions largely define the possibilities and constraints affecting the actors' observed behaviour.

I The Actors

Drawing from the PA literature, we focus primarily on two specific categories of actors: the member states (principals) that design and control IOs, and the IOs themselves (agents) represented by the head of the organisation and the staff. As to the principals, we are agnostic at this stage about the initial motivations of the designers regarding border delineation, as they predominantly focus on the core activities of IOs.[6] Over time, however, principals develop distinct views on the type of border management and shift. In order to understand principals' behaviour we need to focus on how salient a border issue is for them.[7] With increasing salience, principals turn to instruments for influencing the activities of the IO. These range from ex ante tools (selection of agents, definition of mandates), on the spot control (most likely through national representatives within the IO) and ex post control (through sanctioning or non-acceptance of IO outcomes). Not all instruments are similarly effective and their application differs from one IO to another. As there are multiple principals, we differentiate between collective principals (acting as a group) and individual principals. This is important as for instance delegation to agents can only be done through the group of collective principals; however, blocking processes can also be influenced by individual principals (depending on the decision-making rules in an IO).

The second category of actors includes those that patrol and manage the borders (the agents). Given their proximity to the issues, they are in a privileged position for any discussion and action on borders. In particular, they benefit from information asymmetry. Yet their role is only of analytical interest if IO staffers have some discretion (Elsig 2010b; Elsig 2012).[8] PA frameworks help us understand variations in

[6] E.g. when the WTO was created most attention was paid to core rights and obligations related to trade liberalisation; little attention was paid to design explicit relationships with other IOs. Negotiations rarely prioritise border questions and when they do negotiators cannot anticipate how future events will 'test' the border.

[7] We abstain from offering a mapping of principals' preferences. This would go beyond what this chapter can possibly achieve.

[8] For a discussion on the differences between autonomy, discretion, slack and slippage, see Hawkins et al. (2006: 8).

bureaucratic autonomy across IOs, the type of strategies applied by bureaucratic actors and the conditions under which this type of actor merits attention (Nielson and Tierney 2003).[9] Where proponents of the PA literature disagree is on the incentives that drive the agents. Early work used simple models in which agents' individual motivations (utility) were measured by income, gaining reputation within an IO and budget maximisation (e.g. Niskanen 1971; Vaubel 2006). Recent studies pay more attention to an armoury of agent strategies (Hawkins and Jacoby 2006) and focus increasingly on a combination of rational and organisational factors that drive behaviour (Elsig 2010a). In a twist to the PA issue, recent work sees agents as strategic 'orchestrators' working with third parties (such as other IOs) to achieve the IO goals (Abbott et al. 2014). As to the incentive structure, we side with newer approaches towards bureaucratic actors. In terms of border politics we suggest that, first and foremost, actors exhibit loyalty to the IO itself and to the regime's guiding principles. We therefore expect them to be inclined to defend borders. At the same time, given incentives to broaden one's portfolio (and to elevate one's position within an organisation) bureaucratic actors will seek ways to widen the scope of their jurisdiction (and this may at times be easier through interaction with other IOs than within the existing one). Which of two expectations about bureaucratic behaviour is more likely to be met (defending borders or enlarging the portfolio) largely depends on the conditions we discuss below. These affect the incentives of patrolling agents, strengthening one group (e.g. those interested in broadening the mission) to the detriment of the other group.

II Conditioning Factors

In addition to a simple PA set-up where actors follow their preferences, we conceptualise a set of factors that are likely to impact on principals' and agents' interest aggregation leading to different border dynamics. At this stage, we suggest bivariate relationships between explanatory and outcome variables. We pay little attention to interaction effects.[10]

[9] An agent-driven mission creep is not likely in the context of the WTO – with the partial exception of dispute settlement (Elsig 2010b).

[10] Further, we do not differentiate between causal effects and causal mechanisms (van Evera 1997; King, Keohane and Verba 1994; Goertz and Starr 2003). To reduce complexity, we posit that explanatory variables act independently to produce, each on its own, a particular effect (causal equifinality).

Variables define opportunities and constraints for actors navigating along the borders and affecting the nature of cooperation and the likelihood of border shifting in a certain direction.[11] The aim is to offer a framework, mapping key variables, and suggesting causal explanations for border dynamics. In the selection of variables, we build upon a number of prominent research programmes.

1 Delegation

We first consider how delegation affects preference aggregation within IOs. We expect the extent to which the group of collective principals of an institution delegate authority to an agent to affect the shape of borders. Delegation can take various forms (Pollack 1997; Abbott et al. 2000). Examples include delegation to an arbitrating agent to assist in dispute settlement, or granting discretion to IO bureaucracies to implement policies, as in the case of the International Monetary Fund (IMF) where staffers put into effect the Fund's policies (enforcing agent) (Hawkins et al. 2006).[12] Delegation usually increases obligations to comply with rules. Delegation helps to address time-inconsistency problems and strengthens implementation, as blocking the enforcement of agreed concessions will be tempered. Differences in the extent of delegation across the institutional border are likely to affect stability of the border as such differences strengthen or weaken some agents more than others.

To capture the effects within a dyadic relationship between two IOs we suggest two different situations: (a) symmetry in the extent of delegation; (b) asymmetry of delegation, where one side of the border is clearly characterised by more (or less) delegation than the other side. A symmetrical level of delegation deprives both sides of their ability to redraw borders. If delegation to agents is high, they face each other with sufficient discretion to pursue their preferences to either enlarge their portfolio or to defend their borders. Given this situation, they realise that accommodation with neighbouring agents is the most efficient outcome leading to a cooperative behaviour and no shift. Their delegated powers also enable them to buffer themselves against the principals' influence. If delegation is low on both sides, agents will similarly abstain from attempting to push other borders and will behave more as work-to-rule agents fostering the status quo. An agreed shift may, however, occur if

[11] These variables could be also characterised as antecedent conditions or partially necessary conditions.

[12] This is in line with Abbott et al. (2000) who distinguish delegation in dispute resolution from delegation in rule-making and implementation.

leading principals on both sides agree on such a move and instruct their agents accordingly.

In the scenario 'asymmetry of delegation', we conjecture conflictual outcomes. Asymmetry in delegation may invite agents to pursue border shift strategies. The borders of the institution with greater delegation tend to be more relevant as members have delegated more discretion to agents within the IO concerned.[13] If, on the opposite side of the border, important individual principals are not keen to let delegation-induced policies creep in from the outside, they either react themselves or instruct their agents to react, most likely leading to a conflictual status quo at the border. Yet, if principals disagree as group and cannot overcome collective action problems to react to border shift, given that the agents are weak, forced shifts will occur.

DELEG_a: *Asymmetry of delegation makes conflictual border outcomes more likely*

DELEG_s: *Symmetry of delegation makes cooperative border outcomes more likely*

2 Control

A second variable relates to principals' control constellation over the institutions. We assume that states are not only vigilant about border dynamics that could jeopardise their 'investment' in a particular forum, but that they will also strategically use their most preferred IO to pursue their interests (potentially affecting the borders). We are particularly interested in examining whether (or not) the same set of actors (in terms of composition of principals) controls organisations on both sides.

As to our conjectures, when different sets of members control an organisation, conflictual outcomes are more likely. Given the incentives to forum-shop, both sides will attempt to enlarge their portfolio.[14] Assuming that collective principals in the 'facing' IOs both overcome collective action problems, a conflictual status quo will be the likely result. Forced border shifts will be the observed outcome if the other IO does not react to evolving intrusiveness. This non-reaction is a result of dissent among principals within an IO or lack of knowledge related to

[13] This delegation may also be ad hoc, related to the collective principals' strategy for shifting the borders.

[14] We assume that different compositions of principals are likely to lead to preference divergence on both sides of the border. This makes cooperative solutions for division of labour between the two sides less likely.

the distributional consequences of such a shift. The first problem for principals' reaction relates to the inherent collective action problem to instruct the agent to push back; the second problem is related to benign neglect. In contrast, when the same type of actors control both sides, this will lead to forms of cooperative border outcomes. States will opt for a controlled shift (when the collective principals on both sides agree on a shift). If collective principals are satisfied with the existing border, the status quo will prevail.

CONTROL_a: *When different members control the organisations on each side of the border, conflictual border outcomes are more likely*

CONTROL_s: *When the same member(s) control the organisations on each side of the border cooperative border outcomes are more likely*

3 Nature of the problem

A constant and major determinant of institutional choice has been the type of problem that interdependent actors face. Going back to early work on regime theory (Stein 1982) as well as the more recent literature on rational design (Koremenos et al. 2001), we consider here two generic problems that plague cooperation – enforcement (with the recurrent temptation to free-ride) and distribution (of costs and gains).[15] Previous work does not suggest any specific link between border dynamics and those two problems. The rational design project connects restrictive membership to situations marked by enforcement problems and broad membership to situations characterised by distributive tensions (Koremenos et al. 2001). For our purposes this could mean that enforcement calls for carefully defined and patrolled borders and distribution for malleable borders. But the rational design project also highlights the difficulty of empirically disentangling the relative importance of each problem for institutional design. To address the latter point, we ask what the dominant concern is along a specific border. Are actors on each side of the border worried about the impact of different solutions to distributive tensions? Or are they mostly worried about the enforcement of solutions? We argue that when collective principals are

[15] Clearly this is a very crude way to address the problem of international cooperation. For a more systematic way to conceptualise it, see Aggarwal and Dupont (1999) and subsequent debates with critics (Aggarwal and Dupont 2002; 2003).

concerned with enforcement, border delimitation matters significantly because it affects monitoring and subsequently sanctioning. We are therefore more likely to see cooperative behaviour. This is most obvious when enforcement is a dominant concern of both sides of the border, but it is also true in the case of asymmetry. Whether we will witness a status quo or shifts, however, depends largely on the implementation mechanisms at the disposal of the IOs for controlling free-riding. If one side can employ stronger compliance mechanisms, this would be more likely to lead to an agreed shift. If mechanisms are equally strong (or weak) we should witness the status quo.

But if principals are mostly concerned with how to come up with solutions to the bargaining process in the first place, we expect discussions on border location to be part of the push and pull process (as typically captured in coordination games). If both sides are equally concerned about distributive tensions, this makes a mutual agreement on the contours of the border difficult and we expect overall a conflictual status quo. If distributional tensions characterise one side more than the other (e.g. if one side feels much more strongly about distributive tensions), this will lead to forced shifts compensating for distributional concerns within an IO.

DISTRIBUTE: *When distribution is the dominant problem underlying border issues, conflictual border outcomes are more likely*

ENFORCE: *When enforcement is the dominant problem underlying border issues, cooperative border outcomes are more likely*

4 How to regulate

Drawing from the literature on epistemic communities and consensual knowledge (Haas 1992), we expect actors' regulatory orientations (and paradigms that have developed within IOs) to shape border outcomes. This goes beyond past experience and speaks to the development of convergence (or divergence) of ideas on 'how to regulate'.[16] This can involve questions of regulatory philosophy (e.g. state-led versus market-led solutions or free trade versus re-regulation), procedural issues (e.g. a strong norm of reciprocity versus differentiated responsibility)

[16] The emergence of paradigms may be driven by 'small world environments' or 'embedded relationships' within regimes (Alter and Meunier 2009).

Table 14.2 *List of Conjectures*

DELEG_a	*Asymmetry of delegation makes conflictual border outcomes more likely*
DELEG_s	*Symmetry of delegation makes cooperative border outcomes more likely*
CONTROL_a	*When different member(s) control IOs on both sides of the border, conflictual border outcomes are more likely*
CONTROL_s	*When the same member(s) control IOs on both sides of the border, cooperative border outcomes are more likely*
DISTRIBUTE	*When distribution is the dominant problem underlying border issues, conflictual border outcomes are more likely*
ENFORCE	*When enforcement is the dominant problem underlying border issues, cooperative border outcomes are more likely*
IDEAS_a	*Ideational divergence on how to regulate makes conflictual border outcomes more likely*
IDEAS_s	*Ideational convergence on how to regulate makes cooperative border outcomes more likely*

Source: Created by the authors.

or whether issues can be regulated unilaterally or multilaterally. We expect that when actors on both sides disagree over the regulatory philosophy (lack of degree of shared norms and rules) conflictual border management is more likely.[17] Influential actors (depending on delegation and control: agents or principals or jointly) on both sides will attempt to impose their views which will lead to a conflictual status quo. Shifts occur when one side enjoys significantly greater attention from principals, which is a function of preference intensity. Lack of the latter will weaken ones side's preparedness to defend the border. In contrast to the conjecture suggesting conflictual border management, consensual knowledge and goals help delineate clearly defined and bounded issue-areas (Haas 1980) based upon explicit agreements. We should thus witness agents and principals working towards cooperative solutions to border problems. We expect periods of status quo replaced by controlled shifts when new regulatory ideas

[17] An example is the difference in the underlying philosophy on regulating food safety between the WTO (scientific risk assessment) and the Biodiversity Convention's Cartagena Protocol (precautionary principle), see Winham (2003).

clearly favour one of the IOs over the other to be more likely to implement a regulatory philosophy.

IDEAS_a: *Ideational divergence on how to regulate makes conflictual border outcomes more likely*
IDEAS_s: *Ideational convergence on how to regulate makes cooperative border outcomes more likely*

D Border Dynamics and the WTO

I The Trade-and Debate in the WTO

The transition from the GATT to the WTO included a major redesign of the dispute settlement mechanism from a diplomatic conflict resolution mechanism to a judicial mechanism with significant delegation. This change set in motion border dynamics and it was suggested that 'other regimes are responding both to WTO normative dominance and linkage by accommodating the WTO' (Kelly 2006: 81). While potential effects of delegation to WTO dispute settlement bodies have been vigorously debated in the legal field (Alvarez 2001; Dunoff 2001; Guzman 2004), empirical evidence on border shifts is far from conclusive.[18] We posit caution before jumping to the conventional conclusion that accommodation has been the only and uniform answer to an expanding multilateral trade regime. Using our conceptual framework presented in the previous section, we highlight the diversity of answers in connection with four different situations of border dynamics (see Table 14.3).

II Conjectures and the WTO Borders: Three Illustrations

Whereas a systematic test of the set of conjectures presented is beyond the scope of this chapter, we briefly discuss their relevance for our understanding of WTO border politics. In this subsection, we suggest an example for three of the four generic outcomes of border politics and contrast the set of expected predictions (derived from our conjectures) with observed outcomes. In the next subsection, we discuss in more detail an example for the fourth generic outcome to further illustrate the dynamics from a PA perspective and the causal mechanisms at work.

[18] In addition, linkage might weaken formerly highly legalised regimes. In this respect, Shaffer and Pollack (2010) argue that through linkage with hard law regimes, soft law regimes may be 'hardened', while hard law regimes may be 'softened'.

Table 14.3 *Border Outcomes in Relation to the WTO*

	Cooperative	Conflictual
Status quo	Monetary policy (IMF)	Cultural diversity (UNESCO)
Shift	IPRs (WIPO)	Food safety (WHO/FAO)

Source: Created by the authors.
Note: The 'facing' IO is shown in parentheses.

IMF–WTO borders are a generally an illustration of a cooperative status quo (upper left cell) (Charnovitz 2002). A number of WTO (formerly GATT) provisions lay down the cooperative framework for interaction.[19] On the IMF side, there is a clear link with trade issues in Article I (ii), which mentions that a key aim of the Fund is to 'facilitate the expansion and balanced growth of international trade', as well in Article IV whereby members of the Fund are not allowed to 'manipulate' their currency in order to gain 'unfair competitive advantage'. As part of the Marrakesh agreement, GATT Members approved a '[d]ecision on achieving greater coherence in global economic policy-making', whereby the WTO 'is called upon to develop its cooperation with the international organizations responsible for monetary and financial matters. In particular, the Director-General of WTO is called upon to review, with his opposite numbers in the World Bank and the international Monetary Fund, the implications of WTO's future responsibilities for its cooperation with the Bretton Woods

[19] Article 3.5 of the WTO charter, specific provisions in GATT and GATS, and in particular Article XV of GATT. According to that article, common members of both GATT and IMF are requested not to frustrate the intent of the GATT provisions by means of exchange action, nor the intent of the IMF articles through trade action (Article XV, p. 4); cooperation with the IMF is sought to the end of a coordinated policy with regard to exchange questions or of quantitative restrictions and other trade measures (Article XV, p. 1); payments and transfers restrictions in connection with imports, applied by a member State inconsistently with the GATT exceptions on quantitative restrictions, should be reported to the Fund (Article XV, p. 5).

institutions.'[20] This search for coherence has also been embodied in the Doha process with the creation in 2001 of a Working Group on Trade, Debt and Finance tasked with promoting cooperation with the Bretton Woods institutions to explore how trade could help debt-ridden countries or more recently how trade could be hindered by financial difficulties. So far, we have witnessed cooperation in WTO dispute settlement cases, where the WTO panels consulted with the IMF (e.g. in disputes covering monetary reserves, balances of payments or foreign exchange arrangements).[21] More recently, border management was strengthened and institutionalised with an IMF/WTO Cooperation Agreement which in addition lays down 'the Fund's obligation to respond to the WTO's request to consult' (Siegel 2002: 572). Close cooperation is also visible in rule-making, encouraged in particular by the Fund's participation in the WTO Committee on Balance of Payments (WTO 1996). A key test of the IMF–WTO relationship has been the long discussion over valuation of China's currency since 2005. Given the strong pressure exerted by the US Congress on the US President and administration to push for action against China, various legal and institutional channels within the IMF and the WTO have been pursued (including the attempt to consider an undervalued currency as a prohibited subsidy under the WTO Agreement on Subsidies and Countervailing Measures), to little avail. The IMF staff has not been given the capacity to really explore deeply the issue by the IMF member countries, and the WTO Members, despite having the capacity to adjudicate the matter, have done little to suggest that trade issues linked to currency manipulation are within the WTO's responsibility.

Reviewing our explanatory variables, a cooperative status quo corresponds to the expected outcome in most conjectures. We witness the same principals controlling both organisations (*CONTROL_s*).[22] Both sides also support a trade-liberalising agenda whether they are ministers

[20] Declaration on the Contribution of the World Trade Organization to achieving greater coherence in global economic policymaking, adopted by the Trade Negotiations Committee on 15 December 1993.

[21] Article XV GATT in terms of case law, see *Korea – Beef*, *Argentina – Footwear*, *India – Quantitative Restrictions*, and *Dominican Republic – Cigarettes*, see Mitchell and Sheargold (2009).

[22] The United States plays a pivotal role in both organisations. Weighted voting and the existence of a super-majority are key features of the IMF. The WTO is member-driven and consensus-oriented, yet, in practice informal decision procedures based on a system of concentric decision-making favour decisions within small and powerful groups.

of finance or trade. They take the view that certain exceptions (e.g. balance of payment restrictions) can be applied under clear conditions (*IDEAS_s*). It is in the interests of leading actors on both sides to support the status quo. As to the cooperation problem, enforcement has been the key concern ever since the creation of the GATT in 1947. Participants in the trade regime need assurance that trade concessions will be implemented and not 'nullified' through other types of domestic regulation. From the GATT/WTO side, the discipline of trade rules would lose much of its meaning if states on the other side of the border could easily manipulate exchange rates. Viewed from the side of the IMF, the manipulation of trade flows through state intervention may prevent market mechanisms from correcting short-term balance of payment imbalances. Hence the need for an international monetary system that should 'promote exchange stability, to maintain orderly exchange arrangements and *avoid competitive exchange depreciation*' (Article I (iii) IMF; italics added). In sum, on both sides, any specific agreement to solve distributive tensions would be rendered moot or severely jeopardised if there was no enforcement on the other side of the border. We therefore expect a cooperative border outcome (*ENFORCE*). Given that implementation tools are strong in both IOs, a cooperative status quo is expected. The conjecture on delegation is more difficult to assess. While the IMF scores high on bureaucratic capacity, WTO staffers play a marginal role in rule-making (Elsig 2011) (*DELEG_a*). However, as cooperation so far has predominantly occurred in the realm of dispute settlement and is in the hands of elected enforcement agents (e.g. panels and the Appellate Body) on the WTO side, asymmetry is less of an issue (*DELEG_s*).

As an illustration of the outcomes of controlled border shifts (lower left cell of Table 14.3) we briefly discuss the relations between the WTO and the WIPO. In the late 1980s, the transatlantic partners (EU and United States) pushed for protection of intellectual property rights (IPRs) to be brought into the WTO rule book. As Abbott put it, 'WIPO was perceived as an ineffectual institution because its governing agreements failed to adequately prescribe the types of IPRs protection sought by the developed countries, and because the WIPO arrangement lacked an effective enforcement mechanism' (2000: 66). While some developing countries (notably India and Brazil) questioned whether the WTO was the right venue for IPRs, the WTO incorporated the protection of IPRs

However, the role of the United States in both organisations has been challenged recently by emerging economies.

into its system. In particular, the new TRIPS Agreement led to additional obligations for countries, backed by the new dispute settlement understanding which made implementation more credible.[23] This controlled shift was accompanied by a collaborative relationship between the two key international institutions. There was extensive inter-institutional cooperation in the run-up to and during the Uruguay Round negotiations (Stewart 1999; Matthews 2002). Also, since the conclusion of the Uruguay Round, inter-institutional cooperation based on explicit agreements has functioned well. Moreover, the shift has potentially increased the capacity of WIPO to act as a norm-setter as demonstrated by the adoption of new treaties in specific areas (Abbott 2000). Sell (2003) argues that there was considerable convergence of views on IPRs among the regime's key actors.

This case seems to be in line with most of our conjectures. Beginning with the question of control, we observe dominance of powerful principals (United States and EU) (*CONTROL_s*) in both organisations around the time of the negotiations. Also, agent autonomy was constrained in both organisations (*DELEG_s*). Both agents were encouraged by principals to explore the linkage. In addition there was strong convergence on the regulatory philosophy (*IDEAS_s*) in which IPRs were framed as key factors for innovation, economic growth, and technology transfer. On both sides of the border, enforcement was the main problem with respect to IPRs, given that the dominant incentive to produce certain goods stems from the ability to selectively exclude users (*ENFORCE*). The stronger compliance mechanisms of the WTO could be interpreted as a pull-factor in the direction of a cooperative shift.

Border politics of culture (the WTO with the United Nations Educational, Scientific and Cultural Organization (UNESCO)) is a case of conflictual status quo (upper right cell of Table 14.3). The conflict dates back to the Uruguay Round negotiations, when, in the area of audiovisual services, the question was raised whether states could opt out to protect domestic cultural content. The discussions oscillated between legitimate concerns for freer trade and the legitimate concerns about cultural exceptions. While the UNESCO side of the border was concerned about an alleged dominance of the trade discourse, it moved away from a doctrine of cultural exception and towards the notion of cultural diversity in the second half of the 1990s (Graber 2006). In other words, the

[23] For a critical account discussing why few cases have been brought under the TRIPS Agreement, see Pauwelyn (2010).

UNESCO regime attempted to move from a defensive to an offensive stance, pushing for culture to be incorporated into the definition of a commodity. In the course of this rhetorical turn, we witnessed that actors within the cultural protection regime vigorously reacted against a perceived hierarchy of international norms and engaged in pushing the border back to the original status quo ante. What could be interpreted as the result of this counter-strategy was the work on (and subsequent adoption of) a new Convention on the Protection and Promotion of the Diversity of Cultural Expressions (CCD) in 2005.[24] Not surprisingly, one of the major contentious issues was how the UNESCO Convention would overlap with free-trade rules as stipulated by the WTO (Pauwelyn 2005).

Given our explanatory factors, we expect mostly conflictual borders. We posit more asymmetry (than symmetry) in delegation (*DELEG_a*). The WTO Secretariat had no mandate (and low autonomy) to push the borders in this area; there is a more elaborate executive structure in the UNESCO system. Therefore, bureaucratic agents within UNESCO had more leeway than WTO staffers in negotiations. Different groups of principals control the organisation (*CONTROL_a*); in particular, the United States was not able to sufficiently influence the outcome of the Convention. The United States had not been part of UNESCO since 1984 and only joined again in late 2001. Therefore, it was less capable of influencing the evolving agenda through targeted strategies, including coalition-building. At the later stage, it largely tried to block the process. Yet, the willingness of the majority of principals on the UNESCO side to defend the border contributed to the conflictual status quo. Turning to the nature of the problem, the dominant concern is distribution (*DISTRIBUTE*). Discussions focused on the specific bundles of trade liberalisation commitments, in particular whether there could be specific protection for cultural goods. Finally, clear ideational divergence on how to deal with the culture–trade nexus is an important factor reflected in the literature (*IDEAS_a*).

III *Conjectures and the WTO Borders: A Focus on the WTO–Codex Border Dynamics*

We have illustrated examples that fall into three of the four outcome categories. In this subsection, WTO–Codex border relations are

[24] On the negotiations, see Moghadam and Elveren (2008). The United States and Israel voted against the Convention.

discussed in more detail to flesh out the nature of cooperation, the interests of principals and agents and the types of shifts and the causal processes that unfolded. Border politics between the two organisations in the 1990s corresponded to what we call a forced border shift (lower right cell of Table 14.3). In the meantime, cooperation has again stabilised on a more cooperative modus.

The Codex Alimentarius Commission, an institution jointly set up by the WHO and the Food and Agricultural Organization of the UN (FAO), specialises in setting international food standards. As a standards developing organisation (SDO), it elaborates standards that are agreed upon in several Committees where – prior to the WTO linkage – health experts from governmental agencies met in a club-like environment (Cosbey 2000). In the second half of the Uruguay Round negotiations on the new Agreement on the Application of Sanitary and Phytosanitary Measures (SPS Agreement) the GATT Secretariat, strongly encouraged by GATT Members, looked for specific SDOs to be 'endorsed' with regard to internationally agreed standards (Elsig 2012). On the side of the GATT, key principals favoured Codex (over other potential SDOs) (Büthe 2009). On the side of Codex, Members (the principals) followed more of a benign neglect approach. Many health ministries involved in Codex activities did not follow these discussions closely. However, some staffers of the Codex Secretariat (the agent) were interested in getting the attention of the GATT negotiators (see Büthe 2008).[25]

The linkage to Codex that the WTO agreement eventually made changed the nature of norm-setting. Standards that were originally seen as optional were hardened (see Shaffer and Pollack 2010) as governments became suddenly obliged 'to use international standards ... as the technical basis for health and safety regulations' (Büthe 2008: 226). A shift therefore occurred, in particular, within the national levels of policy-making in the field of food safety and at the level of intergovernmental cooperation. At the national levels, agents working in regulatory agencies within states (e.g. on health) were increasingly influenced by bureaucratic agents from trade ministries. In the preparation of the work of specific Codex Committees, internal coordination increased with the role of trade interests. At the international level, standard-setting became heavily politicised at the domestic and at the international level. 'In light

[25] Representatives of one of Codex's parent organisations (the FAO) were interacting closely with WTO negotiators 'praising the unique scientific expertise of Codex committees' and successfully 'built "a constituency among developing countries"' (Büthe 2009: 11; quoted in Elsig 2012).

of the new role of Codex under the SPS Agreement, proceedings of the Commission have often become trade battlegrounds' (Silverglade 2000: 521). In rule-setting, one result of politicisation was increasing recourse to voting procedures, moving away from the consensus principle in the Commission. The shifts towards embracing more trade policy considerations were mostly visible in the work of the various Committees on specific food standards. Technical discourse was increasingly replaced by strategic trade policy interests (e.g. work on food labelling, on cocoa products and chocolate or on natural mineral water, among others). Deliberation was replaced increasingly by tough negotiations (Livermore 2006). Some of the Committees' work became completely paralysed. The Committee on Food Labelling, for example, became deadlocked over finding common labelling standards for products made with genetically modified organisms (see Smythe 2009: 103–107).[26] Similarly, Smythe argues that politicisation is 'reflected in its growing membership of state actors (177), the increased involvement of national trade officials pursuing their interests and the increased attention and involvement of other organisations (e.g. the WTO Secretariat)' (Smythe 2009: 96). Generally, Codex was ill-prepared to face this new situation of increased politicisation, which was a reflection of the forced shift to influence food standard setting via trade interests. Following this conflictual shift and increased politicisation, higher levels of cooperation have resumed. As to politicisation, Codex Members tried to avoid voting, which became practice after the shift and contributed to the polarisation. Also, the relations between the WTO Secretariat and the Codex Commission Secretariat currently have a business-as-usual status. Many informal and formal contacts are established. Secretariat officials regularly receive invitations to participate as observers in each other's work.[27] The mapping of preferences of agents and principals in both organisations shows that principals and agents in the GATT jointly worked to embrace Codex as the leading SDO in the field of food safety, while Codex agents were receptive to gaining more international attention, and most of the Codex principals were taken by surprise, in particular regarding the stark politicisation (Elsig 2015).

Let us turn to our conjectures and highlight the causal mechanisms that unfolded in more detail. In terms of delegation, there is an important

[26] The only result so far has been the adoption in 2011 of a document entitled 'Compilation of Codex Texts Relevant to Labelling of Foods Derived from Modern Biotechnology' (Document CAC/GL 76-2011).

[27] Interview with WTO official assisting the SPS Committee, 23 April 2012.

difference that warrants attention. The GATT Secretariat was requested by GATT Members to explore the linkage. While the GATT/WTO is usually Member-driven, in this case Members overcame collective action constraints and provided the Secretariat with some autonomy. This ad hoc delegation led to activism to explore further relations with the Codex Secretariat. On the Codex side, there was little delegation visible. Representatives of the Codex Secretariat, however, showed some willingness to cooperate, but this occurred without a specific mandate (*DELEG_a*). Agents of Codex did not obstruct the linkage, not least because they expected to gain in reputation from a shift (Büthe 2009; Elsig 2015). At the time of creating a linkage between WTO treaties and the work of this SDO, conflict was not yet apparent (see for instance Dawson 1995). It increased over time through politicisation of the processes and the growing discontent of health officials in Codex Member States. The evidence suggests that delegation supported a shift that was to occur. The shift was then accompanied somehow unintentionally with growing conflict over the intrusiveness of trade policy into the food safety regime.

As to the question of how the set of members that controls the organisation affect border outcomes, we observe that there are important differences between the two sides. In the early 1990s, both organisations were dominated by the United States, the EU and a number of industrialised countries, yet in the GATT negotiations we were already witnessing strong influence (and control over the processes) by a group of emerging developing countries (e.g. India and Brazil). This translates into asymmetry in control (*CONTROL_a*). The EU and the United States (among others) considered that their control was potentially more significant in Codex where developing countries lacked sufficient representation.[28] This forum-shopping idea was behind the transatlantic partners' decision to provide the GATT Secretariat some wiggle room. The incentives for developing countries in the GATT were different. While they did not follow Codex's work closely, they found the prospect of linking to a UN organisation more appealing than 'embracing' other organisations that seemed more dominated by industrialised countries. This might explain a certain benign neglect on developing countries' part leading to a clearly second-best situation for this group of countries. The work of Codex continues to be dominated by the United States and

[28] An additional illustration of asymmetry in control is that the vast majority of Committees in the 1990s were chaired by officials from developed countries (Livermore 2006: 783).

the EU, while developing countries' concerns are not yet sufficiently articulated. Further, we observe increasingly conflictual situations between the United States and the EU over the correct levels of food standards (e.g. on labelling and genetically modified food products; Smythe 2009) and over the basic approach to regulating risk – the EU pushing for the precautionary principle and the United States firmly in line with the WTO's proven-harm principle. Those conflicts have migrated back (a kind of boomerang effect) within the WTO borders through a series of prominent legal disputes, in particular the so-called Biotech case between the EU and the United States (as well as Argentina and Canada).

As to the cooperation challenge, the dominant problem is distribution embodied in the choice of specific standards (*DISTRIBUTE*). Negotiations on regulatory standards have become very conflictual (Krasner 1991; Drezner 2007). In terms of shifts, following the conjecture, the WTO principals felt much more strongly about distributive tensions. This is not surprising, because the export interests of large multinational firms (in the chemical, pharmaceutical, and food industries) lobbied their respective governments to address distributional concerns in their favour. In addition, customers (in particular in Europe) also demanded greater protection of food and health standards. Yet, as agreement on positive rules was difficult in the WTO (and faced much criticism from developing countries), a type of forum-shopping occurred, compensating for the difficulties in addressing distributional concerns within the WTO. Powerful principals could hope that such a shift would enable them to dominate more easily. The shift became conflictual, as described above, as unintended consequences started to affect the functioning of Codex.

Finally, as to the ideational divergence between health officials in Codex and trade officials in the GATT/WTO system (*IDEAS_a*), it was conditioned by the PA constellation. Conflict over the regulatory philosophy surfaced in Codex in the early 1990s. In 1991, the US delegation requested a review of existing standards 'as to their current relevance and sound scientific basis, with a view to facilitating trade' (quoted in Winickoff and Bushey 2010: 6). The majority of Codex Members, however, were sceptical about a change in regulatory orientation. The further politicisation after the linkage was largely a result of diverging interests of distributional outcomes and the right way to regulate. Codex continued to be dominated by health officials who were reluctant to allow trade interests to trump health and food safety concerns. The reason for the lack of counter-pressures (and therefore a push back towards a conflictual status quo) can be found in the explanation that agents in the Codex regime anticipated gains through a linkage, but were institutionally poorly prepared as were the principals to react to the politicisation (Büthe 2008).

E Conclusion

In a world with an increasing number of IOs, there is an urgent need to understand how regulatory borders are drawn and how they evolve. This chapter provides a framework to systematically analyse the politics of border dynamics with an application to the case of the WTO. Whereas our discussions of WTO border dynamics do reveal the relevance of our conjectures and are therefore encouraging signs for further theoretical development, they also suggest interesting implications for the performance of institutions. As the case study of WTO–Codex reveals, a perception of WTO 'dominance' has driven an outward expansion, but the end result may well be a diminished WTO performance in terms of enforcement of existing rules. If so, this would indicate clear externalities from conflictual border dynamics in contrast to more collaborative solutions. In short, this suggests that discussions of performance of organisations would gain from integrating the border dimension.

The chapter ends with reference to two potential extensions of our framework. First – as suggested by historical institutionalists – we need to account for past border management. We should expect that 'past cooperation' affects outcomes at the border. There are different pathways to cooperation, yet cooperation is always shaped by existing institutional platforms and overall experience of actively managing border concerns. Whereas the institutional relationships between the WTO and the IMF have been actively managed over time, institutional relations with other regimes have been more contentious (e.g. cultural rights and the environment) and lack cooperative platforms to tackle obstacles to cooperation.[29] In addition, today's practices tend to imitate past cooperation, whatever the border outcome was. With experiences of conflict-laden past cooperation, the likelihood of conflictual border administration will increase. The second extension concerns the need to move from bivariate to multivariate relations in a future step.

[29] Generally, the contracting parties of the WTO have been reluctant to delegate power to the WTO Secretariat to engage with secretariats of other IOs.

The short case study on Codex and the WTO suggests that when a combination of certain explanatory variables (or a type of conjectural cause) is modelled, this could increase the explanatory power of the conjectures presented for observed border politics. In particular, delegation and control interact in important ways, in addition to concerns about distributional effects and how to regulate an issue area. The case study on the Codex–WTO relations further shows that these variables also affect the border dynamics at different points in time and suggests different causal mechanisms from the original conditions to the final nature and movement of border management.

References

Abbott, Frederick M. 2000. 'Distributed Governance at the WTO-WIPO: An Evolving Model for Open-Architecture Integrated Governance'. *Journal of International Economic Law* 3(1): 63–81.

Abbott, Kenneth, Keohane, Robert, Moravcsik, Andrew, Slaughter, Anne-Marie and Snidal, Duncan. 2000. 'The Concept of Legalization'. *International Organization* 54(3): 401–419.

Abbott, Kenneth, Snidal, Duncan, Genschel, Philipp and Zangl, Bernhard (eds.). 2014. *International Organizations as Orchestrators*. Cambridge: Cambridge University Press.

Aggarwal, Vinod and Dupont, Cédric. 1999. 'Goods, Games and Institutions'. *International Political Science Review* 20(4): 393–409.

Aggarwal, Vinod and Dupont, Cédric. 2002. 'Goods, Games, and Institutions: A Reply'. *International Political Science Review* 23(4): 402–410.

Aggarwal, Vinod and Dupont, Cédric. 2003. 'Comment on "Common Goods, Matrix Games and Institutional Response"'. *European Journal of International Relations* 9(3): 475–478.

Alter, Karen and Meunier, Sophie. 2009. 'The Politics of International Regime Complexity'. *Perspectives on Politics* 7(1): 13–24.

Alvarez, José E. 2001. 'How Not to Link: Institutional Conundrums of an Expanded Trade Regime'. *Widener Law Symposium Journal* 7: 1–20.

Barnett, Michael and Finnemore, Martha. 2004. *Rules for the World: International Organizations in Global Politics*. Ithaca, NY: Cornell University Press.

Büthe, Tim. 2008. 'The Globalization of Health and Safety Standards: Delegation of Regulatory Authority in the SPS Agreement of the 1994 Agreement Establishing the World Trade Organization'. *Law and Contemporary Problems* 71: 218–255.

Büthe, Tim. 2009. 'The Politics of Food Safety in the Age of Global Trade: The Codex Alimentarius Commission in the SPS-Agreement of the WTO'. RWJF Scholars in Health Policy Research Program.

Charnovitz, Steve. 2002. 'Triangulating the World Trade Organization'. *American Journal of International Law* 96(1): 28–55.

Cosbey, Aaron. 2000. 'A Forced Evolution? The Codex Alimentarius Commission, Scientific Uncertainty and the Precautionary Principle'. IISD Paper, Winnipeg: International Institute for Sustainable Development.

Dawson, Richard. 1995. 'The Role of the Codex Alimentarius Commission in Setting Food Standards and the SPS Agreement Implementation'. *Food Control* 6(5): 261–265.

Drezner, Daniel. 2007. *All Politics Is Global.* Princeton, NJ: Princeton University Press.

Dunoff, Jeffrey. 2001. 'The WTO in Transition: Of Constituents, Competence and Coherence'. *George Washington International Law Review* 33: 979–1013.

Elsig, Manfred. 2010a. 'European Union Trade Policy after Enlargement: Larger Crowds, Shifting Priorities and Informal Decision-Making'. *Journal of European Public Policy* 17(6): 781–798.

Elsig, Manfred. 2010b. 'The World Trade Organization at Work: Performance in a Member-Driven Milieu'. *Review of International Organizations* 5(3): 345–363.

Elsig, Manfred. 2011. 'Principal-Agent Theory and the World Trade Organization: Complex Agency and "Missing Delegation"'. *European Journal of International Relations* 17(3): 495–517.

Elsig, Manfred. 2015. 'Orchestration on a Tight Leash: State Oversight of the WTO'. In *International Organizations as Orchestrators*, edited by Kenneth Abbott, Philipp Genschel, Duncan Snidal and Bernhad Zangl. Cambridge: Cambridge University Press, 65–87.

Goertz, Gary and Starr, Harvey. 2003. *Necessary Conditions. Theory, Methodology, and Applications.* New York: Rowman & Littlefield.

Goldstein, Judith, Kahler, Miles, Keohane, Robert and Slaughter, Anne-Marie. 2000. 'Introduction: Legalization and World Politics'. *International Organization* 54(3): 401–419.

Graber, Christoph B. 2006. 'The New UNESCO Convention on Cultural Diversity: A Counterbalance to the WTO'. *Journal of International Economic Law* 9(3): 553–574.

Guzman, Andrew. 2004. 'Global Governance and the WTO'. *Harvard International Law Journal* 45: 303–351.

Haas, Ernst. 1980. 'Why Collaborate? Issue-Linkage and International Regimes'. *World Politics* 32(2): 357–405.

Haas, Peter. 1992. 'Introduction: Epistemic Communities and International Policy Coordination'. *International Organization* 46(1): 1–35.

Hawkins, Darren and Jacoby, Wade. 2006. 'How Agents Matter'. In *Delegation and Agency in International Organizations*, edited by Darren Hawkins,

David Lake, Daniel Nielson and Michael Tierney. Cambridge: Cambridge University Press, 197–228.

Hawkins, Darren, Lake, David, Nielson, Daniel and Tierney, Michael (eds.). 2006. *Delegation and Agency in International Organizations*. Cambridge: Cambridge University Press.

Kelly, Clair. 2006. 'Power, Linkage and Accommodation: The WTO as an International Actor and Its Influence on Other Actors and Regimes'. *Berkeley Journal of International Law* 24(1): 79–128.

Kim, Moonhawk. 2012. 'Disguised Protectionism and Linkages to the GATT/WTO'. *World Politics* 64(3): 426–475.

King, Gary, Keohane, Robert and Verba, Sidney. 1994. *Designing Social Inquiry: Scientific Inference in Qualitative Research*. Princeton, NJ: Princeton University Press.

Koremenos, Barbara, Lipson, Charles and Snidal, Duncan. 2001. 'The Rational Design of International Institutions'. *International Organization* 55(4): 761–799.

Krasner, Stephen. 1983. *International Regimes*. Ithaca, NY: Cornell University Press.

Krasner, Stephen. 1991. 'Global Communications and National Power: Life on the Pareto Frontier'. *World Politics* 43(3): 336–66.

Livermore, Michael. 2006. 'Authority and Legitimacy in Global Governance: Deliberation, Institutional Differentiation, and the Codex Alimentarius'. *New York University Law Review* 81: 766–801.

Matthews, Duncan. 2002. *Globalising Intellectual Property Rights*. London: Routledge.

Mitchell, Andrew and Sheargold, Elizabeth. 2009. 'GATT Art. XV: Exchange Arrangements'. In *Max Planck Commentaries on World Trade Law, Volume 5*, edited by Rüdiger Wolfrum and Peter-Tobias Stoll. Leiden: Martinus Nijhoff, 353–365.

Moghadam, Valentine and Elveren, Dilek. 2008. 'The Making of an International Convention: Culture and Free Trade in a Global Era'. *Review of International Studies* 34(4): 735–753.

Nielson, Daniel and Tierney, Michael. 2003. 'Delegation to International Organizations: Agency Theory and Wold Bank Environmental Reform'. *International Organization* 57(2): 241–276.

Pauwelyn, Joost. 2005. 'The UNESCO Convention on Cultural Diversity, and the WTO: Diversity in International Law-Making?' *ASIL Insights* 9 (35), 15 November.

Pauwelyn, Joost. 2010. 'The Dog That Barked But Didn't Bite: 15 Years of Intellectual Property Disputes at the WTO'. *Journal of International Dispute Settlement* 1(2): 389–429.

Pauwelyn, Joost, Wessel, Ramses A. and Wouters, Jan (eds.). 2012. *Informal International Lawmaking*. Oxford: Oxford University Press.

Pollack, Mark. 1997. 'Delegation, Agency, and Agenda Setting in the European Community'. *International Organization* 51(1): 99–134.

Raustiala, Kal and Victor, David. 2004. 'The Regime Complex for Plant Genetic Resources'. *International Organization* 58(2): 277–309.

Sell, Susan. 2003. *Private Power, Public Law*. Cambridge: Cambridge University Press.

Shaffer, Gregory and Pollack, Mark. 2010. 'Hard vs. Soft Law: Alternatives, Complements and Antagonists in International Governance'. *Minnesota Law Review* 94: 706–799.

Siegel, Deborah. 2002. 'Legal Aspects of IMF/WTO Relationship: The Fund's Articles of the Agreement and the WTO Agreements'. *American Journal of International Law* 96(3): 561–599.

Silverglade, Bruce. 2000. 'The WTO Agreement on Sanitary and Phytosanitary Measures: Weakening Food Safety Regulations to Facilitate Trade?' *Food and Drug Law Journal* 55: 517–524.

Slaughter, Anne-Marie. 2000. 'Governing the Global Economy through Government Networks'. In *Role of Law in International Politics*, edited by Michael Byers. Oxford: Oxford University Press, 177–205.

Smythe Elizabeth. 2009. 'In Whose Interests? Transparency and Accountability in the Global Governance of Food: Agribusiness, the Codex Alimentarius, and the World Trade Organization'. In *Corporate Power in Global Agrifood Governance*, edited by Jennifer Clapp and Doris Fuchs. Cambridge, MA: MIT Press, 93–123.

Stein, Arthur. 1982. 'Coordination and Collaboration: Regimes in an Anarchic World'. *International Organization* 36(2): 299–324.

Stewart, Terence. 1999. *The GATT Uruguay Round: A Negotiating History, 1986–1992*. The Hague: Kluwer.

Van Evera, Stephen. 1997. *Guide to Methods for Students of Political Science*. Ithaca, NY: Cornell University Press.

Vaubel, Roland. 2006. 'Principal-Agent Problems in International Organizations'. *Review of International Organizations* 1(2): 125–138.

Winham, Gilbert. 2003. 'International Regime Conflict in Trade and Environment: The Biosafety Protocol and the WTO'. *World Trade Review* 2(2): 131–155.

Winickoff, David and Bushey, Douglas. 2010. 'Science and Power in Global Food Regulation'. *Science, Technology & Human Values* 35(3): 356–381.

World Trade Organization. 1996. Agreement between the WTO and the IMF and the World Bank. Geneva: WT/L/194

World Trade Organization. 2001. Declaration on the TRIPS Agreement and Public Health. Geneva: WT/MIN(01)/DEC/2.

World Trade Organization. 2004. Doha Work Programme. Decision Adopted by the General Council on 1 August 2004. Geneva: WT/L/579.

15

The GATT/WTO System and National Trade Policies

Which Comes First?

JOSEPH MICHAEL FINGER

A Introduction

The editors of this volume brought together practitioners of several disciplines to contribute to a debate on the World Trade Organization (WTO)'s performance, based on assessments of how the WTO has affected economic, legal and political institutions.[1] This chapter takes up this challenge by applying 'institutionalism' to the examination of the WTO's role and performance. It pays particular attention to the question of how the General Agreement on Tariffs and Trade (GATT)/WTO system relates to domestic institutions, namely its role in the management of trade policy and pressures for trade policy actions within WTO Members. My specific focus is on management of national trade policy in several Latin American countries and in the United States.

The logic for centring the analysis on national policy rather than on the WTO is that it is difficult to examine how the WTO fits into national trade-policy management by studying only the role of the WTO. Studying 'the WTO' imposes implicitly in all countries the same 'model' of the relationship between national policy management and the GATT/WTO system. This is clearly inappropriate and very likely to lead to misleading conclusions.

The chapter summarises the results of several Latin American case studies undertaken by Baracat et al. (2013) that are informative regarding the role played by GATT/WTO rules in influencing national policy institutions in the implementation of trade policy. I also discuss the imposition in 2001 of safeguards against imports of steel by the United

[1] See Chapter 2 by Elsig, Hoekman and Pauwelyn.

States. The case studies suggest there is a complementary relationship between the WTO and national policy institutions. In the case of the Latin American countries, the liberalisation that began in the 1990s has been sustained in some countries and reversed in others. In some of the cases – e.g. Peru – leaders used the WTO system to support reform that made sense at home. In others – e.g. Argentina – policy-makers characterised the WTO system's economics and its procedures as contrary to Argentina's interests. In this policy environment, WTO legal strictures had limited impact. These cases suggest that Latin American reform is about liberalisation that is 'unilateral' rather than based on a reciprocal exchange of 'concessions'. The US safeguards case illustrates how reciprocity dynamics embedded in WTO rules played a key role in helping the US government manage pressures for protection, resulting in the lifting of restrictions only thirteen months after they were imposed. This case shows how interrelated WTO and national processes have become in the modern practice of trade diplomacy.

Overall the cases make evident that different 'models' apply in different Latin American countries as well as between Latin American countries and the United States. While the choice of countries reflects my recent research and knowledge of US trade policy institutions, they serve to illustrate the point that the relationship between WTO rules and membership and national trade policy is not a uniform one.

Within the overall lesson of the complementarity of the GATT/WTO system and national trade policy management, the comparative advantage lesson of the Latin American studies is that trade reform is at its core a national decision. The comparative advantage lesson from the US safeguards study is the symbiosis of national and international processes for trade policy management. The common element that emerges is that what matters is not so much the WTO rules and processes as such, but the willingness and interest on the part of governments to use the WTO as a mechanism to manage protectionist pressures.

Before reviewing the various cases – the Latin American ones quite briefly, as they have been summarised in Baracat et al. (2015) – I will offer a brief discussion of institutionalism. This is a conceptual approach that my Latin American colleagues and I have found useful in studying national trade policy management – and provides an alternative way to think about trade diplomacy. My intent here is not to dispute the concepts used by Elsig, Hoekman and Pauwelyn in Chapter 2, but rather to expand on them. After reviewing the case studies, I discuss how they support the lessons noted in the above paragraph. I will close with some recommendations for further work to broaden the examination of the GATT/WTO system, particularly how it relates to national trade policy management.

B An Institutionalist Framework for Examining Domestic Policy Management

The editors in Chapter 2 bring together the different perspectives of economics, legal analysis and international relations. Their idea is that from these differences will emerge new and productive perspectives on the role of the WTO in creating and preserving a liberal international trading system. In the same spirit I introduce here some of the basic ideas of institutionalism.

Consider these alternative visions of a liberal international economic order:

- **Vision One**, in which authority over the instruments of trade control is ceded to a supranational authority, examples being trade among the fifty states of the United States or among the twenty-eight Member States of the European Union.
- **Vision Two**, in which no national government imposes more than minimal restrictions on the freedom of its citizens to engage in economic transactions with citizens of other countries.

The first vision frames the challenge of trade liberalisation as an international issue of providing a global public good (Zedillo 2007: 2). It reflects a legal rather than a behavioural perspective – the WTO is the supreme trade law to which national policy must align itself.

The second is more accepting of existing legal realities – and, I will argue below, of behavioural realities as well. It emphasises the domestic management of trade policy and how that management draws on the GATT/WTO system to build and maintain an open economy.

I A Hudecian Perspective

In much of his work Robert E. Hudec framed the GATT/WTO agreements as a commitment by participants to apply only approved methods of trade control, and to subject these controls to a long-term process of discipline through reciprocal negotiations.[2] In the language of

[2] E.g. in Hudec (2011: 119–120). Kennedy and Southwick (2002) provide a bibliography of Hudec's work.

mathematical programming, Hudec's view might be thought of as the logical 'dual' to the more familiar view of the GATT/WTO system as a process of negotiating trade disciplines.

How does the GATT/WTO system help domestic actors to advance liberal trade policies? My colleagues and I (Baracat et al. 2013; 2015) found that Hudec's perspective offered a productive way to examine, for example, how the GATT/WTO system supported the *domestic politics* of eliminating the plethora of restrictions that had accumulated in Latin American countries and of creating and operating within rules-based national decision mechanisms that take into account the positive impacts of integration into the global economy.

II Hudec and Institutionalism

David Palmeter (2003), in a perceptive tribute to Robert Hudec, pointed out that much of Hudec's work is grounded in a mode of thought Palmeter identifies as 'American Legal Realism', whose counterpart in economics he points out is institutionalism. The work I will cite is thus based on a mix of 'American Legal Realism' and institutionalism.[3]

Much of contemporary analysis (and many of the chapters in this volume) accept what Kyle Bagwell and Robert Staiger (2010) label 'the political economy of trade reform'. This view presumes that governments make trade-policy decisions through international negotiations and hence that trade policy reform results from the momentum of the WTO system rather than from the efforts of national reformers. This approach, we found, did not provide an adequate framework for examining how the GATT/WTO system interacts with the domestic political economy of trade reform. The story, we found, should be understood from a perspective that gives credit where credit is due. It is about how the energy and skill of people, of *local reformers*, drew from many things, including the GATT/WTO system, to change domestic trade policy management.

The core ideas of institutionalism concern organisations, habits and rules.[4] This approach takes into account social structures, norms and

[3] This has a long history – see e.g. Hamilton (1937). My training, mostly as an undergraduate at the University of Texas in the 1950s, was before the 'new institutional economics' established itself. I find the ideas in the 'new' to be much the same as those in the 'old' institutionalism; the differences are mostly matters of academic politics.

[4] See e.g. Eisenstadt (1968); North (1990); Williamson (2000); as well as more recently Acemoglu and Robinson (2010).

values, not just economic 'parameters' such as geography, technology or factor proportions as shaping human decisions. The 'parameters' that explain differences in economic outcomes lie at a higher level of social structure – the level of spirit – than economics usually takes into account.[5] Institutionalism facilitates an impetus towards specific and historically located approaches; its pattern of thought tends to be inductive; reasoning from examples towards generalisations rather than deductively from hypothesised structures. It tends to be somewhat existential, generalising upwards for the functions of organisations rather than reasoning downwards from objectives. As such, it facilitates separating normative analysis from positive or behavioural analysis.

III An Illustration of the Difference

Consider the following two statements: (i) international institutions are purposefully designed to uphold the rule of law; and (ii) in their introduction of rule of law into national management of trade policy, reformers have found the WTO supportive. These statements differ in several ways. The first reflects Vision One of a liberal international economic order, the second, Vision Two. The second is at the core of the institutionalist perspective applied by Baracat et al. (2013), is about synergy and indicates 'ownership' by the subject, as opposed the 'authority' of the superior agency that is implicit in the first. The second is about giving credit where credit is due, the recognition of national reformers as the 'heroes' of the story. This is more than a matter of getting it objectively correct, it is about incentive to continue with good policy management at home.

The same deconstruction could be applied to the statement: 'To the extent international courts embed their judgments in domestic legal orders they enable national actors to remedy potential treaty violations at home and avoid the need for international litigation.' 'Embeddedness' and 'ownership' look the same, but they feel different and they motivate differently.

C Latin American Experience: Reform Is About Domestic Institutions

Robert Hudec's perspective leads directly to one of the important conclusions emerging from Baracat et al. (2013): for a country to use the

[5] Williamson, an institutional economist who has won an economics Nobel Prize, elaborates on the various levels of social structure and analysis in Williamson (2000).

modern value-chain economy as a vehicle for development, WTO rules and other policy disciplines must have operational content in national institutions.[6] Recourse, say, to overcharge of a customs duty through the exporting country's rights under WTO tariff bindings would take years, and thus would be of no commercial value either to the exporting company or to the importing company. Likewise for misuse of other trade controls – those the GATT/WTO system allows and those it does not. 'Locking in' is about national institutions.

As to accepting international legal obligations and WTO enforcement (the dispute settlement process) locking things in, Argentina, a WTO Member since 1995, had accepted all the legal obligations of its agreements. Baracat et al. (2015) show that Argentina's trade practices (involving inter alia restrictive import licensing, the use of trade-related investment measures (TRIMs), safeguard actions and restrictions on agricultural trade) that were eventually challenged as WTO-illegal in 2012 had been in place at least since 2003 and would be subject to WTO-authorised disciplinary action no earlier than mid-2016. WTO rule-of-law was difficult to apply because Argentina's restrictions, while real in practice, had a vague existence in law or regulation. Baracat et al. (2015) refer to Argentina's practices as the output of the 'informal sector of government'; the WTO Panel and Appellate Body reports on the Argentinian cases label them 'unwritten measures'.[7] The absence of rule-of-law in national policy management elevates trade policy to the level of elective, presidential, politics.

In Peru, as in the other Latin American countries we examined,[8] adopting GATT-sanctioned trade remedies – that included the rule-of-law disciplines included in GATT/WTO requirements – facilitated the closing down of a plethora of administrative mechanisms that had accumulated over time. Dealing with these one by one would have been impossible. This done, to sustain the liberalisations, reformers had to ensure that *all* the politics of protection was channelled through these instruments – to ensure that *only* GATT-sanctioned instruments were used.

Although this did not happen in Argentina, Peru has been one of the most successful countries in maintaining discipline over new restrictions and in confining protectionist pressures within formal trade remedy

[6] This work has been updated in Baracat, et al. (2015). I take up here only this key point.

[7] The cases include DS 438, DS 444, DS 445, and DS 446 (regarding various Argentinian import procedures, licensing requirements, domestic content and other trade policies).

[8] Finger and Nogués (2006) examined Argentina, Brazil, Chile, Colombia, Costa Rica, Mexico and Peru. The follow-up study, Baracat et al.(2015), looked at Peru and Argentina.

mechanisms. The 2015 WTO Director-General's Report on trade measures (WTO 2015a, the press release for which was titled 'Increasing stockpile of trade-restrictive measures "a cause for concern"') reports no new restrictions by Peru. To the contrary, it lists a number of Peruvian liberalisations: elimination of import tariffs on 1,089 tariff lines, elimination of import clearance duties and termination of two anti-dumping measures.

A critical aspect of how Peru has sustained its trade reforms is that leaders there have insisted that all pressures for protection be channelled through formal processes. *All* the new trade controls that Peru has imposed since its reforms of the 1990s have been anti-dumping or countervailing measures (Global Trade Alert data – Baracat et al. 2015 provide details); the numbers indicate a good deal of discipline. As of 30 June 2015, Peru had 1 countervailing and 8 anti-dumping measures in force, as compared with 258 anti-dumping and 60 countervailing measures for the United States, 224 anti-dumping measures for India, 158 anti-dumping measures for Brazil, 101 anti-dumping and 4 countervailing measures for China and 98 anti-dumping and 15 countervailing measures for the EU (WTO 2015b, c).

Leaders interviewed by Baracat et al. (2013; 2015) indicated that there have been pressures for off-the-books actions, some of them from powerful Peruvian interests. Saying 'No. Use the trade remedy process,' has been in significant part an exercise in political courage by high officials.[9]

D US Safeguards on Steel Products: The Synergy of WTO and National Institutions

The US steel industry has been one of the more frequent appellants for import restrictions, always alert for a political opportunity. President George W. Bush's seeking 'trade promotion authority' in 2001 provided such an opportunity. The Doha negotiations were under way, and scheduled to end by 1 January 2005. Trade negotiations are a prestigious platform for a US President; those in a position to give this authority to the president will bargain for something in return.[10]

[9] Harberger (1993) also notes the importance of political courage in sustaining economic reforms.

[10] In President Kennedy's time, Robert Kerr of Oklahoma chaired the US Senate committee that handled trade negotiating authority. His asking for public works rather than trade protection shows that the payoff for trade authority is fungible, not restricted to a deal on trade policy.

The steel-producing states of Pennsylvania, Ohio and West Virginia had been hotly contested in the presidential election of 2000 and were shaping up as battleground states for the Congressional elections of 2002. When campaigning in these states, Richard Cheney, the Republican vice-presidential candidate, had emphasised the willingness of a Bush–Cheney administration to vigorously enforce US anti-dumping laws on behalf of steel producers.

I Pre-empting Anti-dumping

The steel industry had traditionally petitioned for and received protection through the unfair trade laws; anti-dumping and countervailing duties.[11] US unfair trade laws, however, allow the president no discretion. If the dumping and injury determinations are affirmative, the restriction is automatic.

To pre-empt anti-dumping or countervailing duty petitions from the industry, in June 2001 the United States Trade Representative (USTR) petitioned the US International Trade Commission (USITC) to undertake a safeguards investigation. An affirmative USITC determination would leave the final decision to the President; it would also provide for several events through which resistance to import restrictions might come forward. These events are taken up below.

II Affirmative Determination from the USITC

General conditions indicated that the industry had a good case. Employment at furnaces, mills and foundries dropped from almost 470,000 people in 1995 to fewer than 400,000 in 1999 and more than 30 steel companies had gone bankrupt between 1997 and 2001. No one was surprised when in December 2001 the Commission submitted to the president affirmative determinations on sixteen different categories of steel products.

An affirmative determination by the USITC in a safeguard case provides the president the legal authority to restrict imports but it does not mandate such action. The president could impose or not impose

[11] Bown (2004: 28) reports more than 200 anti-dumping or countervailing duty investigations in the 1990s that led to restrictions on steel imports. Finger and Murray (1993) document the use of anti-dumping cases in the 1980s to pressure the US government to negotiate export restraints from major suppliers.

restrictions – of whatever form he chose, on whichever of the covered products he chose.

After the Commission returns an injury determination it then turns to deliberations and recommendations over remedy. The president is not required by law to follow the Commission's recommendations, but the deliberations over remedy do serve a useful function. They provide a venue for interested parties to enter into the debate over what the president's action will be.

III *Managing the Application of Safeguard Restrictions*

Another element of judicious management was that the period for which the President imposed restrictions (a combination of tariff rates and quantitative restrictions) was three years *and one day*. Why the extra day? As mandated by the WTO safeguard agreement, US safeguard law specifies that when restrictions of more than three years duration are imposed, there must be a mid-term review. The review provides another focal point, along with the opportunity (in US law) for the president to ease or withdraw the restrictions.

Exporters affected by the restrictions immediately claimed that unless satisfactory compensation was provided, they would retaliate.[12] The WTO safeguards agreement suspends the right to compensation or retaliation only if the safeguard measures are taken in response to an absolute increase of imports, and the USITC report[13] itself provided a basis to argue that there had not been an absolute increase of imports. Over the period the USITC used for its investigation, 1996–2000, imports tended to peak in the middle, declining sharply in 1999 and 2000.

To deal with such threats, the president's March 2002 order instructed the USTR to consider exemption requests from other countries.[14] Steel-using companies had been an organised political element throughout. The resulting consultations were driven by partnerships of steel-using US companies combined with their foreign sources so that, politically speaking, the outcome of these consultations represented a balancing of the three interests at play: US producers, US steel users and foreign

[12] Under the Agreement on Safeguards (Article 8.2), exporters can retaliate 120 days after the date of imposition of the restrictions.

[13] United States International Trade Commission (2001).

[14] The initial order had already exempted free-trade agreement partners Canada, Mexico, Israel and Jordan, together with a number of smaller developing countries.

exporters. As a result of these negotiations, some 37 per cent of US steel imports subject to the March 2002 order were exempted.[15]

Taking user interests into account did not begin with the steel case. For more than a decade, US administrative practice has incorporated the concept of 'short supply'. Even an anti-dumping restriction can be suspended if the administering agency determined that the product subject to restriction was important to a US buyer and that domestically produced substitutes were unavailable or 'in short supply'.

IV WTO Case

In May 2002, a number of exporting countries (Brazil, China, the European Communities, Japan, South Korea, New Zealand, Norway and Switzerland) requested consultations with the United States concerning the WTO-legality of the measures. When these consultations and the exemptions negotiated with USTR (re: the previous paragraph) did not resolve the issue, the exporters requested that a panel be established. The Panel found against the United States, the United States appealed and the Appellate Body (AB) upheld the Panel on every major point. The AB's report was adopted by the WTO Dispute Settlement Body on 10 December 2003.

Although some had questioned the earlier claim of exporters to a right to retaliate – and no country had retaliated – it was clear that exporters now held a right to do so. (There remained, of course, the procedures through which the WTO would sanction acting on this right.) Exporting countries soon began to publicly identify US exports on which they might retaliate, focusing on US producers/exporters in sensitive states and Congressional districts. In short, they followed the same politics as the steel industry had used to put pressure on the President to restrict imports.

V USITC Mid-term Review

In March 2003 the USITC announced the opening of its mid-term review.[16] Shortly after announcing this investigation, the Commission received a request from the US House of Representatives, Committee on

[15] Hufbauer and Goodrich (2003: 4).

[16] US law requires that the mid-term review be completed by the midpoint of the restrictions in place. That would have been July 2003.

Ways and Means, to investigate also the impact of the import restrictions on US steel-consuming industries.

The Commission's conclusions on the impact on US steel producers were even-handed. The president could draw on the report to support either a decision to continue the restrictions or to terminate them. As to the need for continuing protection, the report pointed out continuing weaknesses in demand for vehicle parts, appliances and construction. While profitability had improved, it was not up to the level in the base period chosen for comparison. Selling prices were well short of their 2000 and 2001 levels. On the other hand, imports had fallen in many categories not covered by the restrictions, and there was an indication that world demand was picking up. Moreover, the restructuring of the industry was continuing. Several more of the less-efficient factories had been closed, four of the largest steel producers had merged into two and these had announced significant investments to increase productivity.

The companion report on the effects on steel-consuming industries was in structure the mirror image of an injury investigation: it measured how the restrictions had affected employment, wages, prices, profitability, sales, productivity and capital investment in steel-using industries and in port facilities. (Facilities relevant to internal distribution – of imported or domestically produced products – were not included.) A survey of steel-using companies (in parallel with a survey of US producers) added information on such factors as abrogation of contracts by export suppliers when the restrictions were applied and the continued availability of inputs needed to produce their outputs.

VI Decision to Terminate the Restrictions

The study sparked a surge of articles and press statements that provided the political basis for a presidential decision to terminate the restrictions. Perhaps the threat of retaliation from foreign exporters did influence the decision, but the announcement that the restrictions would be terminated did not mention that factor.

The announcement[17] began with a review of the circumstances that warranted safeguards: thousands of jobs were at stake, many steel firms were bankrupt or facing bankruptcy; this was caused by a surge in imports due in part to global overproduction. In response the president

[17] USTR (2003).

decided that the US steel industry needed breathing space – the chance to adapt.

Turning to the present, the announcement reported that 'as the ITC's analysis clearly demonstrated, the safeguard worked'. The lines that followed (one-third of the announcement) reported the mid-term review's findings on aspects including restructuring, higher productivity, profitability and US exports at a historically high level. The announcement went on to explain that the risk of a foreign surge of exports had abated; demand was up in China, Russia and other parts of the world.

The announcement then turned to user costs:

> In the first 21 months of the safeguard, the benefits to the industry outweighed the marginal costs to consumers. Going forward, however, this is not the case. For these reasons, the President has concluded that the safeguard has done its job and can now be lifted. (USTR 2003: 3)

As to lessons one might draw from this case, the first is that an institutionalised role for user costs is emerging in US administrative procedures, although this role is not mandated by WTO rules or even by US law. Given the role that import users forged for themselves in this case, it is not likely that their interests could be passed over in the next safeguard case taken up in the United States. Institutionally speaking, their success in the steel case is more appropriately interpreted as building political capital rather than as using it.

Foreign exporters' interests also have a role. In practice, the influence of foreign exporters on the United States' decision depended on the partnerships (foreign exporters and US users) that US process allows. In appearance, removing the restrictions was a concession to the interests of US users, not to those of the foreign exporters. USTR Zoellick's announcement of the termination of the steel safeguards mentioned twice the costs to users. Although the WTO decision and the USITC mid-term review created a synergetic relationship between domestic users and foreign exporters, the final announcement did not mention the cost to US exporters of potential retaliation.

Note that the managerial skill of the US administration in taking up this issue as a safeguard case rather than an anti-dumping case and in using the various events during the process that allowed termination of the restriction at a minimal loss of domestic political capital, was critical.

E The WTO and the Practice of Diplomacy

I *'War is the pursuit of diplomacy through other means'*[18]

This statement from the Prussian general and military theorist Carl von Clausewitz is often cited as an expression of pragmatic, even macho, determination to achieve ends without regard to means. Broader reading of Clausewitz, however, brings out a more complicated meaning. Clausewitz elaborates that war is 'a continuation of *political* intercourse' (my emphasis) different from diplomacy as normally conceived only by 'the peculiar nature of its means'.[19]

Clausewitz elaborates that the means (i.e. war) should not be allowed to develop their own ends, that ends are established in the wider context of politics or diplomacy. He cautions that war is a means that, when applied, is particularly likely to bring forward other ends.

II *WTO Is Part of Diplomacy*

The first point I draw from this citation is a reminder that the WTO is a part of diplomacy, and its accomplishments and failings should be gauged against such broad standards, i.e. the WTO is the pursuit of diplomacy through other means.

Applying such standards, does the United States' experience with safeguards indicate success or failure? In 1962, when US President John Kennedy wanted trade negotiating authority it cost him protection for the textile industry that lasted 40 years. In 2001, when US President George W. Bush wanted such authority it cost him protection for the steel industry that lasted 13 months. That I judge to be a victory for diplomacy, a victory in which the tools provided by the WTO played an important role.

Judith Goldstein and Robert Gulotty (Chapter 4) remind us that GATT's first round achieved little more than tariff bindings and reductions of rates that contained much 'water'. Lawrence Krauss (1959) found no trade impact from these 'concessions'. In discussion I cited this as success for diplomacy. It helped to establish an institution that would later achieve trade-stimulating results. The US Congress was passively hostile to the GATT as it was; constituents inconvenienced by increased imports might have tipped the Congress into active hostility.

[18] von Clausewitz (1989: Chapter 1, Section 24).
[19] ibid.

Other outcomes are more difficult to judge. Elsig et al. (Chapter 2) report that the rate of compliance with adverse WTO rulings by panels and the AB is impressively high, more than 80 per cent, but Tobias Hofmann and Soo Yeon Kim (Chapter 5) find that this compliance has not led to increased imports. What is the explanation for this finding? Do governments immediately replace discredited restrictions with new ones? Is there sufficient 'water in the law' to enable legal demands to be met without changing the economics?[20]

III National Decisions Anchored in National Interests

This cautions us to note that unless national decisions are 'anchored' in national interests rather than in international obligations, they will drift towards 'water in the law' solutions. Likewise, international negations will drift towards 'water in the law' agreements. (Presuming, of course, that 'national interests' are correctly, not mercantilistically, conceived and that the WTO system is part of the advancement of this conception.) This argues for a Vision Two view of a liberal international economic order.

IV A Theoretically Consistent Rationale

Similarly, I am troubled by the idea that because analysis must have a theoretically consistent rationale, analysis of the WTO should pay obeisance to bargaining models. I offer two references that explain why I am troubled. The first is on the negative side, the second on the positive side. Although Donald Regan (2006; 2015), in two patiently reasoned papers, has demonstrated that terms-of-trade bargaining models and international negotiations are entirely different subjects, most writers in all of the disciplines covered by the concept paper seem obligated to express a cultural obeisance to such models. On the positive side, I concluded from my looks at their use and at their analytical literature that trade remedies serve the WTO system well, although they are an embarrassment to both legal and economic theory (Finger 2012).

[20] Raymond Vernon, a renowned economist of a previous generation, spent six months at the US Treasury Department in the 1970s when I worked there. I recall him observing that: 'The objective of trade policy seems to be to have the greatest appearance of policy without any policy.' That was a fair assessment of how, at the time, the Treasury Department wanted the trade remedies to function.

Institutionalism, with its focus on function rather than on purpose, provides a theoretically consistent rationale for my conclusion.[21]

V *Are 'Reciprocity' and 'Objectives' Theoretically Consistent Rationales?*

Operationally speaking, in the GATT/WTO system, agreement defines reciprocity, not the other way around. An agreed outcome from a negotiating round, the system presumes, is an outcome that each Member considers advantageous; by whatever standard or with reference to whatever objective the Member chooses to apply. GATT's tradition of decision by consensus reinforces the idea that an agreement is an outcome that each Member considers to be to its advantage – through a mechanism that does not demand shared purpose.

Thus reciprocity as the basis for agreement may not be compatible with agreement having a theoretically consistent rationale – if that rationale is a matter of agreed objective. Reasoning from a base objective may impose on the analysis of GATT/WTO agreements something that negotiators had to avoid in order to achieve agreement.

F Recommendations and End

A year or so after Robert Hudec's *Developing Countries in the GATT Legal System* was reissued, my wife asked me if it was selling well. My reply: 'No. Only two people in the world think about things this way and one of us is dead.'

How to relaunch an analysis of the WTO's performance that includes how it has impacted on and supported national institutions? More Hudec, more institutionalism and more studies of national institutions are my recommendations.

I end the chapter by responding to the question I posed in its title, 'Which comes first, the GATT/WTO system or national trade policies?'

My answer[22] is that in institutional economics, the chicken–egg question is not 'which came first?' but 'what process explains the evolution of both?'

[21] Elsig et al. (Chapter 2) use the word 'goal' (or 'goals') 47 times, the word 'objective' (or objectives) 40 times. The word 'function' (or 'functions') appears only 20 times.

[22] Borrowing from Geoffrey Hodgson (1998: 185).

References

Acemoglu, Daron and Robinson, James. 2012. *Why Nations Fail: The Origins of Power, Prosperity, and Poverty*. New York: Crown Business.

Bagwell, Kyle and Staiger, Robert W. 2010. 'The World Trade Organization: Theory and Practice'. *Annual Reviews of Economics* 2: 223–256.

Baracat, Elías A., Finger, J. Michael, Thorne, Raúl León and Nogués, Julio J. 2013. *Sustaining Trade Reform: Institutional Lessons from Argentina and Peru*. Washington, DC: World Bank (https://openknowledge.worldbank.org/handle/10986/15794).

Baracat, Elías A., Finger, J. Michael, Thorne, Raúl León and Nogués, Julio J. 2015. 'Trade Reform and Institution Building: Peru and Argentina under the WTO'. *World Trade Review* 14 (4): 579–615.

Bown, Chad. 2004. 'How Different Are Safeguards from Antidumping? Evidence from US Trade Policies Toward Steel'. Econometric Society 2004 North American Summer Meetings.

Eisenstadt, Shmuel. 1968, 'Social Institutions'. In *International Encyclopedia of the Social Sciences* 14, 409–429. New York: Macmillan and the Free Press.

Finger, J. Michael. 2012. 'Flexibilities, Rules and Trade Remedies in the GATT/WTO System'. In *The Oxford Handbook on The World Trade Organization*, edited by Martin Daunton, Amrita Narlikar and Robert Stern. Oxford: Oxford University Press, 418–440.

Finger, J. Michael and Murray, Tracy. 1993. 'Antidumping and Countervailing Duty Enforcement in the United States'. In *Antidumping: How It Works and Who Gets Hurt*, edited by J. Michael Finger. Ann Arbor, MI: University of Michigan Press, 241–254.

Finger, J. Michael and Nogués, Julio. 2006. *Safeguards and Antidumping in Latin America Trade Liberalization*. Washington, DC: Palgrave Macmillan and World Bank.

Hamilton, Walton. 1937. 'Institution'. In *Encyclopedia of the Social Sciences*, Vol. 8. New York: Macmillan, 84–89.

Hodgson, Geoffrey M. 1998. 'The Approach of Institutional Economics'. *Journal of Economic Literature* 36(1): 166–192.

Hudec, Robert E. 2011. *Developing Countries in the GATT Legal System* (reissue). Cambridge: Cambridge University Press.

Kennedy, Daniel L. M. and Southwick, James D. 2002. *The Political Economy of International Trade Law: Essays in Honor of Robert E. Hudec*. Cambridge: Cambridge University Press.

Krauss, Lawrence B. 1959. 'United States Imports and the Tariff'. *American Economic Review Papers and Proceedings* 49: 542–551.

North, Douglas C. 1990. *Institutions, Institutional Change and Economic Performance*. Cambridge: Cambridge University Press.

Palmeter, David. 2003. 'Robert E. Hudec – A Practitioner's Appreciation'. *Journal of World Trade Law* 37(4): 703–717.

Regan, Donald H. 2006. 'What Are Trade Agreements For? Two Conflicting Stories Told by Economists, with a Lesson for Lawyers'. *Journal of International Economic Law* 9(4): 951–988.

Regan, Donald H. 2015. 'Explaining Trade Agreements: The Practitioners' Story and the Standard Model'. *World Trade Review* 14(3): 391–417.

US International Trade Commission. 2001. 'Steel'. USITC Pub. 3479, Inv. No. TA-201–73, December.

United States Trade Representative. 2003. *Statement by USTR Zoellick on Termination of Steel Safeguards*. Press Release. 12 December 2003.

von Clausewitz, Carl. 1989. *On War*, Vol. 1. Edited and translated by Michael Eliot Howard and Peter Paret. Princeton, NJ: Princeton University Press (originally published in German in 1832).

Williamson, Oliver E. 2000. 'The New Institutional Economics: Taking Stock'. *Journal of Economic Literature* 38 (3): 595–613.

World Trade Organization. 2015a. Report to the TPRB from the Director-General on Trade-Related Developments. WT/TPR/OV/W/9. 3 July 2015.

World Trade Organization. 2015b. Report (2015) of the Committee on Subsidies and Countervailing Measures. G/L/1133, G/SCM/146. 29 October 2015.

World Trade Organization. 2015c. Report (2015) of the Committee on Anti-Dumping Practices. G/L/1134, G/ADP/22. 30 October 2015.

Zedillo, Ernesto. 2007. 'Introduction'. In *Global Trade and Poor Nations: The Poverty Impact and Policy Implications of Liberalization*, edited by Bernard Hoekman and Marcelo Olarreaga. Washington, DC: Brookings, 1–8.

INDEX

www.ingramcontent.com/pod-product-compliance
Lightning Source LLC
LaVergne TN
LVHW011532200926
848484LV00001B/238
* 9 7 8 1 1 0 7 1 9 3 2 2 2 *